American
Evangelicalism

American Evangelicalism

Embattled and Thriving

Christian Smith

with Michael Emerson, Sally Gallagher,
Paul Kennedy, and David Sikkink

The University of Chicago Press
Chicago and London

Christian Smith is assistant professor of sociology at the University of North Carolina, Chapel Hill, and the author of *The Emergence of Liberation Theology: Radical Religion and Social Movement Theory* and *Resisting Reagan: The U.S. Central America Peace Movement, 1981–1990,* both published by the University of Chicago Press.

The University of Chicago Press, Chicago 60637
The University of Chicago Press, Ltd., London
© 1998 by The University of Chicago
All rights reserved. Published 1998

Printed in the United States of America

07 06 05 04 03 02 01 00   2 3 4 5

ISBN 0-226-76418-4 (cloth)
0-226-76419-2 (paper)

Library of Congress Cataloging-in-Publication Data

Smith, Christian (Christian Stephen), 1960–
    American evangelicalism : embattled and thriving / Christian Smith . . . [et al.].
        p.   cm.
    Includes bibliographical references and index.
    ISBN 0-226-76418-4 (alk. paper). — ISBN 0-226-76419-2 (pbk. : alk. paper)
    1. Evangelicalism—United States.   2. United States—Religion.   I. Title.
BR1642.U5S62   1998
280'.4'097309045—dc21   98-11077
                                                                              CIP

For Emily,
the love of my life

CONTENTS

TABLES AND MAPS

Tables

Map

This book tells a particular story about contemporary American evangelicalism in the hopes of stimulating thinking in new directions about the prospects for traditional religion in the modern world. Our approach is sociological, one that tries to attend to both social structural and cultural factors which seem to shape this religious tradition and others around it. In contrast to other stories that are sometimes told, our story suggests that American evangelicalism as a religious movement is thriving—not only that, it is thriving very much because of and not in spite of its confrontation with modern pluralism. In this way, we are seeking to extend the insights of the "new paradigm" in the sociology of religion, in ways that are not unfriendly to, but which move beyond the economistic, rational-choice language employed by many current new-paradigm advocates.

Furthermore, although our story is primarily about evangelical vitality, we also examine in our final chapter aspects of what we see as evangelicalism's relative ineffectiveness at social change. In their faith-based strategic endeavor to transform the world "for Christ," evangelicals often appear to be less than conquerors. We will suggest that the fact of evangelicalism's simultaneous movement strength and strategic debility is thickly ironic, insofar as both often derive from the same subcultural origins. The sources of movement success, in other words, can be mixed blessings, also contributing to a degree of movement ineffectiveness.

Knowing that the matters about which we write are remarkably complex, we view our own theoretical approach as incomplete and provisional rather than comprehensive or conclusive. Nonetheless, we hope that this work helps significantly to advance our understanding of the issues at hand.

There is one important clarification about our use of the words "thriving" and "vitality." We mean them only as descriptions of the social, human dimensions of religion which sociologists can properly access. We do not intend them to imply any kind of moral superiority or essential religious integrity or faithfulness.

Finally, a host of people deserve our thanks. Recognition and gratitude must go first and foremost to Joel Carpenter and the Pew Charitable Trusts for having enough interest and confidence in this research project to fund it. Needless to say, none of the publications from this project would have been remotely possible without Joel and Pew's generous support of our research. For this gift, we are deeply grateful. Naturally, the views expressed in this book are those of the authors and do not necessarily reflect the views of The Pew Charitable Trusts.

Those who worked directly on different phases of the data gathering also deserve recognition for their contribution. Besides the named co-authors of this book, Mark Regnerus, Ray Swisher, Kathy Holladay, Bob Woodberry, Sharon Erickson Nepstad, Carolyn Pevey, Curt Faught, Pam Paxton, and Nancy Thompson contributed significantly to the research project in various ways. This was a genuine team effort, and each participant's contribution was of great value. Dave Sikkink, too, deserves special mention for the intelligent insights, technical skills, and long hours he devoted to help make this research project a success.

We are also greatly indebted to a number of scholars and friends who read and critiqued either individual chapters or the entirety of this manuscript during its writing. These include Robert Wuthnow, Roger Finke, Stan Gaede, Grant Wacker, George Marsden, Dan Olson, Tom Tyson, and Clark Roof. Their advice helped strengthen this work considerably. As is customary to express, however, none of them should be held responsible for any of this work's errors or faults.

Thanks must also go to many of the staff at the UNC Institute for Research in Social Science. First, Bev Wiggins was an indispensable source of advice and support, especially in the early stages of the project. Ruby Massey did a super job administering the grant budget. Angell Beza assisted us in designing our survey. And Paul Mihas, Ken Hardy, José Sandoval, Sue Dodd, Gary Gaddy, and Ed Bachman made valuable contributions in assorted ways as well. We would have been profoundly disadvantaged without the resources which the UNC IRSS put at our disposal.

Many thanks to Sherryl Kleinman, Peter Bearman, and Judith Blau for their valuable advice and support along the way. Vickie Wilson, Karen Sikkink, Laura Hoseley, and Joni Emerson deserve recognition for long hours of tape transcribing they performed for the project. Thanks to Elizabeth

Earle, Kent Walker, and Don Wood for their helpful assistance with bud-
gets and contracts. And for a variety of kinds of other useful contributions
to our project, thanks to Luis Lugo, Bill Kalsbeek, Bud Kellstedt, Jim
Wiggins, Ron Rindfus, Dick Udry, John Reed, Craig Calhoun, Darren
Sherkat, John Green, Lynn Robinson, Chris Ellison, Jenifer Hamil Luker,
and the participants of the UNC IRSS Faculty Working Group on Religion in American Culture, including Tom Tweed, Laurie Maffly-Kipp,
Grant Wacker, Yaakov Ariel, Mike Lienesch, Russ Richie, and Jack Carroll. We must also acknowledge the members of the Friday AM Judges
coffeeshop graduate workshop on religious research for their creative ideas
and incisive critiques: Dave, Mark, Ray, Bob, Kathy, Curt, and José all deserve credit. And, of course, to the hundreds of churchgoing Protestants
around the country with whom we conducted interviews—and in many
cases, the pastors who granted us access to them—many thanks as well.

No amount of praise could adequately credit the members of our families for facilitating our work, in a variety of ways: Emily, Zachary, Erin,
Bob, Helen, Matt, Joann, Tom, and Rick; Karen, Anna, Nancy, John, and
Faye; Joni, Anthony, Josiah, and Leah; Ed and Andrew; and Jan, Justin,
and Anna. Thanks to all for your support.

Lastly, we wish to honor Curt Faught (1971–1996) for his enthusiastic
participation in this research project, abruptly cut short by unjust tragedy.
We wish, Curt, that you were still here with us. Rest, finally, in peace.

Resurrecting Engaged Orthodoxy

On a snowy day on April 7, 1942, a group of about two hundred Christian men—mostly moderate fundamentalists—met at the Hotel Coronado, in St. Louis, Missouri, to launch a religious movement they hoped would transform the character of conservative Protestantism and literally alter the course of American religious history. Those who met for this "National Conference for United Action Among Evangelicals" were fully aware of the ambitious nature of their purpose: "We are gathered here today," declared the Reverend Harold J. Ockenga (quoted in Carpenter 1988: 19), in the first of three keynote addresses, "to consider momentous questions and possibly to arrive at decisions which will affect the whole future course of evangelical Christianity in America." Heady stuff, indeed. This was no run-of-the-mill religious meeting. These were people who intended to change history.

More than a half-century later, we now see that *they succeeded.* This small gathering of restless fundamentalists helped to launch a new religious movement that reawakened a dynamic, activist American religious tradition and that fundamentally altered the landscape of American religious identity and practice: modern American evangelicalism.

This book is a study of where that evangelical movement has come today. In what follows, we seek to "take the pulse" of contemporary evangelicalism by describing and analyzing the commitments, beliefs, concerns, and practices of the 20 million Americans who identify themselves with the evangelical movement.[1] We particularly focus here on how contemporary evangelicals interact with and attempt to influence the secular culture and society they inhabit and how that shapes evangelical identity itself. One

---

1. Seven percent of American adults in our survey identified themselves as Protestant, churchgoing, and "evangelical." For details, see Appendix A: "Research Methods" and Appendix B: "On Religious Identities."

practical goal is simply to promote a better understanding of evangelical Christians in the United States today—who they are and what they want—for both evangelicals and nonevangelicals alike. Another academic goal is to contribute to scholarly understanding of religious movements, when they arise, why they succeed or fail, what they accomplish. At the broadest level, this book aims to challenge longstanding assumptions about religion and modernity, about the prospects for robust religious faith in modern, pluralistic, secular societies.

To get to this, however, we first need to understand better the significance of the American evangelical movement in particular. We need to grasp more fully the meaning of that historic meeting in St. Louis in 1942. And to do that, we need historical perspective.

The Evangelical Heritage, Modernism, and the Fundamentalist Debacle[2]

When in the early 1940s men such as Harold Ockenga struggled to forge a coalition of conservative Protestants into this newly emerging evangelical movement, they were not creating their movement's vision or purpose from scratch. Rather, they were self-consciously drawing on their own nineteenth-century evangelical heritage and seeking to resurrect its temperament and vision—which had grown dim in the early twentieth century. These founders of modern evangelicalism believed that what conservative Protestantism had become in their lifetimes was not the best of what it had been or could be but a sad deviation from a more impressive, respectable tradition. They were determined to turn things around, to get orthodox Protestantism back on the right track.

In the nineteenth century, before the modernist-fundamentalist battles split the Protestant house in two, conservative Protestantism enjoyed a remarkable public respectability, influence, and relevance. Especially during the Victorian era, broadly evangelical Protestants were confident and engaged socially, culturally, politically, and intellectually. Indeed, they were *the* establishment. As one Presbyterian minister, Isaac Cornelison, noted in his 1891 book, *De Civitate Dei: The Divine Order of Human Society,* "[Prot-

2. Many fine histories of these subjects exist, upon which we drew for the following brief summary, including: Marsden 1970, 1980, 1994; Handy 1960, 1984, 1991; Carpenter 1980, 1984a, 1984b; Hatch 1989; Longfield 1991; Sweet 1984; Szasz 1982; Harper 1996; Wacker 1996; Stone 1996; Finke and Stark 1992. The following section also draws upon: Woodbridge, Noll, and Hatch 1979; Hart and Muether 1995; Tidball 1994; Dayton and Johnston 1991; Sweeney 1992; Moberg 1977.

estant] Christianity in a proper sense is the established religion of this nation; established not by statute law, it is true, but by a law equally valid, the law of the nature of things, the law of necessity" (Cornelison 1891: 362). For much of the nineteenth century, Cornelison's claim would have appeared self-evidently true to very many Americans.

To begin, broadly evangelical Protestants were in control of almost all of the major denominations, along with their seminaries, divinity schools, missions boards, and other agencies. From the nation's theological power-houses—such as Princeton Theological Seminary and Yale Divinity School—respected evangelical theologians such as Benjamin Warfield, Augustus Strong, William Shedd, and Charles Hodge expounded an American Protestant orthodoxy with great intellectual aptitude and confidence. Evangelical Protestantism of this era was institutionally and theologically secure. As to the spiritual devotion of the people, evangelical Protestantism was basking in the luster of wave upon wave of successful revivals and awakenings—from those of Jonathan Edwards to Charles Finney—that had and were converting enormous numbers of previously unchurched Americans into the evangelical Protestant camp. And overseas, nineteenth-century American evangelicals had mobilized a missionary enterprise of vast proportions that was spreading the Gospel in Africa, Asia, the Pacific, and Latin America. Both at home and abroad, it appeared that the Protestant Gospel was on the march, effectively Christianizing America and the world. In 1890, Congregational theologian Lewis French Stearns (1890: 366) proclaimed, "Today Christianity is the power which is moulding the destinies of the world. The Christian nations are in the ascendant[cy]. . . . The old promise is being fulfilled; the followers of the true God are inheriting the world."

Intellectually, nineteenth-century orthodox Protestantism enjoyed and promoted an epistemological worldview that secured the critical importance of the Bible and theology in the scientific enterprise. Believing that all of God's truth was unified and readily knowable, evangelicals employed the dominant Baconian paradigm of scientific knowledge and the epistemology of Scottish Common Sense Realism to demonstrate that faith and science could and must go hand-in-hand. The Bible would reveal God's moral law and certain natural truths; science, for its part, would confirm the teachings of the Bible and expand human understanding beyond what the Bible revealed. Together, the Bible and science were expected to render a rational validation of the veracity of Christianity and lay the foundation for a healthy national moral and social order.

Beyond views of science, for most of the nineteenth century, American public culture was dominated by the concerns and assumptions of evangelical Protestantism. Evangelical leaders engaged in public discourse in a way that effectively prescribed the moral bearing of the nation. Typical of the sentiment of the day was this counsel given in 1891 by University of Pennsylvania sociologist Robert Thompson (quoted in Cornelison 1891: 4) to a class of students at Princeton Theological Seminary: "There is no peace for us but to become a more Christian nation and discovering anew the pertinence of the Ten Words of Sinai and the Sermon of the Foundations to our social condition." Through the work of many Christian preachers, writers, and moralists like Thompson, Christian rhetoric, values, and morals hegemonically permeated public discourse, shaping the focus, content, and limits of imaginable popular debate.

Given its role as primary moral guardian of the nation, it is not surprising that nineteenth-century evangelicalism exerted much control over the American education system, private and public, at all levels. University and college presidents, for example, at even the most prestigious schools, were often not businessmen, but well-educated clergymen. University boards of trustees, too, typically contained many Protestant church leaders and clergymen. Furthermore, college and university curricula typically reflected a Protestant worldview and epistemology, combining classical curriculum with orthodox Protestant theology and piety to train properly the future leaders of America's Christian civilization. At lower levels, too, education included generous doses of training in Christian belief, morals, and virtues. Indeed, public schools were believed to be the primary agency that could unify America under a common Protestant perspective.

Politically and socially, nineteenth-century evangelical Protestants were extremely active in civic reform. Many of the culture's public practices—such as Sabbatarianism—were, of course, already modeled after Christian standards. But postmillennial evangelical Protestants believed that America fully becoming the kingdom of God would require additional social reform efforts. The abolition of slavery was, at least to Northern evangelicals, viewed as a major advance of the kingdom of God in America. Beyond that, evangelical Protestants organized myriad voluntary societies and poured their energies into the causes of hospitals, schools, orphanages, prison reform, temperance laws, peace activism, recreation and leisure organizations, Sunday education for working children, the outlawing of dueling, services to native Americans and the poor, and the reform of prostitutes, drunks, and other dishonorable elements of any Christian civilization. So pervasive and zealous was the activism of Protestant voluntary societies, that one Protestant convert to Roman Catholicism, Orestes Brownson (quoted in Askew and Spellman 1984: 86), complained that, "a peaceable man can hardly venture to eat or drink, to go to bed or get up, to correct his children or kiss his wife," without the guidance and sanction of some voluntary society.

Overarching all of this public influence, respectability, engagement, and relevance that nineteenth-century evangelicals enjoyed and fostered was the pervasive belief that America was truly a Christian nation, blessed by God and destined to become the kingdom of heaven on earth. One Methodist bishop, Matthew Simpson, for example, gloried in 1870 that, "God is making our land a kind of central spot for the whole earth. The eyes of the world are upon us." A Methodist colleague of Simpson's, Edward Thomas, declared then too that soon America would become a nation of one hundred million, "without an adulterer, or a swearer, or a Sabbath-breaker, or an ingrate, or an apostate, or a backslider, or a slanderer; hundreds of thousands of homes without a prodigal, a quarrel, or a heart-burn, or a bitter tear" (both quoted in Handy 1984: 70). Evangelical Protestantism in nineteenth century America appeared to represent the advanced guard of civilization that was leading to the kingdom of God on earth.

But then all that began to change. During the last quarter of the nineteenth century, a series of profound social, demographic, and intellectual transformations began to challenge evangelical Protestantism's security, influence, and relevance. Within the churches, liberal theology, biblical higher criticism, and an increased skepticism about supernaturalism began to question the old orthodox verities. And advocates of the Social Gospel began to devalue, in the eyes of many evangelicals, the importance of individual conversion to Christ in favor of structural reforms. Outside of the churches, the shift from the Newtonian paradigm of science and the collapse of Scottish Common Sense Realism seriously undermined in scientific circles any role for the Bible in scientific inquiry. Naturalistic assumptions about reality were coming to dominate the academy, and the Bible increasingly was seen as little more than human writings full of myths and errors. Darwinian evolutionism was particularly challenging to the traditional evangelical worldview. In academia, businessmen increasingly replaced clergy as leaders of colleges and universities, which were more and more separating specialized disciplines, offering elective courses, and advocating academic freedom to espouse different interpretations of truth. Additionally, orthodox Protestantism's dominance of American public culture was increasingly giving way to a "neutral," "rational" version of cultural discourse that left little room for the voice of religious authority. Furthermore, urbanization and industrialization were creating new, massive social problems that evangelical voluntary societies seemed increasingly unable to address and resolve. An expanding federal government at home and abroad and the rise of secular progressive political movements began taking over causes that evangelicals previously championed. Finally, the American population was changing demographically. New waves of immigration from Eastern and Southern Europe were bringing to these shores masses of Roman Catholics and, to a lesser extent, Jews, who did not automatically share Protestant assumptions and values. And religious groups, such as Latter Day Saints and Roman Catholics, began to challenge Protestantism's social hegemony in the courts. By the turn of the century, it began to seem that conservative Protestantism's widespread public respectability, influence, and security, as the cutting-edge of civilization itself, might have been built on a foundation of sand. And the rains were pouring down.

In the end, the Protestant establishment house did crumble. And the transition from cultural establishment to disestablishment was for orthodox Protestantism a very painful, confusing, and complex process. Suffice it for our purposes to say that some conservative Protestants were persuaded to give up the old orthodoxy and join the cause of the modernists and liberals. The majority appear to have retained most of their orthodox beliefs and simply done their best to ride out the turbulent changes of the times, adjusting as best as possible to the new reality. But a minority of other conservative Protestants, who could not abide this perceived assault on Christian truth and civilization, decided to fight back. In the first two decades of the twentieth century, this group of Protestant church leaders mobilized a coalition of conservatives to combat modernism in the churches and in the schools. Their two strategic goals were, in the North, to wrest control of the major Protestant—particularly Baptist and Presbyterian—denominations from liberal forces and, in the South, to make illegal the teaching of Darwinian evolutionism in public schools. In time, these fighting conservatives were labeled "fundamentalists"—a term coined from a booklet series they published between 1910 and 1915 called *The Fundamentals*—and their movement, "fundamentalism."

The years 1917 to 1925 proved to be decisive in the fundamentalist-modernist struggle. Most of the theological, ecclesiastical, and political conflicts that had been brewing for decades erupted in these years into open, bellicose conflict. The fundamentalists were now engaged in an all-out war against secularists, modernists, and liberals. For a time, it appeared that the fundamentalists would win, saving their denominations from liberal penetration and American society from the onslaught of secularism. But in 1925, both of the fundamentalists' strategic campaigns ended in apparent failures. In the pivotal struggle to oust liberals from leadership in the major denominations, defeat was snatched from the jaws of victory when, at the eleventh hour, the majority of more moderate, inclusive conservatives voted—in the name of tolerance, and against the fundamentalists—not to expel the modernists from their denominations. The fundamentalists were furious, double-crossed by their fellow orthodox believers, who they said betrayed the Gospel into the hands of modernism. And in the Southern campaign against Darwinism, fundamentalists met a seeming defeat in the Scopes Monkey Trial of Dayton, Tennessee. Defense attorney Clarence Darrow and the host of attending national media journalists managed to portray prosecuting attorney William Jennings Bryan and the fundamentalists whose cause he championed as ignorant, reactionary, obscurantist, and intolerant. Although Bryan actually won the legal case, the conviction was soon overturned. Much more importantly, the fundamentalists lost the trial of national media opinion as commentators across the nation now stereotyped them as uneducated, provincial, mulish enemies of progress. The political momentum to prohibit the teaching of evolution collapsed. And in a chance development of immense symbolic significance, William Jennings Bryan died suddenly in Dayton the Sunday after the trial ended. The fundamentalist war to save Christian truth and civilization had been lost.

What happened next is absolutely critical for our story. In the decades that followed the 1925 defeats, particularly by the late 1940s, the fundamentalist movement turned in upon itself and increasingly began to resemble in fact the caricature of fundamentalism that its antagonists lampooned. Having for years championed the necessity of doctrinal purity within the denominations, yet having lost the battle to expel the liberals, the fundamentalists believed they had no choice but to denounce and leave their denominations and to start new, theologically correct denominations and church fellowships. Particularly by the 1940s, *separatism* became a new fundamentalist strategy for dealing with suspect Christians and the modern world. Among some, the doctrine of "double separation" became the litmus test of purity: a good fundamentalist had to separate not only from modernists and liberals but also from any otherwise-orthodox believer who refused to break all ties with liberals. This meant that any moderate conservative who chose to remain within a mainline denomination, or even to cooperate with those who did so, was shunned for consorting with enemies of the Gospel. Fundamentalist bitterness over their betrayal by inclusive conservatives in their former denominations lingered long, and tremendous energy was expended castigating all but the most doctrinally and associationally pure believers. Furthermore, having cultivated for years the faculty for detecting signs of doctrinal compromise in their denominational colleagues, the post-1925 fundamentalists grew hypersensitive even to the slightest hint of theological corruption within their own ranks. Accusations of apostasy, factionalism, heresy trials, schismatic splits, and self-righteous doctrinal legalism became pandemic within the fundamentalist subculture.

Fundamentalism's separatist strategy conditioned its relationship to history and society, too. Nineteenth-century Protestantism's postmillennialism—which had not only come to seem terribly naive by the early twentieth century but had also become associated in the fundamentalist mind with the liberal Social Gospel—was rejected in favor of the more recent theological invention of premillennialist dispensationalism. Premillennialism taught that history and society were, in God's plan, inevitably going to grow worse and worse until, just before things hit rock-bottom, Christ would return to vindicate his faithful remnant people and establish his kingdom on earth. This pessimistic view of history suggested that the only task left for the Church was to remain separate from and unblemished by the world and to "win" as many souls to heaven before the damned ship of history went down. This left less rationale for social reform or political engagement, for the world's demise was an inevitable part of God's plan. Nor was there as much reason to sustain intellectual debate in the universities or through the media from a Christian worldview, since modern society had already rejected the truth, and since such engagement might lead to one's own intellectual and spiritual contamination. The perspective of many fundamentalists became: let the worldly intelligentsia, scholars, universities, media, cultural elite, and politicians—all who had spurned Christian truth and civilization—go to perdition.

Finally, fundamentalist ethics underwent a mutation that reflected its judgmental separatism. The fundamentalist subculture's need to establish and maintain strong identity boundaries prompted the creation of clear behavioral contrasts with "worldliness," defined primarily against progressive cultural expressions of the day. The traditional Christian virtues of charity, humility, patience, and so on were displaced by lists of specific, behavioral rules. What separated God's faithful remnant from the degenerate—

besides doctrinal purity, of course—became simply that true Christians did not dance, smoke cigarettes, chew tobacco, drink alcohol, gamble, wear makeup, "bob" their hair, attend the theater, play billiards or cards, or wear immodest clothing. With these subcultural norms, a powerful legalism permeated fundamentalism that maintained its visible separation from the secular world through rigid, self-enforcing, behavioral social control.

The total effect was powerful and conspicuous. By the end of the 1930s, much of conservative Protestantism—under the banner of fundamental-ism—had evolved into a somewhat reclusive and defensive version of its nineteenth-century self. Organizationally, fundamentalism was expanding and strengthening (Carpenter 1980, 1984a, 1984b). But in spirit and cul-ture, much of fundamentalism seemed to have become withdrawn, defen-sive, judgmental, factionalized, brooding, self-righteous, anti-intellectual, paranoid, and pessimistic. At least that is how things looked to some of the younger, more moderate fundamentalist leaders at the time. The condi-tions were ripe for a countermovement from within.

Resuscitating the Evangelical Vision[3]

Harold Ockenga, J. Elwin Wright, Wilbur Smith, Edward Carnell, Carl Henry, Harold Lindsell, Charles Fuller, Gleason Archer, Everett Harrison, Bernard Ramm, Billy Graham. These are just a few of the names of a group of mostly young, moderate fundamentalists who by the early 1940s had grown weary of their own tradition. After fifteen years of fundamentalist negativity and isolation, this growing network of restless evangelists, schol-ars, and pastors began to formulate a critique of their own fundamentalist subculture and a vision for its transformation.

Three facts particularly bothered this coterie of budding reformers. First, as heirs of the evangelical legacy, they believed in effective evange-lism. They were committed to effectively delivering the Gospel of salvation to the world through smart evangelistic campaigns and crusades. Theoreti-cally, all fundamentalists believed in this. But, it had become increasingly clear to these men that the factionalist, separatist, judgmental character of fundamentalism itself had become an insurmountable impediment to

3. Valuable works on the neo-evangelical movement, from which the following section draws, are Marsden 1987, 1984; Carpenter 1984a, 1984b, 1988; Dayton and Johnston 1991; Wuthnow 1988; Fowler 1982; Quebedeaux 1974; Hunter 1983; Askew and Spellman 1984; Wells and Woodbridge 1975; Henry and Kantzer 1996; Hollinger 1983; Bloesch 1973; Er-ickson 1993; McGrath 1995; Allan 1989; Lightner 1978; Henry 1986; Nelson 1987; Soper 1994; Tidball 1994; Abraham 1984; Nash 1987a.

effectively evangelizing American society for Christ. Fundamentalism, these men realized, had guarded doctrinal purity at the enormous cost of sacrificing the spread of the Gospel—a cost too great to bear. Second, many of this growing network of moderate fundamentalists were promising intellectuals, in love with the life of the mind. Firmly rooted in Reformed faith, and standing in admiration of the intellectual stature of the likes of Princeton theologians Benjamin Warfield and J. Gresham Machen, these young men believed that orthodox Protestantism should be bringing a distinctive and respectable Christian voice to the important intellectual debates of the day. They wanted a true Christian faith that could hold its own in academic circles and thus provide a sound philosophical defense of the Christian world and life view. Naturally, they found the defensive and withdrawn anti-intellectualism of their own fundamentalist subculture, which sabotaged any serious attempt at intellectual engagement with the larger culture, terribly frustrating and embarrassing. Third, many of this group of emerging fundamentalist reformers believed that orthodox Christians needed to be socially and politically active. Theirs was an era of global economic depression, the rise of fascism in Europe, the consolidation of communism in Russia, and the outbreak of an ominous world war. But these conservative believers were convinced that Jesus Christ was the answer for the world's social, economic, and political problems and wanted to see Christians making a real impact on the world. However, they also knew that fundamentalism could never sustain this kind of active engagement in such worldly affairs. Its disengaged separatism, pessimistic premillennial dispensationalism, and concern with maintaining purity apart from the world provided no theological or social basis for such involvement. These three grievances led to one conclusion: for Christians to think and live as Christians should, a reform of or break with the worst features of the fundamentalist movement would be required. Separatism, factionalism, anti-intellectualism, defensiveness, pessimism, isolationism, and paranoia would all have to go. A new tradition, a new subculture, a new vision, and new goals would have to be envisioned, organized, and promoted.

The vision and program these young, restless reformers began to develop in response can best be described as "engaged orthodoxy." In keeping with their nineteenth-century Protestant heritage, they were fully committed to maintaining and promoting confidently traditional, orthodox Protestant theology and belief, *while at the same time* becoming confidently and proactively engaged in the intellectual, cultural, social, and political life of the nation. Their commitment to orthodoxy and engagement, respectively, distinguished these incipient "neo-evangelicals"—as they began to call themselves—from their liberal Protestant cousins, on the one hand, and from their fundamentalist siblings, on the other. This clique of maverick religious activists were convinced that it was possible not only to believe the historically orthodox faith, but to do so in a way that was intellectually respectable, culturally engaged, and socially responsible.

They knew, however, that to make this happen, their vision would have to be institutionalized. They therefore set on a major campaign to organize a national movement. J. Elwin Wright, a leader at Harold Ockenga's Park Street Church in Boston, Massachusetts, had been traveling throughout New England, successfully organizing pastors and churches into the moderate interdenominational New England Fellowship. That accomplished, he and Ockenga set their sights on founding an organization at the national level that would unify and coordinate the voice of neo-evangelicals across the country. Wright criss-crossed the nation, mobilizing scores of sympathetic church leaders to support the neo-evangelical project. These efforts culminated in the 1942 St. Louis meeting at the Hotel Coronado, where the National Association of Evangelicals (NAE) was founded. In a move that shocked fundamentalists, Wright and Ockenga invited Pentecostals, Anabaptists, Holiness, and other nonfundamentalist Christians to attend, many of whom did. At that historic meeting, speakers stressed the need for unity and love among different Protestant traditions for the sake of the Gospel and the world. The founding of the NAE was of great symbolic as well as institutional significance, since it offered an alternative national organization to the fundamentalist's separatist American Council of Christian Churches (ACCC), formed one year earlier by arch-fundamentalist, Carl MacIntire.

The NAE was only the beginning of the organizing. To address their concerns about intellectual respectability and engagement, Harold Ockenga and popular Californian radio evangelist Charles Fuller teamed up in 1947 to found Fuller Theological Seminary in Pasadena, California. Fuller was, in the vision of its founder, to be the "Cal Tech of modern evangelicalism," producing scholarship the quality of which would parallel that of the giants of Princeton Theological Seminary in its former glory days, before orthodox evangelicals were edged out by liberals. Faculty positions at Fuller were filled by the leading lights of the neo-evangelical movement: Smith, Carnell, Archer, Harrison, Henry, Lindsell, and Charles Fuller himself.

On the evangelistic front, Billy Graham began in the late 1940s a series of crusades around the nation that promoted—by fundamentalist standards, at least—cooperation among local organizing churches and an ecu-menical spirit. An archetypal neo-evangelical, Graham was more inter-ested in effectively preaching the basic Gospel to America than in policing strict standards of doctrinal and associational purity. Graham's message was traditional and conservative, indeed, but it focused on the essentials of sal-vation that most conservatives could agree with and avoided overtones of rigidity and legalism.

By 1954, Billy Graham had also begun organizing to launch the publi-cation of a new evangelical periodical that would rival the liberal journal, *Christian Century*. What Graham wanted was something that would, in his words, "plant the evangelical flag in the middle of the road, taking the conservative theological position but a definite liberal approach to social problems. It would combine the best in liberalism and the best in funda-mentalism without compromising theologically" (Marsden 1987: 158). With the help of L. Nelson Bell, Harold Lindsell, and Carl Henry—who became the magazine's first editor—Graham's vision came to fruition in 1956 with the publication of *Christianity Today*, mainstream evangelical-ism's flagship journal.

The NAE, Fuller Seminary, Graham's crusades, and *Christianity Today* were only a few of the important organizational initiatives taken to institu-tionalize the budding evangelical movement. During these and subsequent years, a host of decidedly evangelical organizations were founded, and other, preexisting organizations aligned themselves with the new evangeli-calism. The emerging evangelical educational establishment, for example, eventually came to include not only Fuller Seminary, but, at the graduate level, also Gordon-Conwell Theological Seminary, Trinity Evangelical Di-vinity School, Calvin Theological Seminary, North Park Theological Sem-inary, Covenant Theological Seminary, and Asbury Theological Semi-nary.[4] A host of undergraduate liberal arts colleges also aligned themselves with neo-evangelicalism, including Gordon College, Westmont College, Calvin College, Houghton College, Seattle Pacific University, Bethel Col-lege, Taylor University, Messiah College, Azusa Pacific University, and Wheaton College, to name a few. The growing host of evangelical missions and evangelistic ministries came to include Youth for Christ, Campus Cru-sade for Christ, Young Life, Inter-Varsity Christian Fellowship, The Navi-gators, Teen Challenge, Fellowship of Christian Athletes, World Vision

4. Many of the institutions and undergraduate colleges listed here predated neo-evangelicalism but were drawn into the emerging neo-evangelical movement in the 1950s and 1960s.

International, the Luasanne Committee for World Evangelization, the Overseas Missionary Fellowship, the Evangelical Foreign Missions Association, and the World Evangelical Fellowship, again just to name a few. Joining *Christianity Today* as important evangelical periodicals were *Eternity* magazine, *The Reformed Journal,* the *Christian Scholars Review, Journal of the Evangelical Theological Society, Sojourners* magazine, *Christian Herald* magazine, and *Christian Life* magazine. The growing list of evangelical publishing houses came to include William B. Eerdmans Publishing, Zondervan Publishing House, Inter-Varsity Press, Baker Book House, Word Books, Tyndale House, Crossways Books, Thomas Nelson Publishing, Fleming H. Revell Publishing, Multnomah Books, and Hendrickson Publishing Company. And the multitude of evangelical music production and recording companies include Myrhh, Sparrow, Word, Dayspring, Reunion, Benson, Forefront, Brentwood, and Star Song. Other important evangelical organizations include the Evangelical Theological Society, the National Religious Broadcasters, Evangelicals for Social Action, and the Evangelical Press Association. In a relatively short time, then, the evangelical movement had established an institutional infrastructure of impressive magnitude and strength. The spirit of engaged orthodoxy had become incarnate in one giant, national transdenominational network of evangelical organizations.[5]

Restructuring the Field of Religious Identity

The first neo-evangelical leaders actually were originally somewhat ambivalent about their relationship with their fundamentalist heritage. Theoretically, they would have liked simply to reform fundamentalism, setting the entire fundamentalist movement back on what they saw as the right track. At the same time, they were fully aware of fundamentalism's deeply ingrained flaws and were fully committed, if necessary, to creating a new movement with a distinct name and character. Time would prove the reform strategy impossible and the need to start a new, autonomous movement inevitable. The old wineskins simply could not contain the new wine.

Already in the early 1940s, neo-evangelicalism was taking on a clearly

5. Evangelicalism is not primarily denominationally based but, according to George Marsden, "a transdenominational movement in which many people, in various ways, feel at home. . . . Institutionally, this transdenominational evangelicalism is built around networks of parachurch agencies" (1984: xiv). Evangelicalism today is composed of Baptists, Presbyterians, Methodists, Pentecostals, Charismatics, Independents, Lutherans, Anabaptists, Restorationists, Congregationalists, Holiness Christians, and Episcopalians.

distinct identity, and competition between the old fundamentalist and new evangelical traditions was heating up. Every attempt by the evangelical organizers to move in a more moderate direction was condemned by fundamentalist leaders as the first movement on the slippery slope to godless liberalism. In time, it became clear that evangelicalism would never be able to reform fundamentalism, at least directly, but would have to break with it and construct a more intellectually respectable, culturally engaged, and socially responsible alternative. Although their separation had been in process since the early 1940s, the evangelical-fundamentalist divorce was symbolically finalized in 1957 when Billy Graham invited the relatively liberal Protestant Council of the City of New York to help organize an upcoming evangelistic crusade. Fundamentalist leaders where absolutely flabbergasted and infuriated and denounced Graham as apostate. Graham stayed the course, however, convinced that cooperation, not separatism, would best help spread the Gospel. This was the final, irreparable breach.

It would be inaccurate, then, to portray neo-evangelicalism's break from fundamentalism as a quick and easy achievement. It was, rather, the result of a difficult process over the fifteen-year period between—to draw convenient symbolic markers—the founding of the NAE and the decisive rift over Graham's New York crusade. It would be equally inaccurate to portray evangelicalism's break from fundamentalism as absolute and total. For, despite their breach with fundamentalism, many fundamentalist instincts persisted in the thought of most evangelical leaders, particularly during the earliest years (Sweeney 1992). Nevertheless, it is clear that, over time, evangelicalism and fundamentalism developed into two distinct religious movements with major differences in orientation and style. By the mid-1950s, at the latest, it was clear that the emergence of modern evangelicalism had affected a restructuring in the field of American religious identity.

We must be precise, however, about what this evangelical movement did and did not accomplish. It did not by decree transform entire sectors of separatist fundamentalists into engaged evangelicals overnight. Nor did it thoroughly instill its vision of engaged orthodoxy in every individual who came to be associated with it. Nor did neo-evangelicalism merge the diverse faith traditions that made up its constituency—for example, the Reformed, Pentecostals, Pietists—into one supratradition in a way that negated the differences among them. What the evangelical movement *did* accomplish was to open up a "space" between fundamentalism and liberalism in the field of religious collective identity; give that space a name; articulate and promote a resonant vision of faith and practice that players in the religious field came to associate with that name and identity-space; and invite a variety of religious players to move into that space to participate in the "identity-work" and mission being accomplished there. In so doing, these evangelical activists created a distinct, publicly recognizable collective identity, in relation to which individuals, congregations, denominations, and para-church organizations were thereafter able to recognize and form their own faith identities and action-commitments. The new identity also enabled its promoters to mobilize, consolidate, and deploy resources in a new direction for a new purpose. Religious actors who either already silently occupied this space prior to its public naming, or who subsequently "migrated" to inhabit this newly named religious-identity space were then able to signify to themselves and to other actors in a publicly recognizable way their intentions regarding the character of their own religious beliefs, allegiances, demeanor, priorities, and activities. In this way, evangelicalism created an agenda distinct from fundamentalism's around which a variety of Protestants could rally and establish some degree of commonality and solidarity.

It was as if—on a field in which people cluster around various banners to which they feel some common allegiance—a small group of people broke from the crowd assembled under the fundamentalist standard, moved toward an open space in the field, and planted a new evangelical banner somewhat closer to the liberal flag, under and around which people from various positions on the field then began to gather to establish a new distribution of clustered positions on the field. Alternatively, it was as if— on a field in which competing groups stake out and rope off territory to occupy—the neo-evangelicals who stood in the fundamentalists' territory closest to that of the liberals pulled up the nearby stakes that roped them in, threw the stakes and rope behind them, pounded into the ground new stakes, and roped off a large piece of new territory for themselves—all the while waving occupants from around the field to join them in their newly roped off space (and leaving those left behind in the fundamentalist territory, now sniping at them, to hurriedly pound back down the stakes to form a new boundary of a smaller fundamentalist territory). Neo-evangelicalism created a new identity- and strategy-option for American Protestants which reconfigured the field of American Protestantism and opened up new possibilities for alternative expressions of faith and religious practice.

Assessing Evangelicalism Today

The central question of this study is: what has become of the modern evangelical movement? Sixty years after its founding, where today does the evangelical project of engaged orthodoxy stand? And what does that tell us about the nature of religious movements in America and the prospects for traditional religious faith in the modern world?

Clearly, the world of American culture and society—to which the modern evangelical movement was committed to engaging as a redemptive influence—has been dramatically transformed since the evangelical movement's formative years. American society has undergone an avalanche of social, cultural, technological, and intellectual changes that have profoundly altered the life-experiences of most Americans: the Civil Rights movement; Vietnam; the 1960s counterculture; Watergate; the Sexual Revolution; the legalization of abortion; the rapid expansion of mass-consumer materialism; the explosion of high-tech media and communications systems; the rapid increase of women in the paid labor force; the emergence and growth of the Women's and Gay Rights movements; changing family demographics; growing environmental concerns; the proliferation of therapeutic self-help movements; the election of evangelical President Jimmy Carter; the rise of global militant Islam; a Christian fundamentalist resurgence in national and local politics; the weakening of mainline-liberal Protestant denominations; the Reagan-Bush era; the skyrocketing national debt; the Gulf War; the war on drugs; the fall of communism and emergence of a nebulous post–Cold War geopolitical order; the increasingly globalized economy; a growing interest in Eastern and New Age spiritualities; Music Television; Generation X; the expansion of liberal and libertarian "rights-talk"; the rise of epistemological and moral relativism and individualistic subjectivism; and postmodernism's subversion of faith in science, reason, and foundationalist principles. Few areas of life—whether work, politics, family, leisure, or even notions about the human self and its purpose—have remained untouched by these kinds of social changes. Increasingly, more spheres of life have been opened up for reconsideration and redefinition, and the assumptions, beliefs, values, and behaviors of most Americans have been significantly altered. Our question is: after all of this whirlwind of change, what has become of Harold Ockenga, Charles Fuller, Carl Henry, and Billy Graham's evangelical movement and its vision of engaged orthodoxy?

Many observers, including both academic sociologists (for example, Hunter 1983, 1987) and respected evangelical leaders (for example, Wells 1993; Schaeffer 1984; Noll 1994), view modern evangelicalism as either floundering in its mission or actually disintegrating under the pressures of the modern world around it. Others (for example, McGrath 1995; Nash 1987b; Bloesch 1973) take a more benign view, predicting bright prospects for evangelicalism. Our purpose is to explore these and other possibilities in order accurately to assess and explain the condition of the modern evangelical movement today and to reflect on the possibilities of sustaining traditional religion in modern American society.

To explore these issues as insightfully and thoroughly as possible, our study employed a variety of research methods executed in successive stages over a fifteen-month period. During the summer of 1995, we conducted semistructured, two-hour, face-to-face interviews with 130 churchgoing Protestants in Massachusetts, Minnesota, North Carolina, Alabama, Illinois, and Oregon, sampled to represent the variety of theological and denominational traditions in American Protestantism (for a detailed description of our methodology, see Appendix A). During the first three months of 1996, we conducted a national, random-digit-dial, 160-question telephone survey of a sample of all Americans, with an oversample of churchgoing Protestants ($N = 2,591$) (see Appendix D). During the summer of 1996, we conducted in-depth, two-hour, face-to-face interviews with 178 evangelical Christians from twenty-three states proportionately representing every region of the country (see Map 1.1). Ninety-three of those interviewed were respondents from our nationally representative telephone survey who identified themselves as "evangelicals" and agreed to in-depth follow-up interviews—a nationally representative sample of all American evangelicals. The other eighty-five were sampled from church congregations in eleven locations around the country that had reputations among area clergy for being the most clearly "evangelical" churches in the areas. In addition to interviewing evangelicals, we also interviewed nine survey respondents who identified themselves as "fundamentalists" and six as "liberal Protestants." We called back with follow-up questions about religious doubt and unbelief forty of our survey respondents who reported that they "often" had doubts about their religious beliefs and another thirty-four who reported being raised in a religious family but claim now to be nonreligious. Finally, we also called back respondents from our phone survey with questions about Christian faith and education; we called a sample of fifteen (of twenty total) who home-schooled their children, a random sample of fifty (of 187) who sent their children to Christian schools, and a sample of 130 (of 1,243) who sent their children to public schools. This extensive, multimethod data-gathering effort yielded an enormous body of evidence, of tremendous breadth and depth, about the identities, beliefs, attitudes, commitments, and behaviors of American Protestants, and particularly of American evangelicals.

Much of the analysis of this book is based on a set of religious self-

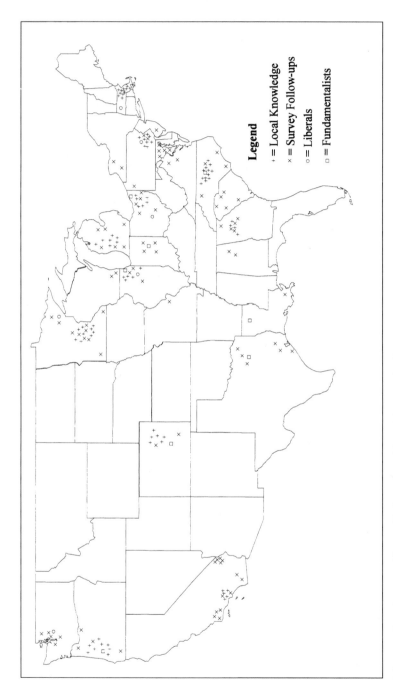

Map 1.1: Distribution of Survey Follow-up and Local-Knowledge Interviewees

identifications—rather than denominational or theological classifications—by which our survey respondents categorized themselves as various kinds of Protestants associated with major historical American Protestant traditions. In this work, we distinguish the identity categories of evangelical, fundamentalist, mainline Protestant, and theologically liberal Protestant. We simply asked the churchgoing Protestants in our survey whether any of these labels described them. If respondents self-identified with more than one, we asked them which of those labels best described them. In this way, our survey respondents' sorted themselves into one of these four identity categories. In the analysis that follows, we employ these identity categories to make a variety of comparisons between the major Protestant traditions in America.[6] (For a detailed explanation of and justification for this religious self-identity measure, see Appendix B.)

In the following chapters, we employ this data to construct an interpretation of American evangelicalism that suggests unexpected conclusions with significant theoretical implications. The next chapter argues that contemporary American evangelicalism is, by a variety of measures, alive and well; indeed, it is thriving. Chapter 3 then reviews and evaluates an assortment of sociological theories of religious vitality which offer to help explain evangelicalism's religious strength. In chapter 4, we propose an alternative theoretical explanation for evangelical vitality—a subcultural identity theory—which appropriates and extends recent theoretical developments in the sociology of religion. Chapter 5 then demonstrates how this theory applies to and explains the case of contemporary American evangelicalism. In chapter 6, we explore in greater depth the problems and prospects of traditional belief plausibility in America. Chapter 7 analyzes ways in which subcultural factors that build evangelical strength also appear ironically to undermine evangelical strategic efforts at social change. Our hope is that, by better understanding evangelicalism, we will also better understand religious movements in America generally, along with the prospects for and significance of traditional religious faith in the modern world.

6. Thus, in the following chapters, when we identify people we interviewed as "evangelical," "fundamentalist," "mainline," or "liberal," we are referring to religious identity traditions with which they themselves personally identified in interviews—*not* to our own *a priori* categorizations of their church denominations or theologies. So, for example, an "evangelical Presbyterian" is someone who attends a Presbyterian church and thinks of himself or herself as an evangelical; a "mainline Lutheran" attends a Lutheran church and considers himself or herself a mainline Protestant; a "liberal Methodist" attends a Methodist church and considers himself or herself a liberal Protestant; etc.

TWO

Evangelicalism Thriving

Contemporary American evangelicalism is thriving. It is more than alive and well. Indeed, we will see in this chapter that it appears to be the strongest of the major Christian traditions in the United States today.

But what does it mean to be a "strong" religious tradition? By what criteria do we measure religious strength? Most of the debates on this topic in the sociology of religion literature revolve around differences in a single dimension of religious vitality: church attendance and membership (for example, Hadaway, Marler, and Chaves 1993; Finke and Stark 1988, 1989a, 1989b, 1992; Finke and Ianaccone 1993; Finke 1989; Finke, Guest, and Stark 1996; Land, Deane, and Blau 1991; Blau, Land, and Redding 1992; Hout and Greeley 1987; Kelley 1972; Bibby and Brinkerhoff 1973, 1983; Bibby 1978). But church attendance and membership is only one possible dimension of a religious movement or tradition's strength. And relying on attendance and membership alone can be very misleading. Hypothetically, a church's pews could be completely filled with regular attenders who are exceptionally uncommitted, uninformed, and apathetic religiously—who perhaps want nothing more than a place to meet useful business contacts and the status they think is associated with being an upstanding, church-going citizen of their community. We wouldn't consider *that* a strong church. Church attendance, then, may be one useful indicator of religious strength; but to make convincing claims about religious strength, we need a better measure than mere attendance.

There are many possible ways to conceive of religious "strength." Some analysts conceptualize the strength of a movement or organization as its ability to maintain social control, group cohesion, and membership-retention by sustaining the intensity of its members' commitment to and readiness to sacrifice for the group (for example, Kanter 1972). Others focus on organizations' assets and long-term probabilities of survival (for example, Marwell 1996: 1099). Yet others emphasize the capacity to satisfy members effectively and to achieve performance goals (for example, Schermerhorn, Hunt, and Osborn 1994: 276–77). Some might measure strength in terms of the religious organization's ability to extract, coordinate, and deploy resources to accomplish its mission (Wuthnow 1988: 495). Others might highlight the ability of the religion to maintain the vitality of members' experiential, ritualistic, ideological, intellectual, and consequential religiosity (Glock and Stark 1965). Kim Cameron (1980; 1986) has attempted to synthesize some of these aspects into a multidimensional approach to organizational effectiveness that emphasizes resource acquisition, constituency satisfaction, internal organizational functioning, and goal accomplishment.

It appears that there exists no one correct definition of strength that applies to all movements, organizations, and communities. How strength is conceptualized and measured depends on the exact nature of the group in question—on its self-definition, values, and purpose. Nonetheless, we can say that a truly comprehensive analysis of religious strength needs to analyze both the organizational and leadership dimensions of a religion, as well as the qualities of the people who constitute the religion's adherents—the first taking a more "top-down," and the second a more "bottom-up" approach.

Since our study focuses primarily on the beliefs, attitudes, opinions, commitments, and behaviors of *ordinary* evangelicals, and not evangelical organizations and leadership, our analysis is limited to the more "bottom-up" approach to measuring the strength of evangelicalism. Nevertheless, to do this, we intend to go well beyond measuring mere church attendance to assess evangelicalism's vitality by examining six distinct dimensions of religious strength: adherence to beliefs, salience of faith, robustness of faith, group participation, commitment to mission, and retention and recruitment of members. For our purposes, then, we will consider any American Christian faith-tradition to be strong when its members (1) faithfully adhere to essential Christian religious beliefs; (2) consider their faith a highly salient aspect of their lives; (3) reflect great confidence and assurance in their religious beliefs; (4) participate regularly in a variety of church activities and programs; (5) are committed in both belief and action to accomplishing the mission of the church; and (6) sustain high rates of membership retention by maintaining members' association with the tradition over long periods of time, effectively socializing new members into that tradition, and winning new converts to that tradition.[1] With these multiple-indicators in mind, we turn now to assess the vitality of the modern evangelical movement.

Adherence to Beliefs

Among all of the major Christian traditions in the contemporary United States, evangelicalism exhibits the highest degree of adherence to many of the traditionally orthodox Christian theological beliefs. Both our survey and interview data bear this out. Table 2.1 shows, for example, that evangelicals stand alone in completely rejecting the idea that the Bible is not inspired by God and are by far the least likely to believe that the Bible may contain errors. Fully ninety-seven percent of evangelicals believe the Bible is God-inspired and without error, a larger number than even that of fundamentalists.[2]

Similarly, evangelicals are the most likely to adhere to a theologically orthodox Christian view of human nature, which holds that, despite being created in God's image, human beings are sinful and in need of God's redemption and restoration. Table 2.1 shows that evangelicals—even compared to fundamentalists—are the least likely to believe that humans are entirely good (which is the only truly nonorthodox position here) and most likely to take the very strong view that humans are entirely sinful. Furthermore, table 2.1 reveals that evangelicals are the most likely to believe that faith in Jesus Christ is the only way to salvation. In addition, almost all evangelicals affirm that they have committed their lives to Jesus Christ as personal Lord and Savior. Interestingly, twice the proportion of fundamentalists than evangelicals believe that there are other ways to salvation, and three times the number of fundamentalists claim that they have not committed their lives to Christ as Lord and Savior.

Table 2.1 shows that evangelicals are by far and away the most likely of all major Christian traditions to affirm a belief in moral absolutes. By more than ten percentage points over fundamentalists, twenty over mainline

1. In chapter 7, we will assess evangelicalism using a very different conceptualization of religious strength: the capacity to influence or change one's cultural, social, or political environment.

2. Fundamentalists do hold to biblical literalism in higher numbers, but biblical literalism is a relatively recent theological emphasis of the early fundamentalist movement (Marsden 1980; Rogers and McKim 1979; Rogers 1977), not a mark of "truer" theological orthodoxy. Indeed, a historically informed perspective suggests that a nonliteral reading of the Bible is a more theologically sophisticated approach more in keeping with the long tradition of Christian orthodoxy.

Table 2.1: Religious Belief Commitments, by Tradition (percent)

	Evangelicals	Fundamentalists	Mainline	Liberals	Catholics
View of the Bible					
Literally true	52	61	35	39	23
True, not always literally	45	31	54	39	51
True, but with errors	3	7	9	15	22
Not inspired by God	0	1	2	7	5
Human Nature					
Sinful	34	27	11	6	3
Good and sinful	48	52	56	64	44
Good	18	22	33	30	53
Hope for Salvation					
Faith in Christ only	96	92	82	72	57
Other ways to salvation	4	8	18	28	43
Committed Life to Jesus Christ as Personal Lord and Savior					
Yes	97	91	87	77	67
No	3	9	13	23	33
View of Morality					
Absolute moral standards exist	75	65	55	34	38
No absolutes, people decide right and wrong for themselves	25	35	45	66	62
How Respondent Knows How God Wants Them to Live					
The Bible	48	41	28	21	7
Knows in heart through personal walk with God	44	48	58	61	71
Church teachings	6	7	10	10	11
Human reason	2	4	4	8	12
N	(430)	(389)	(576)	(431)	(114)

Note: Chi-square for all figures is significant at the .00000 level.

Protestants, and about forty points over liberal Protestants and Roman Catholics, evangelicals reject the idea of moral relativism and individual determinations of morality. Finally, when asked how they know how God wants them to live, evangelicals are the least likely to refer to human reason or to the institutional church's teachings. Instead, evangelicals appeal primarily to the Bible and secondarily to their personal relationship with God as their sources of spiritual and life-direction. While not a strict measure of Christian orthodoxy, per se—since Christian orthodoxy has at various times and places emphasized different combinations of these sources of authority—these results at least indicate an aversion among evangelicals to humanly and institutionally grounded sources of authority in favor of more spiritually grounded ones.

We must pause here, however, and acknowledge certain complications in comparing faith traditions theologically, for different traditions emphasize different points of orthodoxy over others. The idea of committing one's life to Christ as "personal Lord and Savior," for example, casts the broad orthodox demand for faith commitment and discipleship in rhetoric that evangelicals might find particularly familiar. And, as we have noted, different Christian traditions emphasize diverse sources of religious authority—for example, the Bible versus church teachings—over others. Nevertheless, we believe that table 2.1 is highly suggestive regarding evangelicals' concern with commitment to theological orthodoxy generally and that this measure of religious strength is validated by all of the other measures examined below. Thus, while individual measures may only offer tentative indications of religious vitality, this chapter's findings altogether point to a very clear pattern of evangelical strength.

Our in-depth interviews with churchgoing Protestants (see Appendix A) substantiate our survey data on beliefs, confirming that those who identify as evangelicals indeed do manifest very high degrees of concern with adherence to traditionally orthodox Christian theological beliefs. Most evangelicals we interviewed pointed to right beliefs about God, the Bible, and salvation as central to their religious identities and values. Typical in spirit is this Reformed woman's statement, vaguely reminiscent of the Apostle's Creed:

> As an evangelical, I believe that the whole Bible is true. I believe that Jesus Christ is the Son of God, and that he came into the world to save us, and He died on the cross and rose again from the

dead, and He is sitting at our Father's right hand. I also believe it's important to stand up for what you believe.[3]

For most evangelicals, a right view of the Bible is the linchpin of all theological orthodoxy. According to this Christian and Missionary Alliance woman:

> Evangelicals believe that the Bible is the inspired Word of God and the whole truth. Our first tenet is preaching Jesus Christ as the Gospel. The Bible is the basis, the Word of God, taking it literally as God's inspired Word, not adding to it or subtracting from it.

Another theological matter of importance to ordinary evangelicals is salvation. This Pentecostal woman, for example, made a point to underscore her belief in the Reformation principle of salvation by grace through faith alone:

> Evangelical means believing the central Gospel message that nothing people can do can bridge the gap between humans and God but that God in grace himself acted to bridge that gap. We simply can't reestablish that relationship which is broken without God's intervention. That's the Gospel.

Evangelicals also expressed in their discussions concern to maintain right beliefs about the sovereignty of God, the divinity, resurrection, and second coming of Christ, and the reality of heaven and hell.[4]

3. Then, to make clear her theologically Reformed covenantal view of the Bible, she added this clarification: "I also believe the Old and New Testaments are together, there is not a break between them. God had a plan from the beginning."

4. In addition to their concern with theological orthodoxy, however, evangelicals were conspicuous in their insistence that intellectual theological belief, while important, is not enough, but that right theology has to be individually personalized through conversion and firm personal commitment. Explaining what it means to be an evangelical, this Baptist man expressed, "Born again. John 3:16. Conversion, personal relationship with Christ, knowing that he died for your sins, and taking that personally. Taking Scripture at face value, the inerrancy of the Scripture." Evangelicals, in their beliefs, were also generally very concerned to avoid doctrinal legalism or hairsplitting. What mattered most to them was common commitment to what they view as the theological basics. According to this Presbyterian woman, "I'm evangelical with belief in the Bible as the authoritative word of God and the need to share with others about Christ. But I could stand in agreement with someone who professed Christ as Savior and Son of God. Maybe they worship a little differently or have some doctrines I'm not that comfortable with. But we need to look at the essential foundational concepts."

Both our survey and interview data suggest, then, that, if religious strength is measured as adherence to traditionally orthodox beliefs, American evangelicalism stands out as a very strong Christian tradition—the concerns of some evangelical intellectuals (for example, Wells 1993) notwithstanding. Furthermore, an analysis of the relationship between age and theological belief commitments reveals no statistically significant association between the two. That is, nothing in our data suggests that the coming generation of younger evangelicals are less theologically orthodox than their elders—the suggestions of other scholars (for example, Hunter 1987) about generationally progressive theological liberalization also notwithstanding.

Salience of Faith

Evangelicalism stands out as a most religiously vibrant tradition, not simply in its fidelity to orthodox theological beliefs, but also by virtue of the tremendous importance of the religious faith of ordinary evangelicals in their own lives. Evangelicals are distinguished among American Christians for the tremendous significance they report that their spiritual faith plays in their lives. According to table 2.2, fully 78 percent of evangelicals claim that their faith is extremely important to them; no evangelicals at all say that their faith is only somewhat important to them. By comparison, fundamentalists, mainliners, liberals, and Roman Catholics respectively all report lower levels of the importance of their religious faith in their lives.

In our in-depth interviews, the tremendous significance of religious faith in the lives of ordinary evangelicals was obvious and pervasive. In explaining why faith was important to them, most, like this Baptist woman, spoke of the many contributions faith makes to their well-being:

> Faith gives me security. A purpose. Meaning for my life. A reason to be here. A fellowship with Him. A standard to follow. A fundamental life orientation. Absolutely. If for some reason I went emotionally berserk, God would still be with me. I wouldn't lose anything eternally.

Similarly, many, such as this recently converted man involved in a nondenominational evangelical church, point to the importance that faith plays in providing fundamental normative purpose and direction:

> To me, faith is kind of like a guidepost or a direction, a model, a resource on where to go when I'm confused. Without Christ's example, I would not have a role model, which would leave a void.

Table 2.2: Salience and Robustness of Faith Commitments,
by Tradition (percent)

	Evangelicals	Fundamentalists	Mainline	Liberals	Catholics
Importance of Religious Faith					
Extremely important	78	72	61	58	44
Very important	22	27	36	34	48
Somewhat important	0	1	3	8	8
Frequency of Doubts About Own Faith					
Never	71	63	62	44	58
Once or twice	16	20	23	24	19
Sometimes	10	13	11	22	19
Often	3	4	4	10	5
Likelihood that a Christian Revival Will Sweep America in the Coming Years					
Very likely	32	27	18	22	—
Likely	42	34	34	29	—
Unlikely	20	25	36	31	—
Very unlikely	6	13	12	18	—
N	(430)	(389)	(576)	(431)	(114)

Note: Chi-square for all figures is significant at the .000 level.

> Submitting myself to a higher authority, I feel more certain. You know, a desire to have meaning. There's also a sense that behind the miraculousness of people and life, there's a God there who created it all.

For some, like this evangelical Anabaptist, who said she struggles with clinical depression, faith is important for the emotional support it offers:

> Faith gives me the long-term vision. There's nothing more comforting than knowing that there is someone who is all-powerful and in control of all of this junk that is going on. And the fact that He knows me personally. You know there's not a whole lot of places you can get unconditional love. But God is one of the places. And that would be a really devastating thing to give up.

But for the majority, faith is much more than a coping mechanism. Many evangelicals, like this Presbyterian man, point positively to their invaluable relationship with God and with fellow-believers: "Without faith I wouldn't have a purpose for living. I would miss a relationship with God, and I would miss the kind of relationship I have with those in the church, the body of Christ. And there's a whole lot associated with that." Similarly, this woman from a nondenominational "seeker" church, maintains:

> Not having faith would totally reorder my whole life. Even my thought life would be different. My faith is so important to me based on both my relationship with God and Jesus and the Holy Spirit, the whole Trinity. Also very important is the network of relationships that I have with other Christians. All of those relationships would either be eliminated or redefined.

Some evangelicals, like this Pentecostal woman, ground the importance of faith in their lives in their own personal conversion experiences:

> I've had a personal experience with Jesus Christ. God touched me and I was born again. And everything about me changed. It changed my whole life, toward God and the things of God. The Bible came alive to me, when before I never cared.

Others, such as this woman from a Four Square Gospel Church, took a more theologically grounded approach:

> Jesus gave everything for me. He died on the cross for me and shed his precious blood, so that I might have life. If He never did another thing for me, that would be enough. Without faith, I'd feel lost. I wouldn't have him to be there for me.

For a minority of evangelicals, including this Presbyterian woman, the importance of faith to life is explained in terms of the price they are willing to pay for it:

> Faith is costly on a daily basis, not an easy road. It's also costly to forgive. You know? Costly to love. Because it always throws my heart out there, instead of just living for myself. It's costly to serve other people. So I would say it's really reoriented my life.

Likewise, this evangelical Moravian man, who spends a lot of time with his family and volunteering to tutor disadvantaged children, expressed:

> I have changed completely and I'm a completely different person today than I would have been if I was not a Christian. So it has cost

me everything, in a way. And there are also sacrifices I continue to make now that I'm on this road. Like where my money goes: I contribute to my church and other charitable organizations. Also, I spend my time in ways that means I probably forego promotions at work and things like that. Those are costs, because of my faith.

So, for whatever reason and however it is expressed, we see that evangelicals generally are a people whose faith enjoys a place of central importance in their lives. That is a second mark of a strong religious tradition.

Robustness of Faith

Religious strength means not simply that people believe the right things and claim that their faith is important in their lives. It also means that people's religious faith is robust, that it expresses itself with strength and confidence, and that it holds up well under potential pressures and challenges. Therefore, our third measure of religious strength is the degree to which members of a tradition reflect confidence and assurance in their religious beliefs.

In table 2.2, we see that religious faith among evangelicals is subject to the least amount of doubting. Seventy-one percent of evangelicals report never having doubts about their religious beliefs, well above that expressed by members of other traditions. Conversely, evangelicals are the least likely to struggle "sometimes" or "often" with doubts about their faith. As a group, evangelicals appear simply to enjoy a faith that is relatively nonproblematic, for the most part immune from undermining uncertainty, apprehensions, and skepticism. Table 2.2 also shows that evangelicals, among Protestants, remain the most optimistic about the possibility of a Christian revival sweeping America in the coming years. In what would be a major advance in their eyes, evangelicals are anything but pessimistic. In the tables below and in chapters 4 and 5, we will examine other survey evidence indicating the exceptional robustness of evangelical religious faith. For the remainder of this section, however, we examine evidence of robust faith in our in-depth interviews.

We asked evangelicals in our interviews how they knew their faith was true and how often they had doubts about their beliefs. Their answers suggested a variety of bases of assurance and very little doubting. A few constructed rational, historical, or scientific apologetics for their faith. One Presbyterian man working on his MBA at a nationally ranked private university, for example, explained:

The foundations of my faith are historical and biblical. The Bible is a historical document. Christianity is unique, in that the Gospel writers and the apostles who believe the story they are telling had every reason to disbelieve it, mainly to save their lives. Yet they were in the position to really know. Why would these people claiming to have seen the Resurrection be willing to die for a religion if they knew it was a forgery? Why would anyone die for a lie they manufactured?

Most others, like this Baptist man, appeal more to combinations of conversion experiences, subjective spiritual confirmation, and biblical teachings: "I know because of the Holy Spirit. I know when God speaks to me, and I know through his Word where and what I am. And I'm very secure in that." Similarly, this woman attending a nondenominational church, observed: "I know my faith is true because of the confirmation of the person of the Holy Spirit and the difference that I sense spiritually since my rebirth. I also think that the Bible is defensible intellectually." These combinations appear to leave little room for doubts. She continues:

I've never gone through a season of my life where I felt that I was reevaluating everything. Ever since my rebirth experience, I've considered myself a Christian and acknowledged Jesus' lordship in my life and had an established relationship with God. I think that there *has* been more or less intimacy with God, what I would call more or less living out my faith based on choices I made. But no real big doubts.

Likewise, this Baptist woman expressed:

I know my faith is true because I believe what God's Word says. And because I have the Holy Spirit within me who confirms it to my heart. I feel very fortunate. I don't think I've ever doubted the truth of God's Word. I've questioned a lot of things God has done in my life or in the world, you know. But I believe His word, and I believe what He says.

For many evangelicals, this hardy faith sustains and is sustained under even the most difficult circumstances. One Methodist woman we interviewed, for example, had in the previous five years had her husband die after falling into a coma for three weeks, her mother die of breast cancer, one of her sons die, and another son sent to fight in Operation Desert Storm in the Gulf War. On top of that, she herself had recently been diagnosed with skin cancer. She reflected:

Nobody can tell me there isn't a God, because you just don't get through these things without God. It's just too ingrained to me. How do I *not* believe? For what I've been through in the last few years, if I didn't have God I don't know what I'd do, how I would've made it. You don't make it without God, you really don't.

When we asked if these tragedies had ever caused her to question her faith, she replied, "Never, never, no. It's stronger. Faith is my anchor, definitely." Others, like this evangelical Lutheran[5] woman, also professed that their strong faith brings them through even troubling spiritual trials:

It's very upsetting when I don't feel like God is answering my prayers, when I'm praying and praying and praying and I'm getting no answers. Still, I have never questioned whether I should give up my faith. No, never questioned that. My faith is my core, my center, my reason for living. If I didn't have my faith I wouldn't be an entire person. It's the most important thing.

5. Lutherans of all persuasions consider themselves "evangelical" (as with the mainline Lutheran denomination, the *Evangelical* Lutheran Church in America), since the Lutheran Reformation in Germany historically thought of itself as rooted in the *evangelium* (Greek for "good news," or Gospel). In Germany today, the German equivalent, *evangelisch*, is nearly synonymous with the word "Lutheran." This Lutheran appropriation of the term, however, should not be confused with the more specific, American, transdenominational evangelical movement described in chapter 1 and analyzed in this book. These are two different meanings of the same English word. Thus American Lutherans can and often do consider themselves "mainline" or "liberal" *and* "evangelical," in the German Reformation sense, but reject the label "evangelical" in the American conservative Protestant sense associated with *Christianity Today*, Billy Graham, Wheaton College, the National Association of Evangelicals, etc. Lutheran scholar Mark Ellingsen explains: "In North America, the number of Lutherans who [explicitly identify themselves with the American evangelical movement] is infinitesimally small. . . . In fact, the general Lutheran tendency to distance itself from the evangelical movement has led to a kind of linguistic crisis (which connotes elements of an identity crisis) within all segments of American Lutheranism. . . . In English-speaking nations, where there is no distinction between the use of the term *evangelical* by the family of Christians outside the ecumenical establishment (but more aligned with the National Association of Evangelicals [NAE]) and the use of the term by Lutherans, the problem is that the two uses have been collapsed, with the Lutheran use of the term being rendered archaic in the broader culture. For the term *evangelical* has come to be the sole property of the group of theological conservatives clustered around the NAE. It has come to the point where Lutherans in America no longer can lay claim to the title 'evangelical' without being regarded as somehow endorsing the NAE or the theological agenda of the Evangelical Theological Society" (1991: 222–23; also see Noll and Wells 1988: 2–4). Our analysis here employs "evangelical" only to refer to the identity of the transdenominational American evangelical movement; and we identify Lutheran interviewees as "evangelical" only when they identified themselves in their interviews as such in that precise sense.

Although few evangelicals report being harassed for their Christianity at work, those that do show no signs that such opposition undermines their faith at all. This man, for example, who attends a Bible Fellowship Church and works in a machine shop as a janitor, reported:

> I stick my neck out at work. The people at my job are amused by me, they think I'm a walking weirdo. I made it clear from the beginning that I didn't like the hall of pornography others had hung there, and the boss let me take it down. Well, I got a reputation real fast after that. There is ribbing and joking that goes on, with some barb to it.

But none of this seems to bother him:

> That kind of opposition has always been. I made a decision in college to hold the course and stay true to my faith. I have my up days and down days, and I wish that a little gold would pour out of heaven [laughing]. But I trust that God knows more than I do about where my life is going.

He also quickly points out the importance of his Christian presence at work, despite the opposition: "There is a positive side. People at work trust me, they come to me and know I will tell them the truth, and they respect my work ethic. So there is a positive side too. Yet occasionally it does cost to be moral and honest."

Group Participation

Another indicator of religious strength, the approach sociologists have traditionally employed most often, is regular and frequent participation in the activities and programs of the religious organizations of which believers are members. While the previous three measures have indicated the fidelity, importance, and strength of subjective religious beliefs in various ways, this measure considers instead the behavioral performance or enacted expression of religiosity. Strength here is conceived of as faith that is put into practice regularly and frequently through religious organizational channels.

Once again, of all the major American Christian traditions, evangelicalism scores consistently highest in religious group participation. Table 2.3 shows, for example, that, among committed American Christians,[6] evan-

6. We should remind ourselves that these tables contain evidence on only "committed" Christians, defined as those who attend church two to three times a month or more, *or* who say their faith is "extremely" important to them. Because we did not ask "nominal" Protestants their religious identities, our survey does not provide evidence of what proportion of

gelicals by far and away display the highest levels of church service attendance. Fully eighty percent of evangelicals attend church services once a
week or more. Comparatively, only 67 percent of fundamentalists, 63 percent of mainliners, 47 percent of liberals, and 65 percent of Roman Catholics do so. Furthermore, among practicing American Christians who are
married, the spouses of evangelical believers also attend church services
with much greater frequency than those of other traditions. Evangelical
spouses attend church services at least weekly at rates eight, twenty-two,
and thirty-four percentage points higher than the spouses of fundamentalists, mainliners, and liberals, respectively. Evangelicals not only go to
church services more frequently than anyone else, they also attend more
frequently as family units.

We know, however, that most church communities offer other activities
and programs beyond their regular worship services, such as potluck din-
ners, choir practices, social events, Bible studies, and so on. How frequently
do practicing believers in different American Christian traditions participate in the full variety of available church activities? According to table 2.3,
evangelicals again exhibit remarkably high levels of church involvement.
While 69 percent of Roman Catholics, 54 percent of liberals, 45 percent
of mainliners, and 40 percent of fundamentalists participate in church activities besides the Sunday worship services only once a month or less, a
mere 21 percent of evangelicals do so. By contrast, 60 percent of practicing
evangelicals participate in these other activities once a week or more, compared with only 45 percent of fundamentalists, 38 percent of mainliners,
28 percent of liberals, and 19 percent of Roman Catholics. Clearly, evangelicals are extraordinarily involved with the activities and programs of
their churches. This may be because evangelicals simply participate more,
net of opportunities; it may also be because evangelical churches simply
offer more activities in which to participate. Either way constitutes evidence of evangelicalism's significant religious strength.

Finally, viewing religious participation from another angle, evangelicals
also exhibit remarkably high rates of participating in two para-church religious activities that have grown in importance in recent decades: listening

each Christian tradition is "committed" and what proportion is "nominal." Other data, however, indicate that evangelicals exhibit the lowest levels of "nominal" identifiers. The 1996
General Social Survey, for example, shows that, of American Protestants who self-identified
with one of our four identity labels, 75 percent of self-identified evangelicals attend church
two to three times a month or more; compared with 63 percent of self-identified fundamentalists, 58 percent of mainline Protestants, and 32 percent of theological liberal Protestants.

Table 2.3: Religious Practices, by Tradition (percent)

	Evangelicals	Fundamentalists	Mainline	Liberals	Catholics
Respondent's Church Attendance					
More than once a week	48	38	20	14	8
Once a week	32	29	43	33	57
1–3 times a month	12	22	25	33	28
Many times a year or less	5	7	10	14	6
Never	3	4	3	6	1
Spouse's Church Attendance					
More than once a week	40	36	19	9	—
Once a week	31	27	30	26	—
1–3 times a month	14	20	24	29	—
Many times a year or less	5	8	15	20	—
Never	9	8	10	15	—
Attends a different church	1	1	2	1	—
Participates in Church Activities Besides Sunday Worship Services					
Three times a week	17	13	6	5	3
Two times a week	20	14	13	9	0
Once a week	23	18	19	14	16
2–3 times a month	19	15	18	18	12
Once a month	7	11	13	14	11
Few times a year	7	15	19	22	39
Never	7	14	13	18	19
Average Hours per Week Listens to Christian Radio Programs	6.9	4.1	1.9	3.3	—
Average Hours per Week Watches Christian Television Programming	2.6	2.2	1.5	2.0	—
N	(430)	(389)	(576)	(431)	(114)

Note: Chi-square for all figures is significant at the .01 level.

to Christian radio and watching Christian television programs. According to table 2.3, evangelicals listen to Christian radio 1.7 times as much as fundamentalists, 3.6 times as much as mainliners, and more than twice as much as liberals do. Evangelicals also watch Christian television programming significantly more than the others.

Measured in a variety of ways, then, evangelicalism as a tradition consistently displays significantly greater religious strength, as indicated by frequency of religious group participation, than those of the other Christian traditions. These differences were also evident in our in-depth interviews. Indeed, both the number of available activities in evangelical churches and the extent of our interviewees' participation in them were remarkable. This not atypical Baptist woman, for example, stated:

> I'm very satisfied with our church, and I participate in several different ways. I'm on the budget finance committee right now, sing in the choir, am an active member of our Sunday school class, and do service projects. We were looking for a church with happiness, comrades, where people just enjoyed church. So, we have had fellowships and joint classes where couples would get together to know one another better. Then, when the church got too large, we started these small Bible study groups. We take the Scripture and relate it to today's living, real situations. We also work together to know if anybody has a concern and talk about them so we can know how to help each other.

Taking a somewhat more theological approach, this Presbyterian woman noted:

> We are the Church, the body of Christ literally. But we can't be the body apart from others. I just see the power of the Church, of the body of Christ coming together and loving people. There's power in numbers. I've seen it again and again, the way people's hearts are melted just by the love of the body of Christ. So, relationship to church is important. Not to earn our way, but just having it be a part of who we are.

Besides the standard options of choir, potlucks, committees, and ministries, among evangelicals participation in small groups—whether Bible study, fellowship, or prayer groups (see Wuthnow 1994)—emerged as a particularly important practice in dedicated church participation. According to this Reformed man, for example:

> It's important not just to come on Sunday morning and hear the sermon but to be involved in a small group. It's important to gather

and study Scripture. Also, as a church gets bigger, it's very hard to know everybody in a very close way. Small groups give us a chance to really be a part of the lives of these other folks, to know how to pray for each other. In my small group, if anyone has a need, we can help. We also do social activities together, and our kids play together a lot.

And this evangelical Anabaptist woman observed of her small group:

The most encouraging thing has been being in a group of people who believe the essentials that you believe. And then being able to be honest and talk about your shortcomings and your struggles and to be accepted and prayed for, and all that good stuff.

Clearly, evangelicals are creating in their churches opportunities for spiritual nourishment, emotional support, friendships, self-improvement, practical help, and outreach to their surrounding communities. These are generating high levels of church participation and, with it, a strong religious movement.

Commitment to Mission

A fifth measure of religious strength consists of commitment in both belief and action to accomplishing the mission of the religious organization or tradition, whether evangelistic or otherwise. This indicator captures the more outwardly focused dimension of religiosity, the aspect of faith that seeks to achieve its external goals. With the exception of marginal monastic and sectarian religious elements in its history, Christianity in America, both Protestant and Roman Catholic, has characteristically sought actively to exert a public influence on the world. The main thrust of American Christianity over time has been activist: to try to improve America spiritually, morally, and socially, to get involved with the world, to evangelize, disciple, and transform it. In broad terms, then, one way we might measure the strength of an American Christian tradition is by its commitment to achieve these kinds of goals. When we do so, evangelicalism shows itself again to be the strongest of all American Christian traditions, especially when it comes to explicitly religious expressions of activism.

First, we might consider believers' attitudes about faith-motivated social and cultural activism. In our survey, we asked practicing Protestants whether or not they believed Christians should be trying to change American society to better reflect God's will (see table 2.4). Ninety-two percent

Table 2.4: Beliefs about Christian Activism, by Tradition (percent)

	Evangelicals	Fundamentalists	Mainline	Liberals	Catholics
Christians should be trying to change American society to better reflect God's will	92	87	87	76	—
Raising a good family is not a big enough contribution to the world—people need to do more than that	82	74	77	80	67
N	(430)	(389)	(576)	(431)	(114)

Note: Chi-square for all figures is significant at the .001 level.

of evangelicals agreed—5 percent more than fundamentalists and main-liners, and 16 percent more than liberals. The difference between evangelicals and liberals here is especially striking, given liberal Protestantism's long tradition of and reputation for social activism, and evangelicalism's standard critique of liberalism as being too committed to a social Gospel. Evangelicals, it appears, may ironically be the most committed carriers of a new social Gospel (see Regnerus and Smith 1998a; 1998b). We also approached the question from another angle, asking whether or not people were obliged to do more for the world than simply raise a good family. Again, evangelicals were the most insistent that raising a good family is not enough, that people needed to do more for the world than that (see table 2.4).

To probe more deeply practicing Christians' beliefs about *how best* to change American society to better reflect God's will, we asked all of those who espoused this goal to tell us how important they thought various means were to accomplishing it. The results are presented in table 2.5. Evangelicals, compared with those of all other traditions, strongly and disproportionately favored, as methods to change American society, living a way of life radically differently from mainstream America and working for political reforms. Evangelicals and fundamentalists equally, compared with the others, favored converting people to Jesus Christ and defending a biblical worldview in intellectual circles. No statistically significant differences emerged between the various traditions about the importance of giving money to charity and volunteering for local community organizations, al-

Table 2.5: Importance of Alternative Strategies to Change Society, by Tradition (percent)

	Evangelicals	Fundamentalists	Mainline	Liberals	Catholics
Converting People to Jesus Christ					
Very important	91	91	76	76	—
Somewhat important	9	8	22	22	—
Not important	0	1	2	2	—
Christians Living a Way of Life Radically Different from Mainstream America					
Very important	81	69	59	57	—
Somewhat important	16	27	34	38	—
Not important	3	4	7	5	—
Christians Working for Political Reforms					
Very important	69	65	53	49	—
Somewhat important	29	30	40	41	—
Not important	2	5	7	10	—
Defending a Biblical Worldview in Intellectual Circles					
Very important	63	65	46	49	—
Somewhat important	33	30	43	44	—
Not important	4	5	11	7	—
Christians Giving Money to Charity[a]					
Very important	45	38	43	45	—
Somewhat important	47	51	48	46	—
Not important	8	11	9	9	—
Christians Volunteering for Local Community Organizations[a]					
Very important	77	74	73	76	—
Somewhat important	23	24	26	23	—
Not important	0	2	1	1	—
N	(430)	(389)	(576)	(431)	(—)

Note: Chi-square for all figures is significant at the .0000 level, except [a]prob. = n.s.

though evangelicals did rank as highest with liberals on "very important" and lowest on "not important" for both.

Here, then, we see evangelicals again standing out—especially against mainline and liberal Protestants—as very committed to employing a variety of means to try to change American society to better reflect God's will. Again, it is striking that liberals—given their history and reputation—did not distinguish themselves as particularly dedicated to social activism, whether through political reforms, giving money to charity, or volunteering for community organizations. It is also curious—given their heritages—that evangelicals embraced "living a radically different way of life" much more than fundamentalists; and that they chose "defending a biblical worldview in intellectual circles" slightly less than fundamentalists. We will seek to make sense of these unexpected results in chapter 4, where we advance a theory attempting to explain the religious vitality of evangelicalism that we are observing in this chapter.

But talk, one might say, is cheap. What about actions? What about implementation? Which Christian tradition is actually *doing* the work of trying to influence American society? In keeping with all of our findings thus far about religious strength, the evidence suggests that it is the evangelicals who are most walking their talk. We asked our survey respondents whether they had participated in any of twelve different forms of religious, social, and political activism a lot, some, or none in the previous two years. We also asked whether or not they voted regularly in elections. Tables 2.6 and 2.7 show that for almost all of these thirteen distinct forms of activism, evangelicals are the most active of all the comparison groups.

Table 2.6 shows that evangelicals were the most likely to give money to help spread the Gospel, to personally evangelize others themselves, to defend a biblical worldview in intellectual circles, to volunteer for church programs that serve the local community, and to work hard in their daily lives to set Christian examples for others. And table 2.7—which also compares the five major Christian traditions with nonreligious Americans—shows that evangelicals were the most likely to vote in elections, to give money to the poor and needy, to lobby political officials, and to work hard to educate themselves about social and political issues. Among the Christians, evangelicals were the most likely to participate in political protests or demonstrations (only marginally less likely than the nonreligious). And evangelicals were, along with fundamentalists, the most likely to give a lot of money to Christian political organizations or candidates. On only two of the thirteen types of activism—both of which were explicitly disconnected from

Table 2.6: Religious Activism in Previous Two Years, by Tradition (percent)

	Evangelicals	Fundamentalists	Mainline	Liberals	Catholics
Given Money or Time to Help Spread the Gospel in U.S. or Overseas					
A lot	51	35	26	17	16
Some	41	49	56	52	50
None	8	16	18	31	34
Told Others About How to Become a Christian					
A lot	32	25	15	17	8
Some	56	61	53	44	33
None	12	14	32	39	59
Defended a Biblical Worldview in Intellectual Circles					
A lot	44	38	21	16	10
Some	48	45	54	47	46
None	8	17	25	37	44
Volunteered for a Church Program That Serves the Local Community					
A lot	32	26	24	19	17
Some	47	46	47	50	55
None	21	28	29	31	28
Worked Hard to Set a Christian Example					
A lot	82	73	69	58	57
Some	16	26	30	38	41
None	2	1	1	4	2
N	(430)	(389)	(576)	(431)	(114)

Note: Chi-square for all figures is significant at the .01 level.

Table 2.7: Social and Political Activism in Previous Two Years, by Tradition (percent)

	Evangelicals	Fundamentalists	Mainline	Liberals	Catholics	Nonreligious
Vote in Elections	92	85	92	84	89	64
Given Money to Help the Poor and Needy						
A lot	29	23	22	25	22	9
Some	62	67	68	60	72	78
None	9	10	10	15	6	13
Written, Called, or Visited Elected Officials						
A lot	4	6	7	5	7	5
Some	46	38	35	30	32	24
None	50	56	58	65	61	71
Given Money or Time to a Christian Political Organization or Candidate						
A lot	15	15	7	11	13	—
Some	36	39	31	38	42	—
None	49	46	61	51	45	—
Given Money or Time to a Non-Christian Political Organization or Candidate						
A lot	4	3	4	5	9	1
Some	22	27	25	33	34	33
None	75	70	72	63	56	66

Table 2.7: Continued

	Evangelicals	Fundamentalists	Mainline	Liberals	Catholics	Nonreligious
Participated in a Political Protest or Demonstration						
A lot	1	1	0	1	0	3
Some	13	9	6	12	10	12
None	86	90	94	87	90	85
Worked Hard to Educate Self about Social or Political Issues						
A lot	38	36	35	34	35	38
Some	52	53	56	53	56	44
None	10	11	9	13	9	18
Volunteered for a Local Community Organization not Related to Church						
A lot	16	15	17	18	22	9
Some	42	36	41	41	41	37
None	43	49	42	41	37	54
N	(430)	(389)	(576)	(431)	(114)	(60)

Note: Chi-square for all figures is significant at the .01 level.

Christian associations—did evangelicals not distinguish themselves: giving money or time to a non-Christian political organization or candidate and volunteering for a local community organization not related to church. Clearly, the overall pattern here is that evangelicalism is a tremendously activist tradition that is attempting to carry out in practice its mission of "engaged orthodoxy." Measured as commitment in belief and action to accomplish its mission, evangelicalism should be viewed as a very strong religious tradition.

Finally, again, we must note the relative lack of activism among the liberals. If ever liberal Protestantism was distinguished by its social-Gospel activism, it appears to be so no more. The evidence suggests, instead, that evangelicals may be the most committed carriers of a new social Gospel.

These survey findings on evangelical activism were clearly verified in our in-depth interviews. To begin, most ordinary evangelicals believe that their faith has implications for *all* areas of life and that Christians must be concerned about nearly everything. For example, this Presbyterian man answered the question about what things should especially concern Christians:

> Gosh, just about everything should be a concern to us. We're called to love our neighbor. That's society. So anything going on out there affects your neighbor. And we need to love them. So social issues, like hunger or poverty, economic issues, social issues like divorce, crime, abortion, however people are hurting and are affected.

Likewise, this evangelical Pentecostal man answered:

> All things, from the White House to the poor house and all in between. From one country to the next and back again. From the water, the trees, the paved roads, to the buildings. The whole world. Yeah. All of it. There's nothing that should be left out. Political issues, I think, should be a concern. And they should all concern Christians.

One common theme among evangelicals in discussing these matters is a critique of compartmentalized "Sunday-morning" faith. One evangelical Moravian woman, for example, claims, "Being a Christian is more than just the hour you're at church on Sunday. It means making it a part of your life and living your faith, a seven-days-a-week thing." Similarly, this Presbyterian woman explains that, "Part of being evangelical is the desire, the commission to live out faith in everyday life. Not to make it kind of a compartmental piece of our life, but to have it influence everything." Likewise, this Presbyterian man explains:

> Evangelicals try to maintain a biblical worldview that follows the Scriptures and encompasses our ideas on things from education to our stewardship of the earth. Just a whole realm of things, in essence saying our relationship to God affects our everyday living. It's not just a Sunday-only kind of thing.

Given the importance of their faith in their lives, this perspective generates in most evangelicals a genuine heartfelt burden for the state of the world, a tremendous sense of personal responsibility to change society. "I think it's up to the body of Christ to be involved in the world's problems and to pray for changes in the world," claimed one Presbyterian woman. "We can't say, 'the world is always going to be a mess and there is nothing I can do about it.' We need to say, 'yes, it's a mess and what part do I have to play in dealing with that?'"

When we asked evangelicals exactly *why* Christians should be concerned about the world, they almost invariably pointed to religious motivations that transcend immediate self-interest. Some, such as this Pentecostal woman, spoke about the command to love: "Because we love our fellow man, that's one of our first commandments, to love your neighbor as yourself. And if you love that neighbor, you don't want to see them on this earth having all the trouble they are having." Others, like this Baptist woman pointed to the idea of representing Jesus in the world today: "Jesus was right out there with the average person. We are Jesus in the flesh today, and we should be making an influence practically." Still others, like this Reformed woman, focus more on activism as an expression of gratitude to and worship of God:

> Christians should be concerned because Jesus cares for us and because God wants us to be concerned. Not to be self-righteous or to impress other people. We should be involved in the sense of worship and thankfulness for what God has done for us, for me. To respond to these problems is in some way praise or worship to God.

Yet others, such as this evangelical woman involved in an independent church, emphasized engaged social involvement as a way to unlearn selfishness:

I have great respect for Amish and Mennonites and people who believe that they are separate in a totally different societal structure. But my belief is that we're called to have an impact on the world to make a positive change, that we are not placed here on earth just to live for ourselves, for our own satisfaction. The kinds of things we do in the Lord's name are to benefit other people.

She continued:

Jesus wants us to share what we have and care for the widows and orphans. But if there's no activity in my life evidencing that, I have to question whether I really believe it. I have to put my actions where my mouth is. I don't think just talking about things to society can resolve the situation, unless we are also active doing something about it.

Still others, like this Presbyterian man, spoke of the desire to see God's name honored by remaking the world to be more in accordance with God's will: "Christians should have a concern not only for those in the church, but those outside the church. And a concern for seeing God's name honored by all people, eventually, not just the ones sitting next to us in the pew."

Whatever the reason given, however, it is clear that evangelicalism has produced a movement of people who are committed to practical activism toward social reform and evangelism. Tables 2.6 and 2.7 tell us that this "evangelical burden" is expressed as activism through a variety of channels. The notion of "evangelical burden" is well captured in this Presbyterian woman's excited, omniprescriptive account of how Christians should interact with the world:

Read more. You know, try to understand where people are coming from. Translate faith into everyday life. Racial issues. Violence. Domestic violence. I think we don't need to be afraid to address those issues. We need to be unafraid to explore what things mean for my faith today and how can I be more involved on a day-to-day level in some of those issues. Reading the paper. Being more involved in community, whether it's volunteering, whatever.

Often, as with this nondenominational woman, it begins by linking faith commitments to social concerns: "We pray as a family about social problems. And in our small group that meets weekly, if there's a societal or political issue that concerns somebody in the group, then we will pray about

it together too." For many, including this Baptist woman, activism takes
the form of church-based outreach programs:

> We have a lot of programs that reach out to young people and the
> community. A lot of youth groups, vacation Bible schools, and so
> forth. We also have women's Bible study groups—I lead one of
> those—and Sunday school classes, and we try to get people in-
> volved. The pastor also walks through the community praying for
> every home, every family.

Others work self-consciously from their faith to exert a moral influence
in their local communities. For example, one Presbyterian man I (Smith)
interviewed—who attends a very large evangelical church that has spun off
five daughter congregations in the area—afterward took me on a walking-
tour of his local neighborhood. He pointed out a Lutheran (ELCA) church
with very nice building facilities, but which—he learned by visiting once
out of curiosity—had dwindled to about twenty regularly attending members. Thinking out load, he floated by me the idea of a larger group from
his church joining this congregation to change the orientation of its Gospel
message and style of its meetings and, presumably, its attendance record.
"It could really use some new life," he mused. After depositing his paycheck
at the bank, where he knew the tellers on a first-name basis, he walked us
by his local video store. He told how some months earlier the store had
rearranged its shelving and posters so that violent and obscene photographs
were moved to a child's eye-level. He explained how he had petitioned the
sympathetic store managers repeatedly and written multiple letters to the
store's less sympathetic national headquarters, voicing his moral objections.
He made it his project, a personal, informal crusade. But for months, he
was told it was national store policy that could not be changed. Then, when
returning a video that he decided needed to be his last rented from this
store, a manager came out and told him they had secured permission to
return the store to its original, less offensive, condition. He beamed over
his victory.

Still others, such as this Presbyterian woman—who scheduled our
coffee-shop interview to follow a meeting with one of her employees who
wanted to talk about some personal problems—view their paid jobs as important mission fields:

> I feel called to my work. It's crazy to think I work in an outdoor
> sports store. What does that have to do with God's kingdom?
> Well, living out my faith, being willing to jump into people's lives.

> I consider people at work as those God has called me to, as my little flock to care for. I'm called to love them, put their needs above mine, build friendships, and establish trust. They are people with lots of questions, you know, that maybe I can answer. We are all called to just be light wherever we are.

Evangelicals uniformly spoke of the need to get politically educated and vote in elections regularly. Beyond that, a few evangelicals also mentioned supporting political causes financially and through volunteer work. The range of issues was broad. One older Reformed man declared:

> I am an environmentalist. To me the Bible clearly teaches that we should take care of the world and be good stewards of this beautiful green earth that God has given us. We shouldn't allow it to be fouled and polluted. See, we even have books on owls. My wife is an owl freak. Christians should not be opposed to the environment and it's movement.

One relatively conservative Baptist man, on the other hand, stated:

> I hear from a lot of politically conservative groups. Many of these I try to support. Pat Robertson and the Christian Coalition I think is probably pretty right on. The Public Advocate, too, is sincerely fighting the homosexual community, which has certainly targeted them in turn. And for that I am very empathetic. There are also a couple of legal organizations, like the Christian Action Council, that I support.

In these and many other ways, the evangelicals we interviewed manifest a tremendous amount of religious outreach and involvement in a variety of social and political issues. Historian Mark Noll (1994) observes that evangelicalism possesses a long history of restless public activism. Today, that tradition continues strong, as the "evangelical burden" generates a tremendous amount of energy and action for accomplishing its mission of engaged orthodoxy.

Retention and Recruitment of Members

Finally, we should consider a religious tradition to be strong if it sustains high rates of membership retention, maintaining members' association with the tradition over long periods of time and effectively socializing new members into that tradition. This kind of strength is also evident in successful recruitment of new members to the tradition. Consistent with the findings above, our survey data suggests that, overall, evangelicalism does the best job of all Christian traditions with membership retention and recruitment. Table 2.8 shows, first of all, that, of all of our survey respondents—whatever religion they are now—those who were raised in evangelical families (and fundamentalist as well) were raised in home environments where religion was much more likely to be of great importance. Religion in mainline and liberal families, compared with evangelical ones, was about three times less likely to be extremely important and ten times more likely to have been not important.

These differences may help to explain the second finding reported in table 2.8. Namely, the evangelical tradition features one of the highest intergenerational membership retention rates and a great ability to raise children who do not become theologically liberal or nonreligious when they grow up. Fully 78 percent of those raised in evangelical families grew up to be evangelicals themselves. Comparatively, only 57 percent of fundamentalists, 51 percent of mainliners, 57 percent of liberals, and 28 percent of nonreligious retained the religious tradition (or nonreligion) of their families of origin. Not one respondent raised in an evangelical (or fundamentalist) family became nonreligious (or Roman Catholic) as an adult. By contrast, 16 percent of those raised in liberal Protestant and 11 percent of those raised in fundamentalist families grew up to become nonreligious. Furthermore, those raised in evangelical families who did exit their evangelical upbringing by adulthood tended to switch not "far" away, only to either fundamentalism or mainline Protestantism; a mere 5 percent became liberals. Those raised as fundamentalists, however, grew up to become liberals at more than twice that rate.

Moreover, evangelicalism has tended to have the strongest drawing power for those exiting other traditions of childhood. Those raised in nonreligious families, for example, who became Christians later in life, were more likely to become evangelical Christians than another kind. Likewise, evangelicalism has had twice the drawing power of fundamentalist and mainline Protestantism to recruit the relatively few Roman Catholics who became Protestants as adults. And respondents raised in fundamentalist Protestant families who switched traditions were most likely as adults to become evangelicals (or, in equal numbers to become liberals). Overall, then, none of the other traditions match evangelicalism in either retention or recruitment ability.

Evidence from our in-depth interviews substantiates these survey findings. First of all, it is clear that evangelicals as a whole feel a large responsi-

Table 2.8: Religious Characteristics of Families of Origin, by Tradition (percent)

			Religion of Families of Origin			
	Evangelical	Fundamentalist	Mainline Protestant	Liberal Protestant	Roman Catholic	Non-Religious
Importance of Religious Faith in Family of Origin						
Extremely important	46	46	17	15	23	0
Very important	35	36	35	29	46	5
Somewhat important	18	16	37	47	26	23
Not important	1	2	11	9	5	72
Current Religious Faith of Respondent						
Evangelical	78	12	11	8	4	22
Fundamentalist	9	57	8	9	2	19
Mainline Protestant	8	7	51	7	2	14
Liberal Protestant	5	12	12	57	3	15
Catholic	0	0	14	3	83	3
Nonreligious	0	11	5	16	6	28
N	(221)	(297)	(853)	(277)	(321)	(228)

Note: Chi-square for all figures is significant at the .0000 level.

bility to evangelize those whom they consider to be unsaved. "After you become a Christian, you're supposed to do something with the knowledge that you've gotten," explained one evangelical Moravian woman. "You're supposed to tell someone about it, even though that can be the hardest thing to do." This Pentecostal woman concurs: "Christians who understand the Gospel feel a responsibility to take that Gospel to the world—not coercively, but to share—because we all ourselves have felt the pain of a broken relationship with God, and we see pain around us, and so we feel for it. God has given us a ministry and message of reconciliation." Most evangelicals put this felt responsibility into action. According to our survey evidence (table 2.6), fully 88 percent of evangelicals have proselytized others within the last two years, and more than one-third of them have done so "a lot." Surely, this burden and action contributes to evangelicalism's exceptional capacity to recruit new members to their faith.

The evangelicals we interviewed expressed an equal sense of responsibility to do the best possible job raising and training their children to grow up to be good (meaning, evangelical) Christians. One man, for example, attending an evangelical Anabaptist church claimed that, "Influencing the next generation is one of the most important things. If you have children, I think the most important thing you can do is to raise them to be godly adults." Indeed, it appears that, for evangelical parents, having one's children grow up to leave the faith is considered one of the greatest potential tragedies of life. To prevent that, evangelical parents and churches invest enormous amounts of time, energy, and money into providing children's summer camps; vacation Bible schools; Christian equivalents of Boy Scouts, Girl Scouts, Cub Scouts, and Brownies; Bible videos; Christian fiction; Christian music; family devotions; and bedtime Bible reading and prayer for their children. This evangelical Methodist woman's experience as a child is typical:

> My mother raised me very strict about going to Sunday School. I definitely grew up in the church and Bible school and went through choir and everything. When I was old enough, I taught Sunday School and Bible school myself. I've always been a Christian.

And this evangelical Lutheran woman recalled about raising her own family:

> When our boys were young, we used different family devotional books. When the boys got big enough to read, we'd let them take

turns reading the Bible. One year, our family read the whole Bible
straight through on a schedule. Sometimes the boys wanted to
read with us, sometimes not. We've always been big on the Bible.
Even today, you know, it's not uncommon for somebody to call
who needs a Bible passage, and I have a concordance I can pull out
and find them a verse.

And her spiritual investment in her children continues now that they are
older:

I buy my kids Christian music, and I buy it for myself. I have
Sandy Patti and other Christian artists. If I go to a Christian con-
cert, I buy all their tapes, and we play a lot of that in the car when
we're traveling. I also have the Bible on tape, and we listen to that,
the whole Bible on tape while traveling.

Evangelical churches also typically go to great lengths to support this socializing work of parents by providing Sunday School programs, youth
groups, children's ministries, and social events for their youngsters. One
woman attending an Evangelical Presbyterian Church declared proudly:

Our church is really growing. It has three services and is known as
the young people's church in the area. Even the Washington Post
has written about the youth group we have. We have six hundred
youth in a group called "Ambassadors," which meets every Sunday
morning before the services. And they also have their own social
events.

Finally, numerous evangelical parachurch ministries—such as Young Life,
Inter-Varsity Christian Fellowship, the Navigators, and Campus Crusade
for Christ—also work to make sure that high-school and college-age evangelicals do not stray from the evangelical fold. Many of those we interviewed reported that a church youth-group leader or involvement in one of
these parachurch ministries was crucial in solidifying their own faith. All
of this contributes to evangelicalism's effectiveness in retaining the commitments of its young members into and through adulthood that we see in
the tables above. By these effective efforts at membership retention and
recruitment, evangelicalism remains a very strong religious movement.

By Contrast: Mainliners and Liberals

Our interviews revealed perceptible differences between the evangelicals
and the mainline and liberal Protestants we interviewed on our six mea-

sures of religious strength.[7] It would be wrong to overstate these differences. Clearly, very many mainline and liberal Protestants adhere to essential Christian religious beliefs, experience their faith as very important in their lives, reflect confidence and assurance in their religious beliefs, participate regularly in church activities, are committed to accomplishing the mission of their churches, evangelize others, and raise children who grow up to remain in their religious traditions. Nevertheless, in our interviews, as in our survey results, discernable patterned differences in indicators of religious vitality were apparent. A larger proportion of the mainliners and liberals we interviewed exhibited attitudes and behaviors that might lead to or be associated with lower levels of a religious tradition's strength. And the committed mainline and liberal believers we interviewed more often complained about the state of their churches and denominations than did the evangelicals. In the remainder of this chapter, we consider some of these voices. We are not implying that all mainliners and liberals think and talk these ways, but simply that we heard much more of what follows from mainliners and liberals than from evangelicals.

Adherence to Beliefs

First, a number of the mainline and liberal Protestants we interviewed did not express clear and straightforward commitments to traditionally orthodox Christian theological beliefs and ethics. For some, this took the form of depreciating the idea of the objective truthfulness of Christian beliefs by making ultimate religious truth essentially a matter of personal taste. This self-described liberal Baptist woman, for example, expressed: "I'm open to new ideas; I don't believe my ways are the only ways or are good for everybody. I think everybody has to come to their own understanding of what's right in their religion, and I respect other people's religions very much."[8]

7. As a reminder, "mainline" and "liberal" Protestants in this analysis of interview data are those who identified themselves with these religious identities in our personal interviews. Some of these also identified their own church congregations as mainline or liberal. Most were sampled from what are normally considered mainline Protestant denominations (United Methodist Church, Episcopal Church, etc.) (Roof and McKinney 1987). Some were sampled from among telephone survey respondents who identified themselves as "theologically liberal" Protestants. The mainline and liberal Protestants about whom quantitative data are represented in the tables consist entirely of those telephone survey respondents who identified themselves as "mainline" or "theologically liberal" Protestants. See Appendices A and B for details on our research methodology and use of religious identity labels.

8. Later, she repeated this theme: "I am comfortable with my Christianity. I don't feel like it has to agree or disagree with anybody else's, but that it's my own personal little flavor that's meant for me. I've worked very hard on my beliefs over the years and I really appreci-

More than respectful of other religious beliefs, this woman appeared positively attracted to some of them herself, claiming, for example: "I like some New Age ideas, because they believe they can change their world by making things peaceful and right with themselves. Some of their ideas about love and brotherhood and sharing and improving the world by visualizing or whatever, I think are interesting." Others spoke in ways that tended to erase distinctions between Christianity and other religions. For instance, this mainline Lutheran man remarked:

> In my mind, there's only one God, no matter what you call him. Muslims pray to the same God I do. They call him Allah or whatever, but it's the same entity for all world religions, those that believe in a supreme being. They're talking generally about the same one.[9]

Some, such as this self-described liberal Lutheran took his discomfort with Christian distinctiveness to the point of wanting to eliminate the Christian label entirely:

> I have difficulty with the idea of Christian morality as a standard. I think there is a code of human conduct that, if you like, Christ emulated as a human. But why label it Christian? There are others who can do the same thing. It's a moral code of doing what is right. I don't like putting a Christian tag on it.

Others mainliners and liberals didn't mind the Christian label per se but confessed to not really knowing what they believed. This liberal United Methodist man, for example, disclosed:

> I'm an agnostic Methodist. I was brought up in the Christian condition and have spent some time trying to understand what I really think about Christianity. And at the ripe old age of 67, I still haven't decided what I think. I tend to think of Jesus more as a teacher, rather than a divine. Am I a Christian? I hope so.[10]

---

ated the freedom to develop my own particular style. And I've been able to do that in the church that I belong to. I appreciate the liberating feeling very much."

9. Similarly, this Episcopalian man argued: "I think America is becoming more of a Christian nation than it was before, just by fact that more people aren't as prejudiced about other religions. And I think that's kind of what Christianity should be."

10. Ironically, this man has been a leader in his church: "I've been an officer in the church on various occasions, Chairman of the Board, etc. But I don't really know the Methodist discipline that well, any better than I probably know the Koran."

When asked to describe more clearly what Christianity meant to him, this man had difficultly articulating much more than standard American individualism:

> Be self-sufficient. Be your brother's keeper, I agree up to a point. Be honest. Work hard and be responsible for your own actions. That is what I think Christianity is, or what any good solid religion can contribute.[11]

Yet others, like this Episcopalian man, reinterpreted orthodox Christian theology in fairly heterodox ways: "I think Jesus comes from within. Some people think Jesus is separate, but I don't believe that. I think it's from within, Jesus is within you, you know what I'm saying?" Later in the interview, this man actually defined being a liberal precisely as not standing firmly on one's beliefs: "I have strong beliefs, but I don't always carry them out, so that's how I think of myself as a little liberal."

The mainline and liberal Protestants we interviewed also seemed more prepared than evangelicals to discard or significantly modify some traditional Christian beliefs and ethics on the basis that they made them feel uncomfortable. One mainline Lutheran man, for example, said he didn't believe in the existence of hell. After musing on the idea that there may be some kind of purgatory, he concluded, "I think eventually we all wind up with God." Similarly, one member of a mainline Southern Baptist church described hell in annihilationist terms but concluded that, "Anyway, most people I know believe in some kind of higher power, and I think they will go to heaven." When our discussion turned to the issue of sexual ethics, the same Baptist man argued:

> There's nothing wrong with gay marriages. I know homosexuals from work who are married and their marriages lasted longer than mine did. I have also learned they have the exact same kinds of problems I had in my marriage. I know the Bible says homosexuality is wrong, but I just don't think so anymore. I just don't see it. God wants people to be happy. If that's what makes them happy, then fine.

11. He continued to elaborate this rather human-centered approach to faith and life: "The plain fact is that the only thing that can save us is human action. Now, to what degree people want to believe they're guided by a higher being, to my knowledge there's nothing, no God, that forces me to do anything. He may have given us an inspired book, people argue. But I really go back more to my upbringing and education. So, I think the only think that can save us are humans, and we better get some pretty smart ones in a hurry."

More telling about belief commitments in this argument than the actual content of the ethical conclusion here is the evident overriding moral authority of American cultural pragmatism and individually defined happiness. Any sense of objective and transcendent moral standards, divine revelation, and costly discipleship are notably absent from the moral logic.

Some of the more doctrinally orthodox members of mainline and liberal churches that we interviewed were well aware of and concerned about the lack of commitment to the idea of Christian truth and distinctiveness among their fellow believers. This self-described traditional Episcopalian woman, for example, complained:

> Many mainline churches have become only concerned about the world, and not the personal. Sin and redemption are words that never pass many pastors' lips, although in fact people are hungry for that. The church has gotten to the point where it says, "Do whatever you want, it doesn't matter." But then Christianity feels like a social club, not any kind of life-changing experience. I think that's one fundamental reason why a lot of mainline churches are losing membership.[12]

Such people, however, seemed reluctant to take concrete steps to raise moral expectations or doctrinal standards in their denominations and were left with few solutions for improving their situations.

Salience of Faith

Unlike most of the evangelicals we interviewed, many of the mainliners and liberals we spoke with described their faith as merely part of the ordinary furniture of their lives, simply one of many important facets of their existence. Faith was often conceived of as a rather taken-for-granted aspect of a general lifestyle, not as an intense personal commitment that provided indispensable order and meaning to their lives. This mainline Baptist man, for example, stated:

> Being a Christian hasn't changed much about my life. It was just the way I was raised, what my family was doing. I didn't have any big born-again experience. Church was just a part of our family lifestyle, something we did. It all seemed normal to me, not a big

12. She continues: "I think the Episcopal church has bought a whole mess of left-wing pottage and sticks its nose in where they know nothing about. A lot of mainstream churches have become very kneejerk, making simplistic political pronouncement—you get the feeling that they are not thinking very carefully."

deal. It's important to believe in God and the Bible and all. But that's just one aspect of my life.

In describing exactly why their faith is important to them, mainline and liberal Protestants tended not to say typically evangelical things like, "I couldn't live without it" or "It's the most important thing in the world to me." Rather, they tended to speak more about how faith provides them with personal contentment and enjoyment and how it is all just a relative matter of personal taste. This mainline Lutheran man, for example, explained:

> Faith gives me peace of mind. I enjoy listening to a service, the ritual and the sermon. I enjoy meeting people at church, talking with them, having a cup of coffee with them after church. It just makes my week complete, so to speak. I don't know. It eases my conscience or whatever. It's enjoyable for me. If somebody else didn't really like it very much, fine. I'm not for imposing any kind of religion on anyone. If they don't feel the need for it, then it's up to them.

Similarly, this man, who left the Roman Catholic Church to join the Episcopal Church and later a mainline Lutheran (ELCA) church, said:

> My faith is important to me because it helps me formulate actions and behaviors that not only make me comfortable with who I am, but help me to relate positively to others. When I think of Christianity, I like to think of emulating Christ's life on earth. I am always mindful of the fact that I must be tolerant of all other individuals who may not espouse the same belief system I have. We can all be Christlike and minister to each other. We can all help each other get along through this mortal veil in as comfortable a way as we can. We are all going to end up in the same place: dead. So why not ease the plight of each other as much as we can?

Again, the overarching moral authority here is not a sovereign God's claim on one's life or a call to committed discipleship but one's own personal comfort. Faith is important because it helps people get along and feel good. This Episcopalian man framed his religious practice therapeutically: "I go to church to worship and relax. Church is the only place I can go to and I don't have to worry about any burdens." Another Episcopalian man put the idea into somewhat different words: "Good religion is not about how many people you have going to the church. It should be what it does for you, y'know?" The idea of costly discipleship seemed to many mainliners and liberals a bizarre oddity, extraneous to their lives. As the "Methodist agnostic" we met above argued when we raised the subject, "I don't think Jesus literally meant taking up any cross and denying ourselves. Maybe that was for his disciples, because they weren't such red-hot characters to start with and so weren't giving up a whole lot. But today, there's no preacher or anybody else that's gonna convince me to cash in all my stuff and give it away." Absent from many of these voices—and more present in the evangelical interviews—is the "pearl of great price," the "treasure hidden in the field," a sense that faith is important enough to spend oneself for, to allow it to transform one's very life. Rather, simply, if it works, if it makes you comfortable, fine.

Robustness of Faith

Given their relatively lower levels of commitment to traditionally held orthodox theological truth and the somewhat diminished importance of faith in their lives, it is not surprising that many mainline and liberal Protestants also expressed relatively lower levels of confidence and assurance in their faith. When asked how he knows his faith to be true, for example, this mainline Lutheran (ELCA) man responded: "Nobody really knows if Christian faith is true. I believe the teachings of Christ as I know them through my church; it's the proper way to live, where you don't hurt anybody or take advantage of anybody, or this kind of a thing. And I feel good about it." This liberal United Methodist stated:

> I think, if put to the test, I'll probably pray. But I still feel somewhat that religion is the opiate of the people. Maybe I consider myself too much of an intellectual, which I'm really not, to swallow it totally. So I doubt. Still, every time I get too far afield, I think, "Well, you know, there's got to be something there." I suppose I've always had doubts.

Those who maintain this kind of religious orientation are not surprisingly disinclined to share enthusiastically their religious beliefs with others. This woman from a liberal Presbyterian church, for example, confessed: "I'm not a real banner-carrying type of person. People who know me know that I'm afraid to say what I believe in."

This self-described liberal Lutheran man, a teacher at a local community college, went even further in eschewing confidence and assurance in his faith:

Whether or not my faith is true is not an issue for me. I don't worry
about what is true. I think many things are true. True is what it is
for the moment. And I don't have to feel that it is true, or sell
someone that it is true. Science has taught me that truth is ephem-
eral, it's changing: what is true today is not true tomorrow. There
is no true. True has no meaning for me.

When speaking of his profession, he combined this epistemological relativism with intellectual compartmentalization: "I have never had any intellectual conflicts between my faith and my science, because I am very successful
at wearing a multitude of hats and playing a multitude of roles. I pick up
new ones all the time, and I am very capable with my left brain of pigeon-
holing and dealing for the moment. My faith and science may never come
together, which is fine."

Group Participation

The relatively lower levels of participation by mainliners and liberals in
church activities that we saw in our survey were reflected in our interviews
as well. A number of mainline and liberal Protestants tended to speak more
of church attendance as a weekly routine than as the center of their social
lives or as vital to their spiritual lives. More than evangelicals, mainliners
and liberals spoke of church participation as something they worked
around other priorities in their schedules rather than as a baseline commitment in their lives. Mainliners, and liberals, such as this liberal Methodist,
were simply much more likely than evangelicals to say things like, "I enjoy
going to church. But not every week, because we're simply not around here
a good bit."

From what we could gather about the churches our interviewees attended, compared with evangelical churches, mainline and liberal churches
were more likely to accommodate lower levels of commitment and investment among their members and attenders. One mainline Lutheran man
we interviewed, for example, who, because he is a member of his church
council, might be expected to play a leadership role in building church life,
reported, "Our church does have small groups, Bible classes, and other
things. But I am not a member of any of those, I don't attend any. The only
thing I attend is council meetings."

In some cases, it appeared that mainline and liberal churches were making efforts to get more people involved in programs and activities but with
limited success. Part of their difficulty, it seemed to us, lay in the fact that
mainline and liberal congregations allow or encourage so much theological

and moral diversity in their constituencies. In churches where individual members tend to customize their own beliefs and ethics to suit their felt needs and interests, a congregation may not possess enough personal and religious commonality among members needed to build group solidarity. Furthermore, when faith is constructed as a responsive obligation to God or as a mission to achieve, as in most evangelical churches, a rationale exists for members to invest themselves in the life of the church. But when faith is constructed as a means to enhance personal contentment and enjoyment according to one's personal tastes, it becomes much more difficult to secure investment into the public good of vibrant group life, for people will only participate if it makes them more comfortable.

Again, some of the more committed members of mainline and liberal churches we interviewed were well aware of and frustrated by the lack of commitment to participation on the part of so many of their fellow parishioners. This mainline Lutheran woman, for example, griped:

> You know what we have? We have the same people who are doing all the work, and all the others just come and go. I mean, parents drop their kids off at Sunday School and go home and say they've done their parently duty. They never go to church. I can't tell you to how many I'd like to say, "Hey, we have a church service!" I've tried to get council to have a service during Sunday School, because obviously these parents don't want to be bothered with their kids in church. But ninety percent of the people here, if there's a baptism or confirmation class or first communion, will say, "Oh boy, it's running ten minutes over now, gotta get out of here!" And they walk away and say they did their duty today!

It is understandable that these kinds of attitudes and their resulting frustrations lead to depressed levels, if not downward spirals, of group participation.

Commitment to Mission

In our interviews, we saw major differences in the attitudes of evangelicals versus mainline and liberal Protestants toward trying to exert a distinctive Christian influence on the world, whether through evangelism or social or political activism. Some of those differences seemed rooted in a lack of clear boundaries between Christians and "the world" that might need redeeming or transforming. One mainline Baptist man—who had just returned to the East Coast from a weekend trip to Las Vegas, where he played golf every night until 3:00 A.M., and to which he wanted to return and "do it again right away"—remarked, "I don't think Christians should have to live all that differently from mainstream American culture. What for? I think Christians can be just normal people." Not surprisingly, then, he later declared, "I'm not so sure Christians should be trying to change America particularly. That's not a big responsibility I feel."

Another apparent basis for the relative lack of enthusiasm among mainliners and liberals for missionary or social activism was pessimism about the possibilities for social change, mixed with an anticipation that it would not be personally rewarding. This liberal Baptist woman, for instance, said:

> If we all lived the kind of life Jesus lived, the world would be a far different place. But I don't think that is going to happen. I feel that I cannot go out and march or be proactive. It's not going to do much good for me. I guess it doesn't fit my style.

Finally, the mainline and liberal proclivity for *laissez faire,* individual self-determination of truth, evident in this mainline Lutheran man's statement, also helps to explain the lack of commitment to Christian mission and social influence:

> I hedge at the idea that Christian morality should be the commonly accepted morality of our culture. I would prefer it were that way. But then we have all kinds of groups, and that would be forcing our morality on them. I think we ought to leave people well enough alone. Let them do their own thing as long as it doesn't hurt anyone else.[13]

These factors particularly worked against any sense of commitment to evangelistic missions. For example, this liberal United Methodist man argued:

> I am not a believer in missionaries. If we want to go to Africa and provide medical help and teach people how to farm, great. But if we go to Japan and try to convert Shintoists, no way. If they came here and tried that on me, I'd get mad, and I think they have every right to feel the same. Christianity is great. If I'm anything I'm a

---

13. And the Baptist man above argued: "I think everyone should live exactly as they think. I believe everyone should choose for themselves. I don't want to impose my views and beliefs on anyone. I just live the way I think is right. Let other people do what they want."

Christian. But I think that others have a right to believe for themselves, and if they go to hell, they just took the wrong turn.[14]

Similarly, the liberal Lutheran community-college professor we met above
declared:

> To say that other religions are wrong is self-centered and egocen-
> tric. I am not even comfortable with saying all religions point to
> the same God. Whatever trips your trigger is fine with me, if that's
> your belief system. We are mortal. Who is to say who is right and
> wrong? If it helps you get through your life and helps bring mean-
> ing to your life, then fine.

But even aside from formal church missions programs and a sense of
responsibility for Christian social or political activism, many mainline and
liberal Protestants appeared to make few efforts to figure out how their
faith should or might influence how they live in their daily lives in the
public realm. For example, one police officer we interviewed who attends a
mainline Southern Baptist church observed:

> I don't really know how my faith affects my life at work. I try to be
> a good example and all. But mostly it's just a way to earn a living,
> and just barely at that. I guess some of my colleagues know I'm a
> Christian, because I play for a church softball team. And some-
> times I'll advise someone who's having a hard time to go talk to a
> pastor. But mostly my work is just a job.

The compartmentalization and privatization of faith that we have seen
above surely feeds this lack of connection between faith and the rest of life.
But the cumulative effect is to produce religious traditions with higher levels of disinterest in exerting a faith-based influence on the surrounding
world.

Retention and Recruitment of Members

Finally, compared with evangelicals, the mainliners and liberals we interviewed showed more signs of problems retaining and recruiting members
for their churches. Mainliners and liberals were more likely, for example,
to recall growing up in families where religion was not very important or

14. He continued: "Personally I don't think they're gonna end up in hell. Now, some of
these Muslims may end up in hell, the way some of them are acting. But then again, they
are much more devout in their religion than I am in mine, so who am I to criticize? I just
don't agree with them."

where their parents did not particularly nurture them spiritually. Not atypical of many was the story of this mainline Lutheran man whose family emigrated to the United States from Norway when he was a child:

> My family never had family Bible reading or devotions or prayer time or anything like that. Sometimes a prayer before meals. But I don't recall ever sitting down to a Bible reading at home. No. But when we visited with grandpa two weeks every summer, there was always a daily Bible reading and prayer. That was automatic in his house. But none of that really had any effect on me. I can remember wishing we didn't have to come in for that. It was not something that I enjoyed.

The mainliners and liberals we interviewed also seemed to place much lower priority than evangelicals on ensuring that their own children embraced their own faith. Again, given their commitment to individual choice of truth and aversion to "imposing" their views on others, this makes sense. As this liberal Baptist woman said:

> Some of our children attend church and some don't. We just try to let them know how we feel. But I don't feel like going out there and trying to evangelize the world on a big basis. I just don't, it wouldn't fit me. Lot of my family haven't chosen the same thing we have, but that's okay. We try to accept that.

Similarly, the liberal Lutheran we met above, who doesn't believe in truth itself, told us that one of his children has grown up to be nonreligious and another had converted to an "Eastern" religion. And that was just fine with him.

Furthermore, as far as we could tell through our interviews, many of the mainline and liberal churches our interviewees attended were having difficulty with the retention of adult members. Some of this appeared to be the lack of commitment to programs to integrate newcomers and the lack of accountability in membership. According to this woman who is a member of a liberal Presbyterian church, for example:

> We have a wonderful minister, but lots of times I notice we don't really have the follow-through in place. It's sad because, we may get a family that becomes very involved. Then all of a sudden, they're not there. You ask, "What happened to so-and-so," and you get, "Oh, well they left." And nobody says, "Oh jeez, we just let them leave? Didn't anybody call them?"

Others we interviewed, such as this mainline United Methodist woman, notice that their churches have a hard time identifying an appealing message or style that would attract new adult members in the first place:

> For some reason, I don't know what it is, but mainline Protestant churches as I know them have absolutely turned people off by being too drab and not being at all able to make statements anyone can grab hold of. Fundamentalist churches are growing by leaps and bounds in this city, but not the mainline churches.

Some of these people, such as this mainline Baptist woman, even recognize that the individualism, accommodation, and relativism that they so highly value contribute to their own numerical decline: "Our denomination is not growing much, and I think it's because there is not a definite list of things you do and don't do. It is lot more iffy. And lots of people don't like that." But they are not prepared to take action that might reverse the membership decline of mainline and liberal churches.

To conclude, we want to emphasize again that we are not claiming that most of the mainliners and liberals we interviewed were heterodox, doubting free-riders. Far from it. Many reflected the same levels of religious vitality we noticed among evangelicals. Furthermore, as sociologists, we forswear making judgments about the ultimate truth or spiritual fidelity of any belief, attitude, or behavior of any tradition. Our intent is not to suggest that mainliners and liberals are spiritually inferior Christians. Here we simply recount that we did notice somewhat more frequently among our mainline and liberal Protestants signs of what might, from a sociological perspective, be considered aspects of weakness in a religious movement—as measured by our six dimensions of religious strength outlined in this chapter.

By Comparison: Fundamentalists

Our survey data reveal only marginally lower levels of religious vitality among fundamentalists compared with evangelicals, but lower levels which remain fairly consistent across many measures. In chapter four, we theorize why fundamentalism may have become a somewhat weaker religious movement than evangelicalism. For now, we simply report briefly that we did, in fact, sometimes notice in our interviews modest differences between self-identified evangelicals and fundamentalists regarding our six measures of religious strength. Many of these signs of marginal weakness seemed to revolve around a certain routinization of faith and practice that the fundamentalist subculture appeared to allow or invite—the kind of mentality our evangelical interviewees often disparaged as "cultural Christianity" or "churchianity."

While our self-identified fundamentalists, for example, tended to emphasize their belief in orthodox doctrine, they sometimes didn't reflect the same intensity about the matter and occasionally even showed signs of compromise on or indifference to matters of theological truth. One self-identified fundamentalist Baptist woman we interviewed, for example, stated her willingness to disregard the Bible when it came to an issue with which she disagreed with it: "I feel like homosexuals should not be scorned from the church. I know from the Bible that is certainly not according to biblical teaching, but I'm being very, very tolerant of that anyway."[15] Very rarely did we hear that kind of moral logic—simply setting aside the Bible despite what is perceived to be its clear teaching—from evangelicals.

Similarly, while the self-identified fundamentalists we interviewed generally professed the great value of their faith in their lives, and their confidence and assurance in it, also evident in some fundamentalists was a certain routinization of faith as a taken-for-granted element of a broadly Christian way of life. Furthermore, although our fundamentalists commonly participated in a variety of church activities relatively frequently, we also noticed in some a contentment with habitual Sunday-morning-only church attendance, or less, as an acceptable churchgoing way of life. That mentality is evident, for example, in this self-described fundamentalist member of a Southern Baptist church:

> Probably from when I was a week old and all my life, I was made to go to church. I don't know whether that's good or bad. Of my siblings, I'm the one that goes to church most often, partly to please my mother—it makes her happy to see me in church on Sundays. Now, I don't participate in anything other than the Sunday service. I'm one of those 11 o'clock Sunday-morning type people. But I thoroughly enjoy church, the social aspect of it, the music, sometimes the sermons. Sometimes I would like to get up and say, hey, I disagree with that but I don't do it because that would be totally unacceptable socially. My husband does not go to church as frequently as I do. He likes to go out of town on the weekends, which pulls me away.

Moreover, for those fundamentalists who professed the need proactively to influence the surrounding society as Christians, they did not convey in

15. Later, she explained: "I don't have a problem with other peoples' faith. Whatever you believe, if you believe in God, I don't have a problem with that. I just do have a problem if you don't believe in anything."

their talk the same urgency and fervor that was evident in the "evangelical burden" we observed. And they more often offered reasons why getting involved might be a bad idea. For example, this self-identified fundamentalist Pentecostal man's separatist instincts neutralized his efforts to put into practice his belief that Christians should influence the world around them: "Sometimes I feel a little isolated, because if I really want to live a Christian life, I cannot really get involved in most things. Because at some point it's going to break down into an activity or lifestyle that I'm not comfortable with." Nor did all of those who advocated their tradition's historical mission to remain separate from the world seem to reflect in practice a passionate commitment to that kind of subcultural boundary-maintenance.

Finally, in their talk, fundamentalists tended to be somewhat more reticent about outgoing personal evangelism and building strong churches than were evangelicals. Part of this seemed to derive from their separatist tendencies and part from their difficulty in responding positively to their construction of "soul winning" as a legalistic obligation for pleasing God. Another self-identified fundamentalist Baptist woman we interviewed, for example, confessed her turmoil over her reluctance to share her faith with her friends:

> My walk with God is terrible, because my friends are unsaved and I just go along. I feel badly about that. I can see the Lord shaking his head at me, because I don't speak out like I should. It is hard for me to witness to them, because the Word says to be separate, and if I really lived by that, I wouldn't be fellowshipping with them. When I do say anything and they don't want to talk about it, then I don't press it. I wish I was able to witness like others, but I can't seem to. I'm not good at it. But that's what we should be doing is witnessing. I'm not even good at giving out tracts, in my weakness I can't do it. So I just pray for those people who do.

This tone contrasts with many evangelicals who spoke of evangelism as a natural expression of self, a free response to God's love.[16]

Again, not all fundamentalists spoke in these ways. Very many did

16. Compare the above quote with this from an evangelical Presbyterian woman: "Evangelism means we are all called to be light in darkness. We are all called. I know I can't do anything to earn God's love. It's a gift. My response is to want to love God and to love people, knowing that my love comes from God. If the love comes from God, I'm going to explode if I don't give it away. I'm into lifestyle evangelism, just teaching people to live and breathe their faith. I'm an aroma of life to those that are perishing, though I might not even know who is smelling that aroma. But I believe that I am because God says so. We need to be driven by love, not fear. I don't cram my faith down people's throat. But I also don't hold back integrating my faith, because it's just a part of who I am. I can't hide it."

manifest strong, committed faith. Nevertheless, in these ways, among some self-identified fundamentalists at least, we did notice small but perceptible sociological indications of religious weakness, as measured by our six dimensions of religious strength.

Conclusion

If there in fact remain distinct religious traditions in the contemporary United States, and if we can identify significant differences in the religious vitality of those traditions, the question that confronts us next is, why? How can we account for differences in the vitality of religious traditions? What social forces shape variations in religious strength? We turn now to examine and evaluate alternative approaches to answering those questions.

THREE

Explaining Religious Vitality in America

Ｈow can we explain different degrees of religious vitality reflected in different religious groups? Why do some religious movements seem to thrive while others languish? Viewed from the perspective of committed faith, the relative success of a religious group might be understood as the result of spiritual consequences or the blessing of God. A flourishing religious movement may believe its prosperity is God's reward for obedience or orthodoxy or the natural outcome of having espoused an important spiritual truth or practice. A declining religious group, on the other hand, may view its lack of "success" as an affirming mark of genuine spiritual faithfulness, seeing itself as the "last, true remnant" whose truth the world has not the sense to recognize.

The sociological perspective, however, reveals that differences in vitality among religious groups can also be at least partially explained as the result of *social* forces and structures. Sociological analysis enables us to see that qualitative differences in the histories, organizations, subcultural norms, and social positioning of religious groups can significantly shape their strength. This chapter reviews and evaluates a number of important sociological theories that seek to explain the vitality of religious groups in the United States. The purpose is to know both what theoretical tools are at our disposal that can help us explain why American evangelicalism is thriving and whether the case of American evangelicalism can help us assess the usefulness of existing theories.

Theories of Religious Vitality
Sheltered Enclave Theory

The first theory to consider, which we might label the "sheltered enclave" theory, contends that religions—especially traditional, orthodox religions—survive and prosper when they are sheltered from the undermining effects of modernity. The theoretical foundation for this theory was laid by Peter Berger (1967; also see Berger and Luckmann 1966); but it was a student of Berger's, James Davison Hunter (1983; 1987; 1997), who most systematically and articulately developed and applied it to the case of (for us, significantly) American evangelicalism.

The sheltered-enclave perspective views religions as relatively cohesive moral orders constituted and bounded by their distinctive cognitive content and symbolic boundaries (Hunter 1987). A religious tradition is not merely an organized population of fellow believers but a socially maintained and sacredly defined cultural milieu that sustains a distinct worldview or "sacred cosmos" (Berger 1967). Strong religions are those that offer credible and secure moral orders that make life and the world meaningful and significant for their members.

Credibility and security in this are absolutely critical, for a sacred cosmos that cannot legitimate itself for those who inhabit and sustain it as simply the nature of things, the final truth, "just the way things are," invites doubt. And doubt opens the door for belief implausibility and loss of religious faith. This creates a major problem for religions, however, because every sacred cosmos—indeed every normative order—is a social construction (Berger and Luckmann 1966), and "all socially constructed worlds are inherently precarious" (Berger 1967). Because the sacred cosmos really *isn't* simply the nature of things, but a human construction, any cultural milieu is always in danger of delegitimation; its symbolic boundaries are continually subject to encroachment and erosion.

Of particular danger are the religiously corrosive forces that accompany modernization: functional rationality, cultural pluralism, and structural pluralism (Hunter 1983: 12–13). Modernity's technological production, bureaucratic social organization, rational and utilitarian values, urbanization, cultural diversity, mass media communications, and differentiation of spheres and functions are all thought to undermine the credibility and security of religious worldviews. These forces, according to Hunter, make it,

> increasingly difficult for people to maintain an open attachment to a perspective on reality the antithesis of which is institutionalized in most sectors of social life and taken for granted as the norm. Religious belief and commitment are, as a result, much more tenuous for the man on the street. . . . The net effect is the rendering of a commitment to a certain [religious] world view precarious if not altogether implausible. (1983: 12–13)

This theoretical framework provides Hunter with a very interesting research question: "If modernization secularizes and America is among the most modern societies in the world, how then is it possible that Evangelicalism survives and even thrives in contemporary America?" (1983: 4).

The answer, explains Hunter, is that evangelicals are in their demographic and social location extraordinarily shielded from the religiously corrosive forces of modernity. Using 1978–79 survey data collected by the Princeton Religious Research Center, Hunter shows that evangelicals are—compared with other populations in American society—disproportionately older, less educated, more often female, and more often married; they earn relatively lower incomes; and reside disproportionately in rural and small town areas of the South and Midwest, rather than in large urban centers (1983: 49–60). Hunter concludes: "the Evangelical community as a whole is—perhaps more than any other major American religious body—sociologically and geographically distant from the institutional structures and processes of modernity. . . . Thus one reason for the survival of American Evangelicalism in the modern world may be that its social and demographic distance from modernity allows it to avoid sustained confrontation with modernity's most threatening attributes" (1983: 60). Even so, in Hunter's view, modernity's inexorable advance increasingly threatens evangelicalism, forcing it gradually to bargain away many of the beliefs, norms, and morals that have traditionally made it orthodox and distinctive (1987; 1997).

For our purposes, then, according to this general model, religions that thrive are those able to offer their meaning-seeking members credible and secure moral orders that make life and the world purposeful and significant. And religions become weak and decline when their members are exposed to the social and cultural forces of modernity that disaffirm and undermine the credibility and security of the sacred moral orders they have inhabited, thereby producing doubt, accommodation, and sometimes the complete abandonment of belief. The principle way to avoid that fate is thought to be by remaining demographically and socially distant from the corrosiveness of modernity, within strong enclaves where vibrant sacred moral orders can be sustained.

Status Discontent Theory

A second theoretical school, more narrowly focused, seeks to offer an explanation of why certain religious groups become energized to mobilize their resources for social and political activism. This theory focuses on threats to or anxiety about the social status of religious groups. Originally developed to explain right-wing political extremism (Hofstadter 1955; Lenski 1954; Lipset 1963), theories of status discontent have evolved over the years into explanations for a broader array of religious and political phenomena (for example, Marshall 1986; Wasserman 1990; Zurcher and Kirkpatrick 1976; Zurcher, Kirkpatrick, Cushing, and Bowman 1971; Gusfield 1963; Rohter 1969; McEvoy 1971; Wood and Hughes 1984; Lipset 1960; Brungart 1971; Wilson and Zurcher 1976). Although unfashionable with many sociologists, versions of status discontent theory still find occasional proponents in the sociology of religion literature. Kenneth Wald, Dennis Owen, and Samuel Hill (1989), for example, advance evidence suggesting that status discontent is a significant contributing factor to support for conservative Christian political activism. Louise Lorentzen (1980), too, interprets the rise of conservative Protestant political activism in the United States in the late 1970s and early 1980s as motivated by the desire to counteract status decline resulting from the cultural devaluing of traditional, conservative Protestant lifestyles. Similarly, Ann Page and Donald Clelland (1978) view continuing protests over the content of public school textbooks in Kanawha County, West Virginia, as a "politics of life style concern" struggle between status groups for control of the means of the production of lifestyles (also see Crawford 1980). And many more popular interpretations of the resurgence of conservative Christianity in the United States seem to view it in part as a reflection of status resentment. MIT economist, Lester Thurow (1996: 232), for example, is merely the latest proponent of this approach:

> The rise of religious fundamentalism is a social volcano in eruption. Its connection to economics is simple. Those who lose out economically or who cannot stand the economic uncertainty of not knowing what it takes to succeed in the new era ahead retreat into religious fundamentalism.

Elaborated and applied to the broader question of religious vitality, status discontent theory would suggest that religious identities become more salient, religious commitments more firm, religious practices more consistent, and religious resources more easily mobilized for activism the more a religious group feels a threat to the social status that it previously enjoyed. Conversely, it would suggest that religious groups that perceive no threats to their social status could likely afford to become complacent and routinized.

Strictness Theory

A third theoretical approach to religious vitality focuses not on the macro social location of religious populations vis-à-vis the forces of modernity or other shifting forces that threaten social status, but on the micro-level normative demands and expectations that different religious groups impose on their members. This approach argues, in short, that "strict" religious groups thrive, while "lenient" religious groups languish. The two most important proponents of this theory are Dean Kelley (1972; 1978) and Laurence Iannaccone (1992 and 1994; also see Finke and Stark 1992: 252–55), each of whom offer somewhat different accounts of exactly why strict religions thrive.

In his 1972 book, *Why Conservative Churches Are Growing,* Kelley demonstrates with pages of statistics and graphs that mainline-liberal Protestant churches in the United States since the 1960s have been in numerical decline, while at the same time conservative denominations have been growing rapidly. The reason, he says, is that the former are lenient and the latter are strict. Building, like Hunter, on Bergerian theory, Kelley argues that "the business of religion is meaning," and that religions will only thrive when they can deliver substantial meaning to their adherents (1972: 36–46). But how do religions produce the kind of meaning that satisfies the religious faithful? Not simply by espousing mere concepts and ideas, which Kelley calls "notions": "ideas that do not require anything of those who espouse them, but can be bandied back and forth like verbal playthings" (1972: 52). Rather, religions produce meaning by demanding that their followers respond to their ideas and concepts by committing their time, money, energy, reputations, and very selves in a way that validates and invests in those ideas. Put into a formula, "*meaning = concept + demand*" (1972: 52). According to Kelley (1972: 52–53, italics in original):

> We want something more than a smooth, articulate verbal interpretation of what life is all about. Words are cheap; we want explanations that are validated by the commitment of other persons. . . . What costs nothing accomplishes nothing. If it costs nothing to belong to a community, it can't be worth much. So the quality that enables religious meanings to take hold is not their rationality, their logic, their surface credibility, but rather the *demand* they make upon their adherents and the degree to which that demand is met by *commitment.*

Strict religions are able to provide their adherents rich meaning, according to Kelley, precisely because they are demanding. They demand an absolutism about aims, beliefs, and explanations of life; high levels of conformity; and fanaticism in communications with outsiders. These, in turn, produce high levels of commitment (total solidarity and willingness to sacrifice for the group), discipline (willingness to obey leaders and accept discipline), and missionary zeal (eagerness to spread the faith).

By contrast, "lenient" religious groups are characterized by relativistic beliefs and values, an appreciation for a diversity of views and lifestyles, and an interest in dialoguing with, rather than judging, the views of outsiders. These, in turn, produce lukewarmness (indecisiveness and reluctance to sacrifice for the group), individualism (personal autonomy, resistance to discipline, readiness to leave the group), and reserve (reluctance to share faith with others or insights and convictions with the group). Since lenient groups, by making few demands, fail to authenticate for their followers the meanings their faith espouses, they tend over time to weaken and decline. Strict religious groups, on the other hand, successfully generate satisfying meaning and so thrive and grow.

Laurence Iannaccone (1992; 1994)—who is echoed by Finke and Stark (1992: 252–55)—likewise contends that strict religions thrive but for a somewhat different reason than Kelley sets forth. Iannaccone's theoretical wellspring is not Berger's (1967) sociology of religion but the economic assumptions of rational choice theory. According to Iannaccone, strict religions thrive not so much because they provide richer meaning for the faithful, but because they screen out "free riders"—people who enjoy many of the benefits of the religious group while contributing little to the group. It is not possible in a strict and demanding church, Iannaccone argues (1994), for a member to enjoy worship services and holiday programs, benefit from pastoral counseling and wedding and funeral services, be visited in the hospital, receive the support of a small group, and savor potluck suppers without contributing at least their fair share of time, energy, money, and emotional investment to make it possible to generate those "collective goods" in the first place. Consequently, strict religious groups that screen out free-riders enjoy high degrees of commitment, investment, solidarity, and mutual-rewards—all of which make those groups thrive and grow. By contrast, lenient religious groups are full of free-riders who want to take a lot more than they give (1992). Consequently, there are far fewer religious collective benefits (inspiration, support, fellowship, etc.) to go around, which creates a downwardly spiraling atmosphere of apathy and disinterest—

a sure recipe for organizational decline. This process, Iannaccone claims (1992), applies not only to ordinary church congregations but also to a variety of religious groups, including religious cults.

Competitive Marketing Theory

Another theory of religious vitality that is based on the economic model of rational choice is what we might label the "competitive marketing," "religious economies," or "supply-side" theory of Roger Finke, Rodney Stark, and Laurence Iannaccone (Finke and Stark 1988; 1989a; 1989b; 1989c; 1992; Finke and Iannaccone 1993; Finke, Guest, and Stark 1996; Finke 1989). The theory's basic claim is that religious regulation and monopolies create lethargic religions—Finke and Stark observe that "there is ample evidence that in societies with at least a putative monopoly faith, religious indifference is rife"—but that capable religions thrive in pluralistic, competitive environments (1988: 44). Capable religions thrive because their religious "entrepreneurs" capitalize on unregulated religious environments to aggressively market their religions to new "consumers"; in these environments, religious "firms" (denominations and traditions) that possess superior organizational structures (denominational polities), sales representatives (evangelists and clergy), products (religious messages), and marketing (evangelistic) techniques flourish (Finke and Stark 1989c: 32). Those that do not cannot successfully compete and so decline numerically. Nonetheless, with pluralism and competition, at the aggregate level, the total amount of religious participation in the society increases, since more and more religious consumers are induced into participation by the variety of religious products that satisfy their needs and wants (Finke and Stark 1992).

With this theoretical framework in hand, Finke, Stark, and Iannaccone have sought iconoclastically to overturn much conventional wisdom on religious growth and decline. For example, they offer empirical evidence to show that religion in pluralistic urban areas fares better than religion in small towns and rural areas. The city, in fact, they claim, is not inimical to religion but a conducive environment for religion (Finke and Stark 1988; Finke, Guest, and Stark 1996). They have also argued that, contrary to widespread beliefs, the rate of church attendance over United States history has steadily increased; that, throughout its history, America has become a more, not less, religious nation. This, they claim, is precisely because a more regulated religious economy has given way to a more pluralistic, competitive environment (Finke and Stark 1992). Exemplary of this process, they suggest, was the Second Great Awakening, in which the "upstart" Baptist and Methodist sects—which were better equipped to capitalize on religious pluralism—outstripped in growth the established Episcopal, Presbyterian, and Congregational denominations, which had become comfortable and lazy because of the monopoly status they enjoyed before disestablishment (Finke and Stark 1989c).

From this theoretical perspective, then, religious vitality is a result of unregulated religious environments that stimulate aggressive religious entrepreneurs in search of expanding market-shares to promote more diverse supplies of religious products that satisfy ever-expanding markets of religious consumers. At the macro level, religious vitality is the product of pluralistic, competitive religious economies; and religious weakness is the product of highly regulated religious environments that discourage competition. At the micro level of religious congregations, vitality is the result of skilled and aggressive religious activists marketing their religious products to newly responsive and satisfied market niches of religious consumers; conversely, religious decline at this level is the product of languid religious firms that lack the marketing skills and organizational capacity to generate and sustain thriving religious congregations.

Before evaluating these theories, two observations are worth making. First, the competitive marketing theory is largely compatible with the strictness theories, particularly Iannaccone's version that focuses on screening free-riders (a compatibility fostered by their common rational-choice assumptions). However, these two theoretical approaches focus their causal explanations at somewhat different levels of analysis. Strictness theories locate the crucial variable determining religious vitality and weakness at the level of individual religious congregations and the demands they place on their members; competitive marketing theory, by contrast, focuses on macro religious "economies" and the incentives and opportunities they offer religious entrepreneurs to market their products. Second, and quite important, we should note the stark contrast of the diametrically opposed logics of the competitive-marketing and sheltered-enclave theories: the former claims that religious pluralism promotes religious vitality and monopoly environments impair it, while the later suggests that pluralism undermines religious vitality and monopoly environments promote it. Indeed, their views of the consequences of religious monopoly and pluralism for the life of religious groups are so antithetical that some observers (for example, Warner 1993) claim they represent two opposing "paradigms."

Evaluating the Theories

Which of these theories best help us to explain the case of American evangelicalism thriving? And for which of them does the character of evangelicalism's vitality suggest empirically supportive evidence?

Sheltered Enclave Theory

First, we can observe that, for all of its theoretical elegance and intelligent articulation, the sheltered enclave theory appears to offer little help in understanding our case. If anything, this study's data contradict many of the expectations and conclusions of this approach. Little in our findings suggest that American evangelicalism's vitality is due to any social or geographic distance from modernity. Quite the contrary. Evangelicalism appears to be thriving despite—or, as we will suggest below, perhaps precisely *because of*—the fact that it is very much engaged in struggle with the institutions, values, and thought-processes of the pluralistic modern world.

We have already seen that evangelicals are—almost always *more* than most other Americans—voting in political elections; working hard to educate themselves about social and political issues; lobbying elected officials; participating in public protests and demonstrations; talking with nonbelievers about their faith; getting involved in local community organizations; giving money to help the poor; defending a biblical worldview in intellectual circles; and struggling with the public issues of racism, abortion, and educational policy. Here are people who appear to be quite engaged with the people, institutions, and concerns of the pluralistic, modern world.

More significantly, the demographic and socioeconomic location of contemporary evangelicals largely fails to comport with the expectations of the sheltered enclave theory. Hunter (1983: 58–60; 1987: 9–13, 165–78) maintains that higher education, income, and participation in the paid labor force; residence in urban areas, particularly outside of the South and Midwest; younger age; and being male and unmarried are indicators of proximity to modernity. We are persuaded that higher education and income, work in the paid labor force, and urban residence can serve to operationalize exposure to the technical rationality and cultural and structural pluralism of modernity. However, we remain unconvinced that anything about regional location, sex, marital status, or age—in and of themselves—do so. There appears no compelling reason to believe that (controlling for education, income, work status, and population density of residence) an older, married woman's existence in Atlanta, Georgia (or Yadkin County, North Carolina), for example, is somehow less modern than is a younger, single man's existence in Buffalo, New York (or Northumberland County, Pennsylvania)—particularly in the age of cable and satellite-dish television, the Internet, fax machines, and so on. True, important regional (for example, South versus non-South) variations in religion do exist, but they are essentially historical-cultural differences, not differences in distance from modernity. Granting this assessment of Hunter's measures of proximity to modernity, our data suggest an almost complete lack of correlation between distance from modernity and religious vitality.

Table 3.1 shows that, on average, self-identified evangelicals have more years of education than fundamentalists, liberals, Roman Catholics, and those who are nonreligious; and only slightly fewer years than mainline Protestants. Of all groups, evangelicals are the least likely to have only a high-school education or less; the nonreligious are the most likely. Furthermore, higher proportions of evangelicals have studied at the graduate-school level than have fundamentalists, liberals, or the nonreligious; the same proportion of evangelicals have a graduate-level education as Roman Catholics; and only slightly less have than mainline Protestants. In addition, evangelicals above all groups have made the greatest gains in intergenerational educational mobility—increasing more than twice as many years of education as nonreligious Americans. Furthermore, evangelicals are slightly less likely than fundamentalists, Roman Catholics, and the nonreligious to be engaged in the paid labor force, but more likely than mainline and liberal Protestants.[1] Regarding income, evangelicals are more likely to fall into the $20,000-or-less household income bracket than mainline Protestants, but less likely than Roman Catholics, and much less likely than fundamentalists, liberals, or the nonreligious. At the high end, evangelicals are less likely than mainline Protestants and Roman Catholics to earn incomes of $50,000 or more but more likely than fundamentalists, liberals, and the nonreligious to do so. Thus, in three of the four valid indicators of proximity to modernity—higher education, greater income, and participation in the paid labor force—evangelicals actually prove *more* likely to be exposed to the forces of modernity than are nonreligious Americans and at least not consistently less so, if not often more so, than those of other, less sociologically strong Christian traditions.

Regarding urban residence, table 3.2 shows that evangelicals are, on the

1. Relatively high proportions of evangelicals *are* keeping house, but only slightly more so than liberals.

Table 3.1: Socioeconomic Status and Mobility, by Tradition (percent)

	Evangelicals	Fundamentalists	Mainline	Liberals	Catholics	Nonreligious
Education						
Some high school or less	6	6	5	9	5	19
High school graduate	23	31	25	24	26	24
Vocational-technical degree	7	7	8	7	5	2
Some college	28	30	22	31	30	27
College graduate	21	16	24	17	19	17
Some graduate school	4	3	4	2	2	0
Master's degree	7	5	9	6	12	11
Beyond master's degree	4	2	3	4	1	2
Mean Years of Education	14.2	13.7	14.3	13.8	14.1	13.4
Mean Years Father's Education[a]	11.1	11.3	11.8	11.4	11.2	12.0
Mean Years of Education Gained over Father's Education	3.1	2.4	2.5	2.4	2.9	1.4
Work Status						
Full-time	54	57	49	54	56	61
Part-time	11	11	11	5	12	7
Keeping house	16	10	11	14	9	7
Retired	14	13	23	14	14	4
In school	4	6	4	7	5	14
Unemployed/on leave	1	3	2	6	4	7

Table 3.1: *Continued*

	Evangelicals	Fundamentalists	Mainline	Liberals	Catholics	Nonreligious
Income						
Less than $9,999	5	6	3	10	4	11
$10,000–19,999	10	14	10	19	12	15
$20,000–29,999	19	15	16	19	12	16
$30,000–39,999	21	24	19	12	18	17
$40,000–49,999	12	13	14	11	11	11
$50,000–59,999	12	9	12	9	8	11
$60,000–79,999	11	9	12	9	13	8
$80,000–99,999	3	6	5	5	7	7
$100,000 and More	6	4	9	6	14	4
How Economic Situation Has Changed in Last Ten Years						
Better off	59	62	56	54	54	49
About the same	28	24	31	26	24	36
Worse off	13	14	13	20	22	15
N	(429)	(389)	(576)	(431)	(114)	(60)

Note: Chi-square for all figures is significant at the .01 level, except [a]prob. = .05.

whole, only slightly less likely than nonreligious Americans to live in more urban areas. The same proportion of each group (one percent) lives in truly rural counties (less than 10,000 population). Compared with nonreligious respondents, evangelicals are slightly more likely to live in small-town counties (populations of 10,000–50,000) and somewhat less likely to reside in the most densely populated counties (500,000 or larger). However, evangelicals are more likely to reside in counties with major cities, containing populations between 50,000 to one-half million residents. If urbanization exerts a faith-undermining effect, then, its effect would have to be extraordinarily powerful to operate through these relatively small differences between nonreligious Americans and the strongest of Christian groups, the evangelicals. But if this were the case, it is hard to explain the fact that churchgoing Roman Catholics are much less likely than nonreligious Americans to reside in rural counties and much more likely to reside in the most urban counties. Furthermore, we should also expect to find the powerful secularizing effect of urbanization explaining differences in vitality of faith among religious groups. In fact, we don't. Evangelicals are less likely than either fundamentalists, mainline Protestants, or liberals to reside in counties with populations of less than 50,000. And, of all Protestant groups, evangelicals are the most likely to reside in counties with populations of 100,000 or more. All things considered, then, the urbanization variable also fails to confirm the expectations of the sheltered enclave theory.

Finally, even if we provisionally suppose with Hunter that sex, marital status, age, and region *do* indicate proximity to modernity, we still see (table 3.2) that, while significant differences that the sheltered enclave theory would predict do exist between evangelicals and the nonreligious, parallel expected correlations among religious groups between religious vitality and proximity to modernity fail to materialize. Of all Protestants, for example, evangelicals are the most likely to live in the Northeast, the North Central, and the "Bible-bust" Mountain and Pacific regions[2]; and are by far the least likely to live in the Southeast and South Central states. As to age, evangelicals are more likely than fundamentalists, liberals, and non-Christians to be more than sixty-five years old but less likely than mainline Protestants or Roman Catholics. At the younger end, evangelicals are less likely than fundamentalists, liberals, and non-Christians, but more likely than mainline Protestants and Roman Catholics, to be under thirty-five years old.

2. Indeed, evangelicals are more likely to live in the "Bible-bust" Mountain and Pacific states than are the nonreligious.

Table 3.2: Demographic Characteristics, by Tradition (percent)

	Evangelicals	Fundamentalists	Mainline	Liberals	Catholics	Nonreligious
Sex						
Male	35	43	34	33	30	51
Female	65	57	66	67	70	49
Race						
White	87	81	92	73	84	82
Black	9	14	7	22	2	6
Hispanic	3	1	0	2	9	4
Asian	0	1	1	1	3	4
Other	1	3	0	3	4	4
Marital Status						
Married	78	69	74	57	64	47
Never married	8	18	9	20	16	35
Divorced	6	6	8	13	10	10
Widowed	8	5	9	7	8	5
Separated	1	2	1	3	2	3
Ever Divorced	18	25	20	29	15	33
Age						
17–24	5	9	4	11	5	20
25–34	15	21	9	19	13	25
35–44	23	24	22	25	18	22
45–54	25	18	21	20	30	21
55–64	14	12	20	11	13	7
65–74	11	11	14	9	14	4
75 and older	7	5	10	6	7	1

Regional Location						
Northeast	17	10	13	14	42	31
Southeast	25	36	34	37	9	19
North Central	31	21	24	21	27	27
South Central	12	21	14	16	9	10
Mountain/Pacific	15	12	14	12	13	13
Population of County of Residence						
1–10,000	1	3	2	1	0	1
10,000–50,000	21	24	23	24	12	17
50,000–100,000	16	15	15	21	6	15
100,000–500,000	37	30	24	26	31	36
500,000 or Larger	25	28	26	28	51	31
N	(429)	(389)	(576)	(431)	(114)	(60)

Note: Chi-square for all figures is significant at the .001 level.

Table 3.3: Encapsulation in Christian Networks, by Tradition (percent)

	Evangelicals	Fundamentalists	Mainline	Liberals
How many of important family, friends, and work colleagues are Christians				
Almost all	36	33	41	35
Most	30	33	32	30
Some	33	33	27	33
None	1	1	< 1	2
N	(430)	(389)	(576)	(431)

Note: Chi-square is not significant.

Moreover, evangelicals are less likely than fundamentalists, but more likely than liberals Protestants and Roman Catholics to be male. Finally, while evangelicals are the most likely to be married and least likely to be never married, evangelicals also look remarkably like self-identified mainline Protestants in their marital-status patterns, who display rather lower levels of religious vitality.

One could still argue, however, that evangelicals who are exposed to modernity at a macro-structural level still manage to protect themselves from its effects by encapsulating themselves in micro-level enclaves of Christian relational networks. To check this, we asked survey respondents to think about all of the family, friends, and work colleagues who are important to them and to tell how many of them are Christians. According to table 3.3, no differences exist between the major American Protestant traditions in degree of encapsulation in Christian relational networks.

Overall, then, we see that, in a comparison between groups, the vitality of the evangelical movement shows no clear correlation with demographic factors that might indicate distance from the alleged religion-corroding forces of modernity. Evangelicals appear no less consistently engrossed in the institutional structures and processes of the modern world than any other group in the United States.[3] Evangelicalism's relative vitality, therefore, cannot easily be understood as a product of social and demographic distance from modernity that shields it from sustained confrontation with modernity's faith-threatening attributes. An explanation for evangelicalism's vitality will have to be found elsewhere.[4]

3. Multivariate regression models we ran confirm this finding as well.
4. This raises the question as to why the 1978–79 Gallup data that Hunter analyzed (1983) show such different results from ours. Four factors together may suggest an explanation. First, and probably most important, Hunter operationalized "evangelicalism" using theological criteria, whereas we have relied on religious self-identification, which is likely

Status Discontent Theory

What about status discontent theories? Do they offer an analytically useful explanation for evangelical vitality? Historical studies and our data suggests they do not. To begin, our data fail to support status theories that focus on objective or subjectively perceived economic decline. Evangelicals, we have seen, are no more economically or educationally deprived than others in American society. Nor do they appear to have suffered downward mobility in the recent past. Indeed, again, table 3.1 shows that evangelicals above all groups have advanced most in intergenerational educational mobility. And, as a measure of subjective perception, evangelicals in 1996 were among the least likely to view their financial situation as having grown worse in the previous ten years; evangelicals were also much more likely than the nonreligious to view their economic situation as having gotten better. Hence, neither discontent over real economic status decline nor social-psychological repercussions deriving from perceptions of decline would seem to explain evangelicalism's religious vitality and activism. Arguments like Lester Thurow's (1996) appear far too broad-brushed and reductionistic.

Status discontent theories that focus on concern about status decline resulting from the devaluation of lifestyle by the dominant culture (for example, Page and Clelland 1978; Lorentzen 1980) also seem problematic. For one thing, some scholars have argued that evangelicals in the twentieth century have never enjoyed particularly high social status in U.S. public culture (for example, Smidt 1988). Especially since 1925, the views of evangelicals and fundamentalists alike have been largely ignored or discounted by the institutions of the dominant culture (Marsden 1980: 176–95). According to this logic, status discontent may have energized evangelicals seven decades ago; but there would seem to be relatively little public social status for contemporary evangelicals to be losing today.

Our 178 interviews with evangelicals in 1996 yielded what at first glance appears to be support for lifestyle-defense status-discontent theo-

---

to have produced different groupings (Hunter 1983: 139–41). Second, almost twenty years separate the Gallup survey Hunter analyzed and our survey, and the demographic profile of evangelicals may have shifted somewhat in the intervening years (Hunter himself [1983: 55] suggested such changes were underway in the late 1970s). Third, Hunter's broader religious identity classifications—which did not separate out fundamentalists from evangelicals, nor mainline Protestants from liberals—may have obscured some significant demographic distinctions between groups. Finally, and probably least if at all important, the sampling of the data that Hunter analyzed was "not strictly random" (Gallup 1978: 2), such that Hunter (1983: 142) recognized that, "extreme precision in reporting demographic factors is neither assumed nor guaranteed."

ries. The evangelicals we interviewed (as we will see in the chapter 5) *did* voice grave concerns about what they view as America's turning from the ways of God. However, closer inspection shows significant deviations from the reasoning of lifestyle-defense theories. For one thing, our interviewees generally did not perceive that the dominant culture was preventing *them* from practicing the kind of lifestyle to which they were committed. Nor were their concerns about America turning from God centered on the loss of social status that *they* were suffering or would suffer as a consequence. The issue of evangelical social status was noticeably absent from their language and logic—status concerns hardly seemed to enter their minds, even when we specifically asked about them. Instead, their concerns about America's turn from God focused almost exclusively on the deleterious social and spiritual consequences they believed that *other* individuals and *the nation* as a whole would suffer as a result. We suspect, then, that status-discontent theory will prove unhelpful in explaining evangelical vitality. However, we will keep it in mind, and return in chapter 5 to reconsider its usefulness.

Strictness Theory

Does strictness theory provide a more helpful approach to explaining evangelical vitality? Our data speak less decisively on strictness than they do on proximity to modernity and status discontent. Broadly speaking, it does appear that the church denominations that have been thriving are what one could characterize as strict.[5] And, generally, the evangelicals that we interviewed were definitely living out higher-demand, higher-investment versions of faith than many of the mainline and liberal Protestants we interviewed. A key question, however, is whether this is a mere association or if there is really something about strictness per se that actually *causes* religious vitality. We are tentatively inclined to say, that, in broad terms and over time, when church organizations place relatively high (but not too high) demands on their members, that may serve as a contributing factor to their organizational growth and strength, possibly for both reasons outlined by Kelley and Iannaccone. Over the long run, in other words, relative differences in strictness may help to account for the relative greater strength

5. Both Kelley and Iannaccone's accounts of strictness theory have been criticized on many fronts in the literature (for example, Bibby and Brinkerhoff 1973, 1983; Bibby 1978; Chaves 1989; Hunter 1987: 203–6; Perrin and Mauss 1993; Marwell 1996). However, none of these criticisms—with the possible exception of certain of Marwell's (1996) critiques of Iannaccone—seems decisively to refute the theory.

of fundamentalist and evangelical churches compared with mainline-liberal churches.

However, in considering the usefulness of strictness theory to explain our particular case of evangelical vitality, one significant logical problem presents itself. The evangelical movement has from its very beginning represented and today still represents a self-conscious, strategic attempt to differentiate itself from fundamentalism primarily by *reducing the level of strictness* in its organizational culture at all levels—in small groups, church congregations, parachurch organizations, and denominations. The strictness of which Kelley speaks—absolutism, conformity, fanaticism—much more accurately describes the character of fundamentalism than of evangelicalism. While archetypal fundamentalists are about the business of creating "total worlds" (Peshkin 1986; Ammerman 1987), archetypal evangelicals are about the business of creating "seeker friendly" churches, which are often anything but strict, yet can be very strong (Perrin and Mauss 1993). The difference is strategic: evangelicalism's core task of evangelizing and influencing the secular world encourages the movement to curb absolutism, conformity, and fanaticism, in a way that fundamentalism's core tasks of defending the theological fundamentals against liberalism and remaining pure from the world do not. For to influence the world, one must sustain ongoing interaction with it and not build rigid walls behind which simply to remain separate and preserve orthodoxy. Evangelical leaders all along—from Charles Fuller to Charles Colson—have known this, and have acted accordingly.

But if strictness per se causes religious vitality, then evangelicalism's decrease in strictness relative to fundamentalism should have been accompanied by a diminishing of evangelical vitality. The strictest churches should be the strongest. However, we have seen the opposite: evangelicalism as a religious tradition enjoys a significant margin of vitality above and beyond that of fundamentalism. We must conclude, then, that churches placing high demands on their members *per se* cannot fully explain the religious vitality of the evangelical movement. Something other than strictness, it would seem, must be at work.

Competitive Marketing Theory

Of the four theories reviewed, Finke, Stark, and Iannaccone's competitive marketing theory seems to us to present the best orienting framework and set of assumptions with which to construct an explanation for evangelicalism's vitality. We must acknowledge that our data—which focus primarily on the views and behaviors of ordinary evangelicals, not entrepreneurial elites and organizations—by nature cannot decisively substantiate this theory. And our findings do compel us to develop a theory for our case well beyond Finke, Stark, and Iannaccone's current formulation. Nevertheless, we can begin by observing that what we already know of evangelicalism appears to verify this theory.

Contemporary evangelicalism inhabits a pluralistic, competitive religious economy, on which it has very successfully capitalized. Two distinctive features of the evangelical movement's organizational structure and culture especially help facilitate its growth and vitality through competitive marketing. First, evangelicalism exhibits a tremendous fluidity with which it generates entrepreneurial leaders who promote an immense variety of religious products. Second, evangelicalism successfully incorporates a rich variety of Christian traditions and positions into a common identity-movement without relying on geographical or organizational centralization or uniformity to do so. Both, in our view, help explain evangelicalism's vitality.

First, while the mainline-liberal Protestant traditions operate primarily within—and are therefore bound by the organizational dynamics of—established denominations, evangelicalism by contrast has always been an open and fluid transdenominational identity-movement. Evangelicalism is less an organization than a vast, loose network of small denominations, denominational and nondenominational congregations (about 20 percent of American evangelicals belong to nondenominational church congregations), parachurch ministries, missions agencies, and educational institutions. Consequently, the evangelical field is structurally wide open for inventive leaders to emerge and launch new initiatives. Entrepreneurial evangelical leaders are much freer than mainline or liberal church leaders to generate their own new evangelical churches, colleges, missions boards, parachurch ministries, radio programs, publishing ventures, biblical teachings, and spiritual programs.

A comprehensive list of such instances would literally fill an entire book chapter. Suffice it to recall a few of the best-known examples: Charles Fuller and Harold Ockenga founding Fuller Theological Seminary, J. Elwin Wright establishing the National Association of Evangelicals, Billy Graham and Carl Henry launching *Christianity Today*, Billy Graham generating the Billy Graham Crusades, Bill Bright creating Campus Crusade for Christ, Larry Norman inventing contemporary Christian rock music, John Wimber founding the Vinyard Christian Fellowship, Bill Hybals inventing the Willow Creek Community Church, Millard Fuller developing Habitat for Humanity, Robert Schuller founding the Crystal Cathedral, Ronald Sider inventing Evangelicals for Social Action, Charles Colson founding Prison Ministries, Jim Wallis and the Sojourners community creating *Sojourners* magazine, and on and on. Largely unhindered by established denominational bureaucracies, very little but imagination and the limits of market opportunities restrict ever new waves of evangelical entrepreneurs from creating expansive supplies of religious organizations and products to both appeal to and mobilize a growing number of evangelical believers.

Second, evangelicalism has created a meaningful identity-space on the American religious field that, under one banner, manages to accommodate a remarkable degree of theological and political diversity. Evangelicalism incorporates Baptists, Methodists, Presbyterians, Lutherans, Pentecostals, Charismatics, Independents, Anabaptists, Restorationists, Congregationalists, Holiness Christians, even Episcopalians. It also includes right-wing political conservatives, Republicans, moderates, Democrats, liberals, Independents, and political progressives. Yet it manages fairly successfully to orient this medley of traditions and positions in a common direction with common purpose. No single, authoritative theological or political confession or creed binds this diverse array of believers together and sets them apart from their theological and sociological relatives. Nor is evangelicalism's coherence a product of geographical or organizational centralization or uniformity. Instead, evangelicals are coordinated by a set of minimal, baseline, supradenominational theological beliefs and, perhaps more importantly, by a distinctive, shared sensibility about strategy for the Christian mission in the world. In this, the movement tends to be more inclusively than exclusively oriented—a cultural trait that its founders deliberately intended to cultivate. This relatively successful unity-in-diversity allows the evangelical tradition to capture the allegiance of and orient for active mission an incredibly broad array of Christians, while maintaining a tremendous degree of decentralization.

Elaborating the New Paradigm

In at least these ways, we believe the competitive marketing theory goes a long way toward offering a reasonable and persuasive explanation for evangelicalism's vitality. But we also believe that its basic explanatory approach can and must be further extended to more fully account for other dimensions of evangelical vitality. Finke, Stark, and Iannaccone's version of the theory focuses on inter-religious competition, the entrepreneurial activities of religious elites, and the mobilizing capacity of religious organizations. Our study, however focuses on other dynamics at different levels. We focus on the beliefs and actions, not of entrepreneurial elites, but of *ordinary* evangelical believers. We analyze their relationship, not to their religious competitors, but more broadly to the *socioculturally pluralistic world* they inhabit. And we focus on the effectual character, not so much of the organizational structures that transmit it, but of the nature of the *religious faith itself* vis-à-vis pluralism. These differences compel us to develop the logic of the competitive marketing theory in a new direction—one that is compatible with Finke, Stark, and Iannaccone's current account but which extends it along new dimensions. In so doing, we hope to elaborate the "new paradigm" in the sociology of religion in a way that significantly expands its analytical scope and capacity.

The next two chapters argue that evangelicalism is thriving, not because it has built a protective subcultural shield against secular modernity, but—to the contrary—precisely because it is passionately engaged in direct struggle with pluralistic modernity. We will seek to demonstrate that cultural pluralism—like religious competition—has not damaged evangelicalism but has been a condition in which it has thrived. It is to make that case that we now turn.

FOUR

Toward a "Subcultural Identity" Theory of Religious Strength

For decades, sociologists of religion have operated on the belief that cultural pluralism, social differentiation, and religious diversity within a society undermine the plausibility and strength of religion. The inherent logic of this approach—framed by the theoretical literature on modernization and secularization—has tended to produce fairly pessimistic portrayals of the fate of evangelicalism in the modern world. We have seen, however, that modern American evangelicalism is thriving. This suggests the need to develop an alternative theoretical perspective on the viability of traditional religions in modernity.

In this chapter and the next, we argue that evangelicalism maintains its religious strength in modern America precisely because of the pluralism and diversity it confronts. American evangelicalism, we contend, is strong not because it is shielded against, but because it is—or at least perceives itself to be—embattled with forces that seem to oppose or threaten it. Indeed, evangelicalism, we suggest, *thrives* on distinction, engagement, tension, conflict, and threat. Without these, evangelicalism would lose its identity and purpose and grow languid and aimless. Thus, we will argue, the evangelical movement's vitality is not a product of its protected isolation from, but of its vigorous engagement with pluralistic modernity.

We intend to show how cultural pluralism and structural differentiation work to strengthen the evangelical movement, relative to fundamentalist, mainline, and liberal Protestantism. This chapter begins by elaborating a general theoretical explanation for why traditional religion can survive and thrive in the modern world. We then explore in the next chapter the variety of ways that evangelicals construct subcultural distinction, engagement, and tension between themselves and others in a way that builds evangelical strength.

Basic Principles

The following pages combine a variety of elementary sociological principles into a single theoretical interpretation of the fate of religion in modern society, which we will call the "subcultural identity" theory of religious strength. In simplest terms, we suggest that a religious movement that unites both clear cultural distinction and intense social engagement will be capable of thriving in a pluralistic, modern society. Far from undermining the strength of religion, we propose that the cultural pluralism and social differentiation of modern society provide an environment within which well-adapted religious traditions—like evangelicalism—can flourish. We begin by advancing a number of propositions that elaborate some basic and familiar sociological principles with which we will construct our subcultural identity theory.

Proposition 1: The human drives for meaning and belonging are satisfied primarily by locating human selves within social groups that sustain distinctive, morally orienting collective identities.

Perhaps the most elementary principle of sociology is that individual human identities are not self-engendered or formed in isolation but are always and necessarily constructed through interaction with other humans in the context of relatively stably patterned social groups. It is by being located in social groups—which themselves have formed and sustain meaningful collective identities—that one comes to know who one is, what one should do with one's life, and why. In this way, all meaning and purpose is preceded and sustained by belonging and participation.

One of the primary ways social groups provide their members identity and meaning is by inculcating in them a normative and moral orientation toward life and the world. Human beings, we have argued elsewhere (Smith 1996a), are inescapably normative and moral (as well as instrumentally pleasure-seeking) creatures. Their actions and identities are formed not only by their understanding of what is, but also of what ought to be. By morality, we mean, "discrimination of right and wrong, better or worse, higher or lower, which are not rendered valid by our own desires, inclinations, or choices, but rather stand independently of these and offer standards by which they can be judged" (Taylor 1989: 4).[1] Life and the world

---

1. According to Amitai Etzioni, "Actions are morally right when they conform to a relevant principle or duty" (1988: 12). More precisely, Etzioni writes: "It suffices to consider moral acts as those that meet four criteria: moral acts reflect an imperative, a generalization, and a symmetry when applied to others, and are motivated intrinsically. . . . The *imperative*

are made meaningful, then, and individual identity is constructed precisely by establishing moral bearings, values, and standards that render a sense of location and normative direction for those who embrace them. Charles Taylor elaborates:

> To know who you are is to be oriented in moral space, a space in which questions arise about what is good and bad, what is worth doing and what not, what has meaning and importance for you and what is trivial and secondary. . . . We come here to one of the most basic aspirations of human beings, the need to be connected to, or in contact with, what they see as good, or of crucial importance, or of fundamental value. And how could it be otherwise, once we see that this orientation in relation to the good is essential to being a functioning human agent? (1989: 28, 42)

Three premises, then, are foundational for our argument below. First, nobody has the choice to opt out of commitment to some fundamental moral orientation, of taking a normative "view from nowhere," of living a life neutral and disengaged with regard to fundamental oughts and shoulds. Second, the place where people find, learn, and preserve those moral orientations are in the concrete social groups, actual relational networks, and particular subcultures in which their lives are embedded. And, third, religion is, by its intrinsic character, a natural and primary source of the kinds of morally orienting collective identities that provide people meaning and belonging.

Proposition 2: Social groups construct and maintain collective identities by drawing symbolic boundaries that create distinction between themselves and relevant outgroups.

Collective identities depend heavily for existence on contrast and negation. Social groups know who they are in large measure by knowing who they are not. Ingroups establish what it means to be "in" primarily by contrasting with outgroups whose members are "out." Subcultures recognize

---

quality of moral acts is reflected in that persons who act morally sense that they 'must' behave in a prescribed way, that they are in fact obligated, duty bound. . . . Individuals who act morally are *able to generalize* their behavior—they are able to justify an act to others and to themselves by pointing to general rules. . . . *Symmetry* is required in that there must be a willingness to accord other comparable people, under comparable circumstances, the same standing or right. . . . Finally, moral acts *affirm or express a commitment*, rather than involve the consumption of a good or service. Therefore, they are intrinsically motivated and not subject to means-end analysis" (1988: 42–43).

who belongs by marking boundaries which separate those who do not. Of course, collective identities also comprise positive substantive features. But every "yes" automatically begets some "no," any proximity necessarily establishes some distance, all affirmations inevitably suggest denials. Thus, every collective identity inescapably employs distinction from "nots" to establish its "is." Protestants are not Roman Catholics, blacks are not whites, conservatives are not liberals, men are not women, Southerners are not Yankees, gays are not straight.[2]

The bases of these kinds of identity distinctions are rarely, if ever, essentialistic, immutable differences between groups. Rather, identity distinctions are always created through the use of socially constructed symbolic markers that establish group boundaries. It is through languages, rituals, artifacts, creeds, practices, narratives—in short, the stuff of human cultural production—that social groups construct their sense of self and difference from others. This means that every group's sense of self is always the product, not of the essential nature of things, but of active, continuing identity-work (Schwalbe and Mason-Schrock 1996; Snow and Anderson 1987). That is, collective identity is always an ongoing *social achievement*, accomplished through processes of social interaction, in which identity-signifying symbols are collectively generated, displayed, recognized, affirmed, and employed to mark differences between insiders and outsiders (see Hadden and Lester 1978; Boon 1982).

Reports from a variety of fields in sociology confirm the view that groups construct their collective identities primarily by marking socially constructed symbolic boundaries that create distinction between themselves and others. Many studies of race and ethnicity, for example, suggest that symbolic differentiation is central in the social construction of racial and ethnic identities (Nagel 1994; Hein 1994; Pulis 1993; Bahloul 1995; McMahon 1991; Astuti 1995; Jenkins 1994; Olzak 1983; McCulloch and Wilkins 1995; Steedman 1995; De Vos 1975; Barth 1969). Likewise, scholars of social movements—many of whom increasingly view movements as embodiments of alternative, insurgent collective identities (for example, Melucci 1989; Pizzorno 1978; Touraine 1985)—emphasize the significance of symbolic boundary-marking. Writing about lesbian femi-

2. According to W. A. Elliot, "Group consciousness . . . imports a sense of *us* . . . with a corresponding sense of distinctiveness from others regarded as *them*. . . . People only display attitudes of *us* due to an acquired sense of *we-ness* determined largely by a sense of *they-ness* in relation to others. So-called ingroup and outgroup behavior therefore merely reflects the two sides of group consciousness" (1986: 6, 8).

nist mobilization, for example, Taylor and Whittier (1992) argue that the first step in movement collective-identity formation is the setting of symbolic boundaries: "Boundary markers are . . . central to the formation of collective identity because they promote a heightened awareness of a group's commonalities and frame interaction between members of the in-group and the out-group" (1992: 111). Other studies of the formation of gender identities highlight a similar process (for example, West and Zimmerman 1987; Gerson and Peiss 1985; Schwalbe and Mason-Schrock 1996). Many analyses of youth, religious, music, and other kinds of subcultures likewise emphasize the importance of symbolic boundary-marking in the construction of subcultural identities (for example, Kruse 1993; Fenster 1993; Kane 1994; Lowney 1995; Savells 1993). Indeed, the very idea of a "subculture" itself suggests a peculiar group identity, socially constructed by the making of intergroup distinctions through a process of social interaction (Fine and Kleinman 1979; Short 1995). Regional subcultures, too, rely on symbolic boundary distinctions. John Reed (1982; 1986), for example, argues persuasively that American Southerners maintain their particular southern identity by constructing a variety of symbolic distinctions (in speech, food, etc.) between themselves and Northerners. In a fascinating analysis of a particular Southern subculture, Dennis Covington writes that the custom of religious snake handling emerged as a cultural practice of poor Southern whites to preserve their identity in the face of an encroaching, alien dominant culture:

> Snake handling . . . didn't originate back in the hills somewhere. It started when people came *down* from the hills to discover they were surrounded by a hostile and spiritually dead culture. All along their borders with the modern world . . . they recoiled. They threw up defenses. When their own resources failed, they called down the Holy Ghost. They put their hands through fire. They drank poison. They took up serpents. (1995: xvii–xviii)

This process of identity construction through symbolically bounded group differentiation can be theorized in several ways from a number of different perspectives. From the viewpoint of social psychology, for example, a team of British researchers has advanced a "social identity" theory that explains group behavior through processes of self-categorization and social comparison. According to social identity theory, human beings actively seek to render experience in the world subjectively meaningful, to identify features of the world relevant to their action in specific contexts, and to achieve and maintain individual self-esteem (Hogg 1992: 93; Tajfel and Turner 1986: 16). They accomplish this through the process of "categorization," the cognitive grouping of the self and some class of perceived stimuli as similar, in contrast with other classes of stimuli which are considered different (Turner et al. 1987). Thus, people may differentiate the social categories, for example, of immigrant versus native, moderate versus radical, deserving poor versus undeserving poor, or religious believer versus unbeliever. Categorization employs a process of "accentuation," whereby the perceived similarities and differences thought to distinguish the cognitively constructed categories are exaggerated in ways that stereotypically simplify the potentially infinite variety of perceivable stimuli in one's environment (Abrams and Hogg 1990: 556). So, those for whom the distinction between, for instance, the deserving and undeserving poor is significant, will tend to accentuate the features which in their minds distinguish the two: misfortune versus irresponsibility, natural industriousness versus laziness, etc. Thus, categorization "brings into sharp focus a nebulous world, by accentuating similarities between objects within the same category and differences between stimuli in different categories" (Hogg and Abrams 1988: 19). People establish their own individual and group identities by cognitively constructing such categories and identifying with certain ones of them: "self-categorization is the process which transforms individuals into groups" (Hogg and Abrams 1988: 21). Thus, only through categorization, differentiation, and identification can one know oneself, for example, to be an employed, heterosexual, churchgoing, Irish, Roman Catholic father and husband from the better side of town, and not something else.

But people do not simply categorize, they also always evaluate categories through "social comparison." People—in search of meaning, direction, and self-enhancement—assess different values to differentiated categories (Hogg 1992: 91). Almost invariably, social comparison favors the categories that comprise people's own identities. Thus, our Irish Roman Catholic man certainly believes that being employed, heterosexual, and churchgoing are morally and functionally better than being jobless, gay, and unchurched. This is thought necessary to maintain self-esteem. According to Hogg:

> We not only strive to maximize intergroup differences, but also—very importantly—try to secure an evaluative advantage for the ingroup. Because social categories contribute to the self-concept and thus serve to define and *evaluate* the self, we continually try to make intergroup comparisons on dimensions that already favor the ingroup. We strive for evaluatively positive social identity through positive ingroup distinctiveness. (1992: 91)

Categorization and comparison not only bolster self-esteem, but also serve as the very bases of human knowledge itself. Hogg and Abrams write:

> *All* knowledge is socially derived through social comparisons, and this includes knowledge about the physical world. One's confidence in the truth of one's own views is provided by the establishment of consensus—agreement between people. . . . Through social comparisons we learn about ourselves and obtain confidence in the veracity and utility of our beliefs. That is, we are motivated to make social comparisons in order to be confident about our perceptions of our selves, other people, and the world in general. (1988: 22)

Social identity theory then uses these social-psychological postulates to explain intergroup behavior, group cohesiveness, prejudice, stereotyping, ideology, social conformity, language communication, ethnicity, and other features of social life (for example, see Abrams and Hogg 1990; Turner et al. 1987; Tajfel 1982; Hogg 1992; Tajfel and Turner 1986; van Knippenberg 1989; Hogg and Abrams 1988).

Viewing identity construction through symbolically bounded group differentiation from another perspective, Michael Schwalbe and Douglas Mason-Schrock (1996) take a symbolic interactionist approach which integrates semiotic theory. They suggest that collective identity construction is best understood not as an accomplishment at the social-psychological level, but as an interactive group process. They write, "To understand identity-making, it is necessary to examine not only individual self-presentations, but the joint creation of the symbolic resources upon which those presentations depend—an activity we refer to as subcultural identity work" (1996: 115). This process of subcultural identity work, they argue, consists of four essential elements: defining (creating social representations), coding (creating rules to signify identity with them), affirming (enacting and validating identity claims), and policing (protecting meaning and enforcing the identity code). While arguing the utility of viewing policing as an analytically distinct dimension of identity work, Schwalbe and Mason-Schrock acknowledge that the intergroup differentiation that policing achieves is present throughout the entire process of collective identity work:

> Defining would seem to imply policing from the start, in that the creation of a social representation entails setting boundaries and saying who's in and who's out. Likewise with coding, the rules saying what kinds of enactments are acceptable and what kinds are not. Even affirming can include an element of policing, in that

the wrong people can be kept out of encounters where they might
otherwise have a chance to signify and be affirmed. (1996: 126–27)

By Schwalbe and Mason-Schrock's account, the kind of collective identities that provide people meaning and belonging would simply be impossible to create and sustain without the use of socially constructed symbolic
boundaries, generated through social interaction, that create distinctions
between ingroups and outgroups. Besides these two, other theoretical approaches, including anthropological studies of community[3] and Pierre
Bourdieu's fields theory,[4] suggest a similar perspective.

3. Social anthropologist Anthony Cohen (1985), for example, has written an incisive
essay rethinking the notion of "community" that draws on anthropological work on symbol-
ism, meaning, and ritual. Cohen breaks with older theoretical approaches—such as the early
Chicago school—which conceive of community in largely ecological and structural terms.
Instead, Cohen advocates a view of communities as intersubjective symbolic systems: "The
quintessential referent of community is that its members make, or believe they make, a similar sense of things either generally or with respect to specific and significant interests, and,
further, that they think that that sense may differ from one made elsewhere. The reality of
community in people's experience thus inheres in their attachment or commitment to a common body of symbols" (1985: 16). From this perspective, communities must symbolize and
utilize cultural boundaries to give substance to their shared values and identities. Community, Cohen elaborates,

> expresses a *relational* idea: the opposition of one community to others. . . . It
> seems appropriate, therefore, to focus our examination of the nature of com-
> munity on the element which embodies this sense of discrimination, namely,
> the *boundary*. . . . The boundary encapsulates the identity of the commu-
> nity. . . . Boundaries are marked because communities interact in some way or
> other with entities from which they are, or wish to be, distinguished. (1985:
> 12, italics in original)

Since communities are defined less by location and institution than by constellations of
shared symbols, constructing cultural boundaries which define their perimeters and differentiate them from other symbol systems is essential to the maintenance of meaningful community life. Cohen writes, "People map out their social identities and find their social orientations among the relationships which are symbolically close to them, rather than in relation
to an abstract sense of society. Much like horses dunging out the boundaries of their territory (if readers will forgive the prosaic metaphor), so people put down their social markers
symbolically. . . . They thereby make community" (1985: 28). Thus, Cohen's conception of
community offers a theoretical account of collective identity which parallels the social-
psychological and symbolic interactionist perspectives reviewed above. Again we see that
social groups construct and maintain their collective identities by drawing symbolic boundaries that create distinction between themselves and relevant outgroups.

4. Bourdieu takes a more macro, conflict-structuralist view (1984, 1991; Bourdieu and
Wacquant 1992). He suggests that we understand collective identities as emerging from
struggles over the strategic control of various forms of sociocultural capital between self-
differentiating social groups operating vis-à-vis one another on various fields of conflict. Although Bourdieu's primary interest is not explaining the sources of collective identity, his
analytical framework nevertheless suggests the importance of socially constructed symbolic

To return to our main argument, this proposition—that collective identity is socially constructed through intergroup distinctions marked by cultural boundaries—together with our first proposition, carry implications for understanding the prospects of religion in modern societies. First, they give us reason to consider the possibility that modernity's sociocultural pluralism may actually strengthen, and not undermine, religion. Pluralism may do this by providing a diversity and abundance of ideological and cultural outgroups. In relation to these, religious groups and subcultures may more readily construct meaningful distinction through symbolic boundaries that strengthen their morally orienting collective identities. Second, these propositions suggest a conceptual basis for a theory potentially explaining variations in strength among different religious groups and subcultures. We might hypothesize that religious groups that are more capable of constructing distinct identity boundaries vis-à-vis outgroups will produce more satisfying morally orienting collective identities and will, as a consequence, grow in size and strength (see Olson 1995). By contrast, religious groups that have difficulty constructing identity distinction in a pluralistic environment will grow relatively weaker. We will explore these possibilities below, but first we elaborate other propositions that help lay the basis for the subcultural identity theory we intend to develop.

Proposition 3: Religious traditions have always strategically renegotiated their collective identities by continually reformulating the ways their constructed orthodoxies engage the changing sociocultural environments they confront.

Sociologists of religion need seriously to rethink how they use the idea of religious "accommodation." Far too often, when sociologists see a religious group modifying itself in response to, or incorporating new elements from, its surrounding culture, they automatically label it "accommodation." The typical connotation is that religion—in an ultimately losing, zero-sum struggle against secular modernity—is giving away more and more of its orthodox truth, its distinctive practices and moralities, its previously held cultural "territory." The underlying image is self-defeating survival strategy, reminiscent of Chamberlain's appeasement of Hitler. With each move of accommodation—despite possible simultaneous efforts at resistance—religion has that much less left to bargain away in the future; and the latest

---

distinctions that define collective actors and differentiate them from each other. According to Bourdieu, all cultural practices and symbols serve to reinforce social distinctions between collective actors. These, in turn, structure both different fields of group relations and groups' conflicts over valued material and symbolic resources (also see Swartz 1996).

bargain stands little chance of ultimately satisfying the ever-encroaching demands of the adversary. Religion stands in relation to modernity like someone on a small island in a path of an oncoming hurricane trying to bargain with the sea for its storm surge to abate by throwing shovelsful of sand at the breakers. Each shovel of sand slightly hinders the next wave; all the while, the island shrinks ever smaller.

Much of James Hunter's work on evangelicalism (1983, 1987), for example, is devoted to explicating the delicate balance of resistance toward and accommodation with secular modernity that American evangelicalism attempts to maintain. Yet, Hunter argues, "in this dialectical interchange, it is safe to say that the religious worldview is the weaker partner" (1983: 15). Evangelicalism's cognitive bargaining with modernity, he claims, "results in *cognitive contamination* of the religious worldview. . . . In spite of specific resistance . . . the onus of pressure [is] on the adherents of the religious worldview to accommodate to the cognitive constraints of modernity by modifying the content and style of their beliefs" (1983: 15, italics in the original). Thus, "the larger question that remains to haunt Evangelicalism is what will be the longer term effects of its encounter with modernity" (1983: 101). The answer, according to Hunter, is not hopeful. Hunter reaffirmed this view in his second book: "As religious traditions and the sociohistorical realities of the modern world order confront each other, there is little question as to which of the two gives way to the other. Almost invariably the former yields to the latter" (1987: 48). Indeed, Hunter maintains that evangelicalism's emergence in the latter half of the twentieth century from its "sociocultural ghetto"—in which "isolated and insulated, it was able to successfully maintain a certain version of theological orthodoxy alive and protected" (p. 48)—may be "essential to ensure the very survival and vitality of conservative Christianity in the contemporary world. . . . On the other hand," Hunter notes ominously, this "may signal the beginning of the collapse of traditional theological orthodoxy" (1987: 49).

In a more recent rendering of the accommodation thesis on evangelicalism, Mark Shibley begins his analysis with the assumption that "those churches that survive and grow are those that find ways to accommodate the surrounding culture" (1996: 84). This he finds true of the rapidly growing Vineyard Christian Fellowship Churches, whose members tend to be relatively socially liberal and religiously tolerant. That members of these kind of vibrant California churches can be found at Halloween parties smoking cigarettes, drinking alcohol, and laughing at off-color jokes, claims Shibley, "illustrates the degree to which some evangelical churches accommodate to and tolerate lifestyle choices that would be unthinkable in a more traditional context" (1996: 86). "Perhaps," he suggests, "not only are these churches *in* the modern world, they are *of* the modern world" (1996: 88, italics in original). Thus, Shibley argues more broadly, "while conservative Protestantism has moved into the mainstream of American society . . . the price of success appears to be cultural—if not theological—accommodation" (1996: 134). He concludes, "The new evangelical churches know and accept their marginality in the culture and are growing precisely because they attend primarily to the therapeutic needs of individuals. . . . Evangelical Protestantism . . . is growing today by catering to the culturally hip, and in making the tradition palatable, these new born-again congregations concede moral ground. Thus conservative Protestantism is being transformed" (1996: 137).

But the conventional mentality about religious accommodation is beset by significant theoretical problems, which together predispose the analyst to seeing contemporary religious demise, whether it is real or not. The first problem is the tendency to read religious history ahistorically: reifying the religious group's past into a sort of "golden age" of orthodoxy and ethics, one that never really existed. Set against such a mythical past, it is easy to read the contemporary religious reality as in decline, compromising and surrendering truths and standards to which generations past (supposedly) held firmly. In this way, many accommodation-analyses read like versions of "the Fall" of Adam and Eve—except that while academic history cannot document a perfect Garden of Eden, it can and does document religious histories far more complex, multivocal, and dirty than the ones accommodation-stories need to ring true. Part of the problem here lies in the tendency of accommodation-stories to compare the *normative* views of historical religious elites (for example, Hunter's use of evangelist Billy Sunday on asceticism and hard work [1987: 51–52]) with *empirical descriptions* of contemporary religious believers (for example, Hunter 1987: 53–71). Naturally, the realities of the latter are found lacking when compared with the ideals of the former.

Another problem is that the assumptions of the overarching modernization-secularization theoretical framework tend to disallow any interpretation of contemporary religion other than decline, compromise, and surrender. The accommodation conclusion is baked into the theoretical model's linear and deterministic evolutionary presuppositions (see Hart 1992: 175–77 for an excellent elaboration). In fact, however, what is often viewed as accommodation (for example, the "liberalization" of campus rules at evangelical colleges), when freed of these evolutionary assumptions, can actually be more accurately understood as the *re*sacrilization and *re*enchantment of life (Schmalzbauer and Wheeler 1996). Furthermore, many accommodation interpretations tend to assume, wrongly, that religion and modernity are playing a zero-sum game: that religious groups have a fixed number of orthodox "goods" to try to protect, which are gradually depleted through accommodation. The truth is, religious actors are quite capable of reclaiming and reinvigorating lost and dormant sacred themes, traditions, and practices; of generating new religious goods while relinquishing others; and of using quintessentially modern tools to strengthen and promote their traditional worldviews and ways of life. In many ways, religious agents are more than capable of turning the proverbial "straw into gold."

Ultimately, to employ the idea of accommodation in any useful way, we need to recognize that religious traditions have *always* strategically renegotiated their collective identities by continually reformulating the ways their constructed orthodoxies engage the changing sociocultural environments they confront. "Accommodation," if that is what we should call it, is nothing new. Sociologists above all should know that religions are always in motion, ever reconfiguring their identities and messages vis-à-vis their social environments, whether modern or not. This has always been and always will be. And it is normally a generative process, not a mechanism of decline. Thus, to privilege or condemn the modern point in history as that which somehow decisively depletes religion of its true essence requires a static view not only of the history, but also of "orthodoxy."

Consider Christian history, for example. Clearly, the apostle Paul labored to cast his Jewish-derived *kerygmatic* message in categories and language his Greco-Roman Hellenistic world could understand and embrace. Was this "cognitive contamination," or creative adaptation? Saint Augustine of Hippo reformulated Christian theology in terms of platonic metaphysics, and altered the Christian view of history in a way to make sense of the crumbling of the Roman Empire with which the Church had become closely associated. Was that "accommodation," or strategic repositioning? Likewise, Thomas Aquinas recast the whole of Christian doctrine within the framework of the Aristotelian philosophy that was being enthusiastically rediscovered at the time. Was that the "collapse" of that era's theretofore theological orthodoxy or a proactive and generative reformulation of sacred tradition? The same kinds of questions can be asked of the work of virtually every important leader, theologian, and missionary in church history generally viewed today as orthodox—from Irenaus, Athanasius, and Anselm to John Wesley, Pope John XXIII, and Billy Graham. In fact, the authors of the books of the Bible themselves were clearly engaged—in part—in the task of reformulating their religious traditions in response to new cultural and social-structural circumstances they confronted and historical events they experienced.[5]

Collective identities and worldviews are always the product of dynamic social construction and reconstruction processes (Berger and Luckmann 1966; Berger 1967). So why ought we treat thousands of years of that process as "orthodoxy" and the few most recent decades or years as "accommodation," "cognitive contamination," and the possible "collapse" of orthodoxy? We can do this only if we employ a theoretical framework that predisposes us to see almost all change vis-à-vis modernity as decline. But by recognizing the strategically renegotiated nature of all collective identities throughout all of history, we create the possibility of distinguishing between self-defeating accommodation and creative adaptation, between religious decline and generative innovation.

To be clear: this approach needs not imply a relativism in which any innovation in theology or religious practice might legitimately be called "Christian," for example. For a stable core of constructed religious orthodoxy can be ongoingly sustained in the process of dynamic religious-identity renegotiation. Indeed, the crucial skill of a religious master in any given tradition is to accomplish just that: to sustain the articulation of the tradition's essential orthodoxy in a reformulated way appropriate for their given context. Like all other religions, Christianity does make actual and distinctive truth claims, which genuinely differentiates it from things non-Christian. It is therefore possible really to abandon those distinctives through accommodation-as-loss. The point, however, is that not all religious change in response to modernity reflects this kind of abandonment. Indeed, we suspect that not much of it, particularly among evangelicals, does. Certainly, Californians wearing blue jeans to churches that play electric guitars (Shibley 1996) does not reflect the surrender of core Christian distinctives. Nor does three percent of evangelical college students taking a Barthian view of the Bible (Hunter 1987: 24)—if, indeed, that represents any historical change at all.

5. For example, certain of the Hebrew prophets' reinterpretation of what it means to be God's chosen people in light of the Babylonian exile; and many of the New Testament authors' appropriations of texts from the Hebrew Scriptures in light of the resurrection event and the Jesus movement.

In assessing contemporary religious change, then, we need not choose between a static view of historical orthodoxy and a vacuous religious relativism. The alternative and preferred choice is that which reflects the way most traditional religious groups actually operate in history in the real world: they work fairly successfully to sustain a relatively stable distinctive religious identity while ever reformulating it to engage the conditions of the times. Religious groups in modern society may and sometimes do bargain away their core beliefs. But they also can and do creatively renegotiate and strategically adapt their beliefs and practices to perform more robustly in a modern context. One of the tasks of the sociologist of religion is to recognize and astutely interpret the difference between the two.

Proposition 4: Because the socially normative bases of identity-legitimation are historically variable, modern religious believers can establish stronger religious identities and commitments on the basis of individual choice than through ascription.

Traditional secularization theory has long argued that the modern condition of having to make a personal choice about one's religion intrinsically undermines the plausibility of that religion. According to the theory, in a culturally homogeneous society with a religious monopoly, the religious worldview is apprehended as absolute and immutable. But in a modern, pluralistic society that offers a multitude of religious alternatives from which to choose, any sense of the objective ultimacy and sacredness of any given religious option grows thin and fragile. For what was once seen as standing outside and above the individual, making fundamental moral claims upon that individual, now becomes merely one of many religious commodities on the table from among which the individual chooses, to suit their own subjective needs and preferences. And this commodification of religion diminishes its aura of objective truth and bindingness. According to Peter Berger, "religious definitions of reality have lost their quality of certainty and, instead, have become matters of choice. Faith is no longer socially given, but must be individually achieved. . . . Faith, in other words, is much harder to come by in the pluralistic situation" (Berger et al. 1973: 81).

What is missing from this secularization analysis, however, is a recognition that the socially normative bases of identity-legitimation are historically variable. Precisely because of the "world openness" of human existence (Berger and Luckmann 1966: 47–49), the criteria people use to authenticate and legitimate their identities are culturally relative. In one time and place, a person learns their proper identity-position in their tribe by inducing an ecstatic vision whose meaning is interpreted by a shaman. In another time and place, someone comes to know their rightful identity as a docile peasant by locating themselves in a socially ascribed Great Chain of Being. And so on. In all cases, the validity of the identity is established in relation to normative legitimizers, which themselves are socially constructed, and are therefore culturally and historically relative. So, what may absolutely authenticate and ratify an identity in one culture or historical era may be completely ineffectual or irrelevant in another. And vice-versa.

For moderns—perhaps especially modern Americans—the ultimate criteria of identity and lifestyle validity is individual choice. It is by choosing a product, a mate, a lifestyle, or an identity that one makes it one's very own, personal, special, and meaningful—not "merely" something one inherits or assumes. In the value-epistemology of modern American culture, to believe, to want, or to do something simply because that is what one's parents believe, or what one's friends want, or what somebody else does is considered inferior and unauthentic. It is not enough simply to assume mindlessly the religion of one's family, to absorb uncritically the outlook of one's neighborhood, to follow by default the career path that somebody else has laid out. That is parochial, acquiescent, and artificial. Rather, every such thing must be personalized and substantiated through individual choice. And even if (as is often the case) one chooses what one was already inheriting or assuming, it is only through the observance of individual choice—whether actual or ritualized—that it becomes "real" and personally meaningful (Bellah et al. 1985).

If the primary socially normative basis of modern identity-legitimation is individual choice, then we should find that moderns having to choose their religion makes the religion they choose no less real or authentic to them. For, according to the cultural epistemology, personal choice is the fundamental basis of identity validity. In fact, this is exactly what numerous ethnographic studies of modern religion are showing. In her study of contemporary women's conversion to Orthodox Judaism, for example, Lynn Davidman concludes that, "contrary to the assumptions of many secularization theorists, the awareness of choice does not necessarily weaken the plausibility of any religious worldview. These women's sense of having chosen Orthodoxy actually validated their choice" (1991: 83). Similarly, Nancy Ammerman (1987) has shown how Christian fundamentalists, fully aware of their religious choices and the boundaries that separate them from "the world," remain vibrant in their faith and beliefs. Likewise, Mary Jo Neitz's study of Charismatic Catholics reveals that their awareness of religious choice "did not seem to undermine their own beliefs. Rather, they felt that they had 'tested' the belief system and had been convinced of its superiority" (1987: 257–58). Other studies draw similar conclusions (see, for example, Snow and Machalek 1982).

What can undermine religious faith-plausibility at any given place and time is always a function of the socially constructed, culturally relative bases of identity legitimation. The argument that individual choice itself corrodes religion requires the projection of premodern criteria of identity-legitimacy onto a modern situation. Moderns authenticate themselves through personal choice. Therefore, modern religious believers are capable of establishing stronger religious identities and commitments on the basis of individual choice than through ascription. And we should expect this to be exceptionally true of American evangelicals, whose faith traditionally emphasizes the importance of making a personal "decision for Christ" through an individual conversion experience. For evangelicals, it is precisely by making a choice for Christ that one's faith becomes valid and secure. There is little reason to believe, therefore, that the modern necessity of having to choose one's own religion makes that religion any less real, powerful, or meaningful to modern believers.

Proposition 5: Individuals and groups define their values and norms and evaluate their identities and actions in relation to specific, chosen reference groups; dissimilar and antagonistic outgroups may serve as negative reference groups.

Secularization theory suggests that cultural pluralism corrodes religious certitude in part because constant interaction with people who do not share one's religious faith disconfirms that faith. By structurally ensuring regular association with people who hold different religious beliefs or who are unbelievers, pluralism renders religious worldviews increasingly implausible. In Berger's words, "There are always 'all those others' that refuse to confirm the religious world in question. Put simply in a different way, it becomes increasingly difficult for the 'inhabitants' of any particular religious world to remain *entre nous* in contemporary society. Disconfirming others (not just individuals, but entire strata) can no longer be safely kept away from 'one's own'" (1967: 151). This assumes that the beliefs and judgments of the myriad people with whom a modern religious believer must deal in the course of life impinge sharply on their own consciousness and identity— in a way that erodes the credibility of their faith.

We know, however, from decades of empirical research that human beings do not care what everyone out there in a society may think about them. For "everyone" is too massive and diverse a group to be worrying about their opinions and judgments. Rather, people care what only *certain* other people think of them, those belonging to what sociologists have long called their "reference group" (Schmitt 1972). A reference group is "a set of individuals whose standing or perspective is taken into account by an actor when selecting a course of action or when making a judgment about a specific issue" (Farmer 1992). Reference groups serve for people as sources of norms, values, and standards of judgment, functioning as informal authorities in the process of self-evaluation (Urry 1996; Hyman and Singer 1968).[6] Thus, people know how to appraise themselves, their own identities, decisions, and actions, in large measure by seeing how their reference groups appraise them. And, importantly, what people outside of a reference group think or feel about someone is largely inconsequential for that person's self-evaluation.

Furthermore, people also construct for themselves "negative reference groups": categories of people who are unlike them, who actively serve in their minds as models for what they do *not* believe, what they do *not* want to become, and how they do *not* want to act. Having to interact with others who are dissimilar to oneself, perhaps even antagonistic to one's own religious views, does not necessarily need to disconfirm one's own commitments, practices, and identity. Indeed, they can serve as ongoing reminders of one's desire to be quite different from them.

Viewing the problem of religious belief plausibility through the lens of reference-group theory helps to show why sociocultural pluralism does not necessarily undermine most people's religious beliefs: people can simply construct their reference groups to include enough fellow believers so that their faith continues to be affirmed (see Su 1996). And the views of other people not in their reference group can be, put bluntly, ignored. Indeed, people can put to use those whom secularization theory would presume to be threatening to belief—those who believe differently or do not believe at all—as faith-reinforcing negative reference groups. Furthermore, reference

---

6. The reference-group concept has proved useful in innumerable analyses over decades, including, more recently, the following: Terry and Hogg 1996; Schaffner 1995; John, Shelton, and Luschen 1995; Kelley and Evans 1995; Eshel and Dicker 1995; Radecki and Jaccard 1995; Kelly et al. 1995; Henderson-King and Stewart 1994; Yu and Liska 1993; Christopher, Johnson, and Roosa 1993; Miller, Wlezien, and Hildreth 1991; Agyeman-Duah and Ojo 1991; Cochran and Beeghley 1991; Sapp and Harrod 1989.

groups do not require geographical proximity or routine interaction to function well. With modern transportation and communication systems, people can maintain reference groups with many members spread far and wide and through only occasional interaction. People may even have deceased loved-ones as functioning members of their reference groups ("Wouldn't Mom be proud of me now if she could see what a strong Christian I've become!"). All that is required is that other people whose views and judgments one considers most important are kept in mind as one constructs one's life and identity.

In this light, we suggest employing a new image to think about religion in modernity. Peter Berger (1967) has asked us to imagine religion normally as providing an overarching "sacred canopy" that envelops and protects the members of an entire society from anomic chaos and terror. The "classical task" of religion, he claims, is "constructing a common world within which all of social life receives ultimate meaning binding on everybody" (1967: 133). But the forces of modernity, he observes, tear apart that unified, overarching shelter of meaning, and the sacred canopies collapse. We would like to suggest, however, that in the modern world, religion does survive and can thrive, not in the form of "sacred canopies," but rather in the form of "*sacred umbrellas.*" Canopies are expansive, immobile, and held up by props beyond the reach of those covered. Umbrellas, on the other hand, are small, handheld, and portable—like the faith-sustaining religious worlds that modern people construct for themselves. We suggest that, as the old, overarching sacred canopies split apart and their ripped pieces of fabric fell toward the ground, many innovative religious actors caught those falling pieces of cloth in the air and, with more than a little ingenuity, remanufactured them into umbrellas. In the pluralistic, modern world, people don't need macro-encompassing sacred cosmoses to maintain their religious beliefs. They only need "sacred umbrellas," small, portable, accessible relational worlds—religious reference groups—"under" which their beliefs can make complete sense.[7]

7. This approach comports with phenomenology's insistence that most people spend most of their lives concerned with the problems and issues that arise in what is to them the "paramount reality" of their everyday lives (Schutz 1971: 262). According to Schutz: "The wide-awake man within the natural attitude is primarily interested in that sector of the world of his everyday life which is within his scope and which is centered in space and time around himself. The place which my body occupies within the world, my actual Here, is the starting point from which I take my bearings. . . . We have an immanently practical interest in it, caused by the necessity of complying with the basic requirements of our life. . . . The selective function of our interest organizes the world . . . in strata of major and minor relevance." Few people spend their limited resources worrying about "the big picture," trying to work out in their lives the cognitive and spiritual implications of competing philosophies and ide-

Of course, Berger did say similar things about "plausibility structures." But he made the mistake of assuming that plausibility structures are frail, ever-threatened, precarious: with them, "the subjective reality of the world hangs on a thin thread" (Berger 1967: 17). Surely, they were no match for the inexorable, faith-destructive forces of modernity. Indeed, Berger stressed that all social worlds are innately precarious: "Every nomos is an area of meaning carved out of a vast mass of meaninglessness, a small clearing of lucidity in a formless, dark, always ominous jungle" (1967: 23). With some distance from the fashionable existentialism of the 1960s that shaped Berger's writing, we suggest instead that both humanly constructed sacred worlds and the plausibility structures that sustain them—modern religious believers' "sacred umbrellas"—are relatively sturdy and adaptable. They *have* to be, given the innate human drive for meaning and order that Berger himself so well articulates (1967: 16–28). If humans are, indeed, the kind of creatures Berger says they are, then they simply could not live with the kind of precariousness and looming terror of anomie that he describes. To maintain meaningful sacred worlds that are cognitively and emotionally manageable, modern religious believers—like all people constructing their realities—establish and evaluate their worldviews and life-practices not in relation to everyone conceivable, but to members of their own reference groups. In so doing, they hold over themselves small, portable, and manageable "sacred umbrellas" which can more than sustain the plausibility of their religious beliefs.

Proposition 6: Modern pluralism promotes the formation of strong subcultures and potentially "deviant" identities, including religious subcultures and identities.

Conventional secularization theories of the decline of religion in modern society closely parallel traditional sociological theories of urbanization, which describe an analogous decline of community in modern society. The correspondence of their "decline" stories is not coincidental. Both are based on the same modernization paradigm that emphasizes the power of cognitive rationalization, economic and political integration, organizational bureaucratization, ecological centralization, and social massification to revolutionize social relations and human experience (Black 1967; Brown 1976). Together these relentless processes are thought inexorably to dissolve the variety and idiosyncracies of decentralized, traditional, local premodern

---

ologies. Rather, most people focus on the rather limited worlds of their everyday existences, worlds which they can readily construct to be faith-reinforcing.

cultures into massive, integrated, rational, secular, urban societies. *Gemein-schaft* is displaced by *Gesellschaft* (Tönnies 1963). Folk culture is consumed by urban culture (Redfield 1930). "Status" relations are supplanted by "contract" relations (Maine 1905), as "communal" ones are by "associational" (Weber 1964). All things traditional are squeezed into the "iron cage" of technical rationality and materialism (Weber 1958: 181). Modern urbanites suffer impersonal, transitory, anomic social relations (Wirth 1938). Disconnected and vulnerable, they conglomerate as social atoms in a "mass society" (Kornhauser 1959; Stein 1960). "All that is solid melts into air" (Berman 1982). In this inexorable, pitiless process, both traditional religious faiths and traditional local communities are thought to share the same ultimate fate: decline, disintegration, obsolescence.

We have reason, however, to question the adequacy of this modernization paradigm. In recent decades, social historians and urban sociologists have challenged its view of the fate of community in modern society. And their conclusions about community have significant implications for our understanding of the prospects of religion in modernity.

Historian Thomas Bender, for example, points out that a comparison of social histories of community written by eminent historians shows that traditional community in America suffered decisive historic breakdown in the 1650s, 1690s, 1740s, 1780s, 1820s, 1850s, 1880s, and 1920s (1978: 51). The theoretical problem generating these chronic "community breakdown" stories, Bender argues, is that historians have wrongly conceptualized community as a *fixed location* and have adopted the linear, unidimensional, zero-sum assumptions of the modernization paradigm. But community, Bender contends, is not place: the village, small town, or well-defined neighborhood itself. Rather, community is an experience, a quality of relationship which "involves a limited number of people in a somewhat restricted social space or network held together by shared understandings and a sense of obligation. Relationships are close, often intimate, and usually face to face. Individuals are bound together by affective or emotional ties rather than by a perception of individual self-interest" (1978: 7). According to Bender, reconceptualizing "community" in this way enables analysts to transcend the misleading presuppositions of the modernization paradigm: "Once the notion of community is understood as a social network characterized by a distinctive kind of human interaction . . . one can talk about change without being trapped by the logic of collapse" (1978: 11).

Citing many studies that show community alive and well in the modern city (1978: 26), Bender argues that what modernity actually created was a bifurcated society in which structures of genuine community relationships, on the one hand, and structures of rational, ends-oriented relationships, on the other, exist together: "*Gemeinschaft* and *Gesellschaft* describe ... two patterns of social relations that coexisted in everyone's social experience. *Gemeinschaft* and *Gesellschaft* were not places; they were forms of human interaction" (1978: 33). In other words, structures of intimate, affective, mutual, intrinsically valuable community are entirely compatible with bureaucratic, rational, ends-oriented, urban social structures. According to Bender, "Community is not a specific place or a mere base line for historical change; it is a fundamental and enduring form of social interaction. Thinking of gemeinschaft and gesellschaft in terms of sequence is thus erroneous. They represent instead two different kinds of human collective living in which all individuals are involved" (1978: 43).[8] With this approach, Bender recommends that historical studies of community "focus on tension and interaction rather than upon collapse. Although the equilibrium between community and society shifted, community never disappeared. It, was, however, transformed" (1978: 119). Sociologist Andrew Greeley has argued a similar point:

> The basic ties of friendship, primary relationship, land, faith, common origin and consciousness of kind persist much as they did in the Ice Age. They are the very stuff out of which society is made, and in their absence the corporate structures would collapse.... [They] have of course been transmuted by the changing context.... But ... that ... does not mean that they have been eliminated. It simply means that they operate in a different context and perhaps in a different way.... We have not witnessed a simple, unidimensional, and unidirectional evolution from gemeinschaft to gesellschaft. What has happened, rather, has been a tremendous complexification of society, with vast pyramids of corporate structures being erected on a substratum of primordial relationships. (1972: 35–36)

---

8. This echoes Durkheim's often-overlooked clarification of the relationship between mechanical and organic solidarity: "In the first, what we call society is a more or less organized totality of beliefs and sentiments common to all the members of the group: this is the collective type. On the other hand, the society in which we are solidary in the second instance is a system of different, special functions which definite relations unite. *These two societies really make up only one. They are two aspects of one and the same reality*" (1933: 129, italics added).

We agree with Bender and Greeley and argue that traditional religion, no less than genuine community, has survived modernity's socioeconomic rationalization, centralization, and integration. Indeed, we suggest that religion not only survives modernity, but that in important ways modernity itself actually *promotes* strong religion. Following urban sociologist Claude Fischer, we maintain here that key features of modernity itself actually *foster* the formation of strong religious subcultures.

Fischer's argument (1975, 1982, 1984, 1995) runs as follows. Evidence shows conclusively that socially deviant attitudes and behaviors that contravene standard social norms (for example, alcoholism, illegitimacy, violent protest, drug use, etc.) are significantly more likely to be found in urban than rural areas. Traditional theories of social deviance maintained that weakened interpersonal ties and the breakdown of normative consensus caused by urbanism promote individual impersonality, anomie, and alienation; and these, in turn, foster social deviance (Wirth 1938; Simmel [1905] 1957; Milgram 1970). But, Fischer observes (as Bender did above) that numerous studies of urban life reveal "a wealth of personal ties and thriving primary groups even in the innermost recesses of the large city" (1975: 1321; also see Wellman and Leighton 1979; Lyon 1987; Hochschild 1973; Webber 1963). How then can we explain higher levels of social deviance in cities? According to Fischer, cities produce unconventional behavior, not because primary-group ties are weakened and people feel anonymous and anomic. Quite the opposite: cities produce deviance because their ecological size and density promote a host of strong subcultures which generate unconventional beliefs and behaviors. Urban ecologies do this, first, by providing the "critical mass" for "institutional completeness." According to Fischer:

> Arrival at certain critical levels of size enables a social subsystem to create and support institutions which structure, envelop, protect, and foster its subculture. These institutions (e.g., dress styles, newspapers, associations) establish sources of authority and points of congregation and delimit social boundaries. In addition to the simple fact of the numbers themselves, they make possible and encourage keeping social ties within the group. (1975: 1325–26)

Furthermore, Fischer argues (1975: 1326; also see Fine and Kleinman 1979: 15), urban size and density affects intergroup relations in a way that strengthens distinct subcultures:

> The greater the variety and size of subcultures in a place, the greater the contrast and conflict among them, and, consequently, the greater the subcultural intensity. On the group level, the competition and conflict which coresidence makes possible foster in-group cohesion. . . . On the individual level, contact with, or even simple observation of, strange others will lead . . . to stronger affirmations of own-group standards.

All of this produces what Fischer calls subcultural intensity, "the antithesis of anomie and normlessness. It refers to the presence of, attachment to, and force of subcultural beliefs, values, norms, and customs. In place of the anomic city, it suggests a city of articulated value systems" (1975: 1325). Thus, according to Fischer, it is precisely the manifold robust, unconventional subcultures that urbanization fosters which give rise to higher levels of unconventional attitudes and behaviors observed in cities.

The key insight in Fischer's subcultural analysis of urbanism for better understanding the fate of religion in modern society is this: the ecology of modern urban centers intrinsically promotes the formation of myriad, distinct, vibrant subcultures. Cities, these quintessentially modern places, in fact do not produce the kind of rationalized, integrated uniformity that we might expect to erode distinctive religious beliefs and practices. To the contrary, cities promote cultural and institutional diversity, distinction, and unconventionality. Demographically and institutionally, they positively nourish the kinds of strong subcultures that are needed to sustain particular religious beliefs and practices, both traditional and innovative. The ecological size and density that define urbanization—that central process of modernization—themselves create conditions which are more friendly to the maintenance of religious "cognitive deviance" in distinctive subcultures than those of any premodern society. In short, at least one essential and central feature of modernity itself positively enhances the sociological capacity of religions to survive and thrive in the modern world—particularly those which are well-equipped culturally to construct distinctive subcultural identities.

If this is true, then many of our images of modernity and modernization—for example, as "iron cage," "mass society," "disenchantment," "homelessness" (Berger, Berger, and Kellner 1973), "the 'MacDonaldization' of society" (Ritzer 1993)—mislead us in our attempt to understand adequately the role of religion in modern society. Perhaps a more suitable image for modern society would be that of a large coral reef ecosystem, teeming with an abundance of complex and varied life forms which occupy well-suited niches in mutual coexistence and interdependence. Does this not better depict the sociocultural character of New York City, for example, than representations which suggest uniformity and homogenization? This image of a coral reef ecosystem better helps us analytically to account for the variety of human subcultures which appear more than able to sustain vibrant religious (as well as other kinds of) belief and practice in a pluralistic situation.

Furthermore, this kind of image propels us to be clear in our reasoning about the relationship between cultural diversity and cultural homogeneity. It appears to us, for example, that Berger and Hunter's causal logic contains a contradiction on this point: that modernity both promotes and undermines cultural pluralism. Berger and Hunter argue essentially that the pluralism of believed meaning-systems at the aggregate level undermines the believability of specific meaning-systems at the particular level; it follows that, as people abandon their old increasingly implausible particular meaning-systems, this yields a homogenization of meaning-systems at the aggregate level. That is, modernity engenders cultural pluralism, which corrodes religious particularism, which then produces relatively more cultural homogeneity in the form of common secularism. But it is incoherent to maintain both that modernity sustains cultural pluralism and that it simultaneously erodes it by undermining varieties of "cognitive deviance." If it is true that evangelical faith, for example, grows implausible when confronted with a panoply of religious alternatives, then it is also true that each of those alternatives facing the same pluralistic situation ought to become increasingly implausible for their own adherents as well. The result should be a compression of religious diversity toward secularism and the spread of a more uniform naturalistic outlook.[9] But this, by definition, constitutes an erosion of modern pluralism itself, which seems at odds with Berger and Hunter's basic approach to modernity.

We believe this contradiction suggests the need for an alternative ap-

9. At bottom, the underlying axial image of Berger and Hunter's secularization theory is Max Weber's *disenchantment through rationalization,* which denotes a process of homogenization. The axial image of our analysis, by contrast, is Emile Durkheim's *sociocultural differentiation,* which suggests diversification and multiplicity (see Hogg and Abrams 1988: 15). We think it is a mistake to presume of modernity an increasingly overarching and integrating culture; as Theda Skocpol argued: "Dangerous pitfalls lurk when students of complex, changing, highly stratified sociopolitical orders rely upon anthropological ideas about cultural systems. It is all too easy to suppose the existence of integrated patterns of shared meanings, total pictures of how society does and should work. . . . Most risky of all, one is tempted to treat fundamental cultural and ideological change as the synchronous and complete replacement of one society-wide cultural system by another" (1985: 90).

proach based not on the model of pluralism-fostering-homogeneity, but of pluralism-reinforcing-pluralism. Such an approach must take seriously not only the structural features of modernity but also the cultural capacity of subcultures to construct for themselves distinctive collective identities through symbolic differentiation. As Cohen suggests, modernity's homogeneity,

> may be merely superficial, a similarity only of surface, a veneer which masks real and significant differences at a deeper level. Indeed, the greater the pressure on communities to modify their structural form to comply more with those elsewhere, the more they are inclined to reassert their boundaries *symbolically* by imbuing these modified forms with meaning and significance which belies their appearance. In other words, as the *structural* bases of boundary become blurred, so the symbolic bases are strengthened. (1985: 44, italics in original)

In sum, in our view, Berger and Hunter tend to argue a mechanistic determination of human consciousness by supposedly religiously hostile modern social structures. By contrast, we suggest that the recognition of modernity's positive facilitation of diverse subcultures, which mediate between consciousness and structure (along with the recognition of subcultures' identity construction through symbolic differentiation), will enable us better to account for the *de facto* persistence of religion in modern society and to formulate a theory of which religions are most strong and why.

Proposition 7: Intergroup conflict in a pluralistic context typically strengthens in-group identity, solidarity, resources mobilization, and membership retention.

Traditional secularization theory assumes that when religious individuals and groups conflict with challenging or oppositional features of modernity, as they inevitably do in a pluralistic society, this conflict weakens religion. Religious distinctions are thought to attenuate through encounters with conflicting realities. The prototypical micro-level process is the religious believer coming into contact with other people who espouse conflicting views and values, consequently questioning the legitimacy and veracity of their own religious commitments, and eventually revising or abandoning their religious beliefs and practices as a means to resolving the cognitive or relational conflict. James Hunter, for example, argues that modern pluralism generates, *cognitive dissonance,* an experience of confusion and anxiety about the certainty of his own understanding of reality. At the least, this leads to the questioning of the veracity of his beliefs. . . . Given a major collision of his view of reality with an alien conception . . . it is highly probable that his beliefs will be compromised. He will feel constrained to modify aspects of his worldview to account for this plurality in a conciliatory way. (1983: 13)

A parallel process is also thought to occur for religious groups, which are seen as modifying their distinctives when confronting conflicting features of the modern, pluralistic reality (for example, Berger 1967: 137–53).

Sociologists have long observed, however, that conflict between groups often tends not to weaken, but rather actually to strengthen groups internally. The disagreements and frictions that can arise between different social groups typically bolster their members' identification with, commitment to, and investment in their respective groups. Thus, "problems" for groups externally prove to be beneficial for groups internally. There is nothing quite like an outside threat or enemy to bring people together, make them set aside their internal differences, and increase their dedication and loyalty to the group.

In 1906 William Graham Sumner observed that "the relation of comradeship and peace in the we-group and that of hostility and war towards others-groups are correlative to each other. The exigencies of war with outsiders are what make peace inside. . . . Loyalty to the group, sacrifice for it, hatred and contempt for outsiders, brotherhood within, warlikeness without—all groups together, common products of the same situation" (1906: 12). Two years later, Georg Simmel wrote in a classic essay on social conflict that,

> Conflict has another sociological significance: not for the reciprocal relation of the parties to it, but for the inner structure of each party itself. . . . The group in a state of peace can permit antagonistic members within to live with one another in an undecided situation because each of them can go his own way and avoid collision. A state of conflict, however, pulls the members so tightly together and subjects them to such a uniform impulse that they either must completely get along with, or completely repel, one another. This is the reason why war with the outside is sometimes the last chance for a state ridden with inner antagonisms to overcome these antagonisms, or else break up definitely. (1955 [1908]: 87, 92)

Ralph Dahrendorf observed years later, "It appears to be a general law that human groups react to external pressure by increased internal coherence"

(1964: 58). And in 1956, Lewis Coser published a classic book, *The Functions of Social Conflict,* which insightfully elaborated the arguments that intergroup conflict clarifies boundaries, solidifies identity, increases unity and cohesion, strengthens ideological solidarity and participation, and augments resource mobilization within conflicted groups (1956; also see Duke 1976: 163–72; Turner 1986: 165–83).

In recent decades, social scientists have observed these principles at work in a variety of settings, from ethnic relations (Gerard 1985; Baker 1975; Cornell 1988: 106–27) to military organizations (Elliot 1986: 79–95). Numerous experimental studies in social psychology, particularly, have validated the theory that out-group conflict builds in-group strength (see, for example, Fisher 1990, 1993; Worchel, Coutant-Sassic, and Wong 1993; Hogg 1992; Muscovici, Mugny, and Avermaet 1985; Dion 1979; Tajfel and Turner 1986; Worchel, Lind, and Kaufman 1975; Sherif 1966). Many studies in anthropology, psychology, and political science also support this view (for a review, see Stein 1976; also see Kriesberg 1982: 291–303; LeVine and Campbell 1972). In a summary review of a wide range of literatures on the subject, Stein (1976) concludes, "In sum, then, there is a clear convergence in the literature in both the specific studies and in the various disciplines, that suggests that external conflict does increase internal cohesion."

This elementary principle—that out-group conflict typically builds in-group strength—has tremendous relevance for our understanding of the fate of religion in the modern world. We need not assume that conflict with ideological and subcultural competitors and adversaries that religious groups may confront in a pluralistic society will inevitably weaken their beliefs and practices. Rather, we have reason to believe that such conflict can strengthen religious beliefs and practices—especially within religious subcultures that possess cultural tools which can interpret the conflict in a religiously significant framework. Thus, the very kinds of intergroup experiences that a highly pluralistic situation is apt to engender—suspicion, disagreement, friction, conflict—can actually strengthen the groups' subcultural identities and cohesion. If this were not so, we would not see the common practice among many religious (and secular) groups of rhetorically highlighting their disagreements and tensions with outgroups with whom they view themselves in conflict.

Theoretically, then, religion in modernity does not have to choose between gradual surrender ("accommodation") and defensively hunkering down for a bleak future ("resistance") (Berger 1967: 153; Hunter 1983: 15). As an alternative, religious groups can grow stronger through the tensions and conflicts that arise between themselves and other groups and subcultures in a pluralistic context, which fortify their own identities and their members' commitment, unity, participation, and resource contributions. In this way, modernity's cultural pluralism can actually positively benefit religious subcultures by providing a greater variety of other groups and subcultures against which to "rub" and feel distinction and tension, in a way that strengthens religious subcultural life internally (see Wuthnow 1989a).

Indeed, religious groups that are (more or less self-consciously) savvy to the dynamics of sociocultural conflict, can themselves actually take the initiative to construct situations which strengthen their own religious vitality. Coser writes (1956: 110): "Struggle groups may actually search for enemies with the deliberate purpose or the unwitting result of maintaining unity and internal cohesion. . . . Imaginary threats have the same group-integrating function as real threats." Certainly, many religious elites—no less than many secular ones—tend to fabricate enemies and exaggerate the strengths and threat of their perceived opponents, precisely in order to bolster members' commitment, solidarity, and financial contributions. But whether fabricated and exaggerated, or actual and factual, recognizing that outgroup conflict typically builds ingroup strength helps us to understand better the bases of the persistence of religion in the pluralistic, modern world.

Proposition 8: Modernity can actually increase *religion's appeal, by creating social conditions which intensify the kinds of felt needs and desires that religion is especially well-positioned to satisfy.*

We have argued above that robust subcultures, whose collective identities provide their members meaning and belonging, can and do survive and thrive in modern, urban, pluralistic societies. Part of the reason why moderns persist in constructing distinctive subcultures within which to embed their lives is precisely because certain features of modernity heighten people's felt need for meaning and belonging. The deficiencies of modern *gemeinschaft* beg for subcultural *gesellschaft*. And the collective identities of religious subcultures are often especially well-suited to satisfying these desires and needs that modernity intensifies.

Technologically and institutionally, modernity specializes in the expansion of means to accomplish given ends. But it has little definitive to say about ends themselves. Modernity maximizes material abundance and individual autonomy. But it affords insufficient insight into the rightful purpose and meaning of material things and provides little direction regarding what people should actually do with their freedom. The modern public realm, the system-world of *gesellschaft* simply lacks the force of normative direction that human beings appear to need and want. So, what moderns cannot find in system, they construct in the life-world. Furthermore, the felt sterility of modernity's bureaucracy, materialism, and secularism can make people yearn for a larger significance, for re-enchantment, for higher spiritual purpose. Moreover, modernity's dominant epistemology of individual subjectivism (Bellah et al. 1985) affords what often feels to people to be a flimsy basis for basic morality and values. In addition, insofar as modernity disrupts traditional, location-based structures of community, many people seek out alternative bases upon which to construct new networks of community relations. For these reasons, moderns often reach out to historical religious traditions and millennia-old spiritual heritages that offer normative direction, moral stability, cognitive confidence, and new forms of meaningful community (Davidman 1991).

Indeed, for satisfying these felt needs and desires, religion remains among the best-suited cultural meaning systems available. Religion has long provided answers that are rooted in ultimacy and transcendence to core existential human questions. Religion has always gathered people into face-to-face congregations of memory, meaning, belonging, and mutual support, bound together by the sacred, and not merely members' immediate interests. Religion has long served as the primary basis for making sense of the recurrent, intense, primordial human experiences of birth, love, tragedy, finitude, war, awe, suffering, and death (Bell 1976: 146–71). Religion has for all of history supplied authoritative moral ends—grounded not in individual subjective experience but in the ultimate, the eternal, the transcendent—toward which to live. To the extent that public life in the modern system-world generates in people a sense of rootlessness, alienation, isolation, restless discontent, and insignificance, religion provides a most natural and suitable remedy (Bell 1980). In these ways, modernity actually creates conditions which often increase the demand for religious belief and experience.

A "Subcultural Identity" Theory of Religion

We are now prepared to formulate more precisely a subcultural identity theory of religious strength, informed and undergirded by the propositions explicated above. Our goal here is to extend and elaborate recent empirical and theoretical work in the sociology of religion on the benefits of pluralism for religious groups (Warner 1993). We hope to do so in a way that, (1) more adequately formulates a theoretical account of why and how religion survives and can thrive in the pluralistic modern world; and (2) more adequately explains variations in religious vitality among different religious traditions operating in a given religious field.

To be clear about our position: we think that the explicit rational-choice language that currently dominates thinking in this area offers one potentially valid and insightful way of theorizing the dynamics of religion and pluralism. However, we also view the rational-choice approach as incomplete. We therefore employ in our analysis a noneconomistic language drawn from fields such as cultural sociology, social psychology, and the sociology of group behavior. And we focus on factors and dynamics other than those highlighted by existing economistic analyses of pluralism and religion. Our intention is to offer a theoretical approach that compliments rather than contradicts existing rational-choice perspectives on the beneficial effects of pluralism on religion. In so doing, we hope to persuade people who may have a distaste for the economistic language of exchange-based rational-choice theory (a distaste we ourselves tend to share) that, language aside, the essential argument of the "new paradigm" is correct: pluralism very often and in many ways is positively good for religion (Warner 1993). We also hope to extend the paradigm's scope of analysis beyond inter-religious pluralism and competition to sociocultural pluralism and conflict more broadly; beyond the entrepreneurial work of religious elites to the experience of ordinary religious believers generally; and beyond differences in denominations' organizational structures and marketing techniques to variations in the content of traditions' faith-orientations themselves.

Having unpacked in some detail the eight propositions advanced above, we now need to compact all that we said about them tightly back into a succinct theoretical statement. Keeping in mind our arguments above, we conclude this chapter by proposing this "subcultural identity" theory of religious persistence and strength. The subcultural identity theory of religious *persistence* is this:

Religion survives and can thrive in pluralistic, modern society by embedding itself in subcultures that offer satisfying morally orienting collective identities which provide adherents meaning and belonging.

And the subcultural identity theory of religious *strength* is this:

In a pluralistic society, those religious groups will be relatively stronger which better possess and employ the cultural tools needed to create both clear distinction from and significant engagement and tension with other relevant outgroups, short of becoming genuinely countercultural.

Clearly, this subcultural identity theory suggests that modern pluralism need not undermine religion but can create the conditions in which religion—or at least *certain* religions—can thrive. It plainly shares with Berger and Hunter a central concern with human meaning. But it explicitly nests that problem of human meaning within the larger problem of collective identity. This necessarily shifts the focus of analytical attention away from the supposed quandaries of individual cognitive belief plausibility within modernity and toward the human necessity for distinctive subcultural identity construction.

On the other hand, this subcultural identity theory plainly shares with Finke, Stark, and Iannaccone the view that pluralism often strengthens religion. Yet it compels us to take seriously not only the effects of competition between different religious organizations but more broadly the subcultural experience of distinct religious traditions situated in a complex secular and religious multicultural field. Subcultural identity theory likewise requires that we pay close attention not only to religious groups' organizational structures and promotional techniques but also to the actual substance of the subcultural beliefs and practices of distinct religious traditions. From our perspective, in other words, the *meaning-content* of theologies, customs, worldviews, and rituals actually matter—which requires us to engage in cultural, and not merely ecological and structural, analysis. Moreover, the subcultural identity theory mandates that we analyze religion not only at the elite level of entrepreneurial religious activists but also at the grassroots level of common religious believers. For it is at this level that—depending on how ordinary people utilize their religious traditions' cultural tools more or less effectively to construct distinctive, meaningful, satisfying social identities—religious strength is shaped.

The next chapter employs the subcultural identity theory to explain how and why modern American evangelicalism is thriving. Our argument will represent both an applied illustration of the theory's analytical viewpoint and a specific test-case of its empirical adequacy.

Evangelicalism Embattled

$\mathbf{W}$e discovered in chapter 2 that modern American evangelicalism enjoys a religious vitality—measured sociologically—that surpasses every other major Christian tradition in the country. Whether gauged by belief orthodoxy, salience of faith, robustness of belief, church attendance, participation in social and religious mission, or membership recruitment and retention, the conclusion is the same: American evangelicalism is thriving. Chapter 3 examined a variety of sociological theories that offer to explain differences in religious strength in an effort to see which might best interpret evangelicalism's strength. Some we judged more satisfactory than others. Still, we decided that none of the existing theories was entirely adequate for explaining evangelicalism's vitality. We therefore formulated in chapter 4 an alternative theoretical approach, which we call the subcultural identity theory. It maintains, essentially, that religions can survive and thrive in pluralistic, modern society by situating themselves in subcultures that offer morally orienting collective identities which provide their adherents meaning and belonging. Furthermore, our theory suggests, in a pluralistic society, those religious traditions will be stronger which better possess and utilize the cultural tools needed to create both clear distinction from and significant engagement and tension with other relevant outgroups.

This chapter uses the subcultural identity theory of religious strength to interpret evangelicalism's striking religious vitality, relative to fundamentalist and, especially, mainline and liberal Protestantism. So as not to belabor what is already well known, we begin by simply acknowledging the fact—without spending words to document it—that evangelicalism has constructed for itself a distinctive religious subculture. We also simply recognize that this subculture sustains a distinctive Christian collective identity which serves as a primary source of individual identity, if not as a master status, for those who believe and participate in the subculture. Anyone familiar with evangelicalism is aware of these points. In other words, we will not primarily concern ourselves here with applying or evaluating the subcultural identity theory of religious *persistence*. Rather, we concentrate on employing the subcultural identity theory of religious *strength* to interpret evangelical vitality. Our analysis below suggests that evangelicalism utilizes its culturally pluralistic environment to socially construct subcultural distinction, engagement, and tension between itself and relevant outgroups and that this builds religious strength. Evangelicalism, we contend, flourishes on difference, engagement, tension, conflict, and threat. In chapter 7, we will suggest that some of the factors which foster evangelicalism's vitality also have the ironic effect of undermining evangelical efforts at social influence. But that is something of a different matter. For now, in this chapter, we argue that evangelicalism's conspicuous vitality is not the result of any protective social, demographic, or geographical distance from, or fundamental accommodation to secular modernity. Rather, its strength results from the combination of its socially constructed cultural distinction vis-à-vis a vigorous sociocultural engagement with pluralistic modernity.

Constructing Distinction, Engagement, and Conflict

Distinction, engagement, and conflict vis-à-vis outsiders constitutes a crucial element of what we might call the "cultural DNA" of American evangelicalism. The evangelical tradition's entire history, theology, and self-identity presupposes and reflects strong cultural boundaries with nonevangelicals; a zealous burden to convert and transform the world outside of itself; and a keen perception of external threats and crises seen as menacing what it views to be true, good, and valuable. These, we maintain, go a long way toward explaining evangelicalism's thriving.

Viewed in historical context, one can go to virtually any point in American evangelical history—but particularly beginning with the latter third of the nineteenth century—and readily detect in its elite discourse a sense of crisis, conflict, or threat. In all cases, the perception of crisis serves to invigorate and mobilize evangelical vitality rather than to undermine or disintegrate it. Examples, beginning with the Puritan jeremiads (Bercovitch 1978) and running through to the present day, are innumerable. We limit ourselves here to four. First, in 1885, Josiah Strong, secretary of the Evangelical Alliance, sounded the alarm in his widely read book, *Our Country: Its Possible Future and Present Crisis,* about the "seven perils" to Anglo-Christian civilization: immigration, Romanism, Mormonism, intemperance, socialism, wealth, and the city.[1] "We are living in extraordinary times," Strong declared, arguing that the closing years of his century "are the pivot on which is turning the nation's future. . . . The destinies of mankind, for centuries to come, [will] be seriously . . . determined by the men of this generation" (1963 [1886]: 13). About the threat of immigration, for example, Strong warned, "During the last four years we have suffered a peaceful invasion by an army, more than twice as vast as the estimated number of Goths and Vandals that swept over Southern Europe and overwhelmed Rome" (Strong 1963 [1886]: 42). Evangelicals, Strong warned, needed to act, and act decisively.

Thirty-six years later, Walter Clarke, editor of the Christian periodical *New Era Magazine,* similarly rallied the troops in his 1921 article, "Christians, Save the Christian Sabbath!":

> Presbyterians all, Christians all, you have need to marshall all your forces, all your strength of prayer and works, to save the Christian Sabbath. The Christian Sabbath in America is doomed unless you act concertedly, unless you act at once. If the Christian Sabbath is once lost to America, America is doomed. (quoted in Handy 1984: 171)

Inaugurating the neo-evangelical era, in his keynote address to the 1942 "National Conference for United Action Among Evangelicals" that founded the modern evangelical movement, Harold J. Ockenga warned:

> I see on the horizon ominous clouds of battle which spell annihilation unless we are willing to run in a pack. . . . Evangelical Christianity has suffered nothing but a series of defeats for decades. . . . Analyze this business of the kingdom . . . and see wherein any evidence of strength or power exists in America today. I will tell you where I see an evidence of power. It is in Roman Catholicism. There was a day when Boston was a stronghold of evangelical Christianity. Today Roman Catholicism has a practical monopoly. . . . Along side of Roman Catholicism is that terrible octopus of liberalism. . . . The third great influence which is defeating evangelical Christianity today is secularism. Floods of iniquity have flowed over America since the great war, in a tidal wave of drunkenness, immorality, corruption, dishonesty, and utter atheism. . . .

---

1. In retrospect, Strong is often thought of as a liberal; yet this 1886 writing precedes the modernist-fundamentalist split, thereby making such a label somewhat anachronistic. We ought, rather, to view Strong in the 1880s as part of the evangelical Protestant mainstream.

> Unless we can have a true revival of evangelical Christianity, able to change the character of men and build up a new moral fibre, we believe Christianity, capitalism, and democracy, likewise, to be imperiled. . . . We are standing in the most tremendous danger of all. Already a revolution has taken place in our country. . . . The crisis is greater than any of us realize. Now, if ever, we need some organ to speak for evangelical interests, to represent men who, like myself, are "lone wolves" in the church. (quoted in Carpenter 1988: 20–31)

Finally, Carl Henry, one of the leading lights of the modern evangelical movement, wrote forebodingly in his 1986 book, *Christian Countermoves in a Decadent Culture:*

> We live in a darkening civilization in which worldlings seek to divide Christ's garments among them. . . . Evangelicals are persecuted in atheistic Russia and much of eastern Europe, are beleaguered in China, prohibited from building churches in Saudi Arabia, arrested for distributing literature in Turkey, and no less tragic, are often vilified in the United States. . . . Who can doubt that the new dimensions of shamelessness permeate modern society and that its horizons of licentiousness are reminiscent of pre-Christian paganism? A vocal vanguard vilifies the very norms of civilization; marriage it decries as bondage, sexual lust it defends as freedom. The biblical Elohim it classifies with the Loch Ness monster; references to God it views as escapist or as life-threatening. . . . Without a return to fixed truths and shared values, no shift of emphasis in modern life will count for much, either in politics or anywhere else. The crisis of our culture is more fundamentally theological and ethical than political. Without a basic change of spiritual and moral condition, our nation is imperiled. (1986: 121–32)

American evangelical elite discourse charged with a similar sense of engagement and apprehension can readily be found in almost any historical time period. After reading enough of these narratives, one begins to develop the distinct sense that evangelicalism actually feeds upon such engagement, tension, and crisis for its own vitality.

But concern with difference, engagement, conflict, and threat is not limited to evangelical elites. Ordinary evangelicals socially construct reality using the cultural tools of the very same tradition, though in perhaps less intellectualized or entrepreneurial ways. Here we examine in greater detail some of the more prominent features of distinction, engagement, and conflict embedded in the evangelical subcultural worldview, features which help constitute the core sensibilities of the preponderance of ordinary contemporary evangelicals.

A Sense of Strong Boundaries with the Nonevangelical World

Evangelicals operate with a very strong sense of boundaries that distinguish themselves from non-Christians and from nonevangelical Christians. Evangelicals know who and what they are and are not. They possess clear symbolic borders that define the frontiers beyond which one is not an evangelical. The implicit distinction between "us" and "them" is omnipresent in evangelical thought and speech, so much so that it does not often in fact draw to itself much attention. Yet it subtly and profoundly shapes evangelical consciousness and discourse. No good evangelical operates without this distinction in their cultural toolkit.

Consequently, evangelicals would never accept the minimizing or erasing of distinction between the Christian and non-Christian that we saw some mainline and liberal Protestants recommending in chapter 2. Indeed, when evangelicals use the word "Christian," most likely they are instinctively meaning *evangelical* Christian—or some approximation thereof, such as "real," "born again," or "genuine" Christian, as they might alternatively say. Generally, all of the others, including liberal and mainline Protestants, Roman Catholics, Jehovah's Witnesses, Mormons, and various participants in what some evangelicals call "cultural Christianity" are spoken of as Christian only as a broad religious classification (as opposed to Muslims or secularists, for example). But they are usually not what evangelicals are talking about when they say "Christian" in ordinary parlance. For well-known boundaries distinguish, in their own minds, evangelicals as the real or most faithful kind of Christians from all of the rest. Not that evangelicals are overtly conceited or imperious about it. To the contrary, so pervasive and natural are these identity borders that mark the evangelical identity from others that few of the evangelicals we interviewed seemed even aware of their operation.

Evangelical boundaries with other types of Christians are most often drawn using the all-important symbolic markers of a "personal relationship" with Jesus Christ and obedience to the authority of the Bible. Those lacking the former or disavowing the latter are seen as out of proper identity-bounds. For example, this evangelical Anabaptist man explained, "Being an evangelical, I guess, separates me from the average person that would go to a Protestant church that may not personally have a personal relationship or personal commitment to Christ. The word evangelical to me emphasizes that there is a personal faith, which you may not find in a mainline denomination." Alternatively, this Baptist woman stated, "In terms of liberals, I wouldn't identify myself with someone who doesn't recognize Jesus as the son of God, as both divine and human, or with those who don't see Scripture as the basis of authority." This evangelical Presbyterian man elaborated the point this way:

> There is a distinction between what I would call mainstream Christianity—many of the larger mainline denominations—and an evangelical church. One of those distinctions would be that evangelicals try to maintain a biblical worldview following the inerrant Scriptures. But other churches sometimes ordain clergy who are clearly practicing what the Scripture calls sin, and have no remorse or intention of stopping. First thing I look for in a church is their stand on Scripture. Do they see scripture as God's word? Does the preaching follow that principle?

In these ways, evangelicals draw powerful distinctions between themselves and Christian "others."

Evangelicals also maintain a clear sense of the difference between "Christians" (themselves) and "the world." Evangelicals do not spend a lot of time talking about what is "worldly," mostly because such discourse has been characteristic of separatistic fundamentalism, and evangelicals want to maintain strong boundaries between themselves and such fundamentalists. However, evangelicals are keenly aware that something out there— "the world"—exists, that they stand in opposition to that something, and that they have an obligation to interact with it redemptively. Actually, "aware" may be an overstatement, for distinction with the world is something more consistently lived and breathed by evangelicals, than consciously contemplated. However, its very unassuming nature makes this difference all the more powerful. Evangelicals may not always contemplate their distinction from the world, but they consistently feel it in lived experience. Confused mainliners and liberals may puzzle the question, "Huh? What do you mean 'the world?' This is the world. We are the world." But evangelicals are not confused. They know that out there is an "other" that is fundamentally not who or what they are.

Distinction from "the world" weaves in and through all evangelical talk. While explaining how she has had to sacrifice the acceptance of her own parents and siblings and financial security for being a Christian, this Bible Fellowship woman concluded, "But we are very strong in saying *'we're us.'* We use that with the kids, too, when they want to imitate the world and do things or have things or go places they can't—and we have to say we don't operate according to other people's standards, we operate according to our own." This Baptist man shared: "There are a lot of pressures that we as Christians feel in society because of the values the world espouses today. Look at the pressure to go to the movies that are riddled with sex and unbearable language—that creates real problems and pressures for Christians." And this woman who recently helped to found a nondenominational Charismatic church concluded her discussion about the spiritual dangers of wealth and intellectual pride with the observation, "There are so many things in the world that could become a stumbling block to us, but Jesus forewarns us not to let those things become our god." Evangelicals rarely speak of "the world" as something to escape; rather almost always as something to be present in and engaged with, but not mastered by. So, for example, the same Baptist man above said:

> Christians should look for every opportunity to show they are different. One way to set ourselves apart is by bowing our heads and praying at lunch. When you go out on a business lunch, say "excuse me," and bow your head and pray. It says to people something is different. I think Christians need to look for those opportunities to live a Christian life where people see that you are different.

A Sense of Possessing the Ultimate Truth

For many moderns, not to mention postmodernists, the idea of Truth with a capital "T" has become problematic. The belief that there exists objectively an unchanging foundation or standard that applies to everyone simply feels too narrow, too absolutist, too old-fashioned to maintain comfortably. Not so for evangelicals. American evangelicals believe not only that an unchanging and universal Truth exists, but—more audaciously, perhaps—that *they* are the ones who know it because God has revealed it to them. On this basis, the Carl Henries of the world speak of the "fixed truths and shared values," which they know and hold, as the only solution to society's problems.

Most of those we interviewed simply presumed knowledge of the Truth. In a discussion of politics, for example, this man from a Holiness church mentioned as an aside, "I find that a lot more non-Christians are not principled because they don't have a foundation for truth, everything is relative." However, some, such as this Pentecostal woman, argued the point more explicitly: "Do you just make up your own rules and as long as they seem okay to you then they're fine? No, there are essential truths that apply to all of humanity, because we were all created by God, and his truth is truth." She continued:

> Relativism is a problem, where everyone does their own thing and makes up their own rules and there are no absolute truths or values, and that it is thought anti-intellectual to believe otherwise. Christians need to be equipped to have answers to that, to learn, to study the issues, to know God's word, to be bold and speak out and not be intimidated, and impact the culture. Because we have the truth.

When asked how Christians ought to relate to believers of other religions, this Christian and Missionary Alliance man said, "We should speak the truth. There is only one standard, only one God, and one true path. These people will eventually come to the truth because it is the truth." And to the same question, this Holiness woman stated, "We as Christians have to understand that we have the answer. At the same time, that really offends people when you say you have the only way. We just need to let the truth speak for itself." In fact, most evangelicals are not particularly arrogant or triumphantistic about their belief in knowing the ultimate Truth. For evangelicals, it is merely a basic, if wondrous, fact of life that they have received the Truth. What our interviews revealed about evangelicals' beliefs about knowing the Truth, our survey data substantiate: in table 5.1, we see that evangelicals, compared with all other groups, are by far most likely, for example, to believe in the existence of absolute, unchanging standards as the basis for morals.

Epistemological and moral relativism leave everyone in the same condition—deprived of absolute foundations—and so tend to highlight commonality. But the belief in having come to understand the ultimate Truth necessarily creates distinction between those who know and believe and those who do not. The most extreme expression of this distinction is the traditional Calvinist doctrine of double predestination: some are chosen for heaven, and some for hell. But most evangelicals operate with a much less predetermined, though not a less surely believed and experienced, distinction between the children of light and the children of darkness. And this boundary, this identity distinction, is not seen as merely theological, but as spiritual and, ultimately, eternal.

Table 5.1: Beliefs about Morals and Values, by Tradition (percent)

	Evangelicals	Fundamentalists	Mainline	Liberals	Catholics	Nonreligious
Believe morals should be based on absolute, unchanging standards	75	65	55	34	37	15
Christian morality should be the law of the land, even though not all Americans are Christians	62	58	45	34	23	10
People have the right to live by their own moralities, even if they are not Christian moralities	59	64	64	75	77	—
Which morals should be taught in public schools?						
Christian morals	19	17	9	9	9	1
General morals	52	49	61	59	67	61
Teach morals at home	30	34	30	32	24	38
How different should Christians' values and lifestyles be from the rest of American society?						
Very different	74	61	46	32	—	—
Somewhat different	17	23	29	32	—	—
A little different	3	5	5	10	—	—
Not different	6	11	20	27	—	—
N	(430)	(389)	(576)	(431)	(114)	(60)

Note: Chi-square for all figures is significant at the .0000 level.

A Sense of Practical Moral Superiority

Evangelicals also believe that their practical way of life, their morality, their functional standards—which are seen as deriving directly from the ultimate Truth they understand—simply "work" better than anybody else's. On this point, evangelicals are pragmatists. They believe God has created reality in a certain way and that those whose moral practices violate that reality will unavoidably suffer frustration, malfunction, and, ultimately, spiritual death. To use a typically evangelical type of illustration, it is like driving on the highway: those who observe the rules of the road get where they want to go; those who do not get into accidents. This woman from a nondenominational church said it plainly, "I feel sad about things today, because I believe so strongly that a faith in Jesus as Lord and adherence to a Christian lifestyle is the best and healthiest state to be in. And I think that some of our social problems arise from a cultural drift away from a Christian norm in the past two or three decades." Or as this Charismatic woman remarked, "Sure Christians have answers to today's social problems. Go to the Bible and get your answer. Most definitely."

Table 5.1 illustrates the consequences of this view. Evangelicals are much more likely than any other group to believe that Christian morality should be the law of the land, even though not all Americans are Christians. Conversely, evangelicals are the least likely to agree that people should be able to choose their own moralities, even if they are not Christian moralities. And when it comes to the concrete issue of moral instruction in public schools, evangelicals—even if only a minority—are the most likely to believe that schools should teach distinctively Christian morals. Most of the reasoning behind these attitudes is not a craving for cultural dominance, but a sincere belief that everyone would simply be better off following God's ways. This woman from a nondenominational church, for example, explained, "Based on certain absolutes in the Word of God, there are ways that people can function and live that resolve a lot of things. If you are really giving yourself to loving your neighbor as yourself, it's going to be real unlikely that you are going to pull a pistol out of your pocket to resolve a dispute." This man from an independent Charismatic church spelled out that logic in greater detail:

> The Bible offers the solution. Talking about abortion and teen pregnancy, if you save yourself for marriage, you won't have teen pregnancy. Then your abortion rate is going to drop. You apply Thou Shalt Not Kill to your life, then you aren't going to have

people out here murdering and killing. The solution is for people
to live up to the morality that God has laid out in the Bible.

Analogously, this man involved in an evangelical seeker-church argued:

> In a Christian community you have more sharing, compassion,
> concern for others. A lot of the problems in our world stem from
> competition, putting down other people, self-concern, greed. And
> for a Christian, all that becomes much less a priority. I think that
> if people became Christians and desired to be like Christ, you
> would see the competition and intolerance going away. Not to say
> that Christians right now don't compete or aren't intolerant. But
> that should be the direction they are headed.

Not all evangelicals are this optimistic. Some more readily admit that
Christianity may not have all the answers. Yet, even in the speech of these
more doubtful evangelicals, like this Presbyterian woman, a sense of practical moral superiority remains evident:

> I don't think we are ever going to be able to answer all the social
> problems we have in today's world. To think that we can is egotis-
> tical. I think that the difference between us and a secular social
> worker is maybe we have 75 percent success and they have 25 per-
> cent success. Because we can show people Jesus. I don't think there
> is any other answer than that. A changed life is the only way to
> change this world.

This believed moral superiority has the important consequence for
evangelical consciousness of creating a distinction between those seen as
trying to live godly lives and those who are not similarly committed. On
the one hand are Christians living as God intended people to live. On the
other hand are the indifferent, the rebellious, the promiscuous, the selfish,
the backsliders. It is very important to recognize here, however, that what
evangelicals generally view as superior is not their own behavior, per se—
which would constitute "works-righteousness," a serious evangelical sin—
but the moral standards themselves that God has established. For this
reason, despite the not infrequent appearance of a rather arrogant moral
posture, evangelicals are not particularly morally pompous people. They
simply believe that, practically speaking, the way God calls people to live
is good for everybody, whether humans like it or not. Hence, even when
evangelicals admit to moral failure themselves—which they readily do—
the distinction in their consciousness between the narrow road that leads

to life and the broad road that leads to destruction remains intact. What matters then is simply that they, by God's grace, get themselves back on the narrow road. But the distinction between the two roads is never blurred.

A Sense of Lifestyle and Value Distinctiveness

Evangelicals see themselves as living an aberrant way of life from that of the surrounding world. If evangelicals ever viewed themselves as belonging to the cultural mainstream, they do not much think so any longer. Rather, evangelicals see themselves as embracing traditional, common-sense values in a broader culture that has abandoned them in pursuit of narcissistic, licentious, and self-destructive values and lifestyles (see Wacker 1984). On television, in schools, on the news, and at work, evangelicals see and hear a set of values and lifestyle commitments that feel to them fundamentally alien and inhospitable. Thus, evangelicals, like this Baptist man, are increasingly becoming aware of themselves as peculiar, as different, as strangers in their own land: "Strong, Bible-believing evangelical and fundamentalist Christians are in the minority in this society. There has to be some standards, but I certainly don't think our society any longer has the Bible as a standard. I feel constantly under attack through the media and through the workplace." Similarly, this woman who attends an independent "seeker-church" said, "We're almost a persecuted group, to some extent. The apostles all lived in the same kind of society, a small group within a larger secular society. That's the same position we Christians are in." Likewise, this woman who attends a Covenant church remarked:

> I work in a public university environment which is very secular. I only know one or two other Christians there. And the perception of people in the university environment is that Christians are radicals and nonthinkers. And so I do feel very different. But I also feel like, "I'm not the way you characterize me."

Having rejected the fundamentalist strategic option of isolationist separation, however, evangelicals feel compelled to struggle to remain involved with and relevant to the emerging mainstream American culture. But they do so keenly aware of their difference from it. Hence, according to the results in table 5.1, evangelicals, far and above those of any other Protestant tradition, including fundamentalists, believe that Christians' values and lifestyles should be very different from the rest of American society. This self-consciousness about difference shone through in our interviews in a variety of ways. Some, like this Lutheran woman, characterized a Christian's distinctiveness as a matter of commitment and selflessness in relationships:

> I can tell Christians from non-Christians real clearly. The best example comes from my experiences with friends who are non-Christians, who end up in divorce court over small problems. Instead of working it through as a family, they say, "I'm leaving." So the biggest thing I find is that non-Christians are more "me"-oriented than "we"-oriented.

Others, like this Pentecostal woman, focus more on trying to please God by obeying God's will:

> You know we're in the world, but we're not supposed to participate in things that are of the world. When I used to be a thief, I didn't desire the things of God. But now I desire to walk with him, to please him. I don't drink, I don't pollute my body, I don't sleep around. Because that's what the Bible says. You know what I mean?

And still others, such as this Charismatic woman, pointed more to subjective attitudes and emotions she thinks should set Christians apart:

> It's a peacefulness. People in this world are very confused, tense, stressed out, and looking for peace. You can have money, a family, everything, but if you don't have peace, you are not going to be capable of structuring your life in this world. But I know people who have given themselves to Jesus Christ and have found peace. You know, the stress of the world doesn't bother them.

But however evangelicals construct difference from the world, most affirm it as a good sign, believing that faithful Christians will naturally be different from non-Christians. As this man who attends a nondenominational Bible church said, "When I go to work in a secular environment, I feel that I don't fit in. Which is the way it should be." In yet another way, then, evangelicals' lifestyle and value distinctiveness creates significant distinction, engagement, and even conflict—in their own minds, at least—between themselves and outsiders.

A Sense of Evangelistic and Social Mission

We saw in chapter 2 the influential presence in the evangelical subculture of an "evangelical burden" of responsibility to evangelize the world and ameliorate its social and political needs. We saw that evangelicals generally view no sphere or activity of life as outside of God's redemptive plan. As this Baptist woman remarked, "We need to love in the midst of all this hate and be strong in our convictions and ethics and morals and laws based on the Bible. They should show through our lives. Everything down to taxes or business dealings or kids in school, whatever—the world should be able to see it." Again, our survey evidence confirms this view. Table 5.2 shows that, comparatively speaking, evangelicals are extraordinarily likely to believe that religion is not a private matter but that it appropriately belongs as a voice in public debates over social and political issues (also see Regnerus and Smith 1998a). And in their social activism, evangelicals are, among Protestant groups, the most prepared to exert an influence in a way that they know may cause tension and conflict. Furthermore, according to table 5.2, evangelicals are the least likely to try hard not to offend other people with their Christian views. Altogether, we see evangelicalism as a tradition firmly committed to a vigorous evangelistic and social mission.

This construction of determined social responsibility toward the outside world works, again, to create distinction between the agents and the recipients of the work of evangelical mission. The very structure of thought, evident in this Presbyterian woman's statement, clearly differentiates the missionaries from the missionized—when "mission" is directed toward the "unchurched"—the ones who have something to give from those perceived as needing to receive:

> Sometimes I get really excited because I think we have a lot to offer people in a broken world. I know I do. From battered women in my neighborhood, to searching college students I work with, to musicians I play with. God has created us for people who are searching for truth. It's exciting to think I'm out there, even though it's really a difficult place to be. Being a Christian isn't an easy thing and I don't know the easy answers. And I have some very close friendships with people who have completely different belief systems. Sometimes it's really hard to connect with them. But it's important.

Organized evangelical ministries designed for "outreach" work are not frequently distinguished by a strong sense of humble reciprocity with those ministered to, although individual evangelicals in ministry often may be so. More typically, an "us" and "them" mentality prevails, often along with a certain un-self-critical paternalism.

But the evangelical burden creates more than distinction. It prompts

Table 5.2: Beliefs about Cultural Engagement, by Tradition (percent)

	Evangelicals	Fundamentalists	Mainline	Liberals	Catholics	Nonreligious
Religion is a private matter that should be kept out of public debates over social and political issues	25	33	48	61	62	84
Christians need to try to change society using ways they know may cause conflict or set people against each other	37	31	28	23	—	—
Tries hard not to offend people with their Christian views[a]	67	76	72	75	—	—
N	(430)	(389)	(576)	(431)	(114)	(60)

Note: Chi-square for all figures is significant at the .0000 level, except [a]prob. = .082.

evangelicals to work hard to spread their faith. To start with, many evangelicals view themselves as constantly on-stage, being scrutinized, so that they must always be a good "witness." For example, after describing in detail ways that Christians should work to be different from the world in order to influence it, this Congregational man concluded, "A lifestyle that is first of all plugged into God and then into our society can make a difference in ways we don't even notice. People will be watching." Specifically, this Congregational man advocated:

> Humility. Being really sacrificial, especially with our time. Setting aside our materialism and living simpler lifestyles. Those things really go against the grain of what the world out there is seeking. I think they look to people who are really noticeably different by their choice of words, the way they live, their lifestyle, what kinds of things they think of. And prayer, setting aside time for intercessory prayer for others, allowing God to change us so that when we get out there we have a different quality of spirit that is apparent to others. We can be more patient, have a greater love, show a lot more self-control when we pray, when the Word of God penetrates our souls. Otherwise we will be out there acting exactly like everybody else, and we wouldn't make a difference.

Similarly, this Baptist man explained,

> I think people around Christians should know there is something different—in how they respond to people, control their tempers, their tongues, don't use profanity, talking to people in a proper way, not tearing them down, but building them up. Those, I think, set Christians apart. I think Christians also need to deal with problems differently, to show their faith when they are confronted and challenged with problems and view them as opportunities to let the world and those around them know there is something different about them.

Many, such as this Baptist man, who was raised by an alcoholic single mother, strongly advocate not only setting good examples, but also direct evangelization:

> Christians need to share their faith in Jesus Christ in direct testimony without being embarrassed. I always look for the opportunity to share something about my faith in Christ. I spent nine years doing real estate training for about 4,500 people. I always shared my testimony in one course module that was on positive, upbeat

thinking, called "The Winning Attitude." I was able to share my past and how, through a personal relationship with Jesus Christ, my life and attitude have been changed.

The evangelical burden also drives evangelicals beyond personal evangelism to engage society at many levels to try to exert a positive Christian influence. The evangelical vision of engaged orthodoxy fosters a sense of involvement with, challenge from, and struggle on behalf of the outside world. There are friends and colleagues to influence, new ministries and programs to establish, the afflicted to be fed and comforted, and political offices to be filled with wise and godly leaders. All of this requires attention, mobilization, involvement, and persistence. This Baptist man's sense of calling to ministry in the public schools, for example, is archetypical of the evangelical mentality about active cultural engagement:

> We have consistently held that our children should be in public schools. If Christians want public schools to be the way they want them, then Christian children have to be there. I know full well my children are going to receive viewpoints and lifestyles that are clearly in opposition to what my family and I believe. But if we aren't there to present an alternative, people are not going to choose that alternative. In a way, it is a mini-mission field.

This statement exemplifies well the earnest and widespread evangelical sense of personal responsibility for the state of the world, evangelicals' keen awareness of their differences from the world, and their firm commitment nonetheless to engage the world to try to transform it. Below we will suggest that evangelicalism actually benefits from this engagement with what it views as an oppositional-but-needy world, as much or more as it thinks the world benefits from it. For now we need simply to observe that this "evangelical burden" has the practical consequence of continually exposing evangelicals to and involving them with their surrounding culture and society. Far from remaining distant or sheltered from modernity, evangelicals have earnestly embraced the idea of engaged orthodoxy and engrossed themselves in debate with, involvement in, and attempts at the reform of modern institutions and culture. Evangelicals really are, as they might say, "out there, where things are happening."

A Sense of Displaced Heritage

Widespread among evangelicals is the belief that America was founded as a Christian nation, that America is now turning its back on its Judeo-

Christian roots, that mainstream institutions are becoming increasingly anti-Christian, and that as a consequence America is in a state of moral and social degeneration. The view of this Baptist man is typical:

> America was founded on Christian principles. Some of our founding fathers were maybe immoral in some of their lifestyles, but they as a whole founded our nation on "one nation under God." They believed in a supreme being, in God Almighty, and they wanted our nation to espouse those values and beliefs. They put it into our Constitution, the Declaration of Independence, and on the currency. They made it an indelible imprint on our society.

And what about today? He continues, "Today it's shaky. Our nation is on the edge and falling from the true meaning of being a Christian nation. I think it's foundation is being eroded from way down deep."[2] This Charismatic evangelical woman concurs:

> America started really turning away from Christianity back when Darwinism and evolution came in. Then they took the Bible out of the schools, and ever since it seems like America has gone downhill. There used to be higher family values, higher morals, whereas today, you know, anything goes! Even twenty to thirty years ago it was quite different. It is gradually getting worse and worse and worse.

According to table 5.3, evangelicals, more than any other major Christian tradition, subscribe to this general view. Particularly striking are evangelicals' perceptions of hostility from the mass media, public schools, and feminism. In all cases, evangelicals are between one-third to almost three times more likely to view them as hostile to their own values and morals than are mainliners, liberals, Roman Catholics, and nonreligious Americans. Clearly, very many evangelical Christians are feeling displaced, marginalized, and denigrated in important sectors of the world they occupy. This nondenominational woman, for example, observed, "I think Christians are stereotyped and often dismissed as not having much intellectual capacity, if they adhere to a strong Christian viewpoint. I see it on your

---

2. He elaborates: "You look at changes in our legal system, the Supreme Court. As the people who have gotten into power have moved further away from any kind of biblical absolutes, you end up with our Christian nation being developed by people who don't hold Christian values anymore. So the laws of the land change to reflect more of a pagan view, a humanistic view. The laws and the judicial system reflect that, and that's why I think we are teetering on the edge."

basic sitcom, you know? In the media, the entertainment industry, and journalism, Christians are almost always characterized in a negative way." This Pentecostal woman stated:

> Intellectuals who place their faith in human beings and their own ability to control their worlds are hostile towards Christianity. They are intimidated by the idea that anyone would have an absolute belief and absolute truth. Those are the main enemies of Christianity. They have the most power, too, and want to make sure their agenda stays in place. Their ideas have controlled our culture now for thirty years, and they don't want to give that up. Instead of acknowledging that what we believe are absolutes from the beginning of time, they portray us in unfair ways as anti-intellectual or as trying to go back to the conservative 1950s.[3]

For evangelicals, there is bitter irony in this. For in the view of many, it was precisely America's open commitment to its Judeo-Christian heritage that explains its prosperity and freedom. America is thought to have become great because it was founded on Christian principles, recognized God's laws, and fostered a Christian-based culture. But then, at the height of its wealth and power, the nation God blessed turned its back on God and displaced from their rightful place the carriers of the heritage to which it owes its success. From this perspective, America's shift to a post-Christian or, for some, anti-Christian culture reflects an ingratitude toward Christianity and ignorance of the workings of history. Nevertheless, few evangelicals express personal resentment about their perceived displacement. Most simply report feelings of sadness, disappointment, and frustration for and about America.

What makes the displacement of their heritage especially difficult for evangelicals, however, is their commitment to engaged orthodoxy, which means they may not simply withdraw and sulk in subcultural isolation. Instead, evangelicals feel compelled to remain involved in society, to engage the culture, to be "salt and light" to the world, and to transform it for

---

3. From a different perspective, but in agreement on the general hostility toward Christianity, this Baptist man reported, "In our society there is more negative feeling toward Christians than there has ever been in a long time. Christians who take a stand for biblical values against homosexuality are scorned, mocked, really put down, because that is not politically correct anymore. There is real pressure on Christians to abrogate the position of Scriptures, to be socially acceptable. If we don't, then we are considered totally out of line with our society today. Certain groups view us negatively and foster the notion that Christians are backward, wrong, and should change."

Table 5.3: Beliefs about Cultural Displacement, by Tradition (percent)

	Evangelicals	Fundamentalists	Mainline	Liberals	Catholics	Nonreligious
America was founded as a Christian nation	92	84	90	72	79	60
Christian values are under serious attack today	92	88	82	65	—	—
View as hostile to own values and morals						
Mass media	76	72	57	46	47	42
Feminists	66	56	38	25	34	24
Public schools	57	52	35	29	23	20
We are seeing the breakdown of American society today	95	95	90	88	87	71
N	(430)	(389)	(576)	(431)	(114)	(60)

Note: Chi-square for all figures is significant at the .001 level.

Christ. Yet this puts evangelicalism in the position, essentially, of a spurned lover: evangelicals are forever passionately pursuing a culture which increasingly disregards and mistreats them. But the more they are spurned, the more evangelicals believe they need to pursue and influence the culture. Employing even the language of a troubled romantic relationship, this Baptist man maintains, "I think it would take something fairly catastrophic for America to be slapped in the face and realize that our nation has gone away from God, and if they would come back, things would get better." Pursuing a rejecting culture is a difficult task for evangelicals, but one to which they nevertheless appear fully committed.

A Sense of Second-Class Citizenship

One consistent theme we heard from the evangelicals we interviewed was their perception of a double-standard in American public discourse that discriminates against Christians. Time and again we heard evangelicals observe that every racial, ethnic, religious, political, and ideological perspective existing is given fair time and a fair hearing, *except* the Christian perspective. Instead, Christians' views are seen as routinely slighted, whether subtly or blatantly. And this feels like unfair discrimination, an unacknowledged infringement of freedom of speech. According to this Charismatic woman, "Schools have completely removed anything that has to do with Christianity or God or the Bible or any of that. And then they will let in books like *Heather Has Two Mommies,* real secular and anti-moral books." A few evangelicals, like this Presbyterian woman, said they thought some Christians may be partly to blame for creating prejudice against Christians as a whole: "I think many in mainstream society have been wounded by fundamentalist and some evangelical Christians who are not willing to love, who are judgmental. And they carry those wounds and act the same way, judgmental and isolationist." But most evangelicals thought it was simply unjustified discrimination for no good reason.

For some, perhaps many, evangelicals, this creates the feeling of being demoted to second-class citizenship, of being suppressed by a selectively liberal mainstream that lives in denial of that suppression. Many, such as this nondenominational woman, a certified public school teacher herself, see a double-standard in public schools, "Some teachers think it is inappropriate to explain at Easter time that people known as Christians believe in Jesus' resurrection—but they don't have any problem spending a month on Native American spirituality. Christianity is sometimes penalized because it was once the norm, but now is not. It is seen as something not to be addressed in any way in public schools."[4] According to this Presbyterian man:

> The state is involved in almost every facet of society, but with extreme interpretations of separation of church and state, the church is left out. I see it as a discrimination or bias. Even something like Americorp, the national service program, its regulations are written so that volunteers can't volunteer in any program with "sectarian bias." So other volunteerism is being subsidized, but Christian volunteerism is left out. Values are being tilted against Christians, in the name of neutrality.

And this Presbyterian woman lamented:

> Christians are not treated too nicely. I'm thinking of two Chief Justices who are Christians, who spoke up and voted against certain things. Then in the *Washington Post* there were columns after columns laughing about their decisions on these cases. I think Christians are mocked and made fun of by mainstream America. I have even experienced that opposition personally from friends, in subtle ways, thinking me very odd to prefer to go to a church activity over a movie.

A few respond with resentment and anger, but most simply feel frustrated and disappointed. What bothers evangelicals about this is not so much the element of personal offense but the duplicity of a culture which professes openness to all views and the concern that America has gotten so far off-track that it positively discriminates against Christians. According to this Baptist man:

> It frustrates and annoys me probably more that anything. It sometimes angers me, depending on a situation. I may become very frustrated over it, feeling like I want to react strongly and dogmatically. But I feel like I have to be careful in what I say. It does sometimes anger me when I see some of the news reporting on some issues—abortion, homosexuality, free sex. Those things disgust and frustrate me. I have a sense of, what really can be done to stem the tide?

4. From another perspective on the same problem, this Charismatic woman in an independent denomination, observed: "When Christmas comes around, you can't have any mention of what it is about. But you can celebrate Halloween. That feels like discrimination. If schools take Christmas holidays, why aren't the kids being told the real reason why they are off and what we are celebrating? Now it has been turned into the "holiday season," it's not Christmas anymore."

Naturally, this perceived prejudice merely serves to heighten evangelicals' boundaries with the outside world, alienation from mainstream culture, and sense of displacement from their rightful American heritage. The distinction, engagement, and conflict are only intensified.

(For Some) A Sense of Menacing External Threats

Finally, at the farthest extreme of cultural tension and conflict, some, but certainly not all, evangelicals see external threats even more menacing than a displaced heritage and demotion to second-class citizenship. More than a few evangelicals are concerned by what they believe are increasingly powerful, organized groups in America with clearly anti-Christian agendas. To be sure, some evangelicals express tremendous self-confidence and see no particular conspiracy set on undermining Christianity. However, other evangelicals do discern rumblings of what they fear could become a frightful future. And yet others, a definite minority, are convinced that the barbarians are already now battering down the gates.[5]

Some, such as this Baptist man, tend to view the issue in terms of social movements and politics: "Yes, I see groups that are hostile to Christianity, absolutely. The whole homosexual movement is extremely anti-Christian, and very hostile towards anybody who would espouse a Christian view. I think the pro-choice movement is extremely hostile towards Christians and Christian values, because they see their freedom of choice limited by the Christian belief that says life has meaning and value. So they are very strongly against Christian groups." Others—particularly Pentecostals, it

---

5. George Marsden (1980) has suggested that analytical leverage may be gained by thinking about early twentieth-century fundamentalism as functioning as an ethnic group. Interestingly, the subcultural-identity dynamics described above find similar expression in the experience of ethnic minorities in the context of less-than-hospitable majorities. First-generation immigrants, new minorities in a new country, for example, tend to strengthen their sense of ethnic identities (for a classic statement, see Hansen 1952). From the evangelical perspective, perhaps the closest ethnic analogy is with native Americans, who once "owned" North America, but who were invaded and marginalized by an alien culture and displaced from their own land. Interestingly, Cornell (1988) has shown that a "supra-tribal" consciousness and identity-movement—closely analogous to modern evangelicalism's transdenominational religious movement—first emerged in the 1950s, when the United States federal government began a "termination policy" that threatened to dismantle completely the reservation system, the last refuge of autonomous Indian life. That was precisely when astute native Americans first really began to think of themselves more as pan-tribal "Indians" than as members of disconnected, local tribes, as "Menominees" or "Cherokees." It took exactly such an external threat to mobilize a collective Indian identity and resources to counter the threat. The parallel with the evangelical experience is striking.

seemed to us—like this Pentecostal woman, spoke more in terms of a spiritual battle between good and evil forces:

> I think there's a radical atheistic part out there, or your homosexuals, and the rest of them. As far as I know, those are the devil's people. I know they are. But they can be saved. Certainly, some are trying to turn America away from its Christian heritage. Certain radicals. Hey, we are in a battle here, you know, and the devil has his people. The Bible says it. "You are of your father, the devil," Jesus told somebody once. I'm talking about homosexual groups and atheist groups and the very liberal. We are in a spiritual battle on this earth. I see them as hostile and opposed to Christianity. And they try their best to get their laws passed. I am absolutely opposed to their beliefs, although I pray for them. Because they are just deceived by the devil, they don't know. Like I once was. I didn't know.

Throughout this interview, it was clear that many of this particular woman's views—which included conspiratorial theories about the Illuminati—were strongly influenced by Pat Robertson and his television program, *The 700 Club*. Yet others, such as this Presbyterian man, cast the battle more in terms of clashing ideologies and worldviews:

> There are two opposing views, a Christian worldview and a secular worldview. And one is going to be crowded out and denied their freedom to live by the standards they hold to. They might say "well just leave us alone," but the thing is they won't leave the Christian community alone. They are impinging on us. There is a war going on, and when you're in warfare, you battle to take ground, not just hold it. They're not just trying to hold ground, they are trying to take ground, which is our right to live in a Christian society. There are a lot of people that would deny us any rights. They aren't passive, they are active.

Summary

In these and other ways, modern American evangelicalism illustrates and corroborates the basic principles undergirding the subcultural identity theory of religion. Evangelicalism appears, indeed, to construct and maintain its collective identity largely by its members drawing symbolic boundaries that create distinction between themselves and relevant outgroups. It also appears that evangelicalism strategically renegotiates its collective religious identity by reformulating the way its constructed orthodoxy engages the changing sociocultural environment it confronts. For example, issues which in previous decades animated evangelical sensibilities—antimodernism, anticommunism, anti-Catholicism, sabbatarianism—have been gradually supplanted by new, more culturally "relevant" issues: moral relativism, social decay, homosexual rights, etc. Yet, in this process of "accommodation," evangelicals appear no more or less cognitively contaminated or ideologically compromised—judged on their own terms—than they were in previous decades.

Modern American evangelicals are also clearly able to establish strong religious identities and commitments in the face of the inescapable modern fact that each individual can and often must choose their own religion. Evangelicals are aware of alternatives to their own version of faith; indeed they are aware that many others think differently from and even critically of them. Yet, this does very little to undermine their own beliefs and commitments. This evangelical self-confidence appears related to the evangelicals' ability to define their values and norms and to positively evaluate their identities and actions in relation to reference groups of other Christians with similar values of evangelical engagement with the "world"; indeed, the perceived dissimilar and antagonistic outgroups of nonevangelical Christians and non-Christians seem capable of serving evangelicals as negative reference groups. Evangelicals, in other words, have fashioned for themselves a very effective "sacred umbrella" under which to live. It is apparent that modern pluralism facilitates for evangelicalism conditions that promote the formation of a strong religious subculture, which sustains a self-perceived semi-"deviant" identity. Likewise, tension and conflict between evangelicals and relevant outgroups appear positively to strengthen evangelical identity, solidarity, resources mobilization, and membership retention. Finally, these rapid sociocultural changes and the accompanying relativism that typify modernity clearly seem to increase for evangelicals the appeal of their own faith, which satisfies for them the felt needs and desires for stability, assurance, and truth—needs which modernity intensifies. Overall, the subcultural identity theory appears to render a fitting interpretation of modern American evangelicalism.

One Caveat

We have emphasized here the distinction, engagement, and conflict that evangelicals construct in their relations with the outside world because we believe they provide an important key to understanding evangelical religious vitality. But we do not wish to leave the impression that evangelicals are essentially or primarily a defensive, frightened, wounded lot. With different purposes in mind, we could have highlighted much different elements of their stories. We could have emphasized the contentment, openness, self-assurance, and joy that is also evident in evangelicals. We could have told of evangelicals who love rock-and-roll and opera, who have risen to positions of power in public universities, who operate in the world with warmth and amiability and broad-mindedness. The reality, of course, is complex and paradoxical. And all analytical interpretations actively frame and therefore necessarily simplify. Still, we think that the interpretation here is both descriptively accurate and analytically helpful. We only need to remember that to underscore certain real features of a movement or subculture for analytical reasons is not to tell all possible stories. It is simply to draw attention to one set of crucial factors that helps to answer one, specific question—ours being: what explains the vitality of contemporary American evangelicalism?

The Evangelical Subcultural Comparative Advantage

Evangelicalism as a case seems to fit well the expectations of the subcultural identity theory. But can subcultural identity theory also explain the differences in religious vitality in fundamentalist, mainline, and liberal Protestantism which we observed in chapter 2? We think it can.[6]

Fundamentalism

We suggest that the reason why fundamentalism as a religious tradition is somewhat less strong than evangelicalism on all of our measures of religious vitality is because its cultural tendency toward *defensive separatism* reduces its active engagement with the surrounding culture. Historically, fundamentalists have constructed a great deal of tension and conflict between themselves and the outside world. But fundamentalism processed that tension and conflict by erecting high and strong subcultural walls behind which to preserve the purity of faith (Marsden 1980: 176–95). Premillennial dispensationalism gave fundamentalists the theological rationale for withdrawing from political involvement, shunning efforts at social reform, and abandoning the surrounding culture to its inevitable descent into perdition. What mattered was not transforming the world for Christ, but

6. Although we also offered comparative data on Roman Catholics in our tables, the sampling design of our interviews (see Appendix A) does not enable us to do an adequately informed subcultural-identity analysis of American Roman Catholicism. That story will have be written elsewhere.

remaining theologically and morally pure until Christ's Second Coming. Thus, the fundamentalist tradition does sustain clear distinction within a pluralistic environment—one of the two necessary factors that subcultural identity theory suggests generate religious strength. But the fundamentalist tradition lacks the second necessary factor: a sustained, active presence in and engagement with the surrounding culture. Fundamentalism, by choice, lacks the cultural tools to maintain an alert orientation toward social partic-ipation and influence; to reinforce the belief that faith must be integrated into and transform every aspect of human life; to provide for the construc-tion of a vision for an orthodoxy that is engaged with the outside world.

Without this orientation toward active, involved social presence and en-gagement, fundamentalism has become somewhat detached from the po-tential challenges of the world, less compelled to be always on guard, ral-lying for action, strategizing to have an influence, and mobilizing resources to counter threats. Fundamentalism's defensive separatism also reduces its chances of encountering self-identity-reinforcing exposure to and tension with hostile outgroups. Relatively safely protected in a subcultural cocoon, fundamentalism has been able to afford to grow somewhat relaxed, disen-gaged, inward-looking. The felt challenge of mission, burden for history and the world, and urgent need to response to threats and crises—all of which work to energize evangelicalism—begin in fundamentalism to grow dull. The edge of fundamentalism's religious vitality wears off. Under these conditions, defending fundamental doctrinal truths can easily devolve into merely embalming them. The challenge of world evangelism can easily drift into routinized door-to-door "soul winning" rituals. And rather nar-row lists of activities that define "worldliness" can begin to render a host of other culturally mainstream practices available to be uncritically absorbed. Thus, fundamentalism's subculturally constructed isolation and disengage-ment eventually produce detectable traces of religious passivity and slack-ening.

We do not wish to suggest here that all of contemporary fundamental-ism can be characterized as separatistic, isolated, and disengaged. The real-ity is more ambiguous than that. For one thing, significant sectors of fun-damentalism appear to have become "evangelicalized," that is, convinced that social and cultural engagement is valuable and necessary. For another, not everyone who self-identifies as a fundamentalist is closely tied to the fundamentalist movement, ideologically or organizationally. Nevertheless, much of contemporary fundamentalism still retains noticeable vestiges of its separatistic cultural heritage. And those vestiges shape its prevailing outlook and experience. Many recent ethnographies of contemporary fundamentalism report that the tradition still perpetuates its separatist heritage. Nancy Tatom Ammerman's (1987) fine study of a fundamentalist church in Connecticut, for example, reveals that "separation from the world" remains a key tenet among fundamentalists. And Alan Peshkin (1986) characterizes the fundamentalist high school in Illinois which he studied as a self-enclosed "total world" whose members together lead ideologically and relationally isolated lives. Our own interviews with fundamentalists around the country also revealed some of their tendencies toward separatism and disengagement. This fundamentalist Baptist man, for example, argued:

> Many Christians emphasize being involved in the culture and trying to win back or reform the culture. It partly comes from Reformed theology, which says that we're gonna evangelize the whole world and everything is gonna get better. I don't believe that at all. I'm not sanguine about things getting better until the Lord Jesus Christ comes and rules. So I'm not a radical activist at all. I think a lot of efforts to change the world are really misguided. The Scriptures says we're strangers, and our citizenship is in heaven, not this earth. I think we should pray for our leaders, for God to guide them so that they can lead decent lives. But I have no interest in blowing up Satan's ammunition depot. I expect God to do that, in his good time. I have no hope that things are gonna get any better.[7]

Sectors of contemporary fundamentalism do retain at least remnants of the tradition's separatist heritage, if not the entire ideological and lifestyle package. We suggest that this helps to explain fundamentalism's consistently marginally lower levels of religious vitality, compared with evangelicalism, which we saw in chapter 2. Evangelicalism thrives on the combination of both distinction from and engagement with pluralistic modernity. But the fundamentalist cultural toolkit lacks the instruments needed to generate sustained social and cultural engagement with the outside world. And distinction from the world alone is not enough to engender in fundamentalism exceptional religious vitality.

7. He continues: "The Scripture talks about 'tearing down strongholds,' but I think those strongholds are inside of each one of us, not out there [in the world]. That stronghold is what Satan has got inside me, occupying territory which prevents me from appropriating the truth of God's word."

Mainline and Liberal Protestants

If fundamentalism's cultural toolkit generates the deficient subcultural orientation of distinction-without-engagement, mainline and liberal Protestantism are beset by the exact opposite tendency: engagement-without-
distinction. And this cultural orientation appears even more inadequate
than fundamentalism's in its ability to generate religious vitality.

According to our own interview data and evidence from other studies,
faith for mainline Protestants is often viewed as a part of an inherited, general way of life. Being religious is simply part of the common cultural furniture. Christianity tends to consist of a somewhat compartmentalized
churchgoing cultural practice, a way to participate as a good citizen in one's
local community. Conspicuously absent, typically, is the all-encompassing,
fervent, mobilizing, missionary view of faith reflected in evangelicalism.
Instead, mainline Protestants prefer a "quieter," more sedate and respectable expression of Christianity (Sikkink and Smith 1996). Mainline Protestantism thus reflects a relative lack of oppositional engagement in or tension with mainstream society. Indeed, almost by definition, mainline
Protestantism *is* mainstream society. What mutes mainline Protestantism's
capacity to generate religious vitality, then, in our view, is its nearly complete enculturation into the mainstream.

Similarly, what weakens liberal Protestantism as a religious tradition is
its radical cultural accommodation (using that concept self-consciously—
see chapter 4). The liberal Protestant tradition suffers decline, in part, because it has lost a strong sense of Christian distinctiveness in worldview,
ethics, and mission. Many liberal Protestants, we saw at the end of chapter
2, are happy to blur or erase the boundaries between Christianity and other
religions and ideologies (also see Reeves 1996). The publicly oriented,
social-activist aspect of the liberal Protestant heritage appears to have faded
well into that tradition's background (Regnerus and Smith 1998a). What
is left, primarily, it appears, is the tradition's one other characteristic trait:
the desire to reinterpret Christian faith in terms of the categories, values,
and commitments of the modern (and now postmodern) world. Much of
what modern elite sensibilities view as distinctive, oppositional, and unbe-
coming about Christianity has been demythologized out of liberal Protestantism. And with that has gone the cultural basis for a distinctively religious contrast, resistance, tension, or challenge. As a consequence, liberal
Protestantism's religious vitality is low and declining.

Many mainline and liberal church leaders and observers are aware of this dynamic, as Thomas Reeves (1996: 10; also see Newman 1993; Woodward 1993) describes:

> A 1985 study revealed that laity in the United Church of Christ
> ... had a great difficulty in identifying anything distinctive about
> their denomination. The sociologist William M. Newman concluded that little more than freedom of religious choice and religious tolerance, practiced at the local level, could be found. "Of
> course, these themes are entirely consistent with broader civic values in the United States." In 1993, bishops of the United Methodist Church's Executive Committee pushed their official papers
> aside and for three hours spoke earnestly about such questions as,
> "What does it mean to be a United Methodist?" and "What, if
> anything, is distinctive about our church?" ... At the Episcopal
> Church's General Convention of 1994, the House of Bishops fell
> into bitter quarrels about homosexuality, concluding that each
> prelate would deal with the issue as he or she pleased. Two weary
> observers exclaimed: "The Episcopal Church is an institution in
> free fall. We have nothing at all to hold on to, no shared belief, no
> common assumptions, no agreed bottom line, no accepted definition of what an Episcopalian is or believes."

In short, the twin Achilles' heels of mainline and liberal Protestantism's strategy of engagement-without-distinction are enculturation and accommodation. Conversely, the central cultural deficiency in fundamentalism's strategy of distinction-without-engagement is defensive separatism. And creating an alternative that avoids the weaknesses of all of these is the evangelical strategy of engaged orthodoxy, distinction-with-engagement, which is the subcultural combination that best fosters religious vitality.[8]

Summary

A great deal of religious history indicates that religious groups tend to gravitate over time toward one of two distinct positions vis-à-vis their social

---

8. To be clear, again (see the Preface), this analysis makes no judgments about the ultimate spiritual truthfulness or faithfulness of any of these traditions. We are certainly not claiming here that evangelicalism is somehow better or more Christian than fundamentalism or liberalism. Certainly, few people, whether religious or secular, would suggest that external measures of success are reliable indicators of moral or ontological truth. All we, as sociologists, are saying here is that evangelicalism is a stronger religious tradition—as "strength" is viewed, operationalized, and measured sociologically—than are the traditions with which we are comparing it.

environments. Some groups—often labeled "sectarian"—tend to generate high degrees of tension with the societies they occupy and so withdraw from extensive participation in mainstream society. This has been the characteristic historical strategy of the American fundamentalist movement. Other groups—sometimes called "churchly"—greatly reduce any tension between themselves and their surrounding cultures and so integrate comfortably into mainstream society. This has been the characteristic strategy of American mainline and liberal Protestantism. But subcultural identity theory suggests that both tendencies comprise significant cultural deficiencies, which it expects will lead, over time, to decline in religious vitality. The American evangelical movement, by contrast, has been relatively successful because it has managed to formulate and sustain a religious strategy that maintains both high tension with and high integration into mainstream American society simultaneously. Evangelical sensibilities allow neither complete disengagement from nor total assimilation into the dominant culture. This provokes a situation of sustained dissonance, if not outright conflict, between evangelical believers and the nonevangelical world with which they—with tension—engage. And this fosters religious vitality.

In other words, we might say that centripetal forces pull fundamentalists inward, increasing their tension and reducing their engagement with society. Centrifugal forces, however, pull mainline and liberal Protestants outward, decreasing their tension with and increasing their assimilation into society. But evangelicalism uses its cultural tools to construct a subcultural reality in which counterbalancing centripetal and centrifugal forces pull against each other in dynamic tension, maintaining both difference from and engagement with American society. This, we suggest, has been an important element of the evangelical "formula" for success.

Again, the importance of sociocultural pluralism in all of this is crucial. Without pluralism, distinction-with-engagement would be difficult to produce. But, in fact, modernity's pluralism offers evangelicalism a favorable environment within which to construct a thriving subculture. Contemporary pluralism creates a situation in which evangelicals can perpetually maintain but can never resolve their struggle with the nonevangelical world. On the one hand, pluralism does not exterminate evangelicalism; on the other, pluralism does not allow evangelicalism's complete success. Outright persecution is minimized, but anything close to a Christ-centered society is made impossible. This situation, then, continually maintains the contest, the struggle, the tension for evangelicals, who feel compelled to continue to carry on their mission as "salt and light" in the "needy world." And it is precisely the tension-generating confrontation between the activist, expansive, engaging evangelical subculture and the pluralistic, nonevangelical dominant culture that it inhabits—which to evangelicals seems increasingly hostile and in need of redemptive influence—that generates evangelicalism's vitality. It is precisely evangelicalism's heavy exposure to and engagement with modern pluralism—and the attendant distinctions, tensions, and conflicts that necessarily arise—which reinforces evangelical boundaries, identity, solidarity, mobilization, and membership retention.

At the same time, according to the subcultural identity theory, an essential determinant of any religious tradition's ability to adapt and thrive in pluralism is the actual content of its theology, the substance of its social vision, the nature of its cultural strategy for interacting with the surrounding world. Structural and ecological factors alone cannot explain religious strength. The subcultural identity theory also compels us to analyze the cultural content of religious discourse, subcultural narratives, and theological rationales for this-worldly action. In our case, we have seen that evangelicalism's "engaged orthodoxy" has proven effective in engendering religious strength. By contrast, fundamentalism's heritage of defensive separatism appears to have formed a subcultural orientation that has proven less effective. And mainline and liberal Protestantism's cultural bearings have proven even less so.[9]

Closing Theoretical Reflections

We view the subcultural identity theory elaborated in this chapter as highly compatible with the already established "competitive marketing" or "religious economy" theories advanced by Finke, Stark, Ianaccone, and others. Although we ourselves are not enamored with rational choice theories in general, we do view subcultural identity theory as complimenting rather than challenging existing theories which suggest that pluralism benefits religion.

Subcultural identity theory's relationship to both Kelly and Ianaccone's versions of "strictness" theory is more questionable. We suggest that whatever is insightful in theories of strictness may be subsumable within the subcultural theory proposed here. We suspect that perhaps strictness itself is not the cause of religious strength but another *consequence* of some reli-

9. The approach of our argument here is theoretically indebted to Robert Wuthnow's (1987, 1989b) work on ideological selection, which seeks to account for the influence of both social conditions and human agency.

gious traditions' engagement and tension with outgroups in a pluralistic society. It may actually be engagement and tension which generate religious vitality (and strictness), and not strictness itself. If so, then strictness theories may be confusing outcomes with causes and mistakenly attributing causal power to what is merely an associated by-product of intergroup distinction, engagement, tension, and conflict. That, however, is only our suspicion, not our firm position.

What about status discontent theory? By arguing that evangelicalism is thriving, at least in part, because it is self-embattled with oppositional forces, are we merely restating the gist of status discontent theory? Or are we saying something different? We can begin by saying that our subcultural identity theory is fundamentally different in focus and logic from economistic versions of status discontent theory—such as Lester Thurow's crude, mechanistic interpretation of fundamentalism (1996: 232). "Lifestyle defense" versions of status discontent theory, however, seem to us perhaps somewhat more compatible with our approach. Both it and our theory claim that a religious group's perception of outside threats is related to its internal energy and strength. And both suggest that religious groups that perceive no threats to themselves will likely become complacent and routinized. Significant discrepancies between the two theories remain, however, which reflect differences in how they frame the problem conceptually. Lifestyle defense theory tends to portray mobilized religious groups as taking a defensive, reactive posture; and as being exclusively concerned with protecting their own narrow interests and practices. It tends to focus on single, issue-oriented case studies of newly energized religious groups, such as the Kanawa County textbook controversy (Page and Clelland 1978). And it suggests diadic situational structures of single activated lifestyle groups under attack by single dominating adversaries. The subcultural identity theory frames the problem differently. It tends to view strong, activist religious groups as operating out of a more proactive, offensive orientation; and as motivated more by a this-worldly, other-concerned desire positively to influence the world beyond itself. Furthermore, it suggests the need to analyze not simply local, issue-oriented case studies but broad subcultural traditions that interact over time. Finally, the subcultural identity approach presumes not a diadic situational structure, but a multiplicity of collective actors contending together on a complex, multivocal, multicultural field. In these ways, it seems to us that the lifestyle defense theory too narrowly and inadequately frames the causal logic explaining religious vitality and thus offers an insufficient and somewhat misleading explanatory approach to our problem. We therefore suggest, again, subsuming and reorganizing the valuable elements that do exist in lifestyle defense theory into what we think is the broader, more nuanced subcultural identity theory.[10]

It goes without saying that the subcultural identity theory we propose here is most at odds with Berger and Hunter's "sheltered enclave" theory. Little common ground appears to exist between the two.

Conclusion

In this chapter, we have tried to utilize the subcultural identity theory of religious strength to interpret evangelicalism's religious vitality, relative to fundamentalist and, especially, mainline and liberal Protestantism. We have argued that evangelicalism capitalizes on its culturally pluralistic environment to socially construct subcultural distinction, engagement, and tension between itself and relevant outgroups, and that this enhances evangelicalism's religious strength. The evangelical movement, we have claimed, flourishes on difference, engagement, tension, conflict, and threat. Its strength, therefore, should be understood as the result of the combination of its socially-constructed cultural distinction vis-à-vis and vigorous sociocultural engagement with pluralistic modernity.

In chapter 7, we continue our investigation of American evangelicalism by exploring ways in which some of the very same factors that strengthen evangelicalism as a religious tradition may also have the paradoxical effect of undermining evangelicalism's strategic efforts at faith-based social change. But first, in the next chapter, we take a detour, briefly turning our attention away from our analysis of American evangelicalism specifically, in order to survey the issue of religious belief-plausibility in America more generally.

10. The subcultural identity theory would also seem to suggest implications for the old church-sect theory, since both highlight the importance of variations in tension with society for the character of religious groups' experiences. Without spending many words to elaborate, subcultural identity theory appears to suggest that the bipolar, unidimensional spectrum implicit in church-sect theory inadequately portrays the available positions different religious groups might construct. By our account, for example, evangelicalism seems to combine elements of both church and sect into a distinctive orientation not readily located on the church-sect continuum. Rather than conceptualizing religious positions as values on a continuous variable (for example, church-sect, conservative-liberal), we think it is more accurate and fruitful to conceptualize religious positions as categorical variables, whose "values" reflect distinct qualities not reducible to placement on a single scale. Furthermore, our evidence should undercut any lingering notion that the sect inevitably evolves into church. For evangelicalism and fundamentalism both appear to be perpetually sustaining tension with society, even if that tension produces somewhat different outcomes.

Excursus: Belief Plausibility in
Modern America

In the last chapter, we advanced broad arguments about the positive prospects for traditional religion in the modern world. We suggested that well-adapted religions, at least, can not only survive, but may actually thrive in modern society. However, our primary empirical referent so far has been contemporary American evangelicalism, the strongest major religious tradition in America today. One might ask: has our perspective been biased by our focus on a subculture with such religious vitality? By primarily studying such a strong religious tradition, might we be naively misinterpreting religion's prospects more broadly? Perhaps outside of the few very strong religious subcultures like evangelicalism, secularization is proceeding apace, not only at the macrostructural level, but also at the level of individual consciousness. Possibly, outside of evangelical circles, Peter Berger is right: modern pluralism is eroding people's capacity to maintain traditional religious beliefs and practices. We certainly did see, for example, higher levels of doubt about religious faith among members of other religious traditions we surveyed. Does that not undermine our subcultural identity theory and suggest that secularization theory is generally accurate when it comes to religious belief plausibility?

To answer these questions, in this chapter we set aside our focus on American evangelicalism to investigate those Americans at the opposite end of the religious-vitality spectrum. Here we examine practicing American Protestants and all Roman Catholics who reported on our survey that in the last few years they "often"—not "sometimes," "once or twice," or "never"—have had doubts about whether their Christian beliefs are true.[1] We will call them "doubters." We also investigate those among all Ameri-

---

1. The survey question on doubts was only asked of churchgoing Protestants and all Roman Catholics; it was not asked of Protestants who reported infrequent attendance at church services.

cans who reported on our survey that, despite having been raised in a religious family, they now as adults consider themselves not religious. These we will call "defectors." By examining those American Christians whose own faith is most doubtful, and those who have grown up to abandon the religion of their youth, we hope to shed greater light on the dynamics of religious belief plausibility and implausibility in modern America.

To accomplish this, we compiled lists of all doubters and defectors among our survey respondents. Altogether, from our total of 2,591 respondents, 114 Roman Catholics and churchgoing Protestants reported doubting their religious faith "often" (unfortunately, the sampling frame unavoidably omitted nominal Protestants from our sample, which certainly biases the results somewhat[2]; still, we believe this analysis of doubters is useful and instructive, as long as we keep this point in mind). And seventy-six of all respondents reported themselves as being not now religious, despite having been raised in a religious family. We then called back from these lists a sample of forty doubters (35 percent of doubters) and interviewed them over the telephone about the nature, causes, and consequences of their doubts. We also called a sample of thirty-four defectors (45 percent of defectors) and asked about their religious histories and reasons for leaving the faith of their families of origin. We were pleasantly surprised when all but one each of the doubters and the defectors we called agreed to participate in the follow-up interviews (98 percent and 97 percent cooperation rates, respectively), despite the potentially sensitive nature of the questions; and that those we interviewed were very open and candid with their answers. All interviews, which typically lasted about ten minutes each, were tape-recorded and transcribed (Appendix C contains the interview schedules).

Doubters

The conclusions that our investigation of religious doubters support are that relatively few practicing Christians suffer from religious doubt; that the skepticism and uncertainty of most of those few who do doubt "often"

---

2. Although our survey question about doubts was asked of all American Roman Catholics—both active and nominal—for Protestants, unfortunately, it was only asked of churchgoers; because of this unavoidable sampling constraint, we are certainly underestimating here those Protestants whose frequent doubts have resulted in withdrawal from church or have profoundly transformed their religious beliefs. We may also have underestimated the proportion of intense (relative to mild) doubting; but to what extent we cannot know.

actually prove largely nonthreatening to their religious faith; and that almost none of these people's religious doubts appear to be caused by factors having anything to do with features of social life that are uniquely modern—that is, modernity's imposing cultural pluralism, technical rationality, and institutional differentiation.

To begin, according to our survey data, only 5.3 percent of churchgoing American Christians "often" have doubts about their religious beliefs. The majority of practicing American Christians appear fully able to maintain their religious beliefs with few or no doubts. Nonetheless, some American Christians do doubt their beliefs often. Our follow-up telephone interviews with them explored the intensity, focus, causes, and outcomes of their recurrent doubts (see table 6.1).

To begin, we see that most recurrent doubting about religious beliefs is of only mild intensity. Twenty-seven of the forty frequent doubters we interviewed (68 percent) reported that their doubts do not significantly challenge or threaten their faith at all. These people say they do have questions, uncertainties, and reservations about various aspects of their faith. But they never really undermine the security or importance of their belief commitments. One Lutheran woman from New Jersey, a typical example, said, "I do not do anything to try to resolve my doubts, I just live with them. They don't worry me, I have accepted that I'm going to have some doubts. Someday, I will find out if I'm right or wrong." Four of the forty doubters we interviewed (10 percent) reported experiencing doubts at a more moderate level of intensity. Their doubts are more deeply troubling. This Anglican woman from Nevada, for instance, remarked, "At times my doubts really bother me, because I grew up in church all my life, so they kind of go against what I do believe inside. So there is a kind of a conflict there." Nonetheless, she says, her doubts would never make her abandon her faith. At yet a higher level of intensity, four of the forty doubters we interviewed (10 percent of our sample, and one-half of one percent of all practicing Christians) reported suffering profound doubts about their religious faith. These people's doubts are acute and sometimes crippling. One Baptist man from Michigan, for example, was genuinely anguished by the contradictions he feels between a variety of theological teachings he believes and the world which he sees as full of suffering and injustice. He detailed his struggles to us over the phone for more than half an hour, almost begging us for any help or advice we could give him. He lamented,

Table 6.1: Characteristics of Frequent Doubters' Doubts about Religious Faith (frequencies)

Intensity		Focus		Causes		Outcomes	
Intense	4	God	15	Personal Tragedies	5	Easy Continuance	20
Moderate	4	Church	7	Others' Sufferings	6	Difficult Struggle	6
Mild	27	Doctrines	6	Minor Intellectual Questions	8	Withdrawal	8
No Doubts	5	Self	6	Others' Hypocrisy	8	Transform Faith	1
		Don't Know	1	Own Daily Troubles	4		
				Own Flawed Life	3		
				Don't Know	1		
N	(40)		(35)		(35)		(35)

I don't like it. It is nice when you have your beliefs all down and can live life according to this code. But when you are in doubt, like me, you never really know where you are at. That's why I'm trying to explain it all to you. I wish I could come to that nice place where I believe, and can follow my beliefs, and just feel comfortable.

But he simply could not. And many years of Bible study, counseling, discussions with fellow church-members, prayer, and tithing more than ten percent of his income did not seem to have helped. Still, he struggled on in his beliefs and in attending church. Lastly, we discovered in our follow-up interviews that five of the forty "doubters" we called (13 percent) say they actually never really do have doubts. This might be due to social desirability effects (that is, reporting what one thinks the interviewer wants to hear) of our follow-up call, or possibly to interviewer error or respondent fatigue in the original survey. In any case, it suggests that even the best telephone surveys may overreport even the relatively low levels of religious doubting by religious Americans. Fully 80 percent of self-reported frequent doubters among practicing Christians, we see, maintain their religious beliefs in the face of only mild skepticism or uncertainty. And, insofar as our follow-up interviews represent the population of doubters more broadly, we see that only one-half of one percent of churchgoing Christians in America suffer intense religious doubts about their beliefs.

What, then, do our thirty-five recurrent doubters (eliminating the five who do not actually doubt) have doubts about (see table 6.1)? Fifteen of the thirty-five real doubters (43 percent) have doubts about God: Does God exist? How can God allow evil and injustice? Is Jesus really divine? Seven of the thirty-five (20 percent) have doubts about organized religion: Why do priests sexually abuse kids? Why are so many churchgoers hypocrites? Why won't the Church recognize my divorce? Six of the sample of frequent doubters (17 percent) were doubtful about specific theological doctrines: Is there really a heaven? Does the Bible contain errors? Might not other religions be truthful in their own ways? Another six of the doubters actually doubt not their religious beliefs, but themselves: Am I living up to what God expects from me? Do I really understand my faith adequately? Why do I so often fail morally? Finally, one person reported having doubts but could not remember about what, even when we probed.

Most varied were the reasons frequent doubters gave for why they doubt so often (table 6.1). Five of the thirty-five (14 percent) said that personal tragedy and suffering had provoked doubts in them. These included one respondent's daughter being born with Downs Syndrome, heart defects, and a cleft palate; one respondent's favorite college professor and his daughter were killed when their car was hit by a train; and other respondents who suffered untimely deaths of family members, both children and parents. Six of the thirty-five recurrent doubters (17 percent) reported that awareness of *other* people's suffering and injustices made them question God's love and power. A few of these were also troubled by animal suffering. Why would a good and omnipotent personal God allow poverty, disease, violence, and other atrocities to oppress and destroy so many people? Eight of the thirty-five frequent doubters (23 percent) recounted how (what were to them) relatively minor intellectual questions bother them: Will we really meet all of our loved ones in heaven? What happens to sincere unbelievers when they die? Is the Baptist way really better than the Methodist way? Another eight of the doubters (23 percent) are aggravated by what they see as other religious people's hypocrisy. Why do rich churchgoers look down on poor churchgoers? Why did the priest get drunk at my wedding? Four of the thirty-five doubters (11 percent) cited ordinary but fatiguing daily troubles in their own lives for causing doubts. These included the stresses associated with working, moving, changing jobs, losing relationships, paying bills, and disciplining kids. Three of the thirty-five (9 percent) pointed to their own weakness of faith and moral flaws as the sources of their religious doubts. Lastly, one respondent simply could not articulate what caused his doubts.

Finally, we examined the outcomes of our frequent doubters' doubts (table 6.1). Fully twenty of the thirty-five (57 percent) appeared simply to continue on in their religious lives fairly effortlessly, despite their recurrent doubting. Their doubts simply did not significantly burden or trouble them. This man who attends a nondenominational church in Virginia, for example, was typical in this regard: "My doubts don't bother me—we are made to question, that's part of what makes us spiritual beings. I consider myself a strong and confident spiritual person. I talk with family and friends about my doubts, and if we resolve them, fine; and if we don't, that is okay too." On the other hand, six of the thirty-five (17 percent) experience their doubts as difficult, ongoing struggles. While none of these said that they had profoundly revised or abandoned their faith, nor intend to in the future, they all disclosed ongoing emotional and spiritual turmoil. This Roman Catholic woman from Illinois, whose child was born with birth defects, for example, explains:

When bad things happen in your life, you wonder why God would
do such things. I still struggle through. It's like having a fight with
your husband and getting mad and not talking to him for a while:
your religion is there for you, but you are just not really happy with
what is going on. I know this too will pass. But I don't pray as
much as I used to, because I still think there is some anger there.

Similarly, this Pennsylvanian woman (who could not recall her church's
denomination), who had recently suffered many deaths of young ones in
her extended family, said, "When things don't seem to go right, I just look
up and say, 'Hey, are you there? Can you see that I need help here?' Sometimes I doubt if God exists, but I don't give up my faith. God may not
shine on me today, but someday He will." Another strategy for dealing
with frequent religious doubts, however, was to withdraw, at least tempo-
rarily, from church attendance and participation. Eight of our thirty-five
doubters (23 percent) reported pulling away from church when they
doubted. Some of these expressed an interest in returning to church; others
seemed to be headed toward more long-term withdrawal. Finally, only one
of our sample of frequent doubters (3 percent) declared that his doubts
had caused him to radically change his religious beliefs. After this Roman
Catholic man's two-year old son died, he rejected the idea of an immanent,
personal God in favor of an image of God as an impersonal force which
does not dictate events on earth and with which humans cannot communicate. When tragedies happen, he now believes, it is simply bad luck, nothing more. He claims to be more comfortable with these new beliefs.

The relationship between the causes, focus, intensity, and outcomes of
frequent religious doubts appear to be clearly patterned (see table 6.2). For
instance, personal tragedies, suffering in the world, and ordinary life troubles tend to provoke doubts about the existence and character of God: Can
a personal, loving God really exist that would allow such evils? By contrast,
those who are troubled by what they view as other people's hypocrisy tend
to focus their doubts on organized religion: What is the value of a church
whose leaders and members act as badly as everyone else? Those who
struggle at a more intellectual level with their faith tend to focus their
doubts on theological and doctrinal matters, often involving heaven and
hell, predestination, baptism, and the like. Finally, the few whose doubts
are generated by their own spiritual and moral flaws tend to focus their
apprehensions not on the plausibility of their religion or value of their
churches, per se, but on their own abilities to live up to the demands of
their faith.

Table 6.2: Effects of Causes of Frequent Doubters' Doubts about Religious Faith (frequencies)

| | Causes | | | | | |
	Personal Tragedies	Others' Sufferings	Own Daily Troubles	Others' Hypocrisy	Intellectual Questions	Own Flawed Life
Focus						
God	5	6	3	—	1	—
Church	—	—	—	7	—	—
Doctrines	—	—	—	1	5	—
Self	—	—	1	—	2	3
Intensity						
Mild	—	4	3	8	8	3
Moderate	2	1	1	—	—	—
Intense	3	1	—	—	—	—
Outcomes						
Easy Continuance	—	5	2	2	7	3
Difficult Struggle	4	1	1	—	—	—
Withdrawal	—	—	1	6	1	—
Altered Beliefs	1	—	—	—	—	—
N	(5)	(6)	(4)	(8)	(8)	(3)

Note: This table excludes the one case in which the respondent could not articulate the cause or focus of frequent doubts.

The causes of doubt also affect their intensity and consequences (table 6.2). Personal tragedies understandably generate the greatest intensity of doubt and are most likely to produce ongoing, difficult struggles with doubt and, in a few cases, provoke major revisions of belief. In cases of doubt caused by others' suffering and by ordinary life troubles, the intensity of people's doubt decreased and their ability to continue easily in their religious lives, despite their doubts, increased. Doubts generated by others' hypocrisy, intellectual questions, and one's own spiritual flaws are all experienced as mild in intensity. However, perceptions of hypocrisy tend to result in withdrawal from organized religion; while people seem to manage simply to continue on fairly effortlessly in their religious lives when their doubts are rooted in either their intellectual questions or own spiritual flaws.

Returning to our larger question, what does all this tell us about religious belief plausibility in modern America? We have already noted that only 5.3 percent of churchgoing American Protestants and Roman Catholics "often" have doubts about their religious beliefs. And we have seen that relatively few frequent doubters have their faith profoundly undermined by their doubts. Most merely proceed with their lives fairly effortlessly. Even many of those who suffer awful personal tragedies simply struggle on through their lives, holding on stubbornly to their faith. The woman who had recently suffered many deaths of young ones in her extended family stated that doubts are "just part of life" and that she is "not ready to toss in the towel yet." Meanwhile, she is teaching her own children about Jesus and God. The woman whose favorite college professor was killed by a train, and whose mother later unexpectedly died of cancer, although she still struggles greatly, reported that she attends church regularly and serves on the church outreach committee. The mother whose baby was born with multiple birth defects said that she thinks doubting reflects a strong religious faith, that she is not going to give up her religious beliefs, and that she knows that "the only reason I am getting through this time is that God is still with me." And one woman we interviewed whose young son had died said religious doubts were not a threat to avoid but a necessary "working through her faith" (indeed, respondents we asked tended strongly to maintain that doubts more likely reflect a strong and confident faith rather than a weakness of faith).

It is true that a number of those who doubt often withdraw from regular participation in organized religion. But even so, many of these say that they still attend church somewhat irregularly, or that they hope to start attending church again soon, or that they believe they will return to church when they have children. Even some of the people most alienated from church proudly declare their commitment to their religious faith. For example, this Roman Catholic man who complained of rude and abusive priests nevertheless reported, "I don't go to church, but I still believe and pray to the man upstairs, you know what I am saying? Your life doesn't end because you don't go to church—you have to keep in contact with the man upstairs. Without him, your life is nothing." This may not sound like ideal orthodox Christian faith, but then again it hardly represents Berger's (1967) modern human, whose old religious beliefs collapse in the face of modernity's pluralism and rationalization. Mostly, it sounds like a version of the popular religiosity voiced by many ordinary Roman Catholic believers throughout many centuries of Church history. Has all that much really changed with the coming of modern society?

Perhaps the most significant conclusion emerging from these follow-up interviews concerns the causes of people's recurrent doubts: almost none of them have anything to do with features of social life that are uniquely modern. Personal tragedies and heartaches, evil and suffering in the world, human hypocrisy, the daily troubles of life, and feelings of moral and spiritual inadequacy have existed since time immemorial. They are human universals, historical constants, not problems that particularly afflict modern people. We have no sound basis for believing, then, that anything particular to modernity itself has become the cause of a significant decline in the plausibility of religious belief. Even the more intellectually based doubts about certain doctrines that some respondents voiced appear to have little to do with uniquely modern factors. Christian believers throughout centuries have wrestled with problems surrounding baptism, human freedom, God's sovereignty, heaven, hell, and the like. None of this is new. And, in any case, we have seen (table 6.2) that these intellectually driven religious doubts are typically experienced as quite mild and generally produce in the doubters little difficult struggle or belief transformation. It hardly appears these doubts will generate a mass erosion of religious faith.

This interpretation is supported by answers our interview respondents gave to questions about the effects of higher education and religious pluralism on their beliefs. The vast majority of those we interviewed who had gone to college maintained, when asked, that their experience of higher education did nothing to cause them to doubt their religious beliefs. One person did say that some philosophy of religion courses she took in college did cause her to doubt her faith. On the other hand, at least three respondents claimed that their university educations actually strengthened their faith. Likewise, the vast majority of people we interviewed maintained that being aware of so many different religions in society and the world did nothing to undermine their own faith. They said things like, "I don't care what other people say or believe. I am my own person. I believe what I think is right and the way my parents brought me up"; and "I have been to different churches and heard about other people's religions, but I always come back to my own"; and, simply, "I have wondered about it. But then I look at it like, people come from different cultures. And different cultures have different beliefs." Again, people's "sacred umbrellas" appear more than capable of sustaining religious commitments in pluralistic situations. A small handful of respondents did say that their awareness of religious pluralism has caused them to doubt their own beliefs. But in each case, they also stated that their doubts were really little more than minor questions; or that working through their doubts was healthy for their faith; or that they still believed, in the face of religious pluralism, that their own faith was correct and that they would never consider giving up their own beliefs.

These conclusions are also supported by General Social Survey (GSS) data about religious doubting in America (see table 6.3). On a seven-point scale, for example, ranging from "no doubts" to "faith mixed with doubts" (a relatively mild statement about doubting), 61 percent of Americans placed themselves between points one and three, indicating that they have few doubts about their religious faith. More than one-quarter said their faith was completely free from doubts. Regarding the various kinds of problems that may cause people to doubt their faith (table 6.3), again we see that most claim that these concerns never cause doubts. And comparing the distributions of people who do doubt, we see that causes of doubt which are historical universals (evil in the world, personal suffering) are twice as likely to make people doubt "often" as those that are more clearly grounded in modernity (conflict of faith and science, feeling life has no meaning).

If the human condition of life in modernity is one of diminished religious belief plausibility, heightened incapacity to sustain traditional faith, and an extensive erosion of religious conviction at the level of individual consciousness, we have found little evidence of that here. Not simply among the most strongly religious, but even among those who most frequently have doubts about their religious beliefs, we see that, for believers, traditional religious faith remains quite resilient in its plausibility—despite

Table 6.3: The Extent and Basis of Religious Doubting in
America (percent)

To what extent is your religious faith affected by doubts? (scale of 1 to 7)	
1 Faith completely free of doubts	27
2	18
3	16
4	17
5	9
6	5
7 Faith is mixed with doubts	7
Don't Know	< 1
How often have these problems caused doubts about your religious faith?:	
Evil in the world	
Often	11
Sometimes	37
Never	50
Don't Know	2
Personal suffering	
Often	9
Sometimes	44
Never	45
Don't Know	2
Conflict of faith and science	
Often	5
Sometimes	25
Never	65
Don't Know	4
Feeling that life really has no meaning	
Often	4
Sometimes	18
Never	76
Don't Know	2
N	(1,462)

Source: General Social Survey, 1988–91.

modernity's cultural pluralism, technical rationality, and structural differ-entiation. In the words of Clifford Geertz (1983: 80), people are simply quite able to "plug the dikes of their most needed beliefs with whatever mud they can find." And the religious doubts that do trouble some religious people appear to spring not from anything distinctively modern, but from timeless and universal human difficulties, such as tragedy, suffering, and moral hypocrisy.

Defectors

Believers doubting is one thing. But we also know that more than a few Americans with religious backgrounds appear to abandon the faith of their childhoods and live adult lives that seem quite secular. They hardly ever participate in organized religion. And they describe themselves as "not religious" when asked. Our survey data indicate that nine percent of all Americans fall into this category (that is, they were raised to be religious but are now not religious); 1996 GSS data suggest 8.5 percent do.[3] What can we learn from these people about religious belief plausibility and implausibility in American society? To answer this question, we called back for follow-up interviews thirty-four of the seventy-six religious "defectors" who completed our telephone survey. What we learned was instructive.

The first fact that impressed us in our interviews, was what it meant to these defectors to be "nonreligious." For 80 percent of them, it did not mean that they had rejected religious beliefs, or even all religious practices, and adopted naturalistic, secular worldviews. Rather, for four out of five, it simply meant that they had somewhere along their lives stopped going to church and perhaps had developed negative attitudes toward church members and clergy. Our defectors routinely defined their nonreligiosity merely as not attending religious services. They offered a variety of reasons explaining why (which we will examine below), but what the vast majority thought relevant to explain was simply that they were not attending church. But not going to church was an entirely different matter for them than embracing religious beliefs and engaging in other forms of religious practice. Twenty of our thirty-four defectors (59 percent) stated emphatically that they still believed and often prayed to a personal God; many insisted this was the same God in whom they were raised to believe. Two said they now believe in an impersonal God and two said they were simply unsure about God. Of our thirty-four defectors, only six (18 percent) said that they did not believe in any God.[4] Furthermore, at least six defectors stated without prompting that they were now interested in finding a church where they could start attending services routinely. And between our orig-

3. Between 68.5 percent (our survey data) and 72.5 percent (1996 GSS data) of all currently nonreligious Americans report that they were raised in a religious family. Between 92.3 percent (our survey data) and 95 percent (1996 GSS data) of all nonreligious Americans attend church less than once a month.

4. This translates into 1.6 percent of the entire American population, a figure which comports with 1988–91 GSS data, which show 1.7 percent of the American population agreeing with the statement, "I don't believe in God."

Table 6.4: Reasons Why "Nonreligious" Americans Left Their Religions
of Childhood (frequencies)

Just "drifted" away	8
Offended by churches	7
Decided religion is false	6
Lack interest in church	5
Moved locations	3
Work and family commitments	2
Incompatible moral views	1
Has returned to church	2
N	(34)

inal survey and our follow-up interview calls, another defector had *already* started attending church regularly. The vast majority of our religious "defectors," in other words, had not forsaken their religious worldviews and belief commitments and become secularized unbelievers. These who identified themselves as "not religious" are not literally not-religious. They simply had stopped participating in the worship services of organized religion, which is quite a different matter.

The second interesting observation we made in our follow-up interviews concerned the reasons defectors stated why they had discontinued attending the churches in which they were raised (see table 6.4). Again, relatively few of those reasons seemed to have anything to do with any allegedly religiously corrosive forces of modernity. Of the thirty-four defectors we interviewed, eight explained essentially that they simply had "drifted away" from churchgoing. They said things like, "It was gradual, I guess it just evolved on it's own"; "I drifted away, I guess, it wasn't a conscious decision"; and "It's hard to say, I just kind of petered out." When we inquired about possible events or situations that may have caused them to drop out of church, they could not think of any. They had simply gradually stopped going to church, typically in their childhood or teenage years, for no apparent reason.

Seven of our thirty-four defectors left their churches because upsetting events in the past had offended and alienated them. One woman from Texas who was attending a Lutheran church said that when she had a stillborn child at eight months pregnant, her church had told her that since her baby had not been baptized, it was going to hell; she quit church immediately. Another young woman from Massachusetts was raised in a Seventh Day Adventist church; when, unmarried, she got pregnant, she felt the church condemned her, so she quit. "I do not believe in church," she said.

"I just believe in God. Why should you go to a church when you can just have your own beliefs? I feel churches aren't churches anymore, they are more like businesses." One Colorado man, raised Mormon, began doubting church teachings on polygamy and prohibitions against coffee-drinking as a teen; but he dropped out completely, he said, when the church "tried to expel my little sister for some acts my mother was doing. That kind of bummed me out, because my sister was really heavy into the church." An ex-Catholic woman from Rhode Island, twice divorced and now a single mother, reported that she wasn't willing to pay the church to have her previous marriage annulled because that would be tantamount to saying her child is illegitimate; she also said she doesn't accept church teachings about the wife serving her husband. Yet another woman raised as a Roman Catholic says that at age nineteen she was excommunicated from the Church and had her marriage annulled, at the behest of her parents, because she had married the "wrong" guy; that she later divorced the man, she blames on her parents (who have since become Pentecostals) and the Roman Catholic Church. Nonetheless, today she has no doubts about God's existence and attends different kinds of churches sporadically. One woman from Arizona reported being turned off by the Charismatic renewal style of worship that she said took over her Roman Catholic church's service, with all of its "mumbo-jumbo," healings, blessings, and so on. Finally, one woman from Michigan said that the pastor of the nondenominational Protestant church she was attending began to get cultish, demanding that members buy all of his books and give money only to him. A church split ensued, after which this woman was "deprogrammed"; realizing that she was "burned out" on religion, she quit attending all churches altogether.

Fitting most closely the conventional image of nonreligious secularists, six of our thirty-four defectors dropped out of their churches because they had simply decided in their minds that religion was groundless, erroneous, or fraudulent. One hispanic man from Texas, for example, who was raised Roman Catholic, reported that he decided to abandon his religion "by reading the Bible." In 1972, he had gone to Vietnam, where he found himself with plenty of time and nothing to read but a Bible. Upon studying it seriously for the first time in his life, he discovered that, "Catholic beliefs are completely out of whack with what the Bible teaches; I mean like rosaries and saints and all these goodies. The Bible doesn't mention anything to that effect." As a result—he said in a long interview full of antireligious profanity[5]—he "got out of institutional religion altogether," and now calls himself a "secular humanist" (although he still believes in and prays to a "supreme being, but not in the sense of one who got crucified"). Looking back, he says, "I can't blame my family or the military or anybody. I really just did what my mind and my soul and my intelligence guided me to." Another man from Washington, DC, reported that by age twenty-five, he had "gradually come to believe that most of the events in my life are controlled by biology and more concrete things than religion; that there is no evidence or scientific proof that there is a supreme being that controls my destiny." His college education, he said, helped make him doubt God's existence. He told us that he was gay but said this had nothing to do with his nonreligious views. Today he considers himself an atheist but respects all people's right to choose whatever religion they want. The others defectors of this type likewise described themselves as atheists or agnostics who see religion as a human-made control mechanism either to control human fears in a world that is truly absurd or to control the behavior of "the masses"; some also charged that "there is too much damn suffering in the world" to believe in any God.

Offering a completely different explanation for their having dropped out of church, five defectors stated that there was nothing especially wrong with church but that church simply did not particularly interest them. One woman from Indiana said that her church's services were held in Greek, so she didn't understand much of them. Another man from Pennsylvania said that he simply doesn't have the interest to figure out all of the available

---

5. For a sense of his manner: "I am the type of person who will curse God in a minute. I will tell Jesus Christ to go fuck himself. Lots of my friends say that God is going to strike me. Somewhere in the Bible [Jesus] says that if a person doesn't like children, they don't like me. But it is a fact that God doesn't love children. Look at how many damn children are born with every defect. If God loved children, he wouldn't permit that. If he is so merciful, then why doesn't he kill all the rapists in prison? Look at the hypocrisy of religion. I think in the Bible he mentions that no man can build me a church because my church is in heaven. Then look, they build a goddam glass church out there in the middle of a goddam earthquake area. And look at these people that are trying to do all this bullshit. Maybe I will go to hell if there is such a thing. But I am not being sucked in. You can have eyes and not see. Religion is keeping people from knowing what the hell is going on. . . . The Catholic Church is like a mafia thing. And all the Protestants did, the mafia family they broke up, you know. . . . Religion is a dictatorship more than anything else; they want to control the masses. Catholics don't care for communism because it is communism in it's own form, a dictatorship. I consider sex a sacred ritual, and the Catholic religion is telling the Catholics not to use birth control? But look at Mother Theresa, all these countries of the world where so many people are starving. So what is the church trying to do?"

religions. Two mentioned that they do believe in God but that this belief is not terribly important in their lives. And another woman from Texas said that although she reads her Bible frequently and thinks her religion is right and others are wrong, she just doesn't believe that organized religious ceremonies are very important.

Three of our thirty-four defectors said that they stopped attending church when they moved to new places to live and work and simply never found a new church to join. One Protestant woman from Oklahoma seemed rather embarrassed about not going to church and said she probably should start again. Two other defectors reported that work and family commitments kept them from going to church. One from Illinois, who works weekends, said that she could not get time off from her job to attend a Roman Catholic church, but would like to. Another Catholic woman from Ohio told us that the reason she stopped going to church was that "I just had too much to do at home, I guess. Too many children." Nevertheless, she still holds to her religious beliefs and sends her own children to both Catholic schools and church. One defector from Indiana dropped out of his Pentecostal church at the age of sixteen when he realized that he was gay and that his church's incompatible moral views would lead them to condemn him. "They preached that if you are gay, you are doomed to hell. I don't think that way at all." Finally, two of the thirty-four defectors we called reported that they were now either already attending church again or were actively looking for a church to join.

One of the most striking aspects of these defectors' reasons for leaving the faiths of their families is how few of them reflect the problem of cognitive implausibility driven by features of social life that are uniquely modern, in the sense that the modernization-secularization paradigm would suggest. Only six out of thirty-four (17.6 percent), those that decided intellectually that religion is false, reflect clear cases of sacred canopies collapsing under the weight of cultural pluralism, scientific authority, and rationalization. The others suggest causes for defection that could have as likely been operative in medieval Europe or the Hellenistic Mediterranean world: being alienated by an offensive incident with the church; choosing to live a lifestyle incompatible with church ethics; moving to a new city and failing to become integrated into a new congregation; or just losing interest and "drifting away" from church.

Another feature that impressed us, as we reviewed the tapes and transcripts of our thirty-four religious defectors, was the importance of relational networks in influencing religious views and commitments. To begin, relational disruptions and realignments appeared to be frequent causes or facilitators of religious defections. A significant number of people reported that they dropped out of church after getting married or divorced. Some talked of being estranged from their families. Others said that they simply quit at the time they moved out of their parents' houses to start their own jobs and households, whether in the same area or farther away. Yet others pointed to offensive relational conflicts with church leaders, oftentimes over family issues, that turned them away from church participation. Even people's religious beliefs were sometimes directly affected by relational disruptions—as the following exchange with an ex-Catholic woman from Michigan, who had gradually drifted out of church, illustrates:

> Q: In the years after you stopped going to church, did you still believe in God?
> A: Yes, I believed in God, at least up until about four years ago.
> Q: What happened then?
> A: I got divorced.

Studies of religious conversion repeatedly demonstrate the importance of positive, affective network ties to religious groups in facilitating religious conversions. Our interviews suggest that the breaking of relational links—even when the breaks appear to have little to do with religion per se—also often works in the opposite direction. These breaks can be critical juncture-points estranging people from prior religious ties and commitments.

Furthermore, our defectors rarely encountered resistance from family and friends when they dropped out of religious practice. Very many said that their parents themselves were either irregular church attenders or had themselves stopped going to church. Some made a point to say that, even if their parents attended church, religion just wasn't very important in the families in which they grew up. Some respondents reported that their parents were divorced; others mentioned parents who were alcoholics or who died when they were children. Some also said they did not have many friendships; others who did have religious friends said their friends hardly ever talked to them about their religious views and commitments. So when our defectors decided to drop out of religion themselves, almost no one questioned or objected to their decisions. In only two cases out of thirty-four did respondents report that their families did anything significant to try to compel them to maintain their religious involvements. Otherwise, families and friends introduced few negative consequences to sanction their leaving religion. Few relational network-based social controls were exerted to attempt to prevent their defections and maintain their old identity boundaries.

To summarize our conclusions on defectors, then, to the extent that our interviews represent a broader reality, they suggest three things. First, very few "nonreligious" Americans are truly nonreligious—most in fact insist they *are* religious, but simply in a rather individualistic, disaffiliated way. Second, the primary basis of most people's distance from organized religion typically has little to do with cognitive belief implausibility, per se; rather, distance from religion appears to be generated more by relational disruptions and the absence of strong relational ties to religion. Third, modernity itself does not appear to be the driving force at work undermining strong religious faith and practice; the primary reasons why religious defectors in contemporary America do not participate in organized religion are probably not very different from the kinds of reasons that would have estranged people from organized religion throughout human history.

Conclusion

We have just examined those Americans whose religious faith appears most precarious (the recurrent doubters) and those who appear to have rejected their old beliefs (the religious defectors). We have found even in these cases relatively little evidence to support the modernization-secularization paradigm's view of religious belief plausibility in the modern world. A minority of doubters do, in fact, distrust their own religious beliefs because cultural and religious pluralism erode any sense of cognitive certainty. And a small segment of defectors have rejected the faith of their families because their traditional doctrines came to seem unbelievable in a rational, naturalistic, pluralistic, modern world. These cases do exist. But for the majority, doubt and defection appear to be driven by causes much more closely related to factors that are historical constants, not problems that particularly beset modern people. Suffering, tragedies, moral hypocrisy, ordinary life struggles and troubles, offensive church actions, and relational network disruptions—the apparent sources of most religious doubt and defections—are not realities peculiar to modern life. Nor are they essentially cognitive difficulties provoked by the contemporary situation of cultural pluralism, pervasive rationalization, and social differentiation. They are, rather, relational and existential universals with which humans have been struggling from the beginning and will no doubt continue to do so for the indefinite future. This means, on the one hand, that some level of religious doubting and defecting always has existed and will exist. But it also means, on the other hand, that these are not particularly modern problems that pose distinctive or extraordinary threats to the continuance of religious faith in the modern world. The human condition simply appears more stable and most religions appear more resilient than the modernization-secularization paradigm would have us believe.

Addendum: The Assurance of Spiritual Experiences

One final, important factor related to the question of belief plausibility, which we have not yet addressed, deserves mention. Very many modern people have encountered and do encounter what are to them very real spiritual experiences, frequently vivid and powerful ones. And these often serve as epistemological anchors sustaining their religious faith in even the most pluralistic and secular of situations. Research in the sociology of religion sometimes neglects spiritual experiences as a focus of study, perhaps because they seem too individual, subjective, or related to the supernatural for an empirical social science to take seriously. But we ignore and discount people's professed spiritual experiences to the detriment of our sociological understanding. Many individuals describe them as very real and meaningful. And, as W. I. Thomas instructed us long ago, when people believe things are real—whether they are "in actuality" real or not—they are nevertheless in the social world certainly real *in their consequences.* To adequately understand the plausibility of religious faith in modern society, then, we must recognize the role that spiritual experiences play in verifying and validating many people's religious faith.

According to General Social Survey data, a sizeable number of Americans have encountered meaningful spiritual experiences in their lives. In surveys conducted between 1988 and 1991, for example, 36 percent of Americans reported that they have been "born again" or had a "born again" experience, a turning point in their life when they committed themselves to Jesus Christ. Forty-six percent of Americans said they have experienced a turning point in life when they made a new and personal commitment to religion. Thirty percent of Americans reported that most of the time they feel "extremely close" to God, while another fifty percent said they feel "somewhat close" to God (only 1.7 percent said they did not believe in God). Sixty-four percent of Americans said that they believe in religious miracles. And twenty-nine percent maintained that they had at least some time in their lives felt as though they were very close to a powerful, spiritual force that seemed to lift them out of themselves. A people devoid of spiritual experiences Americans are not.

These kinds of reports surfaced, as one might expect, with even greater frequency in our interviews with churchgoing Protestants and even more so in our interviews with evangelicals. And these spiritual experiences clearly served to verify and validate these people's faith. Many, such as this Baptist woman, spoke of an experiential sense of God's presence in their lives: "You definitely feel something. You don't always feel it all the time, God on your shoulder twenty-four hours a day. But you feel Him there often enough to know that it's real." Others, like this Charismatic woman, expressed that God's Spirit authenticates truth in their hearts: "I know my faith is true because I know of the confirmation of the person of the Holy Spirit and the difference that I sense spiritually since my rebirth." Some, such as this highly educated Presbyterian man, hint of God speaking more directly to them: "I feel like I've had some experiences in prayer, some direct spiritual knowledge, which also makes my faith real to me." Very often, when people we interviewed spoke of spiritual experiences that confirmed their faith, they pointed to clear answers to their prayers, which for them were no mere coincidences, but God's direct response to their requests. Sometimes, such answers to prayer concern mundane matters, as in the case related by this nondenominational man:

> I have seen too many prayers answered. The Lord has just been there for us. Even to the point where we will come up short to cover our bills, and Franie [his wife] will say, "I need $100 to cover this," and we will get a check in the mail for that amount, which we hadn't been counting on. The Lord just comes through time and time again.

Other times, as in the story of this Baptist man, answers to prayer concern more weighty matters:

> My son, who is now eighteen, was born four months premature. He was born two pounds, four ounces, and dropped in weight to one pound, fourteen ounces. The doctors told us not to name him when he was delivered, because he wouldn't live. My uncle, a Christian pediatrician, told me, "I know what medicine has to offer, and what God has to offer, and your only hope is God." Well, my son is alive and well today because people prayed. And our faith was strengthened through that.[6]

6. The connection between answered prayers and belief plausibility is illustrated well by this man who attends a Bible Fellowship church: "I have had answers to prayer. No spectacular, you know, gold falling out of heaven, stuff like that. But I have prayed about things, and I am confident that the prayers have been heard and answered. I am unswayed in my belief

This man continued enthusiastically to explain how regular devotion to God affects his daily life:

> I know that my God is alive and well because I see Him working in my daily life, on the job, in my family. I can see an unquestionably direct difference in the days that I read my Bible and pray, compared to days I don't. God's blessing in the littlest of ways is evident on days that I have my devotions. He is very much alive and well. And very obviously an active part of our lives.

Some interviewees, such as this Anabaptist man, reported cases where they believe God clearly guided them to accomplish his purposes in the world:

> When I was overseas one summer, on a short-term mission trip, I was praying, and I felt really led. I really felt, for some reason, that God was impressing on me that there was this particular sister in the States that was having a spiritual struggle and I needed to write a letter of encouragement to her. So I wrote it. Turned out she *was* having a particular spiritual struggle and my letter really encouraged and blessed her. There's just one example of many.

A minority of others recounted much more dramatic spiritual experiences that have for them authenticated beyond a doubt the veracity of their religious faith. One Pentecostal woman, for example, described how decades earlier she had been exorcised of a demon. After years as a singer in show-business, and after multiple abortions, she began to feel what she now says was God calling for her to change her life. Through a long conversion process, she said she discovered that her worldly living had opened her up for a demon to possess her. In one part of her very long and colorful story, she recalled:

> I had a devil in me, talking right out of my mouth. At one point I was laying in front of an alter and there was a group of Christians around me. And this thing was hollering out of my mouth, saying, "I will never come out! I'm not coming out!," carrying on like that. And I noticed that when anyone of those Christians said anything about the blood of Jesus, my lips would absolutely stiffen up, and that thing in me could not talk. I learned then there is a devil, and there are demons.

---

in a supreme being and unswayed that the Bible is the proper communication from that supreme being. That God explains himself, unfolds his perspective of history there, and has directed the affairs of men."

Eventually, she explained (in what turned out to be pages and pages of interview transcripts) that she was freed by Christ from this spiritual bondage. She now looks back in amazement as what she sees as the hand of God in her life: "God did so many real things for me when I was coming through this deliverance thing, so many tangible things that I could put my hand on. He did things right down the line to bring me, just one thing after another. And I learned that he was real." Having finished narrating her own story, she then proceeded to detail how her husband—who was sitting in the room during the interview, continually nodding in agreement—had in recent years once been instantly healed through prayer of a permanent vegetative state after a failed heart surgery, and once been raised from the dead through prayer after a drowning accident.[7] "He had absolutely a real miracle of God," she concluded. "See, that's how we know God is real."

Whether or not this woman really was exorcised of a demon and her husband raised from the dead is irrelevant for our purposes. What *is* relevant is that since *they* believe these things to be true and real, they are, in fact, very real in their consequences: this woman and her husband are absolutely as certain that a loving, saving God exists and touches their lives, and that demonic forces also exist which would seek to destroy them, as is humanly possible to be certain of anything. About these beliefs, they have

---

7. In the first case, she reported, a piece of calcium in his bloodstream that doctors had dislodged during the heart operation had become lodged in his brain, tragically leaving him, according to doctors, in a permanent vegetative condition. But, his wife said, she had faithful people all over the country praying for her husband. And God's Spirit moved her then and there to pray for his healing. She placed her hands on his head and prayed, and immediately, she said, he came to consciousness. The amazed doctors could find no trace of calcium in his brain, and he was soon released from the hospital. In the second incident, she reported, her husband had drown in a community pool while the lifeguard had been not paying attention. Half an hour had elapsed, she recounted, from the time he had collapsed underwater to when he arrived at the hospital, and he still had no pulse and was not breathing. "My husband was dead," she said, recalling her ride to the hospital. "But what I did was just grab right hold of his hand and start calling on Jesus, and rebuking what the Lord was giving me: the devil of death, drowning, destruction. And I just kept coming against them, and kept pleading the blood and calling on Jesus." At the forty-five minute mark, a neurologist emerged from the emergence room, and reported that they managed to revive a faint pulse. But he said that there was no way her husband would not be seriously brain damaged. She grasped her "Jesus" pen, which she always carried with her, and replied, "Yes, there is a way." By the next morning, she reported, her husband was awake and alert. In a short time, he was checked out of the hospital.

not the slightest doubt.[8] And nothing about the modern world would appear to be able to undermine this experientially based certainty.

In chapter 4, we argued that because the socially normative bases of identity-legitimation are historically variable, modern religious believers can establish stronger religious identities and commitments on the basis of individual choice than through ascription. One analogue of that principle in this context is that because the mainstream American cultural tradition is strongly pragmatic and activist—rather than doctrinal and contemplative—first-hand spiritual experiences that "work" for people can provide for them stronger epistemological foundations for personal religious faith than can the narrative elegance or intellectually defensibility of theological systems.[9] As the adage says, "You can't argue with experience." Few ordinary people, religious or otherwise, are theoreticians. And few ordinary religious believers begin or proceed in their beliefs with a "hermeneutic of suspicion." People do not generally adhere to their religious faiths because as cognitive frameworks they are intellectually nonproblematic. They adhere to them because they provide identity, solidarity, meaning, order, and purpose—very fundamental human requisites. Whatever cognitive quandaries modernity imposes on ordinary religious believers, most seem capable of disregarding, defusing, or somehow resolving them in a way that does not seriously undermine their faith.

8. One representative sample of her spiritual effervescence from a long interview full of it: "God is God. And is there anything more important than God? I know there is a God, and that God is God. What could be more important? I'd much rather please the Lord than have him knocking himself out to please me, you know what I mean? Without my faith, I would miss God. I would miss Jesus. I would miss the Holy Spirit. I would miss the gratuity. The sense I have that all is well with me because I am God's child. And one day I am going to leave this place down here and I am going to live for eternity in heaven and all that heaven means. I couldn't imagine. I don't know how I ever lived without God before I got born again."

9. Indeed, faith is often called on to "work" precisely in the worst of times, as exemplified by the words of this recently divorced Presbyterian woman: "Faith has helped me survive some of the really bad things I've been through. There is a God out there. He's there. No question. And I believe He's who He says He is. Sometimes I do waiver. But I don't know if I could even really function without God. It helps to give strength. Hope. Knowing that there's a God in charge of it all. It helps make things meaningful to me and puts things in proper perspective." Even well-educated moderns, such as this Baptist woman who is a professional educator, are able to accept without too much difficulty even very difficult matters of belief: "The Bible says hell was created for Satan and his angels, but that it's also the eternal abode of those who reject Jesus Christ. I wish there wasn't a hell. You know, I'm not sure if I would have planned it that way. But I know God is perfectly right and just in whatever He does. So, yes, I believe it's a literal hell."

SEVEN

Ironies of Subcultural Distinction—
Strength and Ineffectiveness

Creating a thriving religious movement within a pluralistic environment through engagement-with-distinction is one thing, but actually successfully accomplishing one's religious movement's purposes in a pluralistic environment through distinctive engagement may be quite another thing. It would be a mistake to think that evangelicalism thrives in all ways or succeeds in everything it sets out to accomplish. Indeed, we wish to draw attention here to at least one significant way in which American evangelicalism appears to be relatively ineffective: in actually accomplishing distinctively Christian social change. Although evangelicalism does sustain a thriving religious tradition for itself, we will suggest that it does not fare so well when it comes to achieving its goal of transforming the world for Christ. Moreover, this circumstance is not quite as simple as evangelicalism succeeding in some ways but faltering in others. In actuality, the irony of this situation is thick, for the conditions underlying evangelicalism's strength and ineffectiveness are often linked: many of the subcultural distinctives which foster evangelicalism's vitality as a religious movement, we believe, are the very same factors which can foster its ineffectiveness as an agent of social change. The sources of both strength and weakness are often the same. Subculturally engaged distinctiveness, in other words, can cut both ways—it can create certain forms of religious vitality but can also produce other forms of strategic debility. This insight, which qualifies our subcultural identity theory of religious strength, is well worth noting and exploring.

That evangelicals do desire to have social influence, we have seen, is clear. Evangelicals want their orthodoxy to be an *engaged* orthodoxy, one that offers Christian perspectives and answers to pressing social and political problems. From Carl Henry and Harold Ockenga in the 1940s and 1950s, to Francis Schaeffer and Mark Hatfield in the 1960s and 1970s, to

Charles Colson and Anthony Campolo in the 1980s and 1990s, evangelicals have been driven by a vision of redemptive world transformation. In their own words, evangelicals desire to serve "as light to the world and salt in the earth" to "apply biblical ethics to society's most difficult problems" (Woodbridge, Noll, and Hatch 1979: 247). In evangelicalism's earliest days, Carl Henry laid out the challenge: "If historic Christianity is again to compete as a vital world ideology, evangelicalism must project a solution for the most pressing world problems. It must offer a formula for a new world mind with spiritual ends, involving evangelical affirmations in political, economic, sociological, and educational realms, local and international" (1947: 68). More recently, Wheaton College professor Robert Webber has argued:

> The Christian as a redeemed cultural being has . . . an obligation to the created order. Wherever oppression, war, injustice, hate, greed, and other social and moral ills prevail, the created order still shows signs of its bondage to decay and death because of sin. But the Christian witness is calling to live and act redemptively in all structures of life, to bring to bear release from sin and its oppressive effects in the totality of the [human] life . . . in the created order. . . . The mission of the church goes beyond evangelism . . . and education . . . to play a decisive role in the world. The role of the church in the world is, first, to be the presence of a new creation and, second, to bring about the new creation. (1978: 210, 213)

But in their efforts to play a decisive role in the world by bringing about the new creation, evangelicals often employ subcultural tools which may work to build subcultural identity strength but which paradoxically can also prove in the end to limit significantly their own effectiveness in social change. This chapter explores some of the ways this ironic process works, beginning with an evaluative overview of evangelicalism by outsiders.

A First Take: The View from Outside

In our national telephone survey, we asked all respondents who were not conservative Protestants a series of questions about how familiar they were with, what kinds of impressions they had about, and how they evaluated the views of evangelical Christians in America. Their responses are represented in tables 7.1, 7.2, and 7. 3. The first thing we see (table 7.1) is that only a minority of nonevangelical Americans of any religious background

are familiar with what evangelicals stand for. Nearly one-half of all groups
said they were simply not familiar with evangelicalism. Only a small minority reported that they were very familiar with what evangelicals stand
for. Perhaps even more problematic for evangelicals, given their history and
identity, is the fact that only between one-fourth and one-third of nonevangelical Americans claimed to see a difference between evangelicals and
fundamentalist Christians. The majority either said that they did not know
whether there was a difference, or that they did not know what "evangelical" meant, or that they definitely thought there was no difference between
evangelicals and fundamentalists. With most groups, those who said there
was no distinction far outnumbered those who saw a difference. The secular U.S. news media, which is typically quite ignorant about religious matters, is certainly partly to blame for this widespread lack of awareness about
an identity difference that historically and within conservative Protestant
circles today is very real. But, we will suggest below, evangelicals themselves may inadvertently share in the blame as well. In any case, the consequence remains: evangelicals have not been able adequately to establish
outside of conservative Protestant circles an identity which distinguishes
their project of engaged orthodoxy from the very different historical fundamentalist project of defensive separatism. Thus, while evangelicals do perform effective in-group identity work that maintains the vitality of their
movement, their out-group identity work leaves much to be desired. The
nonevangelical American population simply does not understand very
clearly what evangelicals are all about.

How well are evangelical strategies for social influence and change
working from the perspective of outsiders (see table 7.2)? The views reported in table 7.2 are filtered through a sampling bias which favors those
who remain unpersuaded by evangelical appeals and examples—since
those who evangelicals would have already succeeded in converting would
not have been asked these survey questions in the first place. Still, the numbers in table 7.2 offer a mixed review for evangelicals. Positively, between
one-third and one-half of all American who are not conservative Protestants say that they personally know an evangelical Christian—not bad,
given that self-identified evangelicals represent only about seven percent of
the American population. Evangelicals, in other words, are doing a reasonably good job of making themselves known as such in their personal relationships with outsiders (using more inclusive definitions of "evangelical,"
however, [see, for example, PRRC 1996; Woodberry and Smith 1998]—
which tend to estimate their numbers at closer to 20 percent of the Ameri-

Table 7.1: Understanding of Evangelicalism, by Religion (percent)

	Mainline, Liberal and Nominal Protestants	Roman Catholics	Non-Christian
How familiar are you with what evangelical Christians stand for?			
Very Familiar	3	4	7
Somewhat Familiar	25	23	26
A Little Familiar	22	23	21
Not Familiar	48	48	46
Don't Know	2	2	1
In your own mind, is there a difference between evangelical and fundamentalist Christians?			
Yes, there is a difference	30	24	21
No, there is no difference	31	45	48
Don't know what "evangelical" means	21	16	20
Don't know the answer	18	15	11
N	(1,038)	(186)	(164)

can population—makes this finding somewhat less impressive). Furthermore, of those who said that they did personally know an evangelical Christian, the majority—especially of Roman Catholics—reported that the evangelical who they know best actually does set a good example for others by living an especially moral life. On that dimension, particularly among the other Christians, evangelicals score reasonably well. Moreover, almost the exact same proportion of people who reported personally knowing an evangelical also reported that an evangelical had at least once tried to convert them to their faith. Evangelicals, then, do not appear to be slacking off of the task of evangelizing outsiders. For every one (self-identified) evangelical in America, between five and seven nonconservative-Protestants have been proselytized by an evangelical. But the evidence from there becomes somewhat less heartening for evangelicals. According to those who say an evangelical had at some time tried to convert them to their faith, only between ten and twenty percent said that that was a positive experience. About one-half said it was a negative experience. The remainder said it was neither positive nor negative. Evangelicals may be "out there" evangelizing. But when they do so, they are generally not leaving particularly good impressions on those they are proselytizing. This suggests that evangelicals have a real problem knowing how to communicate their message in a manner that will be well-received; or perhaps rather that the

Table 7.2: Experience with Evangelicals, by Religion (percent)

	Mainline, Liberal and Nominal Protestants	Roman Catholics	Non-Christian
Do you personally know an evangelical Christian?			
Yes	38	48	44
No	47	46	48
Don't Know	15	6	8
(If you know an evangelical) Does the evangelical best known set a good example for others by living an especially moral life?			
Yes	68	76	57
No	26	21	40
Don't Know	6	3	3
Has an evangelical ever tried to convert you to his or her faith?			
Yes	36	49	44
No	50	43	44
Don't Know	14	8	12
(If an evangelical tried to convert) What kind of experience was that?			
Positive	11	19	13
Neither Positive Nor Negative	38	31	43
Negative	51	50	44
N	(1,038)	(186)	(164)

character of the evangelical message itself, influenced as it is by important features of the evangelical subculture, tends to be alienating.

Furthermore, nonevangelicals do not appear to believe that evangelicals are offering adequate answers for the problems they confront (see table 7.3). Only about one in four nonconservative-Protestant Americans said that they thought evangelicals generally offer good answers to most people's personal problems and moral questions. Significantly larger numbers said that evangelicals did not. The remainder said either that they simply did not know the answer or that they did not know what "evangelical" means. Even fewer nonconservative-Protestants—only between fourteen and twenty percent—reported that they believed evangelicals generally offer good answers to America's social, economic, and political problems. Between one-third and one-half said that evangelicals did not. Clearly, evangelicals have not persuaded one of their major target audiences—Americans who are not conservative Protestants—that they have solutions either to people's personal problems and moral questions or to America's social, economic, and political problems. Indeed, almost half of non-Christian Americans say that they see little difference between the lifestyles of Christians and those of the rest of Americans—more than forty percent stated that Christians' lifestyles are not very different or only a little different from those of non-Christian Americans. Whether or not this is "actually" true is irrelevant to the question of whether evangelicals are adequately persuading non-Christian Americans that they have distinctive and useful answers to offer for the problems and questions that Americans confront today.

Finally, table 7.3 reports nonconservative-Protestants' overall evaluation of evangelicalism's promise to improve American public life through greater social influence. Once again, almost one-third of nonevangelical Americans simply could not answer the question because they did not know what "evangelical" meant. Of those who felt qualified to answer the question, few thought that America would be much better off if evangelical Christians had more influence on public issues. Most thought that America would be only somewhat better off or somewhat worse off. Roman Catholics, mainline, liberal, and nominal Protestants were moderately positive about evangelical public influence—sizeable numbers said that America would be somewhat better off if evangelicals had more influence on public issues. But non-Christians were decidedly unsympathetic to evangelical public influence. Almost four times the number of them said America would be much worse off rather than much better off if evangelical Christians had more influence on public issues.

How can we explain these results? We did not in this project interview nominal Protestants, Roman Catholics, or non-Christians and so cannot speak for them. However, our interviews with churchgoing mainline and liberal Protestants do provide some insight into why nonconservative-Protestants perceive evangelicals as they do. Consistent with our survey findings, a sizeable proportion of the mainline and liberal Protestants we interviewed did not really know what "evangelical" meant. They simply had no idea and could offer no definition or description. Very many of those who did say they thought they knew what evangelicals were about expressed fairly unfavorable impressions of them. Most relevant for present purposes was that often times *it was precisely things which evangelicals consider strengths or assets about themselves which bothered these nonevangelicals.* In other words, many of the very features which evangelicals view as posi-

Table 7.3: Evaluation of Evangelicals' Influence, by Religion (percent)

	Mainline, Liberal and Nominal Protestants	Roman Catholics	Non-Christians
Do evangelicals generally offer good answers to most people's personal problems and moral questions?			
Yes	25	27	18
No	30	32	47
Don't know what "evangelical" means	28	24	23
Don't know the answer	17	17	12
Do evangelicals generally offer good answers to America's social, economic, and political problems?			
Yes	17	20	14
No	35	34	49
Don't know what "evangelical" means	28	24	23
Don't know the answer	20	22	14
Believes Christians' values and lifestyles are only a little different or not very different from the rest of American society today	32	38	42
How would the United States be if evangelical Christians had more influence on public issues?			
Much better off	6	7	7
Somewhat better off	37	38	28
Somewhat worse off	17	15	12
Much worse off	6	11	26
Don't know what "evangelical" means	34	29	27
N	(1,038)	(186)	(164)

tively distinguishing themselves from others were the points which "turned off" outsiders.

One common theme, for example, was that evangelicals are too verbally or publicly expressive about their faith. One Methodist man, for instance, said, "For me, an evangelical is somebody who sings and shouts and is glad to be Christian and wants everybody to know it." This Methodist woman reported, "Well, evangelicals are a lot more active than I am, going around testifying and all, you know, to your face, like doing evangelism. You know, I don't care for that." And this mainline Baptist woman suggested that "An evangelical believes in doing evangelism, in spreading the good news, going out and getting people. Sometimes I don't approve of their methods, button-holing people and being forceful." A related critical theme was that evangelical faith is too grounded on emotions instead of reason. This mainline Church of Christ man, for example, observed:

> Evangelicals look more to emotions. When I go to [their] churches, at the end of the service a lot of people go forward [for alter calls], asking two to three hundred people to go forward, you know. I've never seen that in my denomination. Reason lasts longer than emotions, because emotions can go every which way all the time.

Churchgoing mainline and liberal Protestants also criticized evangelicals for being too pushy and judgmental. One mainline Baptist woman, for example, who we asked what it meant to be an evangelical, replied, "I really shouldn't even say, cause I'm not that sure of what it means, but those that try to go out and force their beliefs on others rather than just saying, 'This is what I believe and if you want to believe it fine, and if you don't, that's your choice.' That's my idea of an evangelical." Likewise, this Lutheran man said:

> I think evangelical can have a negative connotation, it really can. That you're gonna be out there, you know, pointing your finger and saying, "If you don't believe the way I believe, you're in big trouble." I think we have to be real careful about judging other people's spiritual beliefs, because what [matters] is in their heart and very being, and God is working in their life and it's not necessarily what you're seeing [should be] what you judge them by. So, I don't want to be labeled an evangelical, period. I don't want that to be what people say about me.

This Baptist woman, reported,

> Evangelical to me is maybe [to] stand out and yell at a crowd. I really function more or less on my own belief, and not trying to persuade others, you know. I will state very firmly my religious beliefs, what I feel strongly about. But I am not willing to try and evangelize everybody else.

And one liberal Lutheran man said that evangelical concerns about threats from possible cultural antagonists, such as gay rights activists or New Age religionists, were, in his words, "unfounded paranoia. I think that [evangelicals] are using those excuses as rationalizations to meet their self-serving needs." Of evangelicals who believe that their religion is right and other religions are wrong, this man stated simply that, "That is a self centered, egocentric attitude."

Yet another perception of evangelicals among mainline and liberal Protestants is that they are too pious and perhaps self-righteous. One mainline Baptist man, for example, stated:

> I just don't believe in it. If I understand the definition of evangelical, they are very devout. Is that true? I just think they take it to an extreme. And I just personally don't think it needs to be taken to that extreme of personal devotion, worship styles, proselytizing, all those things.

Similarly, this Baptist woman suggested somewhat disparagingly that an evangelical is, "someone who is quite divine. [Pointing to a painting of an angel on the wall] That's an evangelical picture I have. I would think probably an evangelical is someone close to an angel, and that I'm not." Thus, religious traits that evangelicals may pride themselves on—personal conviction, confident evangelism, moral rectitude, fervent devotion—nonevangelical Protestants often view as unappealing or offensive.

Altogether, these data suggest that American evangelicals have a serious public relations problem. One-quarter to one-third of Americans who are not conservative Protestants do not even know what "evangelical" means. Very many of those who do, remain unfamiliar with what exactly evangelicals stand for. And only a minority of nonconservative-Protestant Americans can distinguish between evangelicals and the fundamentalists from whom evangelicals broke half a century ago. Evangelicals have been reasonably successful in evangelizing significant numbers of nonevangelicals. Unfortunately for them, however, the largest proportion of those they evangelize come away viewing the episode as a negative, not positive, experience. Finally, only a minority of nonevangelicals believe that evangelicals are offering helpful answers either to people's personal problems and moral questions or to America's social, economic, and political problems. The vast majority said either no, evangelicals are not offering good answers or that they simply do not know one way or the other. Either way is bad news for evangelicals.

Evangelicals may believe in the practical moral superiority of their particular Christian way of life. But most other Americans apparently do not see it that way. Evangelicals may think that they have real solutions to offer the world for its problems. But few Americans who are not conservative Protestants see the kinds of solutions that evangelicals are offering as attractive or helpful. It may be that most nonevangelicals are judging mere misperceptions of evangelicals' views and positions; but that does not solve evangelicals' problems here, since perceptions are all that people have to go on. And the worst news for evangelicals is this: at least from what we heard from the mainline and liberal Protestants we interviewed, it was generally not what evangelicals might admit are their worst qualities, but rather what they view as their best features that most alienated outsiders. This is bad news, for when others dislike your faults, you might change yourself and win them over; but when what others dislike about you are your strengths and virtues, there is not much you can do to improve your image.

The Limits of Personal Influence Strategy

The sources of evangelical ineffectiveness with social change, however, run deeper than nonevangelicals simply not liking some of the dominant traits of the evangelical subculture. The problem is not merely that many outsiders are ignorant of and unfriendly to the kind of social solutions that evangelicals tend to offer. A deeper problem is that some of the very social analyses and strategies that evangelicals tend to employ in their efforts at social influence are inadequate for the task of genuine social change. In the pages that follow, we will focus on one inadequate central subcultural tool that evangelicals consistently utilize to try to transform the world for Christ, which we call the "personal influence strategy."

American evangelicals are resolutely committed to a social-change strategy which maintains that the only truly effective way to change the world is one-individual-at-a-time through the influence of interpersonal relationships. Most ordinary evangelicals and leaders alike seem to share this view. "The most important contribution almost all of us make in the world is our interpersonal relations," declared evangelical political scientist Reo Christenson (quoted in Hollinger 1983: 107), for example, in a 1977 discussion about Christian involvement in public policy issues. "Our personal acts of kindness and concern," he said, "have probably a hundred times more actual impact on the lives of others than our advocacy of enlightened social ideals." Similarly, this Moravian man we interviewed contended: "I think the most important thing is relationships. Building relationships, where they know how much I care about them, and that the only reason I'm offering this solution to their problems is because I believe in it so strongly." As one dimension of this strategy, evangelicals generally are convinced that the sheer demonstrational power of a life of good example, through personal relationships, can effect real societal transformation. As this Baptist woman suggested, "I just feel that if each individual lived the Christian life, a lot of these things, it influences society. I think we just need to live the life that Christ wants us to live, the best we can, to influence society in general."

The personal influence strategy, which reflects elective affinities with many other aspects of the evangelical subcultural system—including the theological emphasis on a "personal relationship with God" and the centrality of the nuclear family—is a key analytic and action strategy in the evangelical subcultural toolkit. Indeed, the personal influence strategy is, in the evangelical view, a very important subcultural distinctive of evangelical identity. Evangelicals see the relationalist strategy of social influence as part of what sets themselves apart from others, which creates subcultural distinction and a strong self-identity. Evangelicals think of fundamentalists as different, for example, because they are separatistic and judgmental, not relationally engaged in a positive way. Evangelicals see mainline and liberal Protestants as different because evangelicals think they place too much faith in "social activism" and political reform as the way to change society (ironic, given evangelicals' greater public orientation of faith [see Regnerus and Smith 1998a]). And evangelicals view non-Christians as different in part because they are believed to trust naively in secular education and government programs to improve the world. By contrast, evangelicals see themselves as uniquely possessing a distinctively effective means of social change: working through personal relationships to allow God to transform human hearts from the inside-out, so that all ensuing social change will be thorough and long-lasting. In this way, by creating perceived subcultural distinction, the personal influence strategy serves to bolster the vitality of evangelicalism's subcultural identity, helping to make it a strong religious movement.

As a subcultural tool for social change, however, the personal influence strategy also significantly constrains evangelicals' ability to understand how the social world actually works and limits their capacity to formulate appropriate and useful responses and solutions to social, economic, political, and cultural problems. Because evangelicals typically view the complex, socially structured social world, which they hope to influence, through the simplifying lens of relationalism, they routinely offer one-dimensional analyses and solutions for multidimensional social issues and problems. Evangelicals thus often render themselves, through their personal influence strategy, largely incapable of seeing how supraindividual social structures, collective processes, and institutional systems profoundly pattern and influence human consciousness, experience, and life-chances. Thus, the same subcultural tool which serves to promote the evangelical tradition's strength also undermines its strategic effectiveness.

As a social-change strategy, relationalism is profoundly individualistic. And individualism in evangelicalism runs deep, with roots extending back to most of the historical wellsprings of the modern evangelical tradition: the sixteenth-century Reformation, English and American Puritanism, much of the Free Church tradition, frontier awakening and revivalism, movements of spiritual pietism, and anti-Social Gospel fundamentalism.[1] The individualistic premise underlying relationalism is evident in much of the social analysis of evangelical leaders in the past decades. In 1956, for example, Carl Henry wrote in the premier issue of *Christianity Today:* "The solution to the national problem of freedom is no different than the solution of the individual problem of freedom" (quoted in Hollinger 1983: 108). And in 1960, Billy Graham declared that, "International problems

---

1. Dennis Hollinger (1983) has written a fascinating analysis of how individualism as a metaphysic, value system, and social philosophy has shaped the thought of evangelical leaders from 1956 to 1976. Hollinger demonstrates convincingly that, although evangelical leaders did consistently articulate an explicit social concern, their thinking typically presumed a pervasive individualism which governed the kinds of social analyses they conducted and solutions they offered. They regularly defined their "social" ethic, he claims (1983: 116), as "a personal ethic in social clothing"; took an atomistic view of society and sin which defined structural change as nonessential; espoused liberal laissez-faire capitalism as the solution to all economic problems; and in political theory and public policy analysis championed above all individual freedom, limited government, and conservative, individualistic views of race relations, communism, and foreign policy. George Marsden concurs that, "during most of the twentieth-century, conservative Protestants have espoused a sort of social message that is almost identical with the dominant American social, political, and economic dogmas of the 1870s and 1880s. Free enterprise economics, success-oriented competitive individualism, opposition to expansion of the federal government, extreme fear of socialism . . . all confirm this connection" (1973: 18). In these ways and more, then, Hollinger concludes, leading evangelical thought in these formative years (1956–76) reflected a profound individualism: "a metaphysic with an atomistic worldview; a value system heralding freedom, privacy, autonomy, and self-sufficiency; and a social philosophy with a particular view of the relationship of individuals to society . . . [which] stresses personal morality over social ethics, individual transformation as the key to social change, laissez-faire economics, and a politics extolling freedom of the individual and a limited state" (1983: 44).

are only reflections of individual problems. Sin is sin, be it personal or social. . . . Social sins, after all, are merely a large-scale projection of individual sins" (quoted in Hollinger 1983: 40).[2]

The personal influence strategy and its underlying individualism was
relentlessly evident in our in-depth interviews with ordinary evangelicals
around the country, who spoke on these matters with a remarkable
agreement of viewpoint. To begin, evangelical relationalism repeatedly expressed itself in what Woodbridge, Noll, and Hatch (1979: 246; borrowing
a terms coined by Stark [1971: 102–3]) call "the 'miracle motif' . . . the
idea that if everyone were converted to Christ, social ills would disappear."
Deriving from an atomistic, aggregationist view of society as a mere collection of individual persons in relation to each other, this view believes that
the better individuals become, the better society will become. One Charismatic man we interviewed who is involved in a seeker church stated plainly,
"For me, the solution to the world's problems is becoming a Christian,
okay?" One man in the Church of Christ denomination said, "Just believe
in Christ and live the best you can the way he wants you to, and that would
change the whole world, if they would just do that." This woman from a
Four-Square church said, "I think the Lord is the answer, accepting the
Lord. People will change, be more Christ-like. Some of the things that
people are doing today certainly aren't Christ-like." According to this Baptist man, "A lot of our social problems are spiritual in nature. If we could
turn people who are on drugs, and sexual immorality, and the gangs, if we
could turn those people to Christ, we would change a lot of the social problems, fix a lot of those problems." And this Lutheran woman said in a discussion about how to solve the problems of drugs and welfare, "I just feel
like you're just sort of patching up if there's not a real inner change and
dependence on God." The logic of this belief tends to lead evangelicals
away from political action and toward personal evangelism, influence
through good example, and hope for a national revival. As this man from
an Evangelical Free church argued, "There are a lot of well-intending
Christians that are involved in politics and bringing about social change,
but yet it's like Billy Graham said: there's only one way you're gonna change
the country and change people, and that is through bringing them to a
personal knowledge of Christ." Similarly, this Church of the Nazarene

2. And in 1957, evangelical Richard Body wrote against gambling that, "Although its
greatest temptations are introduced through society, gambling is, oddly enough, undeniably
antisocial. This, of course, follows naturally upon its corruption of individuals, for society is
but the sum of individual human beings" (quoted in Hollinger 1983: 108).

woman observed, "I think Christians have solutions, but not necessarily ones that society would accept probably, because it would require mass conversion." And this evangelical Moravian man automatically equated social change with spiritual revival:

> I'll tell you, there's only one thing that's going to cure America from the position that it's in right now. It is love for everyone, and acceptance that Jesus Christ was God on earth. Those are the only two things that are really going to move us to the point where we need to be as a nation. [So it sounds like you mostly see big change happening person-by-person, one individual at a time?] Absolutely. The only way revival would take place in this country is with each person getting their own relationship with Christ right. That's the only way.

Thus, in the words of Fuller Seminary ethicist Lewis Smedes in 1966: "[Evangelical] social ethics is basically very simple then. The Gospel makes men good. Good men make good societies. . . . We have the presence of good men in possession of revealed moral principles, and ready to go anywhere to preach them. . . . [In reality] evangelicals do not have a social ethic. They have a personal ethic for regenerate individuals. They do not have an ethic that prescribes a way of action and form for human society" (1966: 10, 13).

Evangelicalism's personal influence strategy also manifests itself through the miracle motif's logic of social amelioration, which relies primarily on newly converted individuals voluntarily acting altruistically toward other individuals with whom they have relationships. In Fuller Seminary ethicist Lewis Smedes' words, evangelical social ethics "leaves the social needs of [humans] primarily in the hands of benevolent individuals" (1966: 13). This approach is logically necessary, when governmental, institutional, and other systemic means of providing for human well-being which rely on collective action and compulsion are thought of as either illusory or tyrannical. Consider the words of this evangelical woman who attends a Bible Fellowship church:

> Sure Christians have solutions. I am concerned about people in corporations or the rich in America, those who are at the top. I think we have solutions for their dishonesty and emptiness. They have a lot of [material] things, but they aren't feeling fulfilled, and they aren't giving back. I think we have answers for that, equalizing things a little bit more. Being productive and caring about their

communities, and honesty, and all that. If they met Christ face-
to-face, they would give back. They would understand it as a blessing God has given them to be shared and that our communities
would benefit.

This statement reflects what could be an incipient critique of gross structured economic inequality and an attraction to a more equitable redistribution of wealth. But that potential critical analysis is neutralized by this
woman's *a priori* relationalism. Consequently, she defines the problem not
as objective class privilege and inequality, but as personal dishonesty and
existential emptiness and lack of fulfillment. The solution is not a more
equitable restructuring of income distribution, but for rich people to come
to Christ and then practice voluntary generosity toward those around
them. And the ideal outcome is not fundamental economic justice, but an
increase in rich individuals' productivity, caring, honesty, and thankfulness;
"a little bit more" economic equality; and the benefit of patron communities
which are recipients of the munificence of the newly converted corporate
owning class. Such a "personal benevolence" framing is made inevitable by
the evangelical cultural structure of the personal influence strategy.[3]

Evangelicalism's personal influence strategy underscores the need for an
aggregation of individual spiritual conversions and moral improvements as
the pathway to true redemptive social change. But the miracle motif does
not entirely eschew politics as a sphere within which to pursue social transformation. On the contrary, nearly all evangelicals we interviewed insisted
that Christians should get involved in politics as a means to exert a faith-
based influence on American society. But evangelicals' governing relationalism fostered in their thinking a narrow view of appropriate Christian
political strategy. No evangelicals we interviewed, for example, discussed
the importance of potentially more just or effective procedural changes in
government, such as campaign finance reform, more substantive election

3. To be clear, we are not suggesting here that American evangelicals are profoundly
different in their approach to social change than other Christians or Americans. The evangelical approach to social change is not necessarily qualitatively different from that of most
other Americans of similar socioeconomic status; rather, theirs appears to be an exaggerated
and spiritualized version of the broader culture's individualism (see Emerson 1997). But that
is precisely one of evangelicalism's problems, a reality itself damaging to the evangelical project of engaged orthodoxy. For by evangelicals' own standards—because they view themselves
as possessing the Truth and therefore have something extraordinary to offer the "fallen"
world—evangelicals ought to have developed a theology and strategy for social influence
that is distinctive, cogent, realistic, and effective. Instead, what we often find are one-
dimensional social change assumptions and practices which promise only limited effectiveness.

debates, or alternative systems of electoral representation (such as proportional representation). And very few evangelicals addressed broader normative questions, such as the Christian view of political justice, the promise and deficiencies of the new communitarian movement, or distinctively Christian perspectives on specific policy issues (other than their views on abortion, homosexuality, and prayer in public schools). Instead, the primary evangelical strategy for political reform articulated was to elect good Christians to political office. Since evangelicals typically appeared to view the state merely as a collection of elected individuals making decisions together, what they saw as obviously most needed was simply to put into power moral and trustworthy decision-makers. As this Presbyterian woman stated: "I need to be a good citizen, to know who I need to vote for. The goal is getting good people in there that are going to make a difference, who are going to make wise decisions and not take America down." This Pentecostal man elaborated:

> If there's not Christians standing there [in politics], and there's four hundred [politicians] getting ready to vote, [they will] kill the nation, destroy the nation, for whatever reason. What I'm saying is there is no one there with religious beliefs. And he makes a decision for me and my family. Understand? And there's no God in him. He don't fear the Lord. While I'm sleeping, they're up making a decision over my life and my dollar and what will take place in my home and community? I don't think so. I want somebody there that's at least going to pray, to consult God. If all of our politicians were Christians, what would we have to fear? If there was a problem, when they spoke, we would be quick to listen. Quick to follow. But when they speak now, who really listens? [So the most important thing is to have godly people in positions of power, so they can make the right decisions?] Positions of power, that's right.

And when one Charismatic woman told us that Christians need to pray about political groups such as the National Organization of Women and gay rights organizations, we asked her exactly what Christians should be praying for. She replied: "To make it very, very simple: 'Dear God, in Jesus' name, bad ones out and good ones in. Bad ones out of Congress, mayors, schools, professors. Good ones in.'" In this way, evangelicals extend the miracle motif, virtually unaltered, into the political realm.

This "bad-ones-out-good-ones-in" strategy remains particularly plausible for evangelicals in the context of their penchant for viewing gov-

ernment in exaggerated personalistic terms. Rendered largely incapable by
their own relationalism of seeing the structured, institutional, systemic, bureaucratic, conflictive, processual nature of politics, evangelicals tended to
speak about government as if it were an individual person who could act
Christianly, make biblical decisions, and effect personal changes in the lives
of others. This Pentecostal woman, for example, argued: "We need to make
sure the government is run in a Christian manner. How are you going to
have a good government if Christians aren't participating? We need to have
a voice in making decisions." This man from a nondenominational church
explained: "In politics, the first thing Christians need to ask themselves is,
'What would Christ do?' And seek him in any decision that has to be made.
If in the law-making you could reflect the laws of the Bible, the way that
Jesus has laid it out for us, it's got to be a better place." This Presbyterian
woman stated, "The focus of Christians in politics should be: are you going
to be able to change somebody's life by what you are doing?" And this
Church of Christ man viewed politics as a forum for evangelism: "Why
should Christians be active? Because I think souls should be saved. Everybody has a chance or should find a chance to go to heaven. If I can help
somebody do that by being in the government, being in the community
working, that would make me feel good."

Other subthemes about Christian political strategy—governed by the
evangelical personal influence strategy—emerged in many of our interviews. One was that Christians could exert the kind of influence needed in
government merely by being physically present, since the mere presence of
their moral standards alone would inevitably ameliorate politics. This
woman attending an evangelical Moravian church, for example, remarked,
"What can Christians accomplish in politics? Be a moral presence. There's
probably a lot of corrupt people out there who don't mind stealing money,
tax dollars, however they do it. Christians can be there to say [no]." Another common subtheme was the tremendous importance and effectiveness
of Christians simply taking a public stand and "speaking out" to those
around them. More prevalent in interviews than talk about actual pragmatic political accomplishment was an emphasis on the moral need simply
to stand up and have the Christian voice be heard. This woman from a
Charismatic church, for example, stated that, "Christians have a role in
being very vocal and preventing [bad] things. Whether it is from a pulpit
or political position, or just in whatever area of influence they happen to be
in. Speaking out." Similarly, this Lutheran woman explained why Christians need to get involved for social change: "Well, the influence, speaking
up for what they believe is right, and having an influence with what they

believe." Likewise, this man involved in an evangelical Anabaptist church claimed, "We've got to take a stand politically. We're called to do that. No matter what form or how it's done, there are basic things that we have to stand for that are points of faith on which we have to be firm." And this Presbyterian man said, "We've got to try to help others be aware that there are certain issues that a significant number of us feel strongly about." To a certain extent, this evangelical faith in "speaking out" seemed to reveal an optimism—reminiscent of political science's old pluralist theory (Dahl 1961)—about American democracy's capacity to respond to the concerns of all legitimate political interests. As long as Christians make their views known, democracy will respond fairly. And to a certain extent, it also seemed to reflect a need simply to know that one has taken a stand for what one thinks is right, regardless of actual outcomes and consequences. For when history is written—or perhaps rather when all of history is revealed on Judgment Day—all parties will know that evangelicals indeed stood up and spoke out for what was right.

What was also clear was that most ordinary evangelicals retain a tremendous faith in the standard mechanisms of political expression through the American representative democratic process. Many of evangelicals' cultural antagonists worry that the so-called Religious Right contains an authoritarianism which is prepared to run roughshod over the public system of liberal democracy. While those elements certainly may exist in evangelicalism, almost all of the ordinary evangelicals we interviewed were studiously committed to and confident about expressing their views through voting and polite lobbying. Relatively few expressed interest in protests and demonstrations; others expressed deep reservations about the confrontative actions of Operation Rescue and similar groups. Most were simply devoted to and confident in the standard channels of political influence: individuals voting and lobbying their representatives in a respectful, civil manner. This man who attends an independent evangelical church, for example, expressed:

> We should try to influence the law-making process, it is our right as citizens of the country. I hate to use the word "right." But, nevertheless, we are a democracy, we are supposed to have input. We should be speaking up when we find laws being considered that we don't agree with. Christians should be letting their representatives represent them, verbally, you know.

"I think the vote is certainly important," observed one Congregationalist man. "I think it's getting involved. We have a mandate to exercise our role as members of society with voting, talking to your officials in Congress, the Senate, the statehouse, and so on and so forth." This Presbyterian man emphasized the importance in activism of using "the means we have" and "proper channels": "We should use the means we have to make our views known. Writing the politicians, running for office, thinking that we can be effective there, getting involved in various local things. Fight issues [such as public high schools disallowing prayer in graduation ceremonies, he said earlier] if necessary through the proper channels." And this woman involved in a nondenominational evangelical church said:

> What is the goal for Christians to achieve through politics? I don't know, except one individual at a time. People are influenced by their constituency. If the voice isn't there, they will just totally ignore Christians. There needs to be a voice, and individuals who are actually voting on bills too. They only have one vote, but one person at a time, I believe in that.[4]

Aside from political involvement, when evangelicals contemplated affecting redemptive social change, they typically thought in terms of relationally oriented service projects. Theirs was a model of social transformation as "mercy ministry." Relationalists have difficulty recognizing the potential transformative power of countercultural communities and alternative collective identities and practices which challenge normative systems.[5] Nor are relationalists comfortable employing confrontative tactics and collective decision-making processes that force involuntary individual compliance to common standards (with a few exceptions we will discuss below). Therefore, evangelicals' relationalism often tends to lead them toward social involvements that express philanthropic voluntarism. This Presbyterian man, for example, remarked: "Christians should be involved in social things, maybe more than political. There are needy people, who need food and clothes, in our own backyards, stuff like that. Those are the 'least-of-these-my-brethren' types that really need us to be involved with them now." Similarly, this Charismatic man said: "I think if people are living as Christians, they can't help but influence society. You've got soup kitchens

---

4. One Congregationalist woman said, "I think we need to vote intelligently. That's part of being a good citizen of this country, is to vote intelligently, to do the extra chores it takes to find out who are the candidates and what they stand for."

5. To put this analysis into perspective, we might recognize that the Christian tradition contains many cultural tools which—for those who would wish to make use of them—could lend themselves to profoundly alternative social practices and radical social critiques of mainstream American society and culture. For example, Christians could construct a critique of

and community projects, sharing, giving, helping others, being good role models, helping others come to Christ. I mean they can produce inspirational books, you know, fiction or non-fiction." And this Presbyterian woman expressed:

American individualism by invoking the social interdependence of created humanity; the strongly collectivistic nature of God's ideal ancient Hebrew society; the profoundly collectivist nature of the New Testament view of sin and cosmic redemption; Christ's call to deny the self for the welfare of others; and the Apostle Paul's teachings about mutual submission in church bodies, the interdependence of spiritual gifts, and mutual accountability-in-discipleship (see Wallis 1976; Schnachenburg 1968: 190–228; Ridderbos 1975: 91–93; Walter 1979). Christians could challenge the gross inequities of American market capitalism through appeals to the radical economic restructuring of the Old Testament Law's Year of Jubilee; the many Hebrew prophets' condemnations of economic inequality; Jesus' commands to give away and not accumulate wealth; and the early Church's communal economic practices (see Sider 1980, 1990; Miranda 1987; Vogt 1982). Against the glaring disparities in wealth and power of the existing global economic and political system—over which the United States in part presides—Christians could proclaim as normative the created earth and its fruits as God's gift for the welfare of all humanity; the socially revolutionary teachings of the Sermon on the Mount; the Apostle Paul's egalitarian approach to economic differences between early Church communities (see, for example, the Apostle Paul's teachings in 2 Corinthians 8: 13–15); and the myriad New Testament teachings against excessive wealth and power (see Shaull 1988; Sider 1990; Alexander 1986). In response to the relational transience produced by the extensive geographic mobility exacted by the labor-market dynamics of contemporary capitalism and the prevalent drive for upward social mobility, Christians could bring to bear a biblical call for stable, intentional communities of mutual accountability, servanthood, and love that grow out of long-lasting, covenanted relationships (see Jackson and Jackson 1974; Rasmussen 1993; Gish 1979). Against the persistent attitudinal and structural racism in American society, Christians could employ doctrines such as the organic unity of created humanity; the universal love of God; the social-division-destroying nature of Christ's justification; and the ideal of harmony-amid-diversity in the Church to forge profoundly different racial practices within Christian communities (see Yoder 1972; Cone 1975; Mott 1982). Against an American society whose mass-consumer capitalism generally, and advertising and television industries specifically, can be seen as acting as "pushers" for a culture of rampant addiction to all manner of toys, drugs, and novel experiences, Christians could employ cultural tools to model and call for a radically alternative society of spiritually rooted contentment, self-control, and moderation (see Foster 1978, 1981; Sider 1990; Lasch 1986). Christians could witness against the militarism and violence inhering in the American military-industrial economy, entertainment industry, and superpower foreign policy by drawing on and living out the Old Testament visions of shalom, the messianic Suffering Servant, and swords-into-plowshares; Christ's call to nonresistance, peacemaking, and love for enemies; and the Apostle Paul's teaching to resist the fallen principalities and powers (see Yoder 1972; Sider 1979; Berkhof 1977; Stringfellow 1977; Ellul 1972). Christians could challenge the legitimacy of the standard conception of a business corporation as an entity whose primary purpose is to earn profits for its shareholders by elaborating the biblical theology that all human institutions should exist to serve the welfare of all of the people whose lives they touch and not merely the welfare of the privileged wealthy and powerful (see Miranda 1974; USCC 1986). Christians could subvert the competitive American pursuit of social status by asserting instead in word and structured practice the Christian virtues of

I think Christians have answers, and some of them have to be worked on. Some of the areas I think need to be done more on an individual basis, more active Christian involvement. Let's say for the hungry, evangelical churches find a way to hook up resources so they can help. Or help the inner-city areas by providing more tutoring on a more regular basis for some of the students. To help them see the value of getting an education.

Worthy as these projects may be, none of them attempt to transform social or cultural systems, but merely to alleviate some of the harm caused by the existing system. Again, this general strategy assumes a very personalized, individualistic approach to social change through the influence of relationships. "I can't solve the world's problems, but I can sure love the person next to me that is homeless or beaten up," observed one Presbyterian woman. "Christians do have solutions to the world's problems," she continued, "but I think we are paddling up stream. You know it's not up to me to solve the world's problems, and yet I know I can on an individual basis, I can deal with that."

---

humility, contentment, self-denial, and solidarity with the poor and oppressed (see Kraybill 1978; Dorr 1983). Against the environmental destruction wreaked by mass-consumer capitalism, private industry, and the U.S. armed forces, Christians could demand a social order that takes seriously the goodness of God's natural creation; God's inaugural charge to humanity to serve as responsible caretakers of his earth; and the Judeo-Christian tradition of faithful stewardship over all that God owns and entrusts humans with (see Wilkinson 1980; Granberg-Michaelson 1987). In the face of America's continued behavioral and systemic discrimination and violence against women, Christians could denounce gender subordination as alien to God's created order, the result of sin; stress Jesus' revolutionary treatment of women; preach mutual submission of husband and wife; and live out an alternative social practice in which "in Christ there is neither male nor female" (Bilezekian 1985; Swidler 1987; Haubert 1993). Christians could construct a radical critique of America's national system of government schools and secular mass education—which arguably appear to serve better the needs of parents' corporate employers than the genuine educational and developmental needs of children—by emphasizing biblical teachings about childrens' education being the primary responsibilities of their parents and about education as an inescapably religious process (see McCarthy, Skillen, and Harper 1982; Macaulay 1984; Moore and Moore 1979). And against the centralized bureaucracy and hierarchy that characterizes most every mainstream institution in American society, Christians could point to the kingless, decentralized society which God established in ancient Israel; Jesus' radical teachings on human authority and servanthood; and New Testament teachings about the inclusive, participatory, and egalitarian nature of church, in order to fashion a vision for an alternative, small-scale, decentralized, participatory society (see Yoder 1971; Wallis 1981; May 1991). Were American evangelicals interested in making them, all of these critiques and more are theologically available, given the cultural resources of the broad, historical Christian heritage. It is against these potential alternative practices and critiques that contemporary American evangelicalism's actual individualism and personal influence strategy stand in such stark contrast.

Also indicative of the personal influence strategy that pervades evangelical thinking about social change is the recurrent emphasis on each individual's personal choice about where and how to get involved in social change efforts. Seldom did evangelicals speak about the church having a common, collective calling to model an alternative social order, or to throw its unified weight behind a particular vision of social change. Rarely did evangelicals talk about the need for individual believers to yield their own interests and concerns in order to unite behind one common project, campaign, program, or position. Instead, evangelicals typically underscored the uniqueness of each individual's involvement. As one man from a Congregational church said, "Each person has to decide in his own heart what he or she ought to do." "Christians should be involved," elaborated one Baptist man, "but everyone is going to have different areas where that is expressed, because of gifts and talents. Some definitely have a gift with the political environment and should be active; others have a gift in hospital settings, and that is where they should be." Working to transform the world for Christ thus becomes a personal issue, not a collective calling or mission. As this man from a Bible Fellowship church expressed, "I think Christians should be very much involved, but it is a personal kind of thing. It's great to have organizations available to become part of things, but I think each person has specific, unique gifts that God gives out." This individual self-determination of social involvements is often expressed, as by this Baptist woman, in the theological language of a "calling": "I think if God calls you to be involved in politics, I think it would be great."[6] In discussing the problem of race relations in America, evangelicals would often say, "If people feel called to get involved with racial reconciliation, then that's what they should do." But rarely do evangelicals appear called to tasks which require them to transcend their preexisting interests and abilities. As this Presbyterian woman, for example, remarked: "I think there are definitely people who are called to literally be in politics, and more power to them. I could never do it, I think I'd get too frustrated with the whole system. But I do think Christians need to be involved in politics." Overall, then, evangelicals' emphasis on the need for a diversity of social involvements dramatizes and reinforces their own relationalist worldview's commitment to individual self-determination and diffuse interpersonal influence.

We said above that evangelical relationalism tends to avoid confronta-

6. Others, such as this Presbyterian woman, speak in the more secular language of "skills": "Christians could be involved in politics, if they have the skills, why not? I don't know that everyone should be in politics. Because not everyone has the skills."

tive tactics and collective decision-making processes that force involuntary
individual compliance to common social standards. This statement needs
some nuancing. Evangelicals are not anarchists, antinomians, nor absolute
libertarians. Rather, their relationalism operates from an assumed baseline
standard of a necessary common morality. Evangelicals say that a society's
government must obviously enforce standards against lying, murder, and
stealing, whether certain bad individuals like it or not. For evangelicals,
that standard moral baseline is usually considered to be the Ten Commandments and select other aspects of Old Testament law. This Nazarene
woman, for example, said:

> There are some overarching values, but they're not common just
> to Christianity, but to many different life perspectives. Things like
> most of your Ten Commandments, like "Thou shalt not steal."
> That's pretty common amongst society in general. I mean, there's
> always an element that doesn't go along with that, but for the soci-
> ety as a whole, I think [it embraces] that one, and the prohibition
> against murder. Those kinds of things. A value of honesty I think
> is pretty universal.

Beyond these basics, however, evangelicals tend not to want government
power taking it upon itself to enforce the particulars of morality. For, within
the individualism of the relationalist frame of reference, morality is properly that which individual agents should voluntarily choose and live out for
themselves. So, if one want others to live morally (beyond the minimum
baseline standard), one must persuade them to change their personal commitments so that they as moral individuals choose to do so—hence, the
miracle motif (more on this below).

Three specific issues, however, appear as exceptions to this approach:
the vast majority of evangelicals oppose both abortion and gay rights; and
a sizeable number of evangelicals want to see prayer returned to public
schools. But these are exceptions which prove the rule. For one thing, pro-
life evangelicals view abortion as murder and so see this as an issue which
belongs to the baseline moral standard the state should uphold. Likewise,
homosexuality is understood as absolutely prohibited by Old Testament
law, a practice carrying—in evangelicals' view—disastrous social consequences, and so too part of the baseline standard. Conversely, for those
evangelicals who care about the issue (and not all do), prayer in school is
not seen as an attempt to impose religion in the public arena. Rather, these
evangelicals see the problem as an activist secular government preventing

the American public from exercising its basic rights to freedom of worship and free speech—precisely the kind of thing individualism and relationalism resist. Furthermore, abortion and homosexuality are political issues individualistic evangelicals can readily grasp hold of because they both can be fairly easily viewed, within a relationalist framework, as involving individuals who make what are seen as immoral personal choices that negatively affect others around them. As such, they are much easier for individualistically minded evangelicals to reckon with and take stands on than, say, ozone depletion, the national deficit, dysfunctional campaign finance laws, or the international economic consequences of free trade agreements. Similarly, prayer in school can readily be viewed as an inalienable religious good any individual moral agent should be allowed to enjoy, without the obstruction of the state. For these and other reasons, then, when it comes to these issues, evangelicals appear to have little problem mingling the voluntaristic language of individual moral autonomy with the coercive language of legalized moral norms. This Presbyterian man, for example, spoke in one breath about, on the one hand, influencing others through the sheer persuasive power of demonstrated love, and, on the other hand, the need to use political means to prevent change where there are "clear moral values" involved:

> Well of course Christians should be active. I don't know quite how to answer that, except to say I think that we should try to be a positive influence. We should try to show love and try to demonstrate with our own lives what the Lord has done for us and what he could do for them. And we should get involved in politics to try to be an influence where there are clear moral values involved. Like same-sex marriages. There are moral values involved.

Some evangelicals we interviewed did quietly express doubts about evangelicalism's relationalist approach to social transformation, particularly the miracle motif. When we asked this Presbyterian woman, for example, whether more people becoming Christians would begin to solve social problems, she replied:

> I have worked with lots of Christians who have so many emotional and psychological problems that I . . . It not only has to be a changed life accepting Christ as your Savior, it has to be a changed life following that. There are so many Christians who are dying out there, emotionally and physically. So it is not a pill. It doesn't cure the world. I think there is something missing, something

wrong, something we haven't hit on. My sister is Pentecostal, and she thinks she has found it, this deeper inner-spiritual relationship with God. But I can tell it isn't, when she puts her guard down, the perfect pill that is going to make everything better right now. I think there is something that we are missing, and I don't know what it is yet. My family isn't having any major problems, whereas Jane Doe down the street has the same Christianity, the same faith, and she has a million problems and her life is a mess. I think there are different spiritual battles that are going on which we don't begin to know about. I don't think we will ever know until we are in heaven.[7]

Yet these disclosures of doubt (which appear not to undermine either the individualistic view of social problems as ultimately personal and psychological, nor the doubter's religious faith) were rare. Most evangelicals march on, confident in—though perhaps not very self-aware of—their relationalist outlook.

But, again, this personal influence strategy exacts a cost. It tends to render evangelicals rather blind to the supraindividual social structures, aggregate effects, power dynamics, and institutional systems which profoundly shape human consciousness, experience, and life-chances.[8] Because evangelicals employ the personal influence strategy, it serves to obscure, for them, the effect of forces outside themselves and their interpersonal relationships, along with their capacity to comprehend adequately how the social world actually works and to formulate relevant and responsive solutions to complex social, economic, political, and cultural problems. Thus, while this evangelicals cultural tool of personal influence strategy contributes to a sense of evangelical subcultural distinctiveness and identity strength, it

7. Likewise, this Baptist man remarked, "I don't think we can cure all the world's illness, but I think we can offer some kind of hope to these things. Purely physical standpoint, yeah, I think we can help the homeless. We can provide clothes and housing for them. We can volunteer our time to help. But are we going to cure that problem? No." Similarly, this Pentecostal woman—reflecting an embryonic notion about government as a supraindividual social structure—expressed reservations about the effectiveness of merely electing Christians to political office to bring about change: "I know there are good people who get involved in politics and think they are going to go down there and change everything. And they get caught up in the machine. It certainly is there. And despite all their efforts and all the good intentions, they get caught up in the machine and they find they can really do very little."

8. When evangelicals *do* occasionally perceive the power of social structures, they tend to respond—as did this Charismatic woman in a discussion about corruption in the political system—with individualistic or purely spiritual solutions: "What kind of system change could I envision to deal with political corruption? The second coming [of Christ]."

also simultaneously appears to undermines evangelical influence in the public square.

For Example: A Christian Influence on Business and the Economy

In our interviews, we asked ordinary evangelicals who advocated the need for Christian social influence to explain specifically how they think that influence should work in a number of specific areas—including education, race relations, and the business and economic world. For brevity's sake, we will focus here on how evangelicals think the Christian Gospel should affect the world of work, business, and the economy. Despite our explicitly asking them to think beyond interpersonal relationships and individual morality, evangelicals' vision for Christian influence typically did not move beyond the limits of the personal influence strategy or beyond merely improving the morality of individual businesspeople through the influence of personal associations.

Evangelicals offered a variety of ways that they thought Christianity could or should affect the world of work, business, and the economy. Some, such as this Baptist woman, emphasized bringing in elements of religious devotion, like having prayer and Bible study on the job: "We've got groups that start their day with prayer. There are a lot of businesses that start their days with their employees with prayer. What better way?" This woman from an independent seeker-church said, "There are opportunities, if you are the one that is in charge, to have Bible study on company time, a prayer breakfast, outreach of some kind." One Pentecostal man spoke of the need to "keep it a clean job":

> I don't let them cuss excessively on my job. If they let a few words slip, we don't say a lot. But I can't stand a whole lot of profanity, so I keep that real low key. No drinking, no alcohol, no coming into work drunk. Also, we pray most of the time before we start work in the morning, that God would keep us, protect us. And he does. [Do the non-Christians pray with you?] Yeah. If they don't pray, they bow their heads in respect while we pray.

This woman from a nondenominational church who works in a restaurant reported: "I just try and touch people's lives, like at Easter time, I put a little cross on the menu that says, 'He is Risen.' Nobody has ever given me any guff about it. Just putting 'He is the Reason for the Season' on my menu, small things like that." One Bible Church man said that if a "corporation were really living for Christ" and if its decisions were "based on the leading of the Holy Spirit," there might be the possibility, for example, of General Motors starting a strategic-planning board meeting in prayer. And this Wesleyan man spoke of the need to have faith influence the business decision-making process:

> How you make decisions. If you are setting policies or directions for a company, are you doing it in prayer? Are you looking at the Bible? Or are you doing it all in your own head, with your own will? I think policies should be made with God at your side.

Other evangelicals spoke less about religious devotion on the job and more about how Christianity would make employees more creative, harder workers. One Church of God woman said, "I believe a real Christian is a better worker. Because if they follow the Bible, it says to give an honest day's work for your wages. So I do believe they make better employees." This Presbyterian man said that Christians, "should be the most honest employees they have. If you are working for someone, you shouldn't steal, or take an extra ten minutes for lunch break." This woman from a nondenominational evangelical church explained that Christian faith can produce more creative and efficient employees: "If Christians are asked to be creative, short cuts might be made, a better way to do a job, maybe more organization." She said, for example, that she had developed new, more efficient business forms for her company, "then one day my boss came in and started using some of my forms, and they are still today using eight of the forms that I created." Faith, she said, is what made her help create a more efficient office: "Scripture says to do all you do as unto the Lord, so I was doing my job unto the Lord and not unto man." This woman from a nondenominational church also talked about Christians as better employees:

> If more people at the factory where I work were Christians, we would have less theft of government property. You'd have more people committed to their job too. You know, I work eight hours a day, five days a week. But you look at somebody else, they are over there in the hall all the time, and what are they doing? Where's their work ethic? All that would be different.

Similarly, this Assemblies of God man, a business manager who apparently has had trouble with unreliable employees, argued:

The Bible says you get a day's pay for a day's work, okay? If you're following the Bible, don't come to work late. And be consistent about it, okay? If everybody was in tune with that, this would be an awesome nation for the economy and everything. Because you don't have somebody cheating you out of ten minutes, not wrecking the company van without telling anybody about it. [Are there any things beyond that? Beyond just individuals being honest? For Christianity affecting . . .] The economy? Well yeah, because if everybody is going to be honest, then you're going to have people coming to work on time. Then the whole economy would be better, whether you're Christian or not. But I expect more out of Christians. I don't expect them to keep coming in late. I mean, that's not an option if you're a Christian. But back to the economy issue, if everybody would just do what they're supposed to, when they're supposed to do it, for their employer, we wouldn't have the economy problems.

Some evangelicals said that a Christian influence would not only affect employees but should also affect businesses themselves—mostly making them more fair and honest. One man from an independent evangelical church said, "Business should be fair, should not be taking money under the table, should be paying their taxes." Similarly, this Lutheran woman remarked, "Businesses need to be fair, don't work somebody and not pay them what they should be paid—everybody's entitled to make a living. [Should the rules and practices of the work and business world be shaped by Christianity?] Yeah, Christian morals. Fairness, honesty, treating people the way they should be treated, being paid for a job done." One Baptist woman said that at work, because of her Christian faith:

I am more tolerant and helpful. I told this one man, he was upset about a bill, and I said, "It is an honest bill, and I think you should take it up with the Lord. If you feel you should pay me, then do so, if not, don't. You have to live with your decision." He said, "I don't believe you!," and he paid the bill. So, I think your reaction makes a difference.

One man from a nondenominational church suggested that Christian-influenced businesses might resort to drastic measures to keep bad language out of computer communications. It would be good, he said, "if someone could [program computers] so that if anyone types in a pornographic word, it would cause the computer to automatically wipe out everything on it. If any of a list of pornographic words was typed into the computer, it would just cancel and wipe out everything without giving you time to save anything you had."

But this kind of draconian solution was atypical. For the most part, evangelicals assumed that a Christian influence was best exercised through personal relationships by individuals setting good examples of morality. And the moral virtue that evangelicals extolled above all was honesty— again, despite the fact that we explicitly and repeatedly asked them to think beyond individual morality and honesty (compare to Wuthnow 1994b: 81– 88). More than one out of three evangelicals we interviewed mentioned honesty as a primary way Christianity could influence the world of work, business, and the economy. One man from an independent church, for example, said, "I believe that if we do live morally and honestly it's going to have an impact, more of an impact than people really see. It would make a huge difference. Now whether or not it would clean everything up, I think if everybody lived for the Lord, yes it would." And when we asked one Church of Christ man whether there was more Christianity could do for the economy besides honesty, he answered, "No, because if everybody would be honest, that's all it would take. If everybody was honest in the United States, think of how it would be: great!" And this Baptist woman replied, "You have in a nutshell said the Christian values of honesty in your dealings, and being straightforward. If you do that, most everything will take care of itself."[9]

Consistent with our previous analysis, the assumption that social change is most effectively achieved through the influence of interpersonal relationships was commonplace in evangelical thinking about business and the economy. One Baptist female, for example, said, "Most of it you're gonna see it by one-on-one individuals. A lot of the impact is gonna be by individuals." A woman from a nondenominational church remarked, "I feel that it would have to operate on an individual level. I think the way any

---

9. Employing a logic which parallels the evangelical faith in electing moral individuals to office as a means to influence politics, some evangelicals—such as this Christian Reformed man—emphasized the importance of getting moral businesspeople in positions of leadership: "If you are the President or CEO of a company and a Christian, I would hope to think that your views on how to conduct your business would filter down to the lowest man on the totem pole. You conduct your business, no matter how big, with integrity, you do it so it is a Christian business. That influence gets trickled down, as it is made clear that this is the way we do business here." Similarly, this Baptist woman said, "Christians should get involved in places of leadership, which would be more than an individual participation effect. We have several people that go to church, one is a city manager, one a fire chief, and one on the city council. I would think that would make a difference in the way the government business meetings are run."

one of us treats other human beings, or treats what we do, or sees it in the larger picture, that is so important, and has everything to do with the results." And this Baptist man said, "I look back to Galatians, the fruits of the Spirit: love, joy, peace, patience, kindness, self-control. Imagine men and women with that type of lifestyle in the world. I feel it would make a huge difference." Even when evangelicals spoke about changing business firms, they often presumed an individualistic reductionism which views the moral character of corporations as simply the sum total of the related individuals who work for it. This Assemblies of God woman, for example, argued:

> Instead of people being out for the money and revenge and for achieving the top of the corporate ladder anyway they can get there, Christians are thankful for where they are and the blessings of achievement of success. Success comes through their hard work and dedication. I think that would change a lot. The corporate world wouldn't be so cut-throat.

Whether or not a corporation is cut-throat is determined not by institutional policies, the broader economic environment, marketplace dynamics, legal structures, or the profit motive, but rather by the goodness of the individual employees who work for it. Similarly, by stating that part of a Christian influence would be, "not working so much that it begins to hurt your family and your relationships," one Assemblies of God woman automatically identified the problem as discrete individuals choosing to work too much, not corporate work-hour structures that demand work time away from family. And by saying that, "pornography should not be consumed by Christian believers, [producing] less of a market for this sort of industry," one man from a Bible Church automatically focuses the issue on individual consumer preferences, not society's legal toleration of the pornography industry. So, evangelicals leave the existing larger structures of business and the economy largely unquestioned.[10] What they really considered necessary for genuine change are individual morals through personal relationships.

10. Indeed, some evangelicals were quite explicit in their embrace of existing economic practices. One man from a Congregational church, for example, argued: "The most successful businesses are shaped by Christian values and morals. If you look at it from a long-term economic view, that is the only way to run a successful business. Don't do it for the motive of eternal salvation, do it for the motive of success. There are three things required to be successful: a belief in God, a willingness to work, and knowledge. [What do you mean by success?] Success in my mind in business is generating a fair return for the investors."

So foreign was the idea that Christianity might transform business and economic structures beyond improving individual morals and honesty, that many evangelicals simply could not understand what we were asking. After our repeated attempts to pose the question in different ways, some evangelicals simply said, "I'm really not sure what you're asking," or, "I kind of get the question, I don't know. I'm not sure where you're going with that," or, "I don't know, I'm just drawing blanks here." Others *did* understand what we were asking and, because it seemed to violate the subcultural code of the personal influence strategy, said flatly that Christianity could never affect such changes. In reply to our question about whether the rules and practices of business should be shaped by Christianity, this Church of God woman replied, "Yes, it would be better. But we will never see it." One Assemblies of God woman puzzled, "I'm trying to think of how it could. Unless it were controlled by the church, and that I definitely don't believe in. I don't know any way that it could be." Likewise, this Baptist woman said, "If you have a business, you should be running it to the glory of God. I mean you can still make a profit and not get over on everybody you are doing business with. [So you would be a little less concerned with making all that profit, and more concerned . . .] Should be, but it's not going to happen."

A few evangelicals we interviewed did express what seemed to be rudimentary critiques of the existing economic order or visions of alternatives economic structures. Although somewhat simplistic, they nevertheless suggested genuine attempts to think about how Christianity might challenge or influence the economic world beyond the mere improvement of individual morality through interpersonal relationships. One woman from an independent evangelical church, for example, expressed simple reservations about the competition that permeates the capitalist marketplace: "I think competition is bad, I do. I guess it can be good, but my experience is that it is bad." A few others verbalized implicit and explicit criticisms of the dominant normative cultural conception of business corporations as organizations whose fundamental purpose is to earn profits for investors. One Christian and Missionary Alliance man, for instance, suggested that business firms should prioritize the well-being of employee's families over the profit motive:

> Chick-fil-A is closed on Sunday, and has been very successful, and
> I think that makes a statement to the business world. [The priority

order] is God, your family, and then your business. So, there are people who are doing things right and influencing other companies. One of the principles is putting family first.

And one Pentecostal woman thought that service-oriented businesses—like the ambulance company for which she works—should offer their services on a sliding scale for people who need a service but cannot afford to pay full charges. One Wesleyan man suggested that business firms should not only be concerned with profits but always take an egalitarian approach that serves the welfare interests of all parties involved in any transaction:

> You would treat employees, customers, vendors, and the whole spectrum of people you get involved with as equals, as partners. Not always look at the bottom line, asking, is this a profitable decision? Instead, is it profitable? Is it ethical? Is everybody win-win? Or is somebody on the losing end? And if they are, who and why? And do I really want to do that to them? Is that morally and Christianly ethical for them to lose in that situation? I think the well-being of all people should be considered.

Taking a more specific position, this Baptist woman recommended that business firms return their surplus profits to their local communities: "When they reach their goals, they can turn their profits back into the community through service organizations and helping others, not just the company itself and its employees. My husband did that with a company, so I know it can be done."

But these kinds of suggestions were rare. And sometimes the few that were ventured neutralized themselves through a relationalist logic or an incapacity to connect social criticism with the language of faith. This woman from an independent church, for example, negated her own critique of corporate downsizing by restricting all possible solutions to the problem to voluntary, individual decisions by firms to act differently:

> It would be a lot better if businesses were honest and tried to help people out, and not just be out to make money. I think that a lot of our recession wouldn't have happened if everybody hadn't kept downsizing to make more money, because then their employees all get laid off, and so there's nobody to buy stuff. If companies were to look out for their employees, and to kind of follow the rule "do unto others," I think business would be a lot different. Problem is, you can't regulate this, and it has to be an individual decision.

Analogously, because this Baptist man was unable to recognize the manifold biblical teachings against gross income inequality and for income redistribution (see, for example, Mott 1982: 59–106; Sider 1980, 1990; Miranda 1974, 1987), he appears unable to develop his own thinking about income equity beyond merely "wondering" about it:

> I question, I wonder about the redistribution of wealth and the sharing of wealth—which I know might label me extremely liberal or to the left. But I wonder if there couldn't be redistribution of wealth, whether it is a social program or accelerated tax structures on the rich. I don't know. Obviously, I don't find that in Scripture. But I don't find anything in Scripture that is opposed to it. Tax collectors [in Jesus' day] were fleecing the public, and when they were converted, they gave back ten-fold of what they took. I'm not using that to say we ought to be a socialistic society, but all I'm saying is it causes me to wonder, to think.

In this case, the disjunct between his social critique and his authority of faith, produced in part by the cultural power of the personal influence strategy, undermined a potential alternative vision for the economic order.

The Complication of Voluntaristic Absolutism

The deficiencies of the personal influence strategy as a key evangelical approach to social influence are compounded by its interaction with the conjoining of two other related evangelical subcultural tools into what we might call "voluntaristic absolutism." By this we mean, in short, that many evangelicals think that Christian morality should be the primary authority for American culture and society *and* simultaneously think that everyone should be free to live as they see fit, even if that means rejecting Christianity. Because they often firmly believe both positions simultaneously and cannot make up their minds between them, evangelicals have difficulty formulating a coherent philosophy of or strategic plan for faith-based social influence. This sets up for evangelicals some very difficult strategic quandaries regarding Christian social change.

On the absolutist side, most evangelicals have inherited and embrace the theological notion that there is a transcendent God who establishes supreme and universal standards of morality for individuals and societies. They also generally believe that obedience to God's ways is practically superior and ultimately produces abundant life. Rejecting God's ways, however, produces individual and social degeneration and, finally, death. Most evangelicals, too, are heirs of a faith that for centuries enjoyed the status of *de facto* religious establishment. This absolutist legacy—which mixes essential elements of Christian doctrine with aspects of the historical Protestant experience in America, particularly Puritanism—makes evangelicals want *their* morality and standards to be normative for American society. These standards are not only more familiar and comfortable to them, they are also assumed to provide the only basis for the ongoing prosperity of American civilization. The absolutist impulse is illustrated in this exchange with a Baptist woman:

Q: Would you support a law to recognize homosexual marriages?
A: Well, no. The Christian laws shouldn't do that. I'm totally against gay marriages and lesbians and them wanting to raise kids.
Q: And if they say you're imposing your religious values and morals on them?
A: Well, I'm just telling you what the Word of God says.
Q: But if they said they don't believe in God or the Bible, then you would say?
A: You can't change me, my beliefs.
Q: So you're comfortable using laws to maintain Christian morals?
A: Well, yes.

At the same time, most of the *very same* evangelicals are committed to another belief that is fundamentally incompatible with the idea of absolutism: individual voluntarism. This belief reflects other age-old Christian doctrines colored less by Puritanism and more by the American Protestant experience of frontier revivalism and by less-religious aspects of American culture. Embedded in most versions of evangelical faith are the ideas that each individual must ultimately decide for themselves to follow God or not; that truly meaningful moral actions cannot be forced, but must come voluntarily from the heart; and that Christians ultimately can't make people who do not want to be Christians to act as if they were. As one Pentecostal man said, "I am opposed to shoving anything down people's throats and I think God is too. He gives every person a right to choose. And we should also." Furthermore, American individualism—which most evangelicals, we have seen, endorse—prescribes that individuals should not be coerced by social institutions, especially by the government, and particularly not on personal matters; that freedom to pursue individual happiness is a paramount good; that people shouldn't meddle too deeply in other people's business; and that government usually provides poor solutions to social and cultural problems. This belief in individual voluntarism tends naturally to eschew the domineering spirit of absolutism and instead accepts, if not embraces, social and cultural tolerance and pluralism. People should live how they choose to live and be prepared to answer to God for their own choices. So, in the very same discussion, the very same Baptist woman also affirmed the voluntaristic impulse:

> Q: How do you feel about using laws to set social standards
> about family life or sexual morality?
> A: Well, I don't think the law can do that because that's not the
> law's responsibility. The Bible says it's people's own respon-
> sibility, not the law's. I think that's what has America in
> trouble now: we try to make the law take care of everything.
> I don't agree with using laws for that kind of thing.
> Q: You would rather have people live morally voluntarily, and
> not have the government trying to tell people how to live?
> A: Yes, that's right.

Notice that it is generally not that some evangelicals embrace absolutism and others embrace voluntarism. Most of the evangelicals we interviewed, just like this Baptist woman, embrace both, even if they are not aware of it in these precise terms. And being caught on the horns of this dilemma generally creates within them a powerfully confusing and self-restraining ambivalence about Christian social and political activism. Too much voluntaristic thinking automatically evokes the concerns of absolutism—God's laws are not optional, but binding on all people and nations, for their own good. At the same time, however, mental steps toward absolutism automatically rouse the opposition of voluntarism—you should not force people to live like Christians. And in the end, neither gets very far. And, consequently, evangelicals do not get very far in figuring out how to go about transforming the world.

Historically, this voluntaristic absolutism dilemma was fairly easily resolved in that orthodox Protestantism, although officially disestablished, in fact for centuries dominated America's public discourse and its major cultural institutions. By failing to see the degree to which theirs was an imposed domination, the Protestant establishment had its cake and ate it too: it enjoyed a "Christian America" that it believed was voluntarily chosen by the American people. But since evangelicalism has increasingly lost control of the public discourse produced by major cultural institutions (universities, mass media, etc.) since the turn of the twentieth century, the majority of evangelicals who want to affirm both absolutism and individual voluntarism face an increasingly uncomfortable cognitive dissonance.

We could quote equally well very many of the evangelicals we interviewed—men and women from all social classes and doctrinal traditions—to further illustrate the strategic conundrums that the voluntaristic absolutism dilemma generates for evangelicals who are interested in influencing American culture and society. We will restrict ourselves here, however, to quoting one extended discussion which clearly reveals the strategic confusions which this dilemma creates. We held the following conversation with a well-educated and very socially involved Presbyterian woman:

> Q: To what extent do you think Christian morality should be the commonly accepted morality of the culture? And to what extent do you think it should just be one option among many moral options?
>
> A: Well you can't force Christian morality. I mean it's not going to happen. People are going to rebel anyway. I'm not saying, oh, just make everything free. Because it's going to be a mess anyway. I think it's a hard one. It's really a hard one. I mean these are hard questions, because at the end of the day it's the heart that matters. It's not what's happening on the outside, and yet you [have to] change the outside. Hopefully it will sink in, you know. And people go, well, why isn't this allowed? It's nice to think it would make it more difficult for people that are the same sex to be married and to have to jump more barriers. But what's going to stop them from living out that life style? Nothing.
>
> Q: So, would you say you don't think that's a law worth establishing?
>
> A: I think it is a law worth establishing. But along with the law needs to be involvement, Christians involved in people's lives.
>
> Q: You know that a number of groups in society will say, "Well, you're welcome to believe that. However, we don't share your worldview, we don't believe in the Bible or God, we have a different moral standard. And in this free, pluralistic society, you don't have the right to impose your system on me." What do you say in response to that?
>
> A: This is just a really hard issue. And I don't know that I have any answers to that.
>
> Q: But you think if push comes to shove in the voting booth you would support that law?
>
> A: Right.

Q: So it's okay to say that Christian morality should be the officially accepted standards of our culture?

A: Yeah. Because we are a part of society, and we need to take a stand for what our belief system [says], knowing that we can't instill a belief system into those who don't believe. You know, because it's just going to, I mean what change is going to happen? But if you can instill a belief system, and come in the back door and sit down and talk to people and love people. It's got to be both.

Q: But this law is not instilling a belief system, it's setting up an external standard that will be enforced, whether or not people agree with it. So what principles shape when Christian morality should be official and when you say different people can do different things?

A: Well, that's the hard stance. . . . Because people can be angry at Christians for trying to establish their Christian morals and take it as boxing people in and not giving people freedom of choice. But if Christians are taking a back seat and not voting for those things, it's just the age old. . . . And the question that you're getting at is how are, how can we make a difference? Can we make a difference?

Q: When it comes to laws, that's what I'm trying to get at, enforcing certain standards. Or letting people choose what they want morally, and just working to change people from the inside out? What about that kind of argument?

A: Well I'm the first to talk about going to the heart of a matter. And yet I don't think the answer is therefore just to waive our belief system. I mean if somebody believes for themselves that, you know, people should not have abortions, well then they need to vote that way. I mean it's a personal vote. It's one person's vote.

Q: So the principle is majority rules? Whatever the greatest number of Americans think should be the governing rule?

A: Well, that's what happens. In one sense that's what's going to happen if Christians are taking a stand. I mean you can't enforce law. You can't enforce Christian morals. Because Christian morals are not . . .

Q: You can or can't?

A: You can't. You can and you can't. You can externally, but I believe Christian morals come internally. So you can't change matters of the heart. Apart from loving people on an individual and corporate level.

Q: But you can enforce behaviors that derive from Christian morals?

A: Right. And that's the question of law versus grace. There has to be law. I mean you can't just throw law out the window. You know we're given grace, and that helps us interpret law in a different way. So I think it does say something about taking a stand.

Q: How about Sabbath laws? That's one of the Ten Commandments. Yet Christians don't seem very invested in that issue anymore. Would you support a law that said businesses can't be open on Sunday?

A: I work on Sunday, and there are people in my life that have a hard time with that. In a lot of ways that's an individual thing. In my opinion, a Sabbath, a day of rest doesn't have to be Sunday. I work on Sunday because that's the way it is. I have employees who don't want to work on Sundays, and I don't make them. I respect their beliefs. I think it would come down to what did I individually think about that, and also what does the [church] Body think about that. Then I think of the divorce issue coming up in Ireland. That's another question: do you restrict divorce or do you allow divorce? You can go both ways on every same issue that it boggles your brain. I don't know if this is going to be a whole muddled section for me because it's hard. It's hard.

Q: I'm just trying to figure out how people think through to what extent they want Christian morality to be the official standard in this society by law, and to what extent they are willing to allow moral diversity.

A: That's a hard issue and I don't know that I'd come down. . . . I guess it would depend on the issue. I come down on many sides. Because I do think that we need diversity, and yet I think I'm not into just what ever you do is okay.

Q: But you're not entirely sure where you draw the line or why you fall where you fall between those?

A: Right. . . . We're going to have pluralism. And I'm not saying therefore whatever you want to do, do. I don't fall down on that side of the fence, freedom for everybody to do what you feel. But . . .

Q: But should you fight against pluralism or work with it?

A: We're going to have it, and we're going to take a stand on our belief system, and not cram it down people's throat. Accept people who differ from us, love them, and not fight the same way they fight. Fight with love and forgiveness and commu-

nication and involvement. I mean it's the whole thing of
church and state and all that. I don't think we can enforce . . .
The answer is not to enforce law, because it's going to explode some where. And especially given where America is,
it's like taming a wild lion. It's going to get out of the cage.
It's going to eat the bars. So I'm not saying, oh you know,
we're going downhill so we might as well just sit back. I think
we need to be involved, but yet look at what we are looking
at. I'm not doing a great job of answering, because that's
where I wrestle with these questions. It's a hard thing.

Clearly, this woman is caught on the horns of a strategically debilitating
dilemma. Unable to confidently believe in either absolutism or voluntarism, in either Christendom or pluralism, she is repeatedly thrown back
and forth in her thinking between them, occasionally collapsing in confusion. In this, she is not atypical of evangelicals generally.

Most of the evangelicals we interviewed tried to resolve this confusion
and dissonance by compartmentalizing their beliefs in absolutism and voluntarism and strongly affirming them as separate commitments, thereby
preventing each from having to face the full implications of the other.
When we began to press those we interviewed to decompartmentalize
these conflicting convictions and choose one above the other—as we did
above—they typically fought long and hard to keep them in their separate
compartments. When we persisted, sometimes people simply gave up and,
as did the woman above, said, "I don't know how it fits together. I guess I'll
have to think about it some more." But in the end, the ultimate practical
consequence we saw in most of those we talked with was that faith-based
social and political activism that absolutism tended to encourage was consistently reigned in and subdued by the tolerance and pluralism inherent
in individual voluntarism. Battling to Christianize America just didn't sit
right—which perhaps explains why less than half of the evangelicals in our
survey said that their vote was ever influenced by conservative Christian
political organizations like the Christian Coalition. But then again, letting
Americans do whatever they pleased did not suit the evangelicals well either. Caught on the horns of this dilemma, most evangelicals simply remained strategically stumped. And the evangelical project of engaged orthodoxy remained rather stuck.

Conclusion

Some readers may be inclined to suggest that these evangelical strategic
weaknesses in fact document a process of secularization. Yet, these strategic

problems do not consist primarily of an "external" secularizing force undermining evangelicalism's vitality or authority. Rather, these problems are fundamentally the outworkings of the internal subcultural structures of the evangelical tradition. The individualism of the personal influence strategy, for example, has not been imposed upon a reluctant evangelicalism by encroaching forces of modernity. Rather, it reflects a key cultural element native to a long religious tradition which, in fact, significantly *helped to shape* American modernity. Evangelicalism's problems, in other words, are largely subculturally indigenous, difficulties of their own tradition's making. Recently, some "neo-secularization" theorists (see Chaves 1994; Yamane 1997; also see Hunter 1997) have "circled the wagons" and sought to reconceptualize secularization as a decline in religious authority. This is a helpful theoretical move. But, if anything, in our case, the strategic difficulties that constrain evangelical attempts at social influence demonstrate precisely the powerful authority that evangelical cultural codes still do hold over ordinary evangelicals. The problem is not that evangelicalism is suffering a decrease in its capacity to govern individual consciousness and action. Quite the contrary. Evangelical cultural structures—such as the personal influence strategy and voluntaristic absolutism—retain tremendous authority among the faithful. The problem, rather, is that the subcultural codes which evangelicals employ with great conviction are themselves strategically inadequate for the task of social transformation. It is precisely because the strategically deficient evangelical tradition exercises such authority among its adherents, then, that evangelicals encounter much of the strategic ineffectiveness described above.

The larger theoretical point, however, is that the subcultural distinction that, according to our subcultural identity theory of religious strength, generates vitality in a religious tradition may not be an unambiguous good from that tradition's perspective. Subcultural distinction can be a mixed blessing. For the social forces that can unite people into a movement can also paradoxically undermine their attempts at effective social influence in the public square. In the case of American evangelicalism, we find a religious tradition which, ironically, is often for the very same reasons, yet in different ways, both strong and ineffective.

To recapitulate: pluralistic modernity can promote the vitality of culturally well-equipped traditional religions. Far from necessarily undermining the strength of orthodox faith, modernity creates the conditions in which traditional religion may thrive. Contemporary American evangelicalism is a case in point. Evangelicalism thrives in pluralistic modernity, we suggest, because it possesses and employs the cultural tools needed to create both clear distinction from and significant engagement and tension with other relevant outgroups, short of becoming countercultural. And modern pluralism provides the environment within which that strategy works. By contrast, the classical American fundamentalist strategy of isolationist separatism, and the theologically liberal approach of radical accommodation appear to undermine those traditions' religious strength. Comparatively, distinction-with-engagement appears to be the most effective strategy for maintaining religious vitality in the American culturally pluralistic environment (again, we use the words "thriving" and "vitality" only as descriptions of the dimensions of religion which sociologists can properly access, not as indicators of any kind of moral superiority or true religious integrity or faithfulness).

At least some religious traditions, we should recognize, tend to be extraordinarily adaptable. Religious actors appear to have an incredible capacity to draw on traditional beliefs and practices of faith and adjust them to a variety of social situations, including modern structures, imperatives, and sensibilities. Many religious actors seem to be able rather effectively to fashion and utilize "sacred umbrellas" by lodging themselves in subcultural and organizational niches within the rich cultural complexity and diversity of modernity. They can use them, and the outgroups in relations to which they are constructed, to thrive. Part of religion's adaptability appears to derive from its capacity to sustain itself through rituals, practices, microcommunities, organizational routines, and so on, which serve as powerful plausibility structures—even in the face of potential cognitive challenges to religious modes of thinking and living. We know that religion gets worked out in relational contexts. So it should not be surprising that embeddedness in relational networks of identity and obligation can help to hold the fabric of religious commitment and affiliation tight. Congruously, it is primarily relational disruptions that provoke religious disaffiliation and disenchantment when they do occur.

Still, dynamics of religious vitality do not all necessarily work consistently in the same direction. For religious traditions may contain subcultural contradictions which create strength along certain dimensions but foster weakness along others. In the case of American evangelicalism, some of the identity boundaries which enhance vitality within evangelicalism also appear to serve as barriers to communicating and relating effectively to nonevangelicals. Furthermore, certain of American evangelicalism's subcultural tools which orient evangelicals toward strategies of engagement with their surrounding world seem to undermine their best efforts at exerting an effective influence on the world. In the end, as an internal religious subculture, American evangelicalism thrives. But as a faith-based movement to transform the world for Christ, evangelicalism seems somewhat to falter. And not so much because the secularizing modern world has eviscerated the American evangelical tradition of its religious authority over the faithful; but rather because some of its own authoritatively governing subcultural traditions, such as the personal influence strategy and voluntaristic absolutism, provide inadequate tools for effective social analysis and change.

One broader implication of our subcultural identity theory would appear to be that human diversity and particularity—religious and otherwise—are sustained through interactive distinction, tension, and conflict. We have suggested that the human drives for meaning and belonging are satisfied primarily by locating human selves within social groups that sustain distinctive, morally orienting collective identities. We have argued that social groups construct and maintain collective identities by drawing symbolic boundaries that create distinction between themselves and relevant outgroups. Furthermore, we have observed that individuals and groups define their values and norms and evaluate their identities and actions in relation to specific, chosen reference groups and that dissimilar and antagonistic outgroups may serve as negative reference groups. And we have noted that intergroup conflict in a pluralistic context typically strengthens in-group identity, solidarity, resources mobilization, and membership retention. If so, then a strong connection would seem to exist between the satisfaction of basic human imperatives—meaning, belonging, and identity—and the particularities which distinguish all groups of people and often set them at odds. In the world as we know it, in other words, the myriad distinctions and boundaries that separate and oppose people are not obsolete, superficial differences waiting to be swept away through liberal enlightenment. Rather, they are endemic features of social life, constitutionally implicated in the formation of basic human identities. Hence, we should not only expect religions to survive and, in some cases, thrive into the indefinite future; we should also expect differences, tensions, and conflicts between religious (and nonreligious) subcultures to continue as well. For boundary-setting and intergroup conflicts are not merely signs of groups attempting to achieve divergent instrumental goals. They are also signs of groups—religious and nonreligious—constructing and maintaining their collective and individual identities.

In America, strong traditional religious subcultures, like American evangelicalism, will flourish into the foreseeable future. Far from subverting and corroding orthodox religious traditions, modern American pluralism appears to create an environment in which at least some traditional religions thrive. Those interested in better understanding the workings of the contemporary social world, then, would do well to recognize that religion persists and often flourishes. Having shed some of our illusions about secularization and recognized the persistence of religion in modern and modernizing societies—not only in the United States, but around the globe—we can better come to terms with what will increasingly become a major challenge for any just social order. That is, learning how—in ways that both secular liberalism and religious establishments have failed—to construct common lives together which genuinely respect in the public square the particularities and life-encompassing character of multiple religious traditions, without privileging any religious or nonreligious tradition over any another. This points to developing a structural pluralism (see, for example, Monsma and Soper 1997) that does adequate justice to cultural pluralism.

The data used in this book come from the Evangelical Identity and Influence Project, a three-year, multimethods, national-level study focused on contemporary American evangelicals and their social and religious context. The study was funded by a grant from The Pew Charitable Trusts, of Philadelphia, Pennsylvania. The project's principle investigator was Christian Smith (University of North Carolina, Chapel Hill, NC); co-investigators were Michael Emerson (Bethel College, MN), Sally Gallagher (Oregon State University, OR), and Paul Kennedy (Gordon College, MA). Graduate students who participated in the research include David Sikkink, Raymond Swisher, Mark Regnerus, Robert Woodberry, Kathy Holladay, Sharon Erickson Nepstad, Curt Faught, Carolyn Pevey, and Pamela Paxton. The project was administered through the University of North Carolina (Chapel Hill) Institute for Research in Social Science. In the following pages, we detail the variety of methods by which we, in stages, collected our data.

Summer 1995 Interviews

We began collecting data systematically in the Summer of 1995, seeking first to employ qualitative research methods to familiarize ourselves with the perspectives, beliefs, concerns, and languages of ordinary churchgoing Protestants broadly. We were interested, among other things, in having the questions on our upcoming telephone survey, and the language and concepts with which we would ask them, be appropriate for the population we intended to study. During the summer of 1995, therefore, we conducted 130 two-hour-long, semistructured interviews with a sample of churchgoing Protestants in six different locations around the United States. Our strategy was to capture in our sample the diversity of Protestantism while achieving proportionate representation for relevant theological and denominational traditions.

We attempted to represent the population heterogeneity first by stratifying the sample by race, denominational tradition and, where appropriate, theological orientation (liberal/conservative). This stratification yielded thirteen white categories and three black categories of churchgoing Protestants. For the white Protestants, we created a liberal and conservative category for the following denominational traditions: Baptist, Methodist/Pietist, Lutheran, and Presbyterian/Reformed. In our judgment, the predominantly conservative traditions of Holiness, Pentecostal, and Independent/Nondenominational did not warrant a separate liberal cell. The very small number of conservative Episcopalians we included in the conservative Presbyterian/Reformed group. For the black churches, we viewed Methodist, Baptist, and Pentecostal as sufficiently internally homogeneous in theological orientation to warrant one category for each tradition.

We then determined the number of Protestants in each category and assigned denominations to categories using J. Gordon Melton's *Encyclopedia of American Religions* (1993), the most comprehensive source for denominational information; Martin Bradley et al., *Churches and Church Membership in the United States 1990* (1992); Frank Mead and Samuel Hill's *Handbook of Denominations in the United States* (1990); Melton's *Religious Bodies in the United States* (1992); the *Encyclopedia of African-American Religions* (1993) edited by Larry Murphy, J. Gordon Melton, and Gary Ward; and Wandell Payne's *Directory of African-American Religious Bodies* (1991). We relied primarily on Melton's (1993) reported membership figures to determine the size of the denomination. We determined theological orientation from descriptive summaries of each denomination in Melton (1993), Mead and Hill (1990), Murphy et al. (1991), and Payne (1991). Bradley et al. (1992) provided an estimate of independent and nondenominational church membership. While this estimate is very conservative, independent and nondenominational churches were not likely to have been underrepresented in the sample since we established a minimum number of interviews from each category (explained below), and thus the proportion of nondenominational interviews in our sample far exceeded the numerical proportions in the population as estimated by Bradley.

We conducted a total of 130 interviews, which were distributed evenly among four researchers. The number of interviews in each category was based on the proportion of the population in that category, calculated from the Melton directory. However, in order to adequately account for small but distinct and historically significant denominational traditions, we assigned a minimum of five interviews for each category. According to this criteria, we interviewed five respondents from each of the following categories: Anabaptist, Conservative Presbyterian/Reformed, Conservative Pietist/ Methodist, Liberal Episcopal, Holiness, and Independent/Nondenominational. To achieve this diversity, we partially relaxed the proportionality principle and reduced the number of interviews from the largest three denominational traditions, conservative white Baptist (from 37 to 27), conservative black Baptist (from 21 to 15), and liberal Methodist/Pietist (from 14 to 10). Since we were still conducting a relatively large number of interviews from each of these three categories, we assumed that the marginal gain was higher if twenty interviews were reassigned from these three to the other important, though numerically small, denominational traditions. In the end, each of the six smaller traditions mentioned above gained two to three interviews on average; the three large categories lost a total of twenty interviews; and the rest of the denominational traditions were assigned interviews in proportion to their numbers. For the distribution of number of interviews by tradition and location, see table A.1.

We conducted the interviews in Minneapolis (MN); Chicago (IL); Birmingham (AL); Durham (NC); Essex County (MA); and Benton County (OR). The number of interviews conducted in each area accounted for regional strongholds of denominational traditions. The majority of Lutherans were interviewed in Minnesota, for example, and relatively more black Baptists were interviewed in Birmingham. We split

Table A.1: Summer 1995 Interviews by Denominational Tradition and Location

	Durham	Essex	Benton	Minneapolis	Chicago	Birmingham	Total
White Protestant							
Anabaptist	2		3				5
Baptist (Lib)		3	2				5
Baptist (Con)	9	7	10	3			27
Episcopalian	2	3					5
Holiness	2	3					5
Lutheran (Lib)		2	4	4			8
Lutheran (Con)		3		3			5
Methodist/Pietist (Lib)	7						10
Methodist/Pietist (Con)		2	3				5
Pentecostal	4		5				9
Presbyterian/Reformed (Lib)		4	3				7
Presbyterian/Reformed (Con)	3	2					5
Nondenominational		3	2				5
Black Protestant							
Baptist	3	2		2	2	6	15
Methodist					4	3	7
Pentecostal	3				1	1	5
Total	(35)	(34)	(32)	(12)	(7)	(10)	(130)

the smaller categories, with only five allotted interviews each, among two researchers in order to assure geographical diversity and to keep the number of necessary church contacts from unreasonably proliferating. We compiled sampling frames for each category at each location using lists of local churches drawn from telephone directories and checked for relative comprehensiveness with Bradley et al. (1992). We did not include churches without telephones, or which declined to have their telephone number listed in the telephone directory, in our sample. This created an inevitable sample bias against the poorest churches, separatist churches, and house churches. For the purpose of this research, however, this is an unavoidable and relatively insignificant bias, insofar as we expect these churches to have relatively little influence on the dominant character of Protestantism overall. We randomly selected individual churches from the lists. We then contacted church pastors to secure cooperation and complete lists of church members and regular-attenders. In order better to diversify at the level of individual churches, we limited the maximum number of respondents to four per church. We then systematically selected potential respondents and took a second random sample for alternates. We then checked the list of sampled potential respondents with the pastor to eliminate members completely uninvolved in the church. In fact, only very old respondents who had moved into nursing homes and were incapable of doing an interview needed to be eliminated in this way. We then called those we sampled, obtained informed consent, and arranged interviews. All in all, we interviewed members or regular attenders at forty-four local churches. Only one of the churches we contacted refused to participate. Of the individuals randomly selected from the church lists (or, for blacks, through contacts—see below), our response rate was 94 percent (130 completed of 139 attempted). All interviews were tape recorded and transcribed.

While the sampling methodology worked efficiently for white Protestants, it became increasingly clear that a complete random sample of black Protestants would be difficult to obtain. Many were difficult to contact, as many pastors of black churches held second jobs, most churches did not have secretarial assistance, and many did not have an answering machine. Furthermore, in certain low-income neighborhoods, many black churches held a policy against distributing church membership lists because of threats from collection agencies, the IRS, etc. Moreover, many randomly sampled black Protestants proved unwilling to do interviews with a researcher who called without a personal reference. After multiple unsuccessful call-backs and requests, it became apparent that in some cases the only reasonably effective means of obtaining interviews with black Protestants would be to work through existing social networks of black Protestants with which we did have prior contacts. In the sample of black Protestants, therefore, we sampled seven randomly and seventeen not randomly. However, with blacks, we were able to achieve regional diversity (Chicago, Birmingham, Boston, Minneapolis, and Durham) and to represent the three major traditions proportionate to their numbers in the population.

Finally, the sample also attempted to maintain a rough gender stratification. Other studies—including analyses of General Social Survey data—have shown that the female/male ratio in Protestantism is roughly 60/40. Therefore, in our project, if a researcher was assigned an odd number of interviews for a given category, the "extra" interview was conducted with a randomly selected female. For example, if a random sample from a church list yielded one female, one male, and one couple, a female in the household was contacted for an interview. Although this sample did reflect very much of the theological and denominational diversity within American Protestantism, we do not claim that these 1995 interviews reflect a nationally representative sample of churchgoing Protestants.

1996 RDD National Telephone Survey

In January through March of 1996, we conducted a cross-sectional, nationally representative telephone survey probing the religious and social beliefs, identities, and behaviors of Americans over the age of seventeen years (the survey instrument itself is found in Appendix D). Survey Sampling, Inc., provided the randomly generated sample of telephone numbers representative of all telephones in the United States, excluding Alaska and Hawaii. The sample was arranged in replicates based on the proportion of working telephone exchanges nationwide. Random-digit dialing ensured equal representation of listed, unlisted, and not-yet-listed household telephone numbers. The telephone survey itself was conducted by FGI, Inc., a national survey research firm based in Chapel Hill, NC, using Sawtooth Ci3 CATI software. Prior to the full survey, we conducted a small ($N = 100$) pretest of the survey instrument, using both nationally representative and local sample; based on our pretest results, we revised questions and answer categories as necessary to enhance survey clarity and validity. Also prior to the survey's implementation, interviewers—who came to the project with general training and experience in effective telephone surveying—were given a two-hour, project-specific orientation detailing the overall significance and purpose of the survey, the meaning of specific survey questions and their answer categories, and the proper pronunciation of distinctive religious terms. Throughout the survey, the interviews were monitored, using remote technology, by the investigators and by FGI staff, to ensure data quality. Furthermore, at least five percent of respondents who had completed interviews were called back and again asked key questions to verify answer reliability. All business, government, and other nonhousehold telephone numbers were screened out of the sample. In order to randomize responses within households, and so to ensure representativeness by age and gender, interviewers asked to speak with the person in the household who has the next birthday. The research design included at least, but sometimes more than, ten calls for each number; and at least, but sometimes more than, three callbacks to convert refusals. The response rate for the survey was 69 percent.

The survey included a large oversample of churchgoing Protestants, in order—for comparative purposes—to have large enough samples of important distinct traditions within American Protestantism. However, we did not want to eliminate Protestants whose faith is exceptionally important in their lives, but who might be unable to attend church services for reasons perhaps beyond their control. Therefore, a multidimensional screen was used to target "churchgoing Protestants," which included three questions regarding the respondents' religion, church attendance, and the importance of religious faith in their lives. First we identified Protestant respondents (including those who do not call or think of themselves as Protestants [such as some Baptists], but who are nevertheless involved in Protestant denominations). Of them, only those who reported attending church two to three times a month or more, *or* who said their faith was "extremely important" (and not simply "very important") in their lives were defined as eligible for the oversample. This left, for broader comparison purposes, a smaller set of

Table A.2: Regional Distribution of Evangelicals and Summer 1996
Interviews (percent)

Region	Previous Surveys on Evangelicals				
	National Election Study[a] (90–92)	Green's 4,001 Survey[b] (1993)	Evangelical Influence Survey[c] (1996)	"Ideal" Distribution	Actual Summer 1996 Interviews[d]
Northeast	13	15	16	*15*	17 (+2)
Southeast	17	34	25	*24*	21 (−3)
North Central	44	34	31	*34*	35 (+1)
South Central	10	(included in Southeast)	13	*11*	5 (−6)
Mountain/Pacific	16	17	15	*16*	24 (+6)
Total	(100)	(100)	(100)	(100)	(100)

[a]Evangelical chosen against fundamentalist, Charistmatic, moderate-to-liberal.
[b]Evangelical chosen against fundamentalist, Charismatic/Pentecostal, mainline.
[c]Evangelical chosen against fundamentalist, mainline, and theologically liberal Protestant.
[d]Combines survey follow-up and local-knowledge congregation interviews.

respondents who did not pass the screen but were also interviewed with a subset of the survey's questions. Altogether, 2,087 interviews with churchgoing Protestants and 504 interviews with respondents who did not pass the screen were completed, tallying to a sum of 2,591 total survey respondents. All statistical analyses employed appropriate weighting procedures needed to correct both for household size and for the true proportion of churchgoing Protestants in the American population. Interviews with the oversampled churchgoing Protestants lasted an average of twenty-seven minutes; interviews with respondents who did not pass the screen and answered fewer questions lasted approximately fourteen minutes.

Summer 1996 Interview Sampling Methodology

Our goal for our summer 1996 interviews was to engage in extended conversations a nationally representative sample of evangelical Protestant Christians from all regions of the country. We wanted to collect rich, in-depth, qualitative data from a sufficiently large and rigorously sampled cross-section of evangelicals to be able justifiably to generalize our conclusions to evangelicals nationally. To accomplish this, and to make sure we addressed different conceivable ways of defining and locating "evangelicals," we chose a two-pronged sampling strategy. First, we followed-up with fact-to-face interviews a sample of ninety-three self-identified "evangelicals" from our 1996 RDD telephone survey (22 percent of the 429 total self-identified evangelicals). Second, we employed a "local knowledge" strategy to identify the most clearly "evangelical" churches in thirteen different locations around the country, from which we randomly sampled eighty-five interviewees. Altogether, we interviewed 178 evangelicals from twenty-three states from every region of the country (see map 1.1 and table A.2). In addition, for comparative purposes, from our list of 1996 RDD telephone survey respondents, we interviewed eight self-identified "fundamentalists" and six self-identified "theological liberals."

Survey Follow-Up Interviews

Our intention with these ninety-three interviews was to try to overcome the traditional quantitative-qualitative research divide—and transcend the standard disputes about validity, representation, and generalizability which accompany it—by directly linking nationally representative survey data with in-depth, semistructured, face-to-face interviews. We generated a list of names and telephone numbers of all 429 of our Protestant survey respondents who self-identified as "evangelical" rather than as "fundamentalist," "mainline Protestant," "theological liberal," or "other." Then, each of eleven researchers located in different parts of the United States identified all members of that list to whom they believed they could travel to meet and interview in person (some researchers conducted clusters of interviews in two or more widely separated locations). They then called these survey respondents, explained their desire to arrange follow-up interviews, obtained informed consent, and scheduled times and places for personal interviews. The researchers literally flew and drove all over the country to interview these evangelical survey respondents; altogether, the eleven researchers accrued an estimated 7,500 miles of air travel and 25,000 miles of automobile travel to complete the ninety-three follow-up interviews. Most interviews were conducted in people's homes; some were conducted in restaurants, shopping mall food courts, and public libraries. The average interview lasted two hours and covered questions on the 1996 interview guide located in Appendix C. All interviews were tape recorded and transcribed.

The ninety-three survey follow-up interviewees were not selected randomly from the list of 429 self-identified "evangelicals" but were selected on the basis of geographical availability. However, our data shows that they do represent the national sample of evangelicals that our survey captured: a comparison of the demographic attributes of those ninety-three sampled with the complete survey group of 429 self-identified evangelicals reveals no statistically significant differences between the two groups, with one exception. No significant differences were found between the groups in sex, race, age, education, income, marital status, regional location, or employment status. The only significant difference between the two concerned the population of their county of residence: we interviewed fewer evangelicals located in rural counties and more in urban counties (for reasons obviously shaped by geographical availability). However, although theoretically this difference could indicate a bias in our interview evidence, it is not apparent how it would do so substantively, since no significant differences between the two exist in education, income, region, employment status, etc. We are therefore reasonably confident that on the most important dimensions our survey follow-up interviews reliably represent the nationally representative sample of American evangelicals from our telephone survey.

Local-Knowledge Congregation Interviews

In considering how best to sample "American evangelicals" for in-depth interviews, we were aware of a potential critique of the survey follow-up strategy described above: that respondents who self-identify as "evangelicals" on our survey may not adequately represent the views of "real" or the "most important" evangelicals in the United States. For, one might argue, evangelicalism as a subculture which establishes personal identity is also institutionally located in networks of churches and parachurch organizations.

Therefore, according to this logic, to sufficiently capture the *true* evangelical perspective, it is necessary to tap the views of people that are socially located in evangelical institutions. Although we are unpersuaded that the self-identified evangelicals from our survey somehow do not represent the views of "real" or the "most important" evangelicals (see Appendix B), we nonetheless wanted to take seriously the fact that evangelicalism is, indeed, an institutionally located religious movement. We therefore decided to compliment our survey follow-up method described above with a second sampling strategy that relied on the "local knowledge" of evangelical leaders in given geographical locations.

First, we chose twelve locations in different regions of the country which would be accessible to us to conduct interviews. We then established in each location geographic boundaries that would help define our sampling frames; typically these were county boundaries (for example, of Durham County, Pasadena County, etc.). We then began making telephone calls to three groups of people: (1) pastors of local church congregations which belonged to denominations that were members of the National Association of Evangelicals; (2) pastors of nondenominational churches identified in telephone directories which appeared likely to be evangelical churches; and (3) when available, the community-liaison directors of other local evangelicals organizations, such as city chapters of the National Association of Evangelicals, local evangelical seminaries, and so on. We then asked these pastors and directors to identify for us, to the best of their ability, "the most clearly evangelical churches" in their areas. In cases where they asked us exactly what we meant by "evangelical," we asked them to rely on their own understanding of what "evangelical" means; our only positive clarification was that we were not interested in identifying churches that were clearly fundamentalist, mainline, or liberal Protestant. Almost all of the pastors and directors we called were easily able to list churches which they thought of as obviously "evangelical," although the lengths of their lists varied. In most locations, the general overlap in the lists of the churches was remarkable, indicating a strong and coherent self-awareness within evangelical leadership circles about which churches were and were not evangelical. We continued to call more pastors until our tallies on churches stabilized, when calling additional pastors failed significantly to alter the distribution of the frequencies that specific churches were mentioned. As a general rule of thumb, for every one church from which we intended to sample interview respondents, we called, at a minimum, three pastors to solicit their local knowledge. Oftentimes, however, we called more than that. When we had called a sufficient number of local evangelical leaders to be confident about having identified the most clearly evangelical churches in the area, we selected the churches which had most often been named, as those from which to sample interviewees. Since typically the vast majority of the local-knowledge informants mentioned these churches, we believed that they were clear centers of local evangelical church life.

We then called the pastors of these selected churches, explained the purpose and nature of our research project, and asked for their cooperation in allowing us to interview members of their churches. Ninety-three percent of those pastors agreed to do so. We then systematically selected potential respondents and took a second random sample for alternates. In order better to diversify at the level of individual churches, the maximum number of respondents was limited to three per church. The list of sampled potential respondents was checked with the pastor to eliminate members completely uninvolved in the church. Only one needed to be eliminated in this way. We obtained interviewee's informed consent and scheduled interviews. Altogether, we interviewed members or regular attenders at forty-two local-knowledge evangelical churches. Of the individuals randomly selected from the church lists, our cooperation rate was 99 percent. The average interview lasted two hours and covered the same questions on the 1996 interview guide as were asked of the survey follow-up interview subjects (located in Appendix C). All interviews were tape recorded and transcribed.

We wanted to be able to compare our two interview samples—the survey follow-up sample against the local-knowledge church sample—in order to identify possible differences between the two. To accomplish this, at the end of our local-knowledge interviews we administered four-page written surveys containing forty-four questions from our telephone survey (exact wording), concerning interviewees' demographic traits and social and political behaviors. We then compiled those data into one dataset and ran descriptive statistics to compare with those of our survey follow-up sample. The results, which are found in table A.3, show that our local-knowledge interviewees were, indeed, different than our survey follow-up evangelicals. They are more male, white, married and single, young (ages twenty-five and forty-four), much better educated, more likely to earn middle- and upper middle-class incomes (rather than the very lowest or highest incomes), and more likely to be working or keeping house than to be retired. We expect these differences, particularly in education, to have biased us toward more articulate and sophisticated local-knowledge interviewees, compared with our survey follow-up evangelicals. However, since we view both local-knowledge and survey follow-up sampling strategies as different but equally valid ways to operationalize "evangelical," we do not in our analysis discount the views of either sample group. We simply recognize their relevant divergences.

We were also interested in examining the denominational locations of evangelicals nationally. Table A.4 shows a comparison of data from three national surveys of self-identified "evangelicals" and their relative distributions within various denominations and theological traditions. Table A.4 also compares the distribution of both our summer 1996 survey follow-up interviews and local-knowledge congregation interviews. The denominational distribution for the survey follow-up interviews fairly well reflects the national distributions that the three sets of survey data portray, particularly our Evangelical Influence Survey data, with a few exceptions (we somewhat underrepresented Baptists and overrepresented Pentecostals). Our local-knowledge congregation interviews, however—which were sampled based on the reputations of area churches within evangelical leadership circles—less adequately represented the denominational distribution of evangelicals represented by surveys. The local congregations in the twelve areas in which we conducted interviews that were reputed for being "the most clearly evangelical churches" out of proportion to the national denominational distribution (according to survey data) were nondenominational churches, Presbyterian and Reformed, Congregational, and churches within the Holiness and Pietist tradition. Congregations that were denominationally underrepresented in our local-knowledge sampling were Lutheran, Pentecostal, and Baptist churches. To a certain extent, however, these disproportions are balanced out in our interview data overall by the closer distributions of our survey follow-up interviews.

Table A.3: Comparison of Survey Follow-Up and Local-Knowledge Congregations

	Survey Evangelicals	Survey Follow-Up Evangelicals	Local-Knowledge Evangelicals
Sex			
Female	65	67	51
Race			
White	87	90	96
Black	9	9	—
Other	4	1	3
Marital Status			
Married	78	77	81
Never Married	8	10	12
Divorced	6	6	3
Widowed	8	7	2
Separated	1	—	2
Age			
17–24	5	2	—
25–34	15	12	19
35–44	23	23	44
45–54	25	28	24
55–64	14	19	8
65–74	11	12	4
75 and Older	7	4	1
Education			
Some High School or <	6	1	—
High School Graduate	23	17	10
Vocational-Technical	7	5	3
Some College	28	39	25
College Graduate	21	18	31
Some Graduate School	4	9	11
Master's Degree+	11	11	20
Work Status			
Full-time	54	55	59
Part-time	11	13	13
Keeping House	16	12	19
Retired	14	13	2
Other	5	7	7
Income			
Less than $9,999	5	5	1
$10,000–19,999	10	10	10
$20,000–29,999	19	14	6
$30,000–39,999	21	20	19
$40,000–49,999	12	15	15
$50,000–59,999	12	15	24
$60,000–79,999	11	8	11
$80,000–99,999	3	3	13
$100,000 and More	6	10	1
N	(429)	(93)	(85)

Table A.4: Denominational Location of Evangelicals and Summer 1996
Interviews (percent)

Denomination or Tradition	Surveys Data on Evangelicals			Our Summer 1996 Interviews	
	4,001 Survey[a]	Evangelical Voter[b]	Evangelical Influence Survey[c]	Survey Follow-Up Interviews	Local-Knowledge Interviews
Baptist	28	38	25	18	13
Nondenominational	20	5	19	22	27
Lutheran	19	13	12	12	2.4
Methodist	15	23	7	3	—
Pentecostal	—[d]	8	17	18	2.4
Presbyterian and Reformed	5	10	6	8	20
Holiness and Pietist[e]	8	3	4	7	12
Evangelical Free	—	—	8	9	7
Restorationist	4	—	2	1	—
Congregational	2	—	4	2	13
Episcopalian	1	—	1	1	2.4
Total	(100)	(100)	(100)	(100)	(100)

[a]Four options: evangelical, fundamentalist, Pentecostal/Charismatic, mainline.
[b]"Evangelical" = theologically conservative Protestants who say "no" when asked if they are a fundamentalist.
[c]Four options: evangelical, fundamentalist, mainline, theological liberal.
[d]4,001 offered "Pentecostal/Charismatic" as an alternative self-identity to "evangelical"; 4,001's principle investigator, John Green, says half of pentecostals/charismatics choose "evangelical" if that option is not offered.
[e]Includes Christian and Missionary Alliance, Nazarenes, Wesleyans, Holiness, Moravians.

Fundamentalists and Liberals

In addition to the ninety-three survey follow-up evangelicals we interviewed, we also interviewed, for comparative purposes, eight from our 1996 RDD telephone survey respondents who self-identified as "fundamentalists" and six who self-identified as "theological liberals." The locations of these interviews can be seen on map 1.1. These handfuls of fundamentalists and liberals were chosen for follow-up interviews purely on the basis of geographical accessibility. Although we make no claims about the national representativeness of the religious-identity categories from which they were chosen, we can say that these we interviewed did, in fact, strongly resemble the conventional image of Christian fundamentalists and theological liberals. In any case, we have included their interviews for analysis with those from our summer 1995 interviews who identified themselves as fundamentalists and liberals.

Congregational Observation

In addition to doing interviews and collecting survey data, many of the researchers attended religious services, revival meetings, prayer meetings, and other religious gatherings of many of the people with whom we conducted interviews. The project's principle investigator, for example, attended worship services for all but one of the "local knowledge" interviews he conducted during the summer of 1996. When visiting, researchers typically took field notes on the meetings and often gathered free and purchased booklets, programs, books, and bulletins. Although no systematic method was used to sample congregations for observation, attending these services did prove to be a valuable source of insight about many interviewee's answers, about the subcultures they live within, and more broadly about comparative differences between various Protestant traditions.

Call-Back Interviews with Survey "Doubters" and "Defectors"

In addition to the in-depth interviews and telephone survey described above, we decided to conduct short, unstructured follow-up telephone interviews with another sample of our 1996 RDD telephone survey respondents. We were interested in better understanding which kinds of Americans struggle most with doubts about their religious beliefs, why, and to what effect; and why certain Americans who had been raised in religious families later decided to leave the religions of their childhoods. To accomplish this, we compiled a list of all who reported on our 1996 RDD telephone survey that in the last few years they "often" (as opposed to "sometimes," "once or twice," or "never") have had doubts about whether their Christian beliefs are true. Unfortunately, the telephone survey question about religious doubting was asked only of Roman Catholics and churchgoing Protestants; thus, the sampling frame unavoidably omitted nominal Protestants from our sample, which certainly biases our results somewhat (see our discussion of this problem in chapter 6). Altogether, of our total of 2,591 respondents, 114 Roman Catholics and churchgoing Protestants reported doubting their religious faith "often." We also compiled a list of those who reported on our survey that, despite having been raised within a religious family, they now as adults consider themselves not religious. Seventy-six respondents reported themselves as being not now religious, despite having been raised in a religious family.

We then called back from these lists a sample of forty doubters (35 percent of the survey's sampling frame) and thirty-four defectors (45 percent of the survey's sampling frame) and interviewed them over the telephone about the nature, causes, and consequences of their doubts and about their religious histories and reasons for leaving the faith of their families of origin. All but one of the doubters and the defectors each we called agreed to participate in the follow-up interviews, despite the potentially sensitive nature of the questions; those we interviewed were also very open and candid with their answers. All interviews, which lasted an average of about ten minutes each, were tape-recorded and transcribed (Appendix C contains the interview schedules). The results of our analyses of these short follow-up interviews is found in chapter 6.

The analysis of this book hinges upon the validity of survey-based religious self-identifications, by which our survey respondents categorized themselves as various kinds of Protestants associated with major historical American Protestant traditions. In this work, we have distinguished the categories of evangelical, fundamentalist, mainline Protestant, and theologically liberal Protestant. Since the use of such self-identifications is not well established in sociological research, the following pages are devoted to explaining and justifying our method as well as the validity and advantages of this analytical approach.

Our Starting Point

At the most elementary level, our reliance on survey-based self-identifications is grounded on the simple idea that if a researcher wants to know what or who somebody is, they should ask them (a straightforward idea originally suggested to us in those words by Robert Wuthnow). The standard approaches to using denominations (organizational locations) and theology (belief positions) in religious research, when done well, can offer helpful ways to situate people in religious identity-space. We believe, however, that registering people's identification with different historical religious traditions provides another effective means of mapping the terrain of religious identity. And depending on one's purposes, we think it may be the best way to capture important religious categories that shape social life.

Essential to success with this approach, of course, is offering people identity-maps in surveys which adequately correspond to those which they use in real life to negotiate the religious identity world. People are only able to locate themselves on maps they can recognize. In order to accomplish this, we in this project invested a great deal of time and energy into exploring the ground-level language and structure of religious identities in the American religious field through 130 in-depth interviews with ordinary churchgoing Protestants in various parts of the country during the summer of 1995 (see Appendix A). Through these interviews, we learned that few ordinary Protestants are able to recount the histories of the major American Protestant traditions or to articulate precisely the characteristic features which differentiate them. However, we also discovered importantly that most ordinary Protestants possess or feel definite basic associations with and about the different Protestant traditions, which enabled them to be able personally to identify with some and reject others. Few ordinary conservative Protestants know much about the early twentieth-century history of modernism, fundamentalism, and liberalism; nor can many articulate more than rudimentary definitions of "mainline Protestantism" or "evangelicalism," for example. But they can and do express ideas like, "Liberals compromise biblical teachings because they're so influenced by modern culture." And these sentiments provide them enough information to know that they are definitely not liberals. Likewise, ordinary liberal and mainline (and even evangelical) Protestants can express impressions like, "Bible-thumping fundamentalists are so strict and legalistic, that's not what I believe in at all." Thus, after conducting and analyzing 130 in-depth interviews, we concluded that—while they are ill-equipped to explicate religious history and complex theological controversies—most ordinary Protestants are capable of relying on their own mental and emotional associations and sentiments about various religious traditions to locate themselves accurately on a Protestant identity-map (for results of other projects which employed self-identification with religious traditions, see Green et al. 1996: 174–266; Beatty and Walter 1988).

In other words, we believe that most churchgoing people possess meaningful religious self-identities about which they are sufficiently self-aware to be able, when asked, to place themselves in a multipositioned field of religious identity. We believe this capacity is enhanced by the fact that the Protestant religious identities we employed in this work are rooted in distinct, historical, identifiable religious traditions that have profoundly shaped the contours of American Protestantism for decades (see, for example, Marsden 1980, 1987; Carpenter 1984, 1988; Sandeen 1970; Hutchison 1968, 1976, 1986; Cole 1963; Gasper 1963; Roof and McKinney 1987; Ammerman 1987). We also maintain that through the institutionalization of their own cultural codes and discursive structures, these traditions continue to retain much about their distinctive historical subcultures (although this continuity varies between them), which significantly influence those who locate themselves within them. Thus, to identify oneself as an evangelical, for example, means one's religious orientation and actions are shaped by a tradition and subculture which make them significantly different from someone who self-identifies as, say, a mainline Protestant. It is the distinctive differences between these traditions and the variant social and religious effects they can generate our survey-based self-identification approach intends to tap.

Method and Results

In order to locate churchgoing Protestants within the historical traditions to which they most appropriately belong, we employed measures of religious self-identifications by asking the following four questions on our telephone survey:

I have a few questions about your religious identity and background. Thinking about your religious faith, would you describe yourself as:

. . . *a fundamentalist?:*
    1) YES
    2) NO
    3) UNFAMILIAR WITH NAME (THEY MUST VOLUNTEER)
    4) DON'T KNOW

. . . an evangelical?:
    1) YES
    2) NO
    3) UNFAMILIAR WITH NAME (THEY MUST VOLUNTEER)
    4) DON'T KNOW

. . . a mainline Protestant?:
    1) YES
    2) NO
    3) UNFAMILIAR WITH NAME (THEY MUST VOLUNTEER)
    4) DON'T KNOW

. . . a theologically liberal Christian?:
    1) YES
    2) NO
    3) UNFAMILIAR WITH NAME (THEY MUST VOLUNTEER)
    4) DON'T KNOW

We intentionally included the words "theologically" and "Christian" in the last option to focus respondents on religious, not political liberalism. Notice that respondents were asked about and given a chance to say "yes" or "no" to each identity separately. Notice too that respondents were free to say either that they were unfamiliar with the name or that they didn't know whether they would describe themselves as any of these.

When respondents answered "yes" to only one of these identities, we took that to be their religious self-identity. When respondents answered these four questions with more than one "yes" (that is, they identified with more than one tradition), we then asked this question (only offering the answer category options to which they had said "yes" in the previous four questions):

Which of those would you say best describes your religious identity?:
    1) FUNDAMENTALIST
    2) EVANGELICAL
    3) MAINLINE PROTESTANT
    4) LIBERAL
    5) (THEY VOLUNTEER) OTHER
    6) DON'T KNOW
    7) REFUSED

Notice again that respondents were free to say "something other," or that they simply didn't know which best describes them.

When, however, respondents answered "no" to all in the first set of four questions (that is, on first thought they believed none of the options described their religious identity), we then asked this question to confirm that none of the four identities described them:

Table B.1: Number of Identities Selected from which Primary Identity
Was Chosen (percent)

Number of Identities Originally Chosen	Primary Identity			
	Evangelical	Fundamentalist	Mainline	Liberal
One	33.7	42.6	49.2	41.1
Two	34.6	35.2	33.9	35.9
Three	24.9	14.5	10.7	11.6
Four	2.8	0.7	1.2	0.7
None	3.9	7.0	5.0	10.6
N	(430)	(389)	(576)	(431)

If you had to choose, would any of these describe you at all?:
    1) FUNDAMENTALIST
    2) EVANGELICAL
    3) MAINLINE PROTESTANT
    4) LIBERAL
    5) (THEY VOLUNTEER) NO, NONE DESCRIBE
    6) DON'T KNOW
    7) REFUSED

By answering these questions, churchgoing Protestant respondents sorted themselves into seven different identity categories. The final distribution of identities was: 20.9 percent evangelical, 19.4 percent fundamentalist, 27.3 percent mainline Protestant, 20.4 percent theologically liberal Christian, 5.5 percent "Other," 5.7 percent "Don't Know," and .8 percent "Refused." Those sorted into the last three categories answered "other," "don't know," and "refused" consistently throughout. It is worth observing that a total of 12 percent of churchgoing Protestants would or could not chose one of the four religious identities we offered, suggesting that these survey questions did not unduly pressure respondents into choosing an inappropriate self-identity; when none fit, a significant proportion of Protestants simply said so. This strengthened our confidence that the choices of those respondents who did choose primary identities were not forced or arbitrary.

Table B.1 shows the number of identities respondents selected before choosing their primary identity. Between one-third and nearly one-half of respondents chose only one of the four religious identities and declined the others. These people clearly had the most focused sense of religious self-identity. The vast majority of all types of respondents reflect in their answers a focused enough sense of religious self-identity that they were able either to choose their primary identity outright or to chose it over only one other—68 percent of evangelicals, 88 percent of fundamentalists, 83 percent of mainliners, and 77 percent of liberals originally chose only one or two identities. Only relatively small minorities chose primary self-identities from a choice of four options, or which they had originally said did not describe them. Overall, then, while between one-half and two-thirds felt connected to more than one tradition, the vast majority were able to choose a primary religious tradition with which they identified. We do not inter-

Table B.2: Number of Identities First Selected by
Religious Views (percent)

Number of Identities Originally Chosen	Primary Identity			
	Evangelical	Fundamentalist	Mainline	Liberal
Faith "Extremely" Important				
One	78	67	59	60
Two	77	77	57	55
Three	77	76	72	58
Four	67	75	50[1]	100[1]
None	94	57	83	58
Mean	(78)	(72)	(61)	(58)
Personal Faith in Christ Only Hope of Salvation				
One	95	91	76	70
Two	97	87	79	67
Three	93	97	92	67
Four	92	100[1]	88	100[1]
None	94	96	82	76
Mean	(95)	(92)	(79)	(70)
Bible Completely True and without Error				
One	97	95	87	77
Two	95	91	90	80
Three	98	93	92	74
Four	100	67[1]	86	100[1]
None	100	76	86	76
Mean	(97)	(92)	(89)	(78)

[1]Less than five cases in the cell.

pret multiple identities as a sign of identity confusion or religious weakness, however, since self-identification with more than one religious identity shows no correlation with indicators of religious weakness (compare table B.1 with tables in chapter 2). Instead, we simply view this as reflecting the widely recognized fact that Protestant religious identities in America, though clearly distinct, sometimes partially overlap each other.

Furthermore, our data show that, regardless of how many identities respondents had originally chosen before settling on a primary identity, those who eventually choose the same primary religious identity do not differ significantly from each other on important religious matters. Table B.2, for example, shows comparisons within each of the four religious identities between the number of identities respondents had first chosen and their answers to some basic religious questions. Although differences exist, they show no particular pattern either within or between identities. Furthermore, none of them are statistically significant (with two exceptions—importance of faith for main-

Table B.3: Logistic Regression Odds Ratios Predicting from All Adult
Americans' Primary Religious Identities

Variables	Evangelical	Fundamentalist	Mainline	Liberal
	Exp (B)	Exp (B)	Exp (B)	Exp (B)
Female	1.106	.916	1.519*	1.475*
Age	1.009	.996	1.030***	.996
Education	1.158***	1.023	1.118***	1.051
Income	.897**	.934+	1.020	.961
County Population	1.000	1.000	1.000	1.000
Resident of South	1.113	1.818***	1.782***	1.785**
Race[1]				
Black	1.825*	1.970**	1.115	3.472**
Hispanic	1.239	.549	.543	1.257
Other	.184*	.665	.464	.794
Marital Status[2]				
Divorced	.407**	.591+	.739	1.417
Never Married	.325***	.717	.757	.990
Widowed	.782	.793	.713	1.171
Employment Status[3]				
Keeping House	1.625+	1.215	1.049	1.511
Part-Time Work	1.197	1.209	1.205	.597
Retired	.985	1.237	1.421	1.342
In School	1.474	1.264	1.628	1.057
Unemployed	.961	.959	.994	.979
N	2,304	2,304	2,304	2,304
Chi-Square	57.673	29.324	85.699	59.422
Percent Predicted	93.1	93.4	91.3	93.2

+p < .10 *p < .05 **p < .01 ***p < .001
Notes: [1]omitted category = white. [2]omitted category = married. [3]omitted category = full-time employment.

liners, and view of Bible for fundamentalists—the two cells of which that show large deviations from the mean both containing less than five cases, render the chi-squares for both unreliable). We are confident, then, that respondents' final choices of primary religious identities reflect valid distinctions between the identities and consistencies within them, which are not undermined by variation in scope of identity-focus. In other words, regardless of how focused or singular their identities are, churchgoing Protestants do, in fact, have *primary* religious identities. And these primary identities make their bearers much more similar to others who share those same primary identities than to people with other identities with which they may also have secondarily self-identified.

To acquire a clearer sense of the distinctive traits that characterize respondents who self-identify with these four Protestant traditions, we ran logistic regression models, to

Table B.4: Logistic Regression Odds Ratios Predicting from
Churchgoing Protestants' Primary Religious Identities

Variables	Evangelical	Fundamentalist	Mainline	Liberal
	Exp (B)	Exp (B)	Exp (B)	Exp (B)
Female	.917	.663**	1.274*	1.061
Age	1.004	.988*	1.027***	.991
Education	1.086**	.938*	1.063**	.991
Income	.928**	.977	1.099***	1.001
County Population	1.000	1.000	1.000	1.000
Resident of South	.596***	1.052	1.051	1.022
Race[1]				
Black	.885	.992	.474***	1.807***
Hispanic	2.120*	.568	.652	1.516
Other	.274*	1.053	.929	1.401
Marital Status[2]				
Divorced	.468***	.732	1.034	2.127***
Never Married	.427***	1.083	1.196	1.597*
Widowed	.949	.968	.824	1.538
Employment Status[3]				
Keeping House	1.295	.900	.774	1.330
Part-Time Work	1.115	1.226	1.093	.554*
Retired	.660+	.922	1.045	.953
In School	1.179	1.029	1.154	.940
Unemployed	.975	.979	1.026	1.004
N	1,848	1,846	1,846	1,846
Chi-Square	73.919	39.278	108.031	68.617
Percent Predicted	78.9	79.7	73.1	79.1

+p < .10 *p < .05 **p < .01 ***p < .001
Notes: [1]omitted category = white. [2]omitted category = married. [3]omitted category = full-time employment.

see which factors predict choices of identities (see tables B.3 and B.4). Table B.3 shows factors that predict who *of all Americans* chose each of the four religious identities; table B.4 shows, more importantly, who *of churchgoing Protestants* chose these identities. The results show that, compared with all adult Americans, evangelicals and mainliners tend to be better educated; evangelicals and fundamentalists tend to earn lower incomes; evangelicals are less likely to be divorced or single; all groups but evangelical are more likely to reside in the South; mainliners tend to be older; mainliners and liberals tend to be more female; and all groups but mainliners, particularly liberals, tend to be disproportionately black (while those of "other" race tend not to choose the evangelical identity). The results in table B.4 show similar patterns, except that compared only with other churchgoing Protestants, evangelicals are more likely to be hispanic and retired; fundamentalists are more likely to be male, younger, and less educated; mainliners earn more income and are still unlikely to be black; and liberals are more likely to be divorced and single, still tend to be black, and no longer tend to be female.

Altogether, these data suggest two significant points. First—consistent with our argument in chapter 3—no perceptible pattern of correlation exists between the religious strength or orthodoxy of these traditions and the degree of their members' "exposure to modernity" through education, urbanization, full-time employment in the labor force, and so on (compare tables B.3 and B.4 with tables in chapter 2). The evidence again simply fails to support the modernization-secularization paradigm of Berger (1967) and Hunter (1983, 1987). Second, these identities do not appear to function simply as proxies for other social or economic factors that would suggest an interpretation which contradicts that of this book. Clearly, for example, those who self-identify as liberal tend to be black. But (as we argue below), this does nothing to explain the relatively lower levels of religious vitality among self-identified liberals. Mainline Protestants tend to be better educated, but then again, evangelicals are slightly more so. Again, we suggest that these traditions reflect authentically distinct and meaningful religious identities with which Protestant believers can and do self-identify; they thereby situate themselves in the broader terrain of religious identity in ways that have consequences for their religious commitments and experiences.

Finally, we examined how religious identities are distributed within certain Protestant denominations. Table B.5 shows that many denominations exhibit definite tendencies of their memberships to self-identify with certain traditions, usually in unsurprising ways. For example, those within the United Methodist, PCUSA, Episcopal, UCC, ELCA Lutheran, Disciples of Christ, Reformed, National Baptist (USA), and AME denominations strongly tend to identify as mainline or liberal Protestants. By contrast, those within independent and freewill Baptist churches and the Churches of Christ tend to identify as fundamentalists. "Evangelical" tends to be a favored identity within Pentecostal churches, the Evangelical Free and Covenant Denominations, and PCA, CMA, Nazarene, Wesleyan, and many nondenominational churches. Other denominations—such as the Southern Baptist, American Baptist Association, and American Baptist (USA)—tend to contain a great deal of identity diversity. We should not, however, overstate differences in identity patterns among denominations. Table B.5 confirms what many recent scholars have observed (for example, Wuthnow 1988; Hoge, Johnson, and Luidens 1994; Roof 1993), that denominationalism is declining in importance as a strong differentiator of religious identities. Partly for this reason, we believe that using self-identifications in survey research—as we have done in this project— offers a promising alternative approach to religious measurement that should at least supplement researchers' standard reliance on denomination and theology variables.

Substantive Meanings

We have shown how individuals can self-identify with different Protestant traditions and the statistical congruence and denominational and social locations of those who do. But what actually do these religious categories mean substantively to Protestant believers in the real world? In our summer 1995 interviews, we asked our 130 ordinary churchgoing Protestants about the meaning of the identity-labels we later used in our telephone survey. As mentioned above, we discovered that ordinary Protestants are largely unfamiliar with the histories of the major American Protestant traditions. We

Table B.5: Distribution of Identities within Selected Denominations (frequencies)

Denomination	Evangelical	Fundamentalist	Mainline	Liberal	Other	Don't Know	Total
Southern Baptist	66	77	96	77	18	15	349
United Methodist	25	24	118	50	6	19	242
Nondenominational	44	41	20	23	6	4	138
ELCA Lutheran	26	6	36	21	1	6	96
Miscellaneous Pentecostal[1]	34	21	15	15	8	3	96
Independent Baptist	8	30	10	15	5	6	74
Assemblies of God	34	14	7	4	4	6	69
Presbyterian Church USA	7	3	34	15	2	2	63
Episcopal Church	5	3	31	18	2	3	63
Missouri Synod Lutheran	14	11	18	6	3	3	55
Churches of Christ	7	18	10	7	8	2	52
"Just a Christian"	9	8	12	2	4	2	37
Miscellaneous Baptist[2]	10	12	4	5	—	1	32
Disciples of Christ	1	9	16	3	1	1	31
American Baptist Assoc.	3	8	9	8	2	—	30
Missionary Baptist	2	4	4	8	4	6	28
United Church of Christ	1	—	15	12	—	1	29
National Baptist (USA)	5	2	6	10	2	2	27
American Baptist (USA)	6	4	3	7	2	2	24
Evangelical Free/Covenant	19	2	1	—	1	1	24
PCA	9	4	4	1	1	3	22
Miscellaneous Reformed[3]	3	1	13	2	—	1	20
Free Will Baptist	—	8	4	4	1	—	17
AME	—	4	3	6	1	1	15
CMA	8	2	1	2	1	—	14
Mennonite	4	3	1	1	—	5	14
Nazarene	4	2	2	1	—	3	12
Wesleyan Church	4	2	2	1	3	—	12
AME (Zion)	3	1	1	5	—	2	12

[1] Includes Four Square Gospel, Full Gospel, Pentecostal Church of God, Pentecostal Holiness Church, United Pentecostal International, Church of God (Cleveland, TN), Apostolic Pentecostal, and "Other" Pentecostal.
[2] Includes Primitive Baptist, Baptist Bible Fellowship, Baptist General Conference, Baptist Missionary Association, Conservative Baptist Association, Fundamentalist Baptist, and General Association Baptist.
[3] Includes Christian Reformed Church, Reformed Church in America, and "Other" Reformed.

also learned that many Protestant believers claim not to like religious labels. This conservative Protestant man was typical:

> I have never liked labels. In fact, growing up, when I was a teenager going to the Lutheran church, I pretty much refused to call myself a Lutheran. I didn't like the idea of denominational[ism], that was not the essence of being a Christian. So, some people may call me a Charismatic, some may call me a fundamentalist. I think I am going between them. So I do not label myself.

But these disclaimers only initially obscured what also clearly emerged as a widespread de facto reliance on religious labels and categories. For it also became evident that most individual believers *did* distinguish themselves from other kinds of Protestants in patterned ways; and they did make value judgements about the differences that separated themselves from others. On the surface, people disavowed the importance of religious labels generally, as divisive and superficial. But they also in their talk clearly distinguished between different kinds of groups of believers, had definite ideas about the theological and spiritual boundaries that separated them, and were prepared to evaluate different types of Protestants. Furthermore, when we asked people about specific religious identity labels, they were generally quite able to say whether the label described them or not. Thus, ordinary Protestants were, in fact, able to draw lines that demarcated the field of religious identity in what turned out to be rather standard ways. They often claimed that Christians should get away from labels and "just focus on Christ," or "grow up and work together," or "just love the Lord and each other." But their discourse also implied these be done in the context of their own views of Christ and Christianity. However unintentionally, then, most privileged their own particular religious commitments by presuming them as universal standards. Ordinary churchgoing Protestants, in short, did in fact negotiate their lives and make sense of the religious world with normatively oriented religious categories and labels.

So, what did these labels actually mean? The primary image most Protestants associated with "evangelical" was actively evangelizing, taking a stand in the world for religious commitments. One self-described evangelical woman related it as being, "more outspoken, a little more in the limelight of things, evangelizing, preaching the Word." From the less sympathetic perspective of this man, evangelical means, "those that try to go out and force their beliefs on others, rather than just saying, 'this is what I believe and if you want to believe it, fine, and if you don't that's your choice.' That's my idea of it." Thus—whether viewed positively or negatively—the evangelical label for most conveyed a sense of working to cross the boundary out of the world of faith to have an effect on the world outside. One evangelical saw it as, "bringing truth outside the church into the world itself." Another said that evangelical was, "the desire and really the commission to share with others about our faith and to live our faith in everyday life. Not to make it kind of a compartmental piece of our life, but to have it influence everything." Thus, "evangelical" as an identity label typically suggested a particular orientation of religious practice, an activist faith that tries to influence the surrounding world. For evangelicals themselves, this involves a heartfelt, personal commitment to and experiential relationship with God, from which springs a readiness to take a stand

and speak out for the faith. To many more mainline and liberal Christians, evangelical suggests a more emotional, noisy, and possibly pushy version of faith.

Almost all Protestants expressed different associations with the "fundamentalist" label. In contrast to evangelical's more activist, outreaching connotations, people—fundamentalists and nonfundamentalists alike—generally saw fundamentalist as having a more defensive and boundary-maintaining orientation. Those who took fundamentalist as their own master identity tended to emphasize things like separation from the world, the primacy of the King James Bible, and the defense of the faith against modern, liberal thought. Their commitment was to preserving truth and purity, not to influencing the secular world. But this orientation also served as a foil for many mainline and liberal Protestants, as well as some self-describing evangelicals. From their perspective, fundamentalist means being narrow, closed-minded, and rigid. This mainliner, for example, remarked, "I didn't grow up in the South where they are really hard [rules], you know, no makeup or any of that. . . . A Christian to me is somebody who really believes, who makes sure their life is working toward that, but not the hard-core type of thing, if you understand what I'm saying, you know, no jewelry, no makeup." Many nonfundamentalists, especially evangelicals, associated fundamentalism with artificial or legalistic dictates and regulations, which they counterpose to a "real" faith of the heart. One evangelical woman observed: "There are a lot of rules and regulations that man has put upon man, saying, 'To be this you must do this and this and this; you must follow this doctrine, you've got to do these things, you can't do these things.' That's the difference I see [between fundamentalists and me]." For this reason, many conservative Protestants who otherwise say they do believe "the fundamentals" of the Bible tend to hedge away from that identity. This man, for example, observed, "Well, I avoid fundamental, because it tends to have a negative connotation today, and yet I'm probably fairly fundamental. Although, now I tend to think of fundamental as something fairly legalistic and having some pretty angry attitudes toward other believers, which bothers me, so I can't quite stand in that camp."

"Mainline Protestant" had perhaps the most consistent, though not widely recognized, meaning of the labels we explored. Some Protestants we interviewed, including some actually attending mainline denomination churches, were simply not familiar with the term. But those that seemed unfamiliar generally admitted as much and did not claim that the label described them. Those familiar with the term, however, rather consistently said first that, in their minds, it referred to the older, more established, well-known, larger denominations. They also knew that mainline was definitely not fundamentalist, evangelical, or Charismatic. This man, for example, said, "Yes, I've heard of that term. When I hear it, I think of your old established denominations, you know, it's a distinction between them and your newer faiths, like Pentecostal churches." Thus, "mainline" captures for people a certain institutional approach to Christian faith. For mainliners themselves, this also conveys a faith that is more quiet and respectable than expressive and potentially undignified. One mainliner, for example, observed, "I'm not an evangelical, but neither do I have to have highbrow music all the time, Bach, Beethoven, Handel. . . . Evangelical is a folksier kind of Christianity [than my own], they seem a lot more willing to share personal experiences than we sometimes do." It was not unusual in our interviews for evangelicals to declare things like, "I don't believe that anybody should be a closet Christian," and "If I'm a fanatic, I just love the Lord more than you do; so sometimes, I may tend to be overly fanatic." By contrast, mainliners, such as this United Methodist, emphasized a serious but more reserved spirituality:

> I believe in God and Jesus Christ, and that we should be kind and considerate and try to get people to know the Lord one way or the other. I have a friend who's a Baptist, who is very outspoken about her religion. But I'm very, very quiet about mine. She came to our church for about a year. But she didn't like that we weren't as outspoken as she felt we should be, so she went back to the Baptist church.

In the popular imagination and experience, then, to be mainline is to belong to an old, established denomination, but also to hold a faith that is not particularly outspoken or extraordinary, but is rather quiet and respectable.

Finally, "liberal" also generally evoked a coherent set of meanings. However, these were evaluated very differently by different types of Protestants. For liberals themselves, on the one hand, the label meant, for example, being open-minded and accepting of diversity. One liberal, for example, remarked, "I'm the type of person who accepts all people, all races. I know that people have different beliefs and may not always believe the way I believe, but that doesn't necessarily mean I can't associate with them." Another said, "I have a philosophy based on biblical study: judge not. Liberal is the only category that is not making judgments early on, being open to new ideas, being willing to try new things. Because obviously I don't have all the answers, so I'm trying to find what a Christian should be doing, thinking, feeling." Fundamentalists and evangelicals, on the other hand, use liberal as a foil against which to distinguish their truer, more dedicated faith. One remarked, "In today's society I think a liberal is a person that goes along with the ideas of the time, you know, whatever seems to suit the ideas of man." Another observed, "Absolutely not, I am not a liberal. A liberal is someone who takes the Word of God loosely, takes the Bible loosely. He says that it may not be inerrant, that it may be fallible." The common theme underlying these different evaluations is a genuine openness to having one's own faith significantly influenced by new information gained through personal experience; thus, faith is not the maintenance of a single, fixed truth, but a process of discovery and growth in a situation of diversity.

What is striking about the popular understandings of these labels is that, although most ordinary Protestants know little of their precise meanings, the labels nevertheless do evoke in people certain common associations and images which enable them to plot out maps of religious identity and locate themselves on them. And while these identity-maps can sometimes be rudimentary, maps that even different kinds of Protestants plot out usually look quite similar to each other. What usually differ are not the shape of the maps themselves, but their evaluations of the best identity-locations on the maps. What is also noticeable is that, despite most ordinary people's unfamiliarity with American religious history, the associations and images which for them give meaning to these identity labels do, in fact, roughly correspond to the actual historical experiences and positions of the Protestant traditions these labels represent. People may not know exactly how they came to be fundamentalists or liberals, but their elementary conceptions of and self-identifications with those traditions turn out to be fairly accurate and appropriate. All of this strengthens our confidence in our method of self-identification with major religious traditions as a valid means of measuring important dimensions of American Protestant religious identity and orientation.

Race Effects?

Some early reviewers of this book suggested that racial imbalances between the four Protestant identities might significantly influence the results of the tables found in chapters 2 and 3. Specifically, some suggested that the larger numbers of blacks among liberals and fundamentalists might affect either the overall religious strength or the demographic and socioeconomic characteristics of those traditions. Their suggestion was that once race was controlled for, the evidence might more strongly support Berger (1967) and Hunter's (1983, 1987) modernization-secularization paradigm. From one perspective, we think this critique is simply irrelevant. If particular American Protestant traditions are composed of certain combinations of whites, blacks, and other races which influence their theological views, religious practices, or socioeconomic traits, then so be it. Race simply is partly what constitutes the composition and character of different religious traditions. Nevertheless, we wish to address this concern on its own terms. First, tables B.3 and B.4 demonstrate that among churchgoing Protestants, when race is controlled for in multivariate models predicting choice of primary religious self-identity, no correlation emerges between "exposure to modernity" (through education, urbanization, full-time work, income, or even sex or age) and the religious strength or orthodoxy of different religious traditions. Indeed, evangelicals tend to be more educated and less likely to live in the South; fundamentalists are not significantly different from others regarding incomes, residence in urban counties or the South, nor occupational status; and liberals are neither more nor less educated, wealthy, urbanized, or employed full-time.

Beyond these models, we analyzed possible race effects on religious theology and practice. None alter the findings presented in this book. In fact, blacks tend to be much stronger religiously than whites. We ran logistic regression models on a number of religious dependent variables, which controlled for sex, age, education, income, county population, residence in the South, marital status, and race. In those models, compared with whites, the odds of blacks attending church weekly or more were 1.6 times greater ($p = .008$); 2.3 times greater that blacks would say that their religious faith is extremely important to them ($p = .0000$); 2.6 times greater that blacks believe in a literal reading of the Bible ($p = .0000$); 1.4 times greater that blacks say that they never have doubts about their Christian beliefs ($p = .04$); and 2.0 times greater that blacks maintain that the only hope for salvation is through personal faith in Jesus Christ ($p = .0001$). (The sample populations for these comparisons were all adult Americans for the first two, and all Roman Catholics and churchgoing Protestants for the last three.) Thus, controlling for race would not alter the conclusions we draw from our tables in chapters 2 and 3.

On Subjects' Awareness

We anticipate that some reviewers will critique our use of religious self-identifications on the grounds that—despite our discussion of substantive meanings above—survey respondents who choose a religious identity very likely may not understand what it means and may not really belong in the category they have chosen. For example, critics might claim that many of those in our survey who self-identified as "fundamentalists" probably do not adequately appreciate what a genuine fundamentalist is and should not be counted by social scientists as real fundamentalists. One might suppose that the very fact that these people are slightly less conservative than evangelicals theologically, for example (see table 2.1), indicates that they are somehow not bona fide fundamentalists.

We find this critique problematic, for a number of reasons. First, when one is interested—as we are—in comparing the current theological views and religious practices of members of different Protestant traditions, it is necessary to categorize people into those traditions using measures other than theology and practice. Otherwise, one simply samples on the dependent variable. We believe self-identification is the best way to do that. More fundamentally, this critique is problematic because it assumes a static view of religious traditions. It essentially disallows traditions ever to drift, innovate, adapt, or accommodate. It asserts, for example, that because biblical literalism was a hallmark of fundamentalism (or at least of fundamentalist elites) in the past, that it *must* still be so today; therefore, anyone who is not a literalist cannot, by definition, be a true fundamentalist. Unfortunately, this approach privileges the researcher's preconceptions of the social world over evidence that can emerge from the very empirical reality that the researcher hopes to understand. And so it sets unnecessary limits on what might be discovered empirically. Clearly, we have no fixed foundation by which to type people as "true" or "real" fundamentalists. We only have relatively adequate tools which attempt to measure an identity from different perspectives and for different purposes. Given that methodologically relativistic situation, we would do well to use all of the tools at our disposal when they are analytically appropriate, without automatically disqualifying one based on the assumptions or uses of another.

But, in our view, this critique is ill-targeted for yet another reason. We have relied in this book on survey self-identifications to categorize American Protestants, in our attempt to compare and explain the strength of different religious traditions. We have emphasized the importance of traditions' and movements' abilities to maintain strong subcultural identities by creating and policing identity-distinctions and symbolic boundaries between themselves and outgroups. From this perspective, the possibility that some people may not understand the religious tradition with which they identify themselves, and so do not even "really" belong as a part of that tradition, represents not so much a critique of our method; rather, it represents an indicator of the relative weakness of that tradition. Religious traditions that cannot define coherent identities and police their own boundaries are weak traditions. So, for example, if some Americans place themselves within the camp of Christian fundamentalism, who by fundamentalism's own historical and theological standards would not appear to belong there, this tells us that the fundamentalist tradition is now a relatively weaker tradition than those—like evangelicalism—which better define and police their identity boundaries. And this is important information to know. In the end, rather than categorizing people based on theoretical criteria drawn from our own suppositions about what a particular type of religious person is supposed to look like, we think it preferable to ask directly about self-identity.

Conclusion

Some sociologists of religion treat the field of American Protestantism as a unidimensional spectrum on which identities relate to each other as points on a continuous variable. Most typically, this is conceived of as a liberal-conservative spectrum. We believe, however, that viewing religious identities as continuous variables is an unnecessary methodological oversimplification that tends to neglect important complexities. In our view, this wrongly compresses multidimensional realities into a one-dimensional linear continuum and attempts to correlate features of traditions which are incommensurate. Instead, we think Protestant identities are best conceptualized as distinct categories occupying positions in a two- or possibly three-dimensional identity space. We therefore think religious identities should be treated as categorical variables—like race (white, black, hispanic, asian, other) and marital status (married, divorced, separated, widowed, never married)—whose "values" cannot be appropriately fit on a linear, continuous scale. Such an approach has important implications for how religious identities should be measured and modeled in multivariate analyses. Rather than trying in a regression model, for example, to capture variations in religious identities through a unidimensional conservative-liberal scale, we suggest using discreet identity-categories (evangelical, liberal, fundamentalist, etc.) as dummy variables (see, for example, Regnerus and Smith 1998a and 1998b; Sikkink and Smith 1996).

What constitutes this categorical, multipositioned field of American religious identity is the fact that all of these religious identity-traditions are themselves constituted by characteristic cultural and institutional structures. These structures sustain and promote in their traditions certain distinctive assumptions, beliefs, moods, practices, and interests. They also facilitate the traditions' religious production and self-reproduction over time. When individual believers become situated within any of these traditions, therefore, their own religious attitudes and practices become significantly shaped by those cultural and institutional structures, in ways that eventually tend to distinguish them from other believers who occupy other identity-traditions. For this reason, we suggest that scholars should more frequently and thoroughly utilize individual believer's self-identification with major religious traditions as a measurement which promises to enhance significantly our understanding of the role of religion in human social life.

Summer 1995 Interview Question Guide
Religious Identity

1. How do you identify yourself religiously? Are there any labels that describe you well?
2. Do you consider yourself an evangelical? A fundamentalist? A liberal? A moderate? A charismatic? Reformed? Pentecostal? Bible believer? Just a Christian?
3. What does it mean to you to be a [whatever they named]? (focus especially on evangelical)
4. How does being a [whatever they named] distinguish you from the [what they said they weren't]? What are the differences?
5. In your mind, what are characteristic traits of [whichever said they weren't of: fundamentalists, evangelicals, liberal]?
6. Do you think these kinds of labels and differences among Christians are very important these days? Why or why not?
7. Who are the most important Christian leaders today? Why?

The World

8. How does life as a Christian feel to you in our society these days?
9. What is "the world"? ("do not be of the world," "free from the corruption of the world")
10. How should Christians relate to "the world"?
11. What does it mean to be "in but not of the world"?
12. What specific things should definitely make Christians different from the world? What should set Christians apart?
13. What does it mean that Christians should be the "salt and light" of the world?
14. Do you think that evangelicals have become more worldly in recent years? Why? How?
15. In your normal life, do you actually spend much time thinking about these things [dealing with the world]? Is this much of a concern to you, or not?
16. Do you think "secular humanism" is a threat to America? Christianity? What about New Age religion?

Christian Influence

17. Some Christians like to say that "Jesus Christ is 'the answer' for society or the world's problems today." Do you agree? If so, what exactly does that mean?

18. Do Christians have solutions for today's social problems? What are they? Give examples?

19. Should Christians be involved in society to try to exert a Christian influence? What exactly is that influence? What does it look like?

20. Is working for social change in this world an appropriate activity for the church? Why, or why not?

21. Is it even *possible* for Christians to influence American society today? Or is it somehow "too late" to do that?

22. In your normal life, do you actually spend much time thinking about these things [Christian social influence]? Is this much of a concern to you, or not?

23. How effective do you think conservative Christian activists who have tried to influence society in recent years actually have been?

24. How do you think or feel about Operation Rescue? The Christian Coalition? Chuck Colson's Prison Ministry? Etc.?

25. What are the appropriate *means* by which evangelicals should influence society? And why are they appropriate or not?
    - political/legislative reform?
    - religious conversion of individuals?
    - personal influence of good morals/example on friends, colleagues, acquaintances?
    - affect widespread cultural change of values, morals, commitments? how?
    - other? [try to get at, for example, how they think structurally versus individualistically, etc.]

26. What specifically are the most important *issues* about which Christians should be concerned about making an impact? Probe for the following (first try to discern if social issues are on their agenda; then turn the discussion to focus on social issues):
    - gender relations
    - education of children
    - wealth/materialism/consumerism
    - view of nature and purpose of human self
    - media power
    - racism

27. [Probe for any implicit/underlying individualistic versus communitarian/structural analysis; also for faith-compartmentalization versus integration.]

28. What should be done (by Americans? Christians?) about [the named important issues]?

29. [Commitment to "Orthodox" versus "Progressive" moralities? Investment in culture wars?]

30. [Support for Pat Robertson? Christian Coalition? Etc.?]

Relation to "America"

31. Was America ever a "Christian nation?" What does that mean?

32. Is America *now* a Christian nation? Should it be? Could it be? In what ways? Or is it an un-Christian, post-Christian, anti-Christian nation? How do you feel about that?

33. Some Christians think that Christians "own" America because of its Christian heritage and that they shouldn't let secularists "take" American away from them. Do you agree or disagree with this? Why or why not?

34. Some Christians believe that American society is entering a state of serious, desperate crisis, that it is beginning to fall apart at the seams. What do you think or feel about this? Can you relate to this concern?

35. In your normal life, do you actually spend much time thinking about these things [in relation to America]? Is this much of a concern to you, or not?

Perceptions of Outsiders/Status Decline

36. Do you think there have been significant changes—since, say, the 1960s—in the way Christians are viewed or treated by mainstream America? What are they?

37. Do you think non-Christians listen to and respect what evangelicals (or conservative Christians) have to say these days? Or do they ridicule evangelicalism?

38. Do you feel comfortable expressing your Christian views on issues in public discussions? Why or why not? In which arenas of life (work, friends, etc.)? Why there and not elsewhere?

Implementation

39. What do you actually do to try to influence society? How do you implement your influence-strategies? How do they work out in life?

40. Do you feel satisfied with the attempts you make to influence society as a Christian?

41. How do others react to you when you do these things? Is it effective?

Gender Relations

42. What are your thoughts about the place of men and women in families? [probe for ideas on gender-specific roles, housework, authority, childcare, etc.]

43. What are your thoughts about the place of women in the paid workforce? [probe equal opportunity, gender-appropriate jobs, appropriateness for mothers of young children, etc.]

44. In what ways, if at all, do you see similarities or differences between men and women evidenced in the life of your church? [probe roles, functions, spiritual leadership]

45. How do you see these ideas of men and women that you describe being worked out in your own life? [how evidence? contradict? or?]

Education

46. Are you concerned about the state of public-school education in America today? What concerns you? Why? [probe: moral content of texts/curriculum, sex education, school prayer, tuition vouchers, NEA, etc.]

47. [If "yes"] How did these problems come about? What can be done to fix them?

48. [If "no"] What do you think about the many Christians who are upset with public education in America?

49. Should Christians send their kids to Christian schools? Or should they do home-schooling? Why or why not?

Materialism/Consumerism

50. Do you think that American society is too materialistic or consumption-oriented?
51. Do you think that American Christians are too materialistic or consumption-oriented? Why? With what consequences?
52. Do you view wealth as a blessing from God or as something that is spiritually dangerous?
53. How do you think Christians, especially wealthy ones, ought to respond to poverty in America and in the world today?

The Self

54. Do you think individual self-fulfillment is important? Why?
55. Does the Bible require of Christians self-denial, self-discipline, self-sacrifice? [probe how respondent may attempt to reconcile self-fulfillment and self-denial]

Summer 1996 Interview Question Guide

Quick Ice-Breaker

For how long have you been a Christian? How did you become a Christian? How would you characterize your Christian life over the years?

Identity

Do you consider yourself to be an evangelical? What does "evangelical" mean to you?

What things do evangelicals have in common that might make them different from other kinds of Christians?

(Probe) If you met someone for the first time, how would you know if they were an evangelical? What things would you look for? How would you know if they were not an evangelical? Where are the boundaries?

Do you view evangelical Christians as different than *fundamentalist* Christians in any way? In what ways?

The Big Issues

[Quick] How does it feel to you being a Christian in our society today?

Are there things going on in our society today that you think should be big concerns to Christians? What are they? *WHY* should Christians be concerned about them?

What do you think Christians should be doing with their concerns about these things?

Relation to America/Status Decline

Was America ever a "Christian nation?" In what ways?

How do you think Christians are viewed or treated by mainstream America? Is this a *recent* way of viewing or treating Christians, or has it always been this way? (If recent:) When did these things change and why?

Some Christians think that certain non-Christians are trying to turn America away from its Christian heritage. Do you agree or disagree? Why or why not?

Do you see any groups of people in our society today that are hostile or opposed to Christianity? Who? *Why* do you think they are hostile?

Do you feel hostile or opposed to them? How do you think Christians should respond to them?

(Optional Probe:)   Are there any *religious* groups that you view as hostile to your faith or Christianity?

Christian Distinctiveness

What specific things should definitely make Christians different from the world, from non-Christians? What should set Christians apart? Why those things?

Christian Influence

Do you think Christians have solutions to offer the world for its social problems? What are they?

(Probe)   Some Christians like to say that "Jesus Christ is 'the answer'" for society's or the world's problems today. Do you agree? If so, what exactly does that mean? What is "the answer"? How does that solve the problems?

To what extent should Christians be involved in society to try to exert a Christian influence?

[If say "involved"] *Why* is this important for Christians? Why not simply live faithfully and let the world take care of itself; or let God worry about changing the world?

How should Christians go about trying to exert their Christian influence? What are the best ways to go about it? Why?

What is the top priority for a Christian (rotate order:), helping those in need or personal evangelism? Why?

[Quick] Should Christians be getting involved in politics?

(If yes) What should Christians be trying to achieve through politics? What can politics accomplish for Christians?

(If no) Why shouldn't Christians be involved in politics?

(If yes above) What *can't* politics accomplish for Christians? Any limits or dangers in politics?

To what extent do you think Americans are open or resistant to Christians exerting a Christian influence in society? What about the non-Christians you know in your daily life? Do they seem open to a Christian influence from you?

Pluralism and Morality

How do you feel about the fact that America is a pluralistic nation, that there are many different kinds of people, religions, lifestyles, etc.?

(Probe)   How do you think Christians should relate to others in society who don't accept Christian beliefs and morals?

To what extent do you think Christian morality should be the commonly accepted morality of our culture?

What do you mean by "Christian morality"? *Which* morality? (get specifics).

(If yes) What are specific examples of people who would have to live differently than they do now if Christian morals were the basis of our culture as you think they should be?

e.g., should gay and lesbian marriages not be socially accepted (with insurance, benefits, tax implications)? Why or why not?

e.g., should all businesses be closed on Sundays? Why or why not?

e.g., should all abortions be made illegal? Why or why not?

What do you say to people who say, "America is a pluralistic nation, and Christians
shouldn't impose their beliefs and morality on everyone else"?

What do you say to people who say, "There is one true God and one morality that
applies to everyone for their own good, whether they know it or like it or not. So
those morals, and not others, should govern our society"?

What do you say to people who say, "Each person has to decide for themselves how to
live; nobody can force another to believe or live a certain way; it has to come from
each individual's heart"? Do you agree or disagree? Why?

(Probe)   What do you say to people who say, "I don't believe in God or the Bible, so
don't tell me how I have to live"?

(Probe)   To what extent should Christian morality be made into *laws?* Are there aspects of Christian morality that should *not* be made into laws?

Work/Career/Calling [*Only if work or have worked in paid labor force*]—I'd like to ask
some questions about how you relate your Christian faith to your work life:

Do you view your job as contributing to God's kingdom or God's glory in some way?
(If so, how?) Or is it mostly just a way to earn a living?

(Probe)   Ideally, what would you like to be doing for a job for God's kingdom?

How, if at all, do you see your Christian faith affecting your life at work, on the job?

Do your work colleagues know you are a Christian? How do they know that? How do
they respond to that? What is your experience?

Do you think Christian values and morals should affect the world of work, business,
and the economy, *beyond simply having individuals live morally and honestly?*

Education

What are the most important things for kids to get out of their elementary and high
school education? (Follow-up:) Are there particularly *Christian* goals in children's education?

[Quick] How do you think public schools these days are doing? (If problems) What are
the problems? What are the causes of those problems?

To what extent are public schools hostile to your faith, values, or beliefs? Concrete examples?

(Probe)   Some people believe the "educational establishment" or "educational bureaucracy" are real problems. Do you agree or disagree? Why?

How would you like to see your faith and values reflected in or respected by public
schools? Can you give me specific examples of what that might look like? [explore
problem of pluralism]

(Probe)   Should *Christian morality* be taught in the public schools, or just in the home?
Which Christian morals exactly?

Should Christians be trying to redeem the public schools, to make them more Christian? Why?

IF YES: *How* should Christians be trying to do that? By what means?

If money were not a consideration, where should Christians send their kids to school? Christian schools? Home-schooling? Why or why not? What is good and bad about these schooling options?

Race

Do you think our country has a race problem?

If YES: What is the problem? Why is it a problem?

If NO: Why do you think so many people talk about America as having a serious race problem?

Would you actually call that problem "racism," or just race-relations problems?

IF YES TO #1:   What are some examples of racism/race problems in America today?

Do you think that Christianity has solutions to the problems of race relations? What are they? What should Christians be doing about race problems?

Studies show that, on the average, black people have worse jobs, lower incomes, and poorer housing than white people—but they don't tell us why. Why do *you* think this is? (Probe: not just buzz-words—why? poor education? lazy? discrimination? Or?)

Have you heard of the idea of "racial reconciliation?"

IF YES: What does that mean to you? How do people achieve racial reconciliation?

IF NO: go to next question . . .

Gender Relations

What are your thoughts about the role of men and women in families?

To what extent do you think women and men have different responsibilities when it comes to raising children and earning a living? Why?

(Probe)   What are your thoughts about the extent to which and how *men* should be involved in their families? How should that relate to their jobs in the outside world?

(Probe)   Would you say that, for women, raising children is more important than working a paid job? Or equally important? Why or why not? What about for men?

Some Christians believe that husbands are to be the "heads" of their wives or families or households. Do you agree or disagree?

What exactly does it mean to be "head"? Can you give me a concrete example of how that works?

Do you think that husbands and wives should be mutual, equal partners in everything? What does that mean? (If "yes" to both:) How does that relate to the idea that the husband is the "head"?

(Probe)   (*If believe in headship*) In your mind, what would be lost or go wrong if Christians stopped talking or thinking about the "headship" of husbands? Why would that be bad?

How do you see these ideals of men and women that you describe being worked out in your own life? Where do these things [mentioned meanings of "head"] seem to work *well* in your life? *Not* well?

What does "feminism" mean to you? What do you think of feminism? Some Christians see feminism as a threat. Do you? Why?

Are you familiar with Promise Keepers? (If male) Have you ever attended a Promise Keepers event? What are your thoughts about the Promise Keepers movement?

What Faith Does

How costly has your Christian faith been?

(Probe)   Has being a Christian made you have to change anything big about how you live? Has it made you have to sacrifice or suffer in any way? How?

Why is your faith important to you? What would you miss if you (hypothetically) lost your faith?

Belief Plausibility

How do you know that your Christian faith is true?

Have you ever had doubts about your Christian beliefs? (If yes) What was going on in your life at that time?

(Probe)   Some people say that *knowing there are many different religions* in the world makes them doubt that their own faith is the right one. Is that an issue for you? What do you think about other religions? Are they wrong, or just different?

(Probe)   (Only for college-educated) Some people say that their *education* has caused them to have doubts about their faith. How has your education affected your faith? [Make sure you find out where they went to college]

When you have doubts, how have you resolved them?

(Probe)   Do you talk to others about them? Pray? Or do they simply fade away?

Do you believe in hell? (IF YES:) How does your belief in hell shape the way you think about your neighbors, colleagues, other people *you know?* How does the idea of them maybe going to hell affect your relationship with them in daily life?

(Probe)   How do you *feel* about the fact that there will be a hell for so many people?

Spiritual Context

Is your church evangelical? Is its denomination evangelical (If not: is it difficult to be an evangelical in your denomination?)

Are most of your friends evangelicals? (Extended) family? (Is your family positive or negative about your evangelical faith?)

What do you think of Charismatic Christians?

In what ways are you satisfied or not with your church? Have you switched churches in the past? why?

How large is your church? Is it growing?

Does your church have small groups that meet regularly? Are you a part of one? Are these groups helpful? How so?

Can you think of any national Christian leaders who represent the kind of Christian you are? In what ways do they?

How would you compare your lifestyle as an adult with the lifestyle of the family you grew up in?

Would you say you have done better *economically* than your family while you were growing up?

Did your family have family devotions, Bible reading, or prayer time together when you were young? Did your parents encourage you spiritually?

Are there any Christian magazines that you enjoy reading? Christian radio programs you listen to? What Christian music do you buy or listen to?

Callback Questions for Religious "Doubters" and "Defectors"
Doubters

You indicated in the telephone survey last winter that you often have doubts about your religious beliefs.

1. What causes you to have doubts?
2. What is going on in your life at times when you have doubts?
3. Some people say that knowing there are many different religions in the world makes them doubt that their own faith is the right one. Was this ever an issue for you? Why?
4. Some people say that their education has caused them to have doubts about God? How has your education affected your faith?
5. When you have doubts, how do you resolve them? Do you talk to others about them? Pray? Or do they simply fade away?
6. Have your doubts ever caused you to seriously consider giving up your faith?
7. Are you troubled or concerned about your doubts about God? Do your doubts worry you?
8. Would you say that doubts reflect a strong and confident faith? Or does it feel more like a sign of weak faith?
9. Do most of your friends share your religious beliefs? Your family?
10. Do your family or friends ever voice concerns about your faith? How do you respond to them?
11. How would you describe the spiritual life of your family, growing up? Would you say that your family encouraged you spiritually?

Defectors

You indicated last winter that you do not currently consider yourself a member of any particular religion (for example, as Protestant, Catholic, Jewish, etc.), but that you were raised in a religious family.

1. How would you describe the way that you stopped practicing the religion you were brought up in?
2. How old were you when you stopped?
3. Was it all at once, or a more gradual process?
4. What was going on in your life at that time? (for example: Did you move to a different town? Did you get married to someone of a different faith?)
5. Would you describe leaving the church as a conscious decision on your part, or did it just evolve by itself?
6. (If yes) What were the reasons behind your decision? Were your issues more intellectual or relational or?
7. Would you say that you now believe in God?

(*If they believe in God*)

7a. How would you describe the God in which you believe?
7b. How important to you is your belief in God? Why?
7c. How is your belief in this God different from the religious traditions of which you said you are not a member?
7d. Is there any particular reason why you don't associate with a formal religion?

7e. Do you ever have doubts about your belief in God?

7f. What causes you to have doubts?

7g. What is going on in your life at times when you have doubts?

7h. Some people say that knowing there are many different religions in the world makes them doubt that their own faith is the right one. Was this ever an issue for you? Why?

7i. Some people say that their education has caused them to have doubts about God? How has your education affected your faith?

(*If they do not believe in God*)

8a. Do you consider yourself a spiritual person in any way?

8b. What does "spiritual" mean for you?

8c. Do you consider yourself an atheist?

8d. Do you consider yourself an agnostic? What does agnostic mean to you? What would constitute evidence that might make you come down on one side or the other?

8e. (do not ask of agnostics) How do you know that God does not exist?

8f. Some people say that knowing there are many different religions in the world makes them doubt that their own faith is the right one. Was this ever an issue for you? Why?

8g. Some people say that their education has caused them to have doubts about God? How has your education affected your faith?

8h. Do you ever think that God maybe does exist? What causes you to think this?

(*For everyone*)

9. If you have kids, or if you were to have kids, what do/would you tell them about God?

10. How would you teach them about morality?

11. Are most of your friends religious? Your family?

12. Do your family or friends ever voice concerns about your (lack of) faith? How do you respond to them?

13. How would you describe the spiritual life of your family, growing up?

14. Would you say that your family encouraged you spiritually?

15. Are you a member of any clubs, groups, associations, or other community organizations? How would you describe your level of participation in these groups?

APPENDIX D: TELEPHONE SURVEY— THE PEW "RELIGIOUS IDENTITY AND INFLUENCE" SURVEY

→ Let me begin with a few questions about your *religion:*

Q1: Do you consider yourself to be Protestant, Catholic, Jewish, nothing in particular, or something else?

    1) PROTESTANT [INCLUDES BAPTISTS, METHODISTS, PRESBYTERIANS, REFORMED]

    2) CATHOLIC

    3) JEWISH

    4) NOTHING IN PARTICULAR (NOT RELIGIOUS)

    5) "JUST A CHRISTIAN" [GO TO Q2]

    6) OTHER [GO TO Q3]

    7) DON'T KNOW [GO TO Q4]

    8) REFUSED

Q2: [If Q1 = 5] Would you say that you are either a Catholic or Eastern Orthodox Christian or not?

    1) YES

    2) NO

    3) DON'T KNOW

    4) REFUSED

Q3: [If Q1 = 6] Which religion are you?

    1) ANABAPTIST

    2) BAPTIST

    3) "BIBLE-BELIEVING"

    4) BRETHREN

    5) BUDDHIST

    6) CHARISMATIC

    7) "CHRISTIAN" or "JUST CHRISTIAN"

    8) CHRISTIAN and MISSIONARY ALLIANCE (CMA)

    9) CHRISTIAN SCIENCE

    10) CHURCH OF THE NAZARENE

    11) EASTERN ORTHODOX

    12) EPISCOPAL/ANGLICAN

    13) FUNDAMENTALIST

14) HINDU
15) HOLINESS
16) INDEPENDENT
17) JEHOVAH'S WITNESS
18) MENNONITE
19) METHODIST
20) MORAVIAN
21) MORMON/LATTER-DAY SAINTS
22) MUSLIM/ISLAMIC
23) ORTHODOX, EASTERN/RUSSIAN/GREEK
24) PENTECOSTAL
25) QUAKER/FRIENDS
26) SALVATION ARMY
27) SEVENTH-DAY ADVENTIST/ADVENTIST
28) UNITARIAN-UNIVERSALIST
29) OTHER: _____
30) NO RELIGION
31) DON'T KNOW

Q4: [If Q1 = 7] Is there some other religion I haven't mentioned that describes yours?

1) ANABAPTIST
2) BAPTIST
3) "BIBLE-BELIEVING"
4) BRETHREN
5) BUDDHIST
6) CHARISMATIC
7) "CHRISTIAN" or "JUST CHRISTIAN"
8) CHRISTIAN and MISSIONARY ALLIANCE (CMA)
9) CHRISTIAN SCIENCE
10) CHURCH OF THE NAZARENE
11) EASTERN ORTHODOX
12) EPISCOPAL/ANGLICAN
13) FUNDAMENTALIST
14) HINDU
15) HOLINESS
16) INDEPENDENT
17) JEHOVAH'S WITNESS
18) MENNONITE
19) METHODIST
20) MORAVIAN
21) MORMON/LATTER-DAY SAINTS
22) MUSLIM/ISLAMIC
23) ORTHODOX, EASTERN/RUSSIAN/GREEK
24) PENTECOSTAL
25) QUAKER/FRIENDS
26) SALVATION ARMY

27) SEVENTH-DAY ADVENTIST/ADVENTIST
28) UNITARIAN-UNIVERSALIST
29) OTHER: _____
30) NO RELIGION
31) DON'T KNOW

Q5: How often have you been attending _____ [IF Q1 = 1–2
OR 4–6, THEN: church; IF Q1 = 3, THEN: synagogue] services in the last year?
    1) More than once a week
    2) Once a week
    3) 2–3 times a month
    4) Once a month
    5) Many times a year
    6) Few times a year
    7) Never
    8) DON'T KNOW
    9) REFUSED

Q6: [If Q1 = 1–3 or 5–7] How important would you say your religious faith currently is in your own life?
    1) Extremely Important
    2) Very Important
    3) Somewhat Important
    4) Not Important
    5) DON'T KNOW
    6) REFUSED

→ Now I am going to ask you some questions about your beliefs about *morality and America.*

Q7: Do you think being devoted to raising a good family is a big enough contribution to the world? Or do people have to do more than that?
    1) BIG ENOUGH
    2) HAVE TO DO MORE
    3) DON'T KNOW
    4) REFUSED

Q8: Do you think that the United States was founded as a Christian nation based on Christian principles, or not?
    1) YES
    2) NO
    3) DON'T KNOW
    4) REFUSED

Q9: Do you think religion is a private matter that should be kept out of public debates over social and political issues, or not?
    1) YES
    2) NO
    3) DON'T KNOW
    4) REFUSED

Q10: Do you think that to improve American society you have to change laws and institutions? Or is it enough just to change individuals?

1) INDIVIDUALS AND LAWS
2) JUST INDIVIDUALS
3) DON'T KNOW
4) REFUSED

Q11: Do you think morals should be based on an absolute, unchanging standard? Or do you think there are no moral absolutes, so people have to decide for themselves what is right and wrong?

1) ABSOLUTE STANDARD
2) NO MORAL ABSOLUTES
3) DON'T KNOW
4) REFUSED

Q12: Do you think that *Christian* morality should be the *law* of the land, even though not all Americans are Christians, or not?

1) YES
2) NO
3) DON'T KNOW
4) REFUSED

Q13: Do you think we are seeing a serious breakdown of *American society*, or not?

1) YES
2) NO
3) DON'T KNOW
4) REFUSED

Q14: What would you say is the *biggest* problem with public schools today?: [OPEN-ENDED]

Q15: I'm going to read you four different beliefs about prayer in public school. Please tell me which one best represents your own belief:

1) The first is: prayer should *not* be allowed in public schools.
2) The second is: schools should not sponsor prayer, but kids should be allowed to pray together in groups.
3) The third is: teachers should lead in a *moment of silence* for unspoken prayers.
4) The last is: teachers should lead their classes in *spoken Christian prayers.*
5) NONE OF THESE (THEY MUST VOLUNTEER)
6) DON'T KNOW
7) REFUSED

Q16: Do you think abortion should be legal in *all* cases, *most* cases, only *a few* cases, or *illegal* in all cases?

1) MOST/ALL CIRCUMSTANCES
2) A FEW CIRCUMSTANCES
3) ILLEGAL
4) DON'T KNOW
5) REFUSED

→ Now I want to ask a few questions about *family and work.*

Q17: Do you think that, in general, a marriage should be ended if the marriage be-
      comes empty and unfulfilling, or not?
     1) YES
     2) NO
     3) DON'T KNOW
     4) REFUSED

Q18: Do you think that husbands and wives should be *equal* partners in everything in
      marriage, or not?
     1) YES
     2) NO
     3) DON'T KNOW
     4) REFUSED

Q19: Are you currently: married, widowed, divorced, separated, or have you never
      been married?: [IF 3 AND 4, CODE AS 3]
     1) MARRIED
     2) WIDOWED
     3) DIVORCED
     4) SEPARATED
     5) NEVER MARRIED
     6) REFUSED
     Q20: [If Q28 = 1–2] Have you ever been divorced?
          1) YES
          2) NO
          3) REFUSED

Q21: How many children do you have?: [INCLUDING STEPCHILDREN]
     0) NONE
     1) ONE
     2) TWO
     3) THREE
     4) FOUR
     5) FIVE
     6) SIX
     7) SEVEN
     8) EIGHT
     9) NINE
    10) TEN OR MORE
    11) REFUSED
     Q22: [If Q21 = 1] How old is your child?:_____
     Q23: [If Q21 = 2–10] How old is your oldest child?: _____
     Q24: [If Q21 = 2–10] How old is your youngest child?: _____
     Q25: [If Q22 = 5+] Did your child attend public school for all of his or
          her years in school, not counting preschool?
          1) YES
          2) NO

3) DON'T KNOW

4) REFUSED

Q26: [If Q25 = 2] What other kind of school has your child attended?:
(IF 2 OFFERED, TAKE HIGHEST LISTED):

1) WAS HOME SCHOOLED

2) PRIVATE CHRISTIAN (PROTESTANT OR INDEPENDENT)

3) CATHOLIC SCHOOL

4) PRIVATE (NONRELIGIOUS)

5) OTHER

6) DON'T KNOW

7) REFUSED

Q27: [If Q23 = 5+] Did your children attend public school for all of their years in school, not counting preschool?

1) YES

2) NO

3) DON'T KNOW

4) REFUSED

Q28: [If Q27 = 2] What other kind of school have your children attended?: (IF 2 OFFERED, TAKE HIGHEST LISTED):

1) WAS HOME SCHOOLED

2) PRIVATE CHRISTIAN (PROTESTANT OR INDEPENDENT)

3) catholic school

4) PRIVATE (NONRELIGIOUS)

5) OTHER

6) DON'T KNOW

7) REFUSED

Q29: Are you working full-time, part-time, going to school, keeping house, retired, or something else? (IF 2 ANSWERS OFFERED: "Which do you spend more time doing?"):

1) FULL TIME

2) PART TIME

3) IN SCHOOL

4) UNEMPLOYED

5) ON LEAVE

6) RETIRED

7) KEEPING HOUSE

8) OTHER: _____

9) NOT APPLICABLE

10) DON'T KNOW

Q30: [If Q29 = 1–2 or 4–5] What is your occupation? (PROBE:) What do you do for a living? What kind of work do you do? Who do you work for? (OPEN-ENDED): _____

Q31: [If Q29 = 6] What was your occupation? (PROBE:) What did you do for a living? What kind of work did you used to do? Who did you work for? (OPEN-ENDED): _____

Q32: [If Q19 = 1] Is your _____ [If Q34 = 1: wife;
If Q34 = 2: husband] working full-time, part-time, going to school,
keeping house, retired, or something else? (IF 2 ANSWERS OFFERED:
"Which does _____ [If Q34 = 1: she;
If Q34 = 2: he] spend more time doing?"):
    1) FULL TIME
    2) PART TIME
    3) IN SCHOOL
    4) UNEMPLOYED
    5) ON LEAVE
    6) RETIRED
    7) KEEPING HOUSE
    8) OTHER: _____
    9) NOT APPLICABLE
    10) DON'T KNOW

Q33: What year were you born?: _____

Q34: [IF NOT SURE ABOUT RESPONDENT'S SEX] And are you male or female?
    1) MALE
    2) FEMALE
    3) REFUSED

Q35: How many people who live in your household are 18 years old or *older,*
including yourself?: _____

→ Now the rest of this survey contains questions that we are asking of the *Christians*
we are interviewing:

Q36: Do you think that human beings are basically good, basically sinful, or both
good *and* sinful?
    1) GOOD
    2) SINFUL
    3) BOTH GOOD AND SINFUL
    4) DON'T KNOW
    5) REFUSED

Q37: Do you believe that the Bible is the inspired word of God, or not?
    1) YES, INSPIRED
    2) NO, NOT INSPIRED
    3) DON'T KNOW
    4) REFUSED

    Q38: [If Q37 = 1] I'm going to read you three views about the Bible.
    Please tell me which one best reflects your own view:
        1) The first is: the Bible is true in all ways, and to be read *literally,*
        word for word.
        2) The second is: the Bible is true in all ways, but *not always* to be
        read literally.
        3) The third is: the Bible is true primarily about *religious* matters,
        but may contain errors about other things.
        4) DON'T KNOW

     5) REFUSED

     6) DON'T KNOW

Q39: Would you say that you have committed your life to Jesus Christ as personal Lord and Savior, or would you not describe your religious faith that way?

     1) YES, HAVE COMMITTED LIFE

     2) NO, WOULDN'T DESCRIBE THAT WAY

     3) DON'T KNOW

     4) REFUSED

Q40: Do you think that the only hope for salvation is through personal faith in Jesus Christ, or are there also other ways to salvation?

     1) YES, CHRIST ONLY HOPE

     2) NO, OTHER WAYS

     3) DON'T KNOW

     4) REFUSED

Q41: How often in the last few years have you had doubts about whether your Christian beliefs are true?

     1) Often

     2) Sometimes

     3) Once or twice

     4) Never

     5) DON'T KNOW

     6) REFUSED

Q42: How do you know how God wants you to live?: (PROMPT: Which do you think is the *most* important?)

     1) From Church teachings.

     2) Or, from the Bible.

     3) Or, through human reason.

     4) Or, you know in your heart through your personal walk with God.

     5) DON'T KNOW

     6) REFUSED

     7) DON'T KNOW

Q43: [IF Q5 = 1–6] What is the denomination of the church you attend?: [IF 2 OFFERED, ASK: "Which one do you *most* attend or are you *most* involved in?"]

     1) ANABAPTIST

     2) ANGLICAN/CHURCH OF ENGLAND

     3) ASSEMBLY OF GOD

     4) BAPTIST

     5) BRETHREN

     6) CATHOLIC

     7) CHARISMATIC

     8) "CHRISTIAN" OR "JUST CHRISTIAN"

     9) CHRISTIAN AND MISSIONARY ALLIANCE (CMA)

    10) CHRISTIAN SCIENCE

    11) CHURCH(ES) OF CHRIST

    12) CHURCH OF GOD

    13) CHURCH OF THE NAZARENE

14) CONGREGATIONALIST
15) DISCIPLES OF CHRIST
16) EPISCOPALIAN/ANGLICAN/CHURCH OF ENGLAND
17) EVANGELICAL COVENANT CHURCH
18) EVANGELICAL FREE CHURCH
19) FOUR SQUARE
20) FREE METHODIST CHURCH
21) HOLINESS
22) INDEPENDENT
23) JEHOVAH'S WITNESS
24) "JUST PROTESTANT"
25) LUTHERAN
26) MENNONITE
27) METHODIST
28) MORMON/LATTER DAY SAINTS
29) NONDENOMINATIONAL or INTERDENOMINATIONAL PROTESTANT
30) PENTECOSTAL
31) PRESBYTERIAN
32) QUAKER/FRIENDS
33) REFORMED
34) ROMAN CATHOLIC
35) SALVATION ARMY
36) UNITARIAN-UNIVERSALIST
37) UNITED CHURCH OF CHRIST (UCC)
38) WESLEYAN CHURCH
39) OTHER (SPECIFY): _____
40) DON'T KNOW
41) REFUSED

Q44: [IF Q5 = 7–9] With what church denomination are you most closely affiliated?:
[If 2 offered, ask: "Which one are you *most* connected to or involved in?"]

1) ANABAPTIST
2) ANGLICAN/CHURCH OF ENGLAND
3) ASSEMBLY OF GOD
4) BAPTIST
5) BRETHREN
6) CATHOLIC
7) CHARISMATIC
8) "CHRISTIAN" OR "JUST CHRISTIAN"
9) CHRISTIAN AND MISSIONARY ALLIANCE (CMA)
10) CHRISTIAN SCIENCE
11) CHURCH(ES) OF CHRIST
12) CHURCH OF GOD
13) CHURCH OF THE NAZARENE
14) CONGREGATIONALIST
15) DISCIPLES OF CHRIST
16) EPISCOPALIAN/ANGLICAN/CHURCH OF ENGLAND

17) evangelical covenant church
18) evangelical free church
19) four square
20) free methodist church
21) holiness
22) independent
23) jehovah's witness
24) "just protestant"
25) lutheran
26) mennonite
27) methodist
28) mormon/latter day saints
29) nondenominational or interdenominational protestant
30) pentecostal
31) presbyterian
32) quaker/friends
33) reformed
34) roman catholic
35) salvation army
36) unitarian-universalist
37) united church of christ (ucc)
38) wesleyan church
39) other (specify): _____
40) don't know
41) refused

Q45: [if Q43 or Q44 = 4] With which Baptist group is your church associated? Is it Southern Baptist Convention, the American Baptist Churches in the USA, the American Baptist Association, the National Baptist Convention USA, an independent Baptist church, or some other Baptist group?

1) american baptist association
2) american baptist usa
3) baptist bible fellowship
4) baptist general conference
5) baptist missionary association
6) conservative baptist association of america
7) free will baptist
8) fundamentalist baptist (no denominational ties)
9) general association of regular baptists (garb)
10) independent baptist (no denominational ties)
11) missionary baptist
12) national baptist convention usa
13) primitive baptist
14) progressive national baptist convention
15) reformed baptist
16) southern baptist

17) OTHER (SPECIFY): _____

18) DON'T KNOW; "JUST BAPTIST"

Q46: [IF Q43 OR Q44 = 27] Is that the United Methodist Church, African Methodist Episcopal Church, the Free Methodist Church, or some other Methodist group?

    1) AFRICAN METHODIST EPISCOPAL

    2) AFRICAN METHODIST EPISCOPAL ZION

    3) FREE METHODIST CHURCH

    4) UNITED METHODIST

    5) OTHER (SPECIFY): _____

    6) DON'T KNOW; "JUST METHODIST"

Q47: [IF Q43 OR Q44 = 31] Is that the Presbyterian Church in the U.S.A., the Presbyterian Church in America, the Orthodox Presbyterian Church, the Evangelical Presbyterian Church, or some other Presbyterian group?

    1) EVANGELICAL PRESBYTERIAN CHURCH (EPC)

    2) ORTHODOX PRESBYTERIAN CHURCH (OPC)

    3) PRESBYTERIAN CHURCH IN AMERICA (PCA)

    4) PRESBYTERIAN CHURCH IN THE USA (PCUSA)

    5) OTHER (SPECIFY): _____

    6) DON'T KNOW; "JUST PRESBYTERIAN"

Q48: [IF Q43 OR Q44 = 25] Is that the Evangelical Lutheran Church in America, the Missouri Synod, the Wisconsin Synod, or some other Lutheran group?

    1) EVANGELICAL LUTHERAN CHURCH IN AMERICA (ELCA; formerly the Lutheran Church in America, American Lutheran Church)

    2) MISSOURI SYNOD

    3) WISCONSIN SYNOD

    4) OTHER (SPECIFY): _____

    5) DON'T KNOW; "JUST LUTHERAN"

Q49: [IF Q43 OR Q44 = 33] Is that the Christian Reformed Church, the Reformed Church in America, or some other Reformed group?

    1) CHRISTIAN REFORMED CHURCH (CRC; sometimes called "Dutch Reformed")

    2) REFORMED CHURCH IN AMERICA (RCA)

    3) OTHER (SPECIFY): _____

    4) DON'T KNOW; "JUST REFORMED"

Q50: [IF Q43 OR Q44 = 5] Is that the Church of the Brethren, the Plymouth Brethren, United Brethren in Christ, or some other Brethren group?

    1) CHURCH OF THE BRETHREN

    2) PLYMOUTH BRETHREN

    3) UNITED BRETHREN IN CHRIST

    3) OTHER (SPECIFY): _____

    4) DON'T KNOW; "JUST BRETHREN"

Q51: [IF Q43 OR Q44 = 14] Is that the United Church of Christ or just a Congregational church?

    1) UNITED CHURCH OF CHRIST (UCC)

    2) JUST CONGREGATIONAL

    3) DON'T KNOW

Q52: [IF Q43 OR Q44 = 8] When you say "Christian," does that mean the denomination called the "Christian Church (Disciples of Christ)," or some other Christian denomination, or do you mean to say "I am just a Christian"?

    1) DISCIPLES OF CHRIST

    2) "JUST A CHRISTIAN" [GO TO Q61]

    3) OTHER CHRISTIAN DENOMINATION

       (SPECIFY): _____

    4) DON'T KNOW

Q53: [IF Q43 OR 44 = 11] Is that the Church of Christ or the United Church of Christ?

    1) CHURCH(ES) OF CHRIST

    2) UNITED CHURCH OF CHRIST

    3) OTHER (SPECIFY): _____

    4) DON'T KNOW

Q54: [IF Q43 OR 44 = 12] Is that the Church of God of Anderson, Indiana; the Church of God of Cleveland, Tennessee; the Church of God in Christ; or some other Church of God?

    1) ANDERSON, IN

    2) CLEVELAND, TN

    3) IN CHRIST

    4) OTHER (SPECIFY): _____

    5) DON'T KNOW

Q55: [IF Q43 OR Q44 = 21] Is that the Christian and Missionary Alliance, the Church of the Nazarene, the Salvation Army, the Wesleyan Church, the Free Methodist Church, the Church of God (Anderson, IN), or some other Holiness group?

    1) CHRISTIAN AND MISSIONARY ALLIANCE (CMA)

    6) CHURCH OF GOD (ANDERSON, INDIANA)

    2) CHURCH OF THE NAZARENE

    5) FREE METHODIST CHURCH

    3) SALVATION ARMY

    4) WESLEYAN CHURCH

    7) OTHER (SPECIFY): _____

    8) DON'T KNOW; "JUST HOLINESS"

Q56: [IF Q43 OR Q44 = 30] Probe: What kind of church is that? What is it called exactly? Is that part of a larger church or denomination? What is that church called?

    1) APOSTOLIC PENTECOSTAL

    2) ASSEMBLIES OF GOD

    3) CHURCH OF GOD (CLEVELAND, TENNESSEE)

4) church of god (huntsville, alabama)
5) church of god in christ
6) church of god in christ (international)
7) church of god in prophesy
8) four square gospel
9) full gospel
10) pentecostal church of god
11) pentecostal holiness church
12) spanish pentecostal
13) united pentecostal church international
14) other (specify): _____
15) don't know; "just pentecostal"

Q57: [if Q43 or Q44 = 7] Is that a Charismatic church associated with any denomination, a Pentecostal church, or a nondenominational Charismatic church?

1) associated with denomination [Return to Denomination question]
2) pentecostal [Go to If Pentecostal]
3) independent charismatic
4) don't know; "just charismatic"

Q58: [if Q43 or Q44 = 1] What kind of Anabaptist church is that? [If need prompts:] What is it called exactly? Is that part of a larger church or denomination? What is that church called?

1) amish
2) brethren; brethren in christ
2) church of the brethren
3) mennonite church; mennonite brethren
4) moravian
5) quaker/friends
7) don't know; "just anabaptist"

Q59: [if Q52 or Q53 = 24] Does your church have any denominational affiliation at all?

1) yes, it does [go to Q42; second time through go to Q61]
2) no, it doesn't [go to Q61]
3) don't know [go to Q61]

Q60: [if Q43 or Q44 = 22] Is that an independent fundamentalist church, independent Charismatic church, independent evangelical church, or what?

1) independent fundamentalist
2) independent charismatic
3) independent pentecostal
4) independent evangelical
5) other: _____
6) don't know/"just independent" [go to Q61]
7) refused [go to Q61]

Q61: [IF Q19 = 1 AND Q5 = 1–6] How often does your _____
[If Q34 = 1: wife; If Q34 = 2: husband] attend the same church that
you do?
- 1) More than once a week
- 2) Once a week
- 3) 2–3 times a month
- 4) Once a month
- 5) Many times a year
- 6) Few times a year
- 7) Never
- 8) ATTENDS A DIFFERENT CHURCH REGULARLY (THEY
  VOLUNTEER)
- 9) DON'T KNOW
- 10) REFUSED

Q71: [IF Q61 = 7] Does your _____ [If Q34 = 1: wife; If
Q34 = 2: husband] consider _____ [If Q34 = 1: herself;
If Q34 = 2: himself] a Christian or not?
- 1) YES
- 2) NO
- 3) DON'T KNOW
- 4) REFUSED

Q62: [IF Q19 = 1 AND Q5 = 7–9] How often does your _____
[If Q34 = 1: wife; If Q4 = 2: husband] attend church services?
- 1) More than once a week
- 2) Once a week
- 3) 2–3 times a month
- 4) Once a month
- 5) Many times a year
- 6) Few times a year
- 7) Never
- 8) ATTENDS A DIFFERENT CHURCH REGULARLY (THEY
  VOLUNTEER)
- 9) DON'T KNOW
- 10) REFUSED

Q73: [IF Q62 = 7] Does your _____ [If Q34 = 1: wife; If
Q34 = 2: husband] consider _____ [If Q43 = 1: herself;
If Q43 = 2: himself] to be a Christian or not ?
- 1) YES
- 2) NO
- 3) DON'T KNOW
- 4) REFUSED

Q63: Do you think that the husband should be the head of the family, or not?
- 1) YES
- 2) NO
- 3) DON'T KNOW
- 4) REFUSED

→ [If Q63 = 1 THEN DO Q64–Q66 ROTATED]: What do you think it means to be the head of the family?

Q64: Does it mean that the husband should be responsible to give spiritual direction for the family, or not?
    1) YES
    2) NO
    3) DON'T KNOW
    4) REFUSED

Q65: Does it mean that the husband should be the final authority in decision-making, or not?
    1) YES
    2) NO
    3) DON'T KNOW
    4) REFUSED

Q66: Does it mean that the husband should be the primary breadwinner, or not?
    1) YES
    2) NO
    3) DON'T KNOW
    4) REFUSED

Q67: Do you think that women should be allowed to hold the position of head pastor, or not?
    1) YES
    2) NO
    3) DON'T KNOW
    4) REFUSED

Q68: How many hours *per week* do you usually watch *religious* television programs?:

_____

Q69: About how many hours per *week* do you listen to religious *radio* programs?:

_____

→ Now I have some questions about the *influence of Christians in America.*

Q70: Do you think that if enough people became Christians, many of America's social problems would naturally begin to solve themselves, or not?
    1) YES
    2) NO
    3) DON'T KNOW
    4) REFUSED

Q71: Do you think that everyone should have the right to live by their own morality, even if it's not Christian morality, or not?
    1) YES
    2) NO
    3) DON'T KNOW
    4) REFUSED

Q72: Do you think that Christian values are under serious attack in the United States today, or not?

    1) YES

    2) NO

    3) DON'T KNOW

    4) REFUSED

Q73: Do you try hard not to offend people around you with your Christian views, or not?

    1) YES

    2) NO

    3) DON'T KNOW

    4) REFUSED

Q74: Do you think Christians should be trying to change American society to better reflect God's will, or not?

    1) YES [SKIP TO Q79]

    2) NO [DO Q75–Q78]

    3) DON'T KNOW [SKIP TO Q79]

    4) REFUSED [SKIP TO Q79]

[If Q74 = 2 DO Q75–Q78] For each of the following, please tell me if it's a reason that *you* think Christians should *not* be trying to change society: [ROTATE]

    Q75: Christians should focus on saving souls instead:

        1) YES, YOU AGREE

        2) NO, YOU DISAGREE

        3) DON'T KNOW

        4) REFUSED

    Q76: The Bible prophesies that the world will grow worse and worse and we can't change that:

        1) YES, YOU AGREE

        2) NO, YOU DISAGREE

        3) DON'T KNOW

        4) REFUSED

    Q77: Christians should not be trying to impose their religion on American society:

        1) YES, YOU AGREE

        2) NO, YOU DISAGREE

        3) DON'T KNOW

        4) REFUSED

    Q78: Christians should separate from the world and live radically different lifestyles:

        1) YES, YOU AGREE

        2) NO, YOU DISAGREE

        3) DON'T KNOW

        4) REFUSED

[IF Q74 = 1 THEN DO Q79–Q84] [rotate them]

Q79: How important is *converting people to Jesus Christ*, as a way to change American society?
   1) very important
   2) somewhat important
   3) not important
   4) DON'T KNOW
   5) REFUSED

Q80: How important is *Christians giving money to charity*, as a way to change American society?
   1) very important
   2) somewhat important
   3) not important
   4) DON'T KNOW
   5) REFUSED

Q81: How important is *Christians volunteering for local community organizations*, as a way to change American society?
   1) very important
   2) somewhat important
   3) not important
   4) DON'T KNOW
   5) REFUSED

Q82: How important is *Christians working for political reforms*, as a way to change American society?: (IF NEED CLARIFY: "the kind of reforms you would support"):
   1) very important
   2) somewhat important
   3) not important
   4) DON'T KNOW
   5) REFUSED

Q83: How important is *defending a biblical worldview in intellectual circles*, as a way to change American society?
   1) very important
   2) somewhat important
   3) not important
   4) DON'T KNOW
   5) REFUSED

Q84: How important is *Christians living a way of life radically different from mainstream America*, as a way to change American society?
   1) very important
   2) somewhat important
   3) not important
   4) DON'T KNOW
   5) REFUSED

Q85: [IF Q74 = 1] Do you think that sometimes Christians need to try to change society using ways that they know may cause conflict and set people against each other, or not?

1) YES
2) NO
3) DON'T KNOW
4) REFUSED

Q86: Do you think churches and denominations should take stands on social, economic, and political issues? Or should taking stands *always* be left up to individual Christians?

1) CHURCHES AND DENOMINATIONS
2) INDIVIDUAL CHRISTIANS
3) DON'T KNOW
4) REFUSED

Q87: Do you think that racism is a top priority that _____
[IF Q1 = 1–2 OR 5 THEN: Christians; IF Q1 = 3–4 OR 6–8 THEN: people]
should be working to help overcome, or not?

1) YES [DO Q88–Q91]
2) NO [SKIP TO Q92]
3) DON'T KNOW [DO Q88–91]
4) REFUSED [DO Q88–91]

→ [IF Q87 = 1 THEN DO Q88–Q91] _____ [IF Q1 = 1–2 OR 5 THEN: Christians; IF Q1 = 3–4 OR 6–8 THEN: people] disagree about the best way to work against racism. For each of the following possible ways, please tell me if you think it's a Very Important, Somewhat Important, or Not Important way that _____ _____[IF Q1 = 1–2 OR 5 THEN: Christians; IF Q1 = 3–4 OR 6–8 THEN: people] should work against racism?: [rotate]

Q88: Try to get to know people from another race?
1) Very important
2) Somewhat important
3) Not important
4) DON'T KNOW
5) REFUSED

Q89: Work to racially integrate _____ [IF Q1 = 1–2 OR 4–6, THEN: church; IF Q1 = 3, THEN: synagogue] congregations?
1) Very important
2) Somewhat important
3) Not important
4) DON'T KNOW
5) REFUSED

Q90: Work to racially integrate residential neighborhoods?
1) Very important
2) Somewhat important
3) Not important

　　　4) DON'T KNOW
　　　5) REFUSED
Q91: Work against discrimination in the job market and legal system?
　　　1) Very important
　　　2) Somewhat important
　　　3) Not important
　　　4) DON'T KNOW
　　　5) REFUSED
Q92: How often have you relied on conservative Christian leaders or political organizations, such as the Christian Coalition, to help you decide how to vote in an
election? Often, sometimes, or never?
　　　1) OFTEN
　　　2) SOMETIMES
　　　3) NEVER
　　　4) DON'T KNOW
　　　5) REFUSED
　　　[ROTATE Q93–Q95]
Q93: In general, do you think *feminists* are hostile toward your moral and spiritual values or not?
　　　1) YES
　　　2) NO
　　　3) DON'T KNOW
　　　4) REFUSED
Q94: In general, do you think the *mass media* is hostile toward your moral and spiritual values or not?
　　　1) YES
　　　2) NO
　　　3) DON'T KNOW
　　　4) REFUSED
Q95: In general, do you think the *public schools* are hostile toward your moral and spiritual values or not?
　　　1) YES
　　　2) NO
　　　3) DON'T KNOW
　　　4) REFUSED
Q96: Thinking about all the people in America who consider themselves Christians,
how different do you think their values and lifestyles *actually are* from the rest of
American society today?
　　　1) Very different
　　　2) Somewhat different
　　　3) A little different
　　　3) Not very different
　　　4) DON'T KNOW
　　　5) REFUSED

Q97: How different do you think Christians' values and lifestyles *should be* from the rest of American society?
    1) Very different
    2) Somewhat different
    3) A little different
    3) Not very different
    4) DON'T KNOW
    5) REFUSED

Q98: How likely or unlikely do you think it is that a Christian revival will sweep America in the coming years?: [IF SAY "REVIVAL SWEEPING AMERICA NOW" = 1]
    1) Very likely
    2) Likely
    3) Unlikely
    4) Very unlikely
    5) DON'T KNOW
    6) REFUSED

→ [IF Q19 = 1 THEN DO Q99–Q105] Now I have some questions about how you and your _____ [If Q34 = 1: wife; If Q34 = 2: husband] make decisions.

Q99: How satisfied are you with the way that you and your _____ [If Q34 = 1: wife; If Q34 = 2: husband] make decisions in your marriage?
    1) Very satisfied
    2) Somewhat satisfied
    3) Somewhat dissatisfied
    4) Very dissatisfied
    5) DON'T KNOW
    6) REFUSED

Q100: Who usually takes the lead in spiritual matters in your family, you or your _____ [If Q34 = 1: wife; If Q34 = 2: husband]?: ("spiritual matters" = praying, going to church, talking about spiritual things)
    1) RESPONDENT
    2) THEIR [HUSBAND/WIFE]
    3) BOTH EQUALLY (MUST VOLUNTEER)
    4) DON'T KNOW
    5) REFUSED

→ Who would you say has more "say-so," you or your _____
[If Q34 = 1: wife; If Q34 = 2: husband], when it comes to making decisions . . .
Q101: . . . about important financial matters?
    1) ME
    2) [HUSBAND/WIFE]
    3) BOTH EQUAL (THEY MUST VOLUNTEER)
    4) DON'T KNOW
    5) REFUSED

Q102: [IF Q30 = 1–10] . . . about child rearing?
    1) ME
    2) [HUSBAND/WIFE]
    3) BOTH EQUAL (THEY MUST VOLUNTEER)
    4) DON'T KNOW
    5) REFUSED

Q103: . . . about how to spend leisure time?
    1) ME
    2) [HUSBAND/WIFE]
    3) BOTH EQUAL (THEY MUST VOLUNTEER)
    4) DON'T KNOW
    5) REFUSED

Q104: [IF Q38 = 1–5 OR 7] . . . about who should work outside the home?
    1) ME
    2) [HUSBAND/WIFE]
    3) BOTH EQUAL (THEY MUST VOLUNTEER)
    4) DON'T KNOW
    5) REFUSED

Q105: When you and your _____ [If Q34 = 1: wife; If Q34 = 2: husband] disagree about *important decisions* that need to be made, who usually gives in and goes along with what the other thinks, you or your _____ [If Q34 = 1: wife; If Q34 = 2: husband]?
    1) RESPONDENT GIVES IN
    2) HUSBAND/WIFE GIVES IN
    3) BOTH/EQUAL (THEY MUST VOLUNTEER)
    4) DON'T KNOW
    5) REFUSED

→ Now I have some questions about children's education. People disagree about what the top priorities should be for a good education. From this list of competing ideas, I want you to tell me how high a priority you think each should be for children's education: [ROTATE Q106–Q109; ALWAYS LEAVE Q110 LAST]
[First screen] The first one is _____. Would you say that is a Top Priority, a Second Priority, or Not a Priority for a good education for children?
[Second–Fifth screen] What about _____?
(PROMPT IF NECESSARY: Top Priority, Second Priority, or Not a Priority?)

Q106: learning job skills to get ahead in life:
    1) TOP PRIORITY
    2) SECOND PRIORITY
    3) NOT A PRIORITY
    4) DON'T KNOW
    5) REFUSED

Q107: learning to get in touch with who they are and express their feelings:
    1) TOP PRIORITY
    2) SECOND PRIORITY
    3) NOT A PRIORITY

    4) DON'T KNOW

    5) REFUSED

Q108: learning to understand and respect other races, religions, and cultures:

    1) TOP PRIORITY

    2) SECOND PRIORITY

    3) NOT A PRIORITY

    4) DON'T KNOW

    5) REFUSED

Q109: learning to obey authority:

    1) TOP PRIORITY

    2) SECOND PRIORITY

    3) NOT A PRIORITY

    4) DON'T KNOW

    5) REFUSED

Q110: learning to think about life from a _____ [IF Q1 = 1–2 OR 5 THEN: Christian; IF Q1 = 3–4 OR 6–8 THEN: religious] perspective:

    1) TOP PRIORITY

    2) SECOND PRIORITY

    3) NOT A PRIORITY

    4) DON'T KNOW

    5) REFUSED

→ Thinking about religion and public schools:

Q111: Do you think public schools should teach students about the major religious traditions, or not?

    1) YES

    2) NO

    3) DON'T KNOW

    4) REFUSED

Q112: Do you think public school instruction should include Christian views of science and history, or not?

    1) YES

    2) NO

    3) DON'T KNOW

    4) REFUSED

Q113: I'm going to read you two ways that Christian parents might choose to deal with moral issues in public schools. Which one most appeals to you?

    1) The first is: elect people to school boards who will put morality and values back in schools.

    2) The second is: try through relationships to have a positive moral influence on students, teachers, and parents.

    3) BOTH EQUALLY (THEY MUST VOLUNTEER)

    4) NEITHER (THEY MUST VOLUNTEER)

    5) DON'T KNOW

    6) REFUSED

Q114: I'm going to read three views about teaching morality in public schools.
Which do you *most* agree with?
   1) First: public school teachers should teach *Christian* values and morality.
   2) The second is: public school teachers should teach *general* morals, but
      not of a particular religion.
   3) The third is: morals should be taught in the home, *not* in public schools.
   4) NONE OF THEM (THEY MUST VOLUNTEER)
   5) IT DEPENDS (THEY MUST VOLUNTEER)
   6) DON'T KNOW
   7) REFUSED

Q115: When it comes to educating children, do you think that Christians should
focus on:
   1) Working with the public schools?
   2) Or, building strong Christian schools?
   3) Or, home schooling their children?
   4) DON'T KNOW
   5) REFUSED

→ Now I want to ask you about some of the *activities* you are involved in. For each one,
please tell me whether you have done the activity within the last *two* years a Lot, Some,
or None?

Q116: Given money or time to a Christian *political* organization or candidate?
   1) A LOT
   2) SOME
   3) NONE
   4) DON'T KNOW
   5) REFUSED

Q117: Given money or time to *non-Christian* political organization or candidate?
   1) A LOT
   2) SOME
   3) NONE
   4) DON'T KNOW
   5) REFUSED

Q118: Written, called, or visited elected officials?
   1) A LOT
   2) SOME
   3) NONE
   4) DON'T KNOW
   5) REFUSED

Q119: Participated in public protests or demonstrations?
   1) A LOT
   2) SOME
   3) NONE
   4) DON'T KNOW
   5) REFUSED

Q120: Tried to educate yourself about a political or social issue?
1) A LOT
2) SOME
3) NONE
4) DON'T KNOW
5) REFUSED

Q121: Volunteered for a _____ [IF Q1 = 1–2 OR 4–6, THEN: church; IF Q1 = 3, THEN: synagogue] program that serves the local community?
1) A LOT
2) SOME
3) NONE
4) DON'T KNOW
5) REFUSED

Q122: Volunteered for a local community organization not related to _____ [IF Q1 = 1–2 OR 4–6, THEN: church; IF Q1 = 3, THEN: synagogue]?
1) A LOT
2) SOME
3) NONE
4) DON'T KNOW
5) REFUSED

Q123: Worked hard in your daily life to set a _____ [IF Q1 = 1–2, 5: Christian; IF Q1 = 3–4, 6–8: good] example for people around you?
1) A LOT
2) SOME
3) NONE
4) DON'T KNOW
5) REFUSED

Q124: Tried to defend the merits of a biblical world view to non-Christians?
1) A LOT
2) SOME
3) NONE
4) DON'T KNOW
5) REFUSED

Q125: Told teens or adults explicitly about how they could become a Christian:
1) A LOT
2) SOME
3) NONE
4) DON'T KNOW
5) REFUSED

Q126: Given money or time to a Christian organization to help spread the gospel in the U.S. or overseas:
1) A LOT
2) SOME
3) NONE

    4) DON'T KNOW

    5) REFUSED

Q127: Given money to an organization that helps poor and needy people:

    1) A LOT

    2) SOME

    3) NONE

    4) DON'T KNOW

    5) REFUSED

Q128: How often do you go to church activities other than your Sunday morning worship service, such as potlucks, Bible studies, choir practice, small groups, etc.?

    1) 3 times a week

    2) 2 times a week

    3) Once a week

    4) 2–3 times a month

    5) Once a month

    6) Few times a year

    7) Never

    8) DON'T KNOW

    9) REFUSED

→ I have a few questions about your *religious identity and background.* Thinking about your religious faith, would you describe yourself as:

Q129: a fundamentalist?

    1) YES

    2) NO

    3) UNFAMILIAR WITH NAME (THEY MUST VOLUNTEER)

    4) DON'T KNOW

Q130: an evangelical?

    1) YES

    2) NO

    3) UNFAMILIAR WITH NAME (THEY MUST VOLUNTEER)

    4) DON'T KNOW

Q131: a mainline Protestant?

    1) YES

    2) NO

    3) UNFAMILIAR WITH NAME (THEY MUST VOLUNTEER)

    4) DON'T KNOW

Q132: a theologically liberal Christian?

    1) YES

    2) NO

    3) UNFAMILIAR WITH NAME (THEY MUST VOLUNTEER)

    4) DON'T KNOW

Q133: [IF Q129–Q132 ANSWERED MORE THAN ONE "YES" (1)] Which of those would you say *best* describes your religious identity?: [SCREEN SHOWS JUST THE "YESES" GIVEN IN Q129–Q132]
   1) Fundamentalist
   2) Evangelical
   3) Mainline Protestant
   4) Liberal
   5) (THEY VOLUNTEER) OTHER (SPECIFY): _____
   6) DON'T KNOW
   7) REFUSED

Q134: [IF Q129–Q132 ANSWERED NO "YESES" (ALL 0)] If you had to choose, would any of these describe you *at all?*
   1) Fundamentalist
   2) Evangelical
   3) Mainline Protestant
   4) Liberal
   5) (THEY VOLUNTEER) NO, NONE DESCRIBE
   6) DON'T KNOW
   7) REFUSED

Q135: Do you consider yourself a Charismatic Christian or involved in the Charismatic movement, or not?
   1) YES
   2) NO
   3) UNFAMILIAR WITH NAME (THEY MUST VOLUNTEER)
   4) DON'T KNOW
   5) REFUSED

Q136: Which of these terms *best* describes the religion of the family you were raised in: fundamentalist, evangelical, mainline Protestant, liberal Christian, Catholic, Jewish, not religious, or something else?
   1) FUNDAMENTALIST
   2) EVANGELICAL
   3) MAINLINE PROTESTANT
   4) LIBERAL CHRISTIAN
   5) CATHOLIC
   6) JEWISH
   7) NOT RELIGIOUS
   8) SOMETHING ELSE? (SPECIFY): _____
   9) DON'T KNOW
   10) REFUSED

Q137: How important would you say religion was in your family while you were growing up?
   1) Extremely important
   2) Very important
   3) Somewhat important
   4) Not important

     5) DON'T KNOW

     6) REFUSED

Q138: Think for a moment about all the family, friends, and work colleagues who are important to you. How many of them are Christians? Almost all, most, some, or none?

     1) ALMOST ALL

     2) MOST

     3) SOME

     4) NONE

     5) DON'T KNOW

     6) REFUSED

[ONLY NONCONSERVATIVE-PROTESTANTS GET Q139–Q147b]

→ Now I have a few questions about your views of *evangelical Christians:*

Q139: Has an evangelical Christian ever tried to convert you to their faith?

     1) YES

     2) NO

     3) DON'T KNOW

     4) REFUSED

     Q140: [IF Q139 = 1] Was that a positive, negative, or neither-positive-nor-negative experience for you?

        1) POSITIVE

        2) NEITHER POSITIVE NOR NEGATIVE

        3) NEGATIVE

        4) DON'T KNOW

        5) CAN'T REMEMBER

        6) REFUSED

Q141: Do you personally know an evangelical Christian from work, school, your neighborhood, or somewhere else?

     1) YES

     2) NO

     3) DON'T KNOW

     Q142: [IF Q141 = 1] Thinking about the evangelical Christian you know the best, would you say that this person sets a good example for others by living an especially moral life, or not?

        1) YES, AGREE

        2) NO, DISAGREE

        3) DON'T KNOW

Q143: Do you think evangelical Christians generally offer good answers for most people's *personal* problems and moral questions, or not?

     1) YES

     2) NO

     3) DON'T KNOW WHAT EVANGELICALS MEANS/WHO THEY ARE [IF = 3 SKIP TO Q146]

4) REFUSED

5) DON'T KNOW THE ANSWER

Q144: Do you think evangelical Christians generally offer good answers for America's *social, economic, and political* problems, or not?

1) YES

2) NO

3) DON'T KNOW

4) REFUSED

Q145: How much better or worse off would the United States be if evangelical Christians had more influence on public issues? Much better off, somewhat better off, somewhat worse off, or much worse off?

1) MUCH BETTER OFF

2) SOMEWHAT BETTER OFF

3) SOMEWHAT WORSE OFF

4) MUCH WORSE OFF

5) DON'T KNOW

6) REFUSED

Q146: In your mind, is there a difference between fundamentalist Christians and evangelical Christians, or are those just two different names for the same group of Christians?

1) THERE IS A DIFFERENCE

2) SAME GROUP

3) DON'T KNOW WHAT EVANGELICALS MEANS [IF Q146 = 3 SKIP TO Q148]

4) REFUSED

5) DON'T KNOW THE ANSWER

Q147b: How familiar are you with what evangelical Christians stand for?

1) Very familiar

2) Somewhat familiar

3) A little familiar

4) Not familiar

5) DON'T KNOW

6) REFUSED

→ I only have a few questions left, and then we'll be done. Can you tell me:

Q148: What race do you consider yourself?

1) WHITE

2) BLACK

3) AFRICAN-AMERICAN

4) ASIAN

5) HISPANIC [IF = 5 THEN AUTOMATIC "YES" (1) ON Q149]

6) other: _____

7) REFUSED

8) DON'T KNOW

Q149: [IF Q148 = 1–2] Are you of hispanic descent?
    1) YES
    2) NO
    3) DON'T KNOW

Q150: How much education do you have?
    0) NO SCHOOL
    1) 6TH GRADE OR LESS
    2) SOME JR-HI/HIGH SCHOOL
    3) HIGH SCHOOL GRADUATE, OR EQUIVALENT/GED
    4) VOCATIONAL-TECHNICAL DEGREE (1–2 YEAR)
    5) SOME COLLEGE
    6) COLLEGE GRADUATE
    7) SOME GRADUATE SCHOOL
    8) MASTERS DEGREE (M.A., Master of Divinity, J. D., Professional Training, etc.)
    9) GRADUATE BEYOND MASTERS DEGREE (M.D., PH.D.)
    10) DON'T KNOW
    11) REFUSED

Q151: Did you ever attend a Christian grade or high school for at least one year?
    1) YES
    2) NO
    3) CATHOLIC SCHOOL (MUST VOLUNTEER)
    3) DON'T KNOW
    4) REFUSED

Q152: Did you ever attend a Christian college, a Bible college, or a Catholic university for at least one year? (IF "YES": Which?)
    1) CHRISTIAN COLLEGE (ONLY IF SURE IT WAS)
    2) BIBLE COLLEGE
    3) CATHOLIC UNIVERSITY
    4) NO
    5) DON'T KNOW
    6) REFUSED

Q153: How much education did your father have?: (IF DIDN'T HAVE FATHER, THEN MOTHER)
    0) NO SCHOOL
    1) 6TH GRADE OR LESS
    2) SOME JR-HI/HIGH SCHOOL
    3) HIGH SCHOOL GRADUATE, OR EQUIVALENT/GED
    4) VOCATIONAL-TECHNICAL DEGREE (1–2 YEAR)
    5) SOME COLLEGE
    6) COLLEGE GRADUATE
    7) SOME GRADUATE SCHOOL
    8) MASTERS DEGREE (M.A., Master of Divinity, J.D., Professional Training, etc.)

9) GRADUATE BEYOND MASTERS DEGREE (M.D., PH.D.)
10) DON'T KNOW
11) REFUSED

Q154: What state did you live in when you were 16 years old?: [SYSTEM: TRANSLATE INTO FIPS CODES]

1) ALABAMA
2) ALASKA
3) ARIZONA
4) ARKANSAS
5) CALIFORNIA
6) COLORADO
7) CONNECTICUT
8) DISTRICT OF COLUMBIA
9) DELAWARE
10) FLORIDA
11) GEORGIA
12) HAWAII
13) IDAHO
14) ILLINOIS
15) INDIANA
16) IOWA
17) KANSAS
18) KENTUCKY
19) LOUISIANA
20) MAINE
21) MARYLAND
22) MASSACHUSETTS
23) MICHIGAN
24) MINNESOTA
25) MISSISSIPPI
26) MISSOURI
27) MONTANA
28) NEBRASKA
29) NEVADA
30) NEW HAMPSHIRE
31) NEW JERSEY
32) NEW MEXICO
33) NEW YORK
34) NORTH CAROLINA
35) NORTH DAKOTA
36) OHIO
37) OKLAHOMA
38) OREGON
39) PENNSYLVANIA
40) RHODE ISLAND

41) SOUTH CAROLINA

42) SOUTH DAKOTA

43) TENNESSEE

44) TEXAS

45) UTAH

46) VERMONT

47) VIRGINIA

48) WASHINGTON

49) WISCONSIN

50) WEST VIRGINIA

51) WYOMING

52) FOREIGN COUNTRY

53) DON'T KNOW

54) REFUSED

Q155: [IF ANSWER TO Q154 SAME AS STATE LIVE IN NOW (KNOWN THROUGH FIPS CODE)] Do you live in the same town you lived in when you were 16, a nearby town, or a town farther away?

1) SAME TOWN

2) NEARBY TOWN

3) FARTHER AWAY

4) DON'T KNOW

5) REFUSED

Q156: Do you usually vote Republican, Democrat, or do you not usually vote?

1) REPUBLICAN

2) DEMOCRAT

3) INDEPENDENT (THEY MUST VOLUNTEER)

4) DON'T VOTE

5) DON'T KNOW

6) REFUSED

Q157: Compared to ten years ago, would you say your financial situation has gotten better, worse, or has it stayed about the same?

1) BETTER

2) WORSE

3) ABOUT THE SAME

4) DON'T KNOW

5) REFUSED

6) DON'T KNOW

Q158: Now here is the very last question. I'm going to read you a list of income categories. Please *tell me to stop* when a category I read best describes your *total household income before taxes:*

1) Less than $10,000

2) Between 10,000 and 20,000

3) Between 20,000 and 30,000

4) Between 30,000 and 40,000

5) Between 40,000 and 50,000

6) Between 50,000 and 60,000

7) Between 60,000 and 70,000

8) Between 70,000 and 80,000

9) Between 80,000 and 90,000

10) Between 90,000 and 100,000

11) More than $100,000

12) DON'T KNOW

13) REFUSED (PROMPT IF NECESSARY: "Remember, your answers are totally anonymous, and we don't need to know your exact income, just income bracket within ten thousand dollars. It would really help us out. . . ."

[WAIT FOR YES OR NO BEFORE READING ANSWER CATEGORIES])

Q159: Okay, thank you very much. I really appreciate you taking the time to answer our questions. You have been very helpful. One last thing: we may want to follow-up these questions sometime in the future. If we do, may we contact you again?

1) YES

2) NO

Q160: [IF Q159 = 1] Great. Could you give me your first name so we can ask for you if we call?: _____

REFERENCES

Abraham, William. 1984. *The Coming Great Revival: Recovering the Full Evangelical Tradition.* San Francisco: Harper and Row.

Abrams, Dominic, and Michael Hogg, eds. 1990. *Social Identity Theory.* New York: Springer-Verlag.

Agyeman-Duah, Baffour, and Olatunde B. J. Ojo. 1991. "Interstate Conflicts in West Africa; The Reference Group Theory Perspective." *Comparative Political Studies* 24: 299–319.

Alexander, John. 1986. *Your Money of Your Life.* New York, NY: Harper and Row.

Allan, J. D. 1989. *The Evangelicals: An Illustrated History.* Grand Rapids: Baker Book House.

Ammerman, Nancy Tatom. 1987. *Bible Believers: Fundamentalists in the Modern World.* New Brunswick: Rutgers University Press.

Askew, Thomas, and Peter Spellman. 1984. *The Churches and the American Experience.* Grand Rapids: Baker.

Astuti, Rita. 1995. "The Vezo Are Not My Kind of People." *American Ethnologist* 22, no. 3 (August): 464–83.

Bahloul, Joelle. 1995. "Food Practices among Sephardic Immigrants in Contemporary France: Dietary Laws in Urban Society." *Journal of the American Academy of Religion* 63 (3): 485–97.

Baker, Donald. 1975. "Race, Power, and White Siege Cultures." *Social Dynamics* 1, no. 2 (December): 143–57.

Balmer, Randal. 1996. *Grant Us Courage.* Oxford: Oxford University Press.

Barth, Fredrik. 1969. *Ethnic Groups and Boundaries.* Boston: Little Brown.

Beatty, Kathleen, and B. Oliver Walter. 1988. "Fundamentalists, Evangelicals, and Politics." *American Political Quarterly* 16, no. 1 (January): 43–59.

Bell, Daniel. 1976. *The Cultural Contradictions of Capitalism.* New York: Basic Books.

———. 1980. "The Return of the Sacred?" In Daniel Bell, *The Winding Passage.* New York: Basic Books.

Bellah, Robert, Richard Madsen, William Sullivan, Ann Swidler, and Stephen Tipton. 1985. *Habits of the Heart.* Berkeley: University of California Press.

Bender, Thomas. 1978. *Community and Social Change in America.* Baltimore: Johns Hopkins University Press.

Bercovitch, Sacvan. 1978. *The American Jeremiad.* Madison: University of Wisconsin Press.

Berger, Peter. 1967. *The Sacred Canopy.* New York: Anchor.

Berger, Peter, and Thomas Luckmann. 1966. *The Social Construction of Reality.* Garden City: Doubleday.

————. 1995. *Modernity, Pluralism and the Crisis of Meaning: The Orientation of Modern Man.* Gutersloh: Bertelsmann Foundation Publishers.

Berger, Peter, Brigitte Berger, and Hansfried Kellner. 1973. *The Homeless Mind: Modernization and Consciousness.* New York: Vintage Books.

Berkhof, Hendrik. 1977. *Christ and the Powers.* Scottdale, PA: Herald Press.

Berman, Marshall. 1982. *All That Is Solid Melts into Air: The Experience of Modernity.* New York: Simon and Schuster.

Bibby, Reginald W. 1978. "Why Conservative Churches Really Are Growing: Kelley Revisited." *Journal for the Scientific Study of Religion* 17: 129–38.

Bibby, Reginald W., and Merlin Brinkerhoff. 1973. "The Circulation of the Saints: A Study of People Who Join Conservative Churches." *Journal for the Scientific Study of Religion* 12: 273–83.

————. 1983. "The Circulation of the Saints Revisited." *Journal for the Scientific Study of Religion* 22: 153–62.

Bilezikian, Gilbert. 1985. *Beyond Sex Roles.* Grand Rapids, MI: Baker Book House.

Black, Cyril. 1967. *The Dynamics of Modernization.* New York: Harper.

Blau, Judith, Kenneth Land, and Kent Redding. 1992. "The Expansion of Religious Affiliation." *Social Science Research* 21, no. 4: 329–53.

Bloesch, Donald. 1973. *The Evangelical Renaissance.* Grand Rapids: Eerdmans.

Boon, James. 1982. *Other Tribes, Other Scribes.* Cambridge: Cambridge.

Bourdieu, P. 1984. *Distinction: A Social Critique of the Judgement of Taste.* Cambridge: Harvard University Press.

————. 1991. "Genesis and the Structure of the Religious Field." *Comparative Social Research* 13: 1–44.

Bourdieu, P., and L. J. D. Wacquant. 1992. *An Invitation to Reflexive Sociology.* Chicago: University of Chicago Press.

Bradley, Martin, et al. 1992. *Churches and Church Membership in the United States 1990.* Atlanta: Glenmary Research Center.

Brown, Richard. 1976. *Modernization: The Transformation of American Life.* New York: Hilland Wang.

Bruce, Steve. 1988. *The Rise and Fall of the New Christian Right.* Oxford: Clarendon Press.

Brungart, R. 1971. "Status Politics and Student Politics: An Analysis of Left- and Right-Wing Student Activists." *Youth and Society* 3 (December): 195–209.

Cameron, Kim. 1980. "Critical Questions in Assessing Organizational Effectiveness." *Organizational Dynamics* 9, no. 2 (Fall): 66–80.

————. 1986. "Effectiveness as Paradox: Consensus and Conflict in Conceptions of Organizational Effectiveness." *Management Science* 32, no. 5 (May): 539–54.

Carpenter, Joel. 1980. "Fundamentalist Institutions and the Rise of Evangelical Protestantism, 1929–1942." *Church History* 49 (1): 62–75.

————. 1984a. "From Fundamentalism to the New Evangelical Coalition." In *Evangelicalism and Modern America*, edited by George Marsden. Grand Rapids: Eerdmans.

————. 1984b. "The Fundamentalist Leaven and the Rise of an Evangelical United Front." In *The Evangelical Tradition in America*, edited by Leonard Sweet, pp. 257–88. Macon, GA: Mercer University Press.

————, ed. 1988. *A New Evangelical Coalition.* New York: Garland.

Chaves, Mark. 1994. "Secularization as Declining Religious Authority." *Social Forces* 72, no. 3 (March): 749–75.

————. 1989. "Secularization and Religious Revival: Evidence from U.S. Church Attendance Rates, 1972–1986." *Journal for the Scientific Study of Religion* 28: 464–77.

Christopher, F. Scott, Diane Johnson, and Mark Roosa. 1993. "Family, Individual, and Social Correlates of Early Hispanic Adolescent Sexual Expression." *The Journal of Sex Research* 30 (1): 54–62.

Cochran, John, and Leonard Beeghley. 1991. "The Influence of Religion on Attitudes Toward Nonmarital Sexuality: A Preliminary Assessment of Reference Group Theory." *Journal for the Scientific Study of Religion* 30: 45–63.

Cohen, Anthony P. 1985. *The Symbolic Construction of Community.* New York: Tavistock Publications.

Cole, Stewart. 1963. *The History of Fundamentalism.* Hamden: Archon.

Cone, James. 1975. *God of the Oppressed.* New York, NY: Seabury Press.

Cornelison, Isaac. 1891. *De Civitate Dei.* Philadelphia: John Wattles.

Cornell, Stephen. 1988. *The Return of the Native: American Indian Political Resurgence.* New York: Oxford University Press.

Coser, Lewis. 1956. *The Functions of Social Conflict.* New York: The Free Press.

Covington, Dennis. 1995. *Salvation on Sand Mountain: Snake Handling and Redemption in Southern Appalachia.* New York: Penguin Books.

Crawford, Alan. 1980. *Thunder on the Right: The "New Right" and the Politics of Resentment.* New York: Pantheon.

Dahl, Robert A. 1961. *Who Governs?* New Haven: Yale University Press.

Dahrendorf, Ralf. 1964. "The New Germanies." *Encounter* 22: 50–58.

Davidman, Lynn. 1991. *Tradition in a Rootless World: Women Turn to Orthodox Judaism.* Berkeley: University of California Press.

Dayton, Donald, and Robert Johnston. 1991. *The Variety of American Evangelicalism.* Knoxville: University of Tennessee Press.

De Vos, George. 1975. "Ethnic Pluralism." In *Ethnic Identity,* edited by George De Vos and Lola Romanucci-Ross, pp. 5–41. Palo Alto, CA: Mayfield.

Dion, K. L. 1979. "Intergroup Conflict and Intergroup Cohesiveness." In *The Social Psychology of Inter-group Relations,* edited by W. G. Austin and Steve Worchel, pp. 211–24. Monterey, CA: Brooks/Cole.

Dorr, Donald. 1983. *Option for the Poor.* Maryknoll, NY: Orbis Books.

Duke, James. 1976. *Conflict and Power in Social Life.* Provo, UT: Brigham Young University Press.

Durkheim, Emile. 1933. *The Division of Labor in Society.* New York: Free Press.

Ellingsen, Mark. 1991. "Lutheranism." In *The Variety of American Evangelicalism,* edited by Donald Dayton and Robert Johnston, pp. 222–44. Knoxville: University of Tennessee Press.

Elliot, W. A. 1986. *Us and Them: A Study of Group Consciousness.* Aberdeen: Aberdeen University Press.

Ellul, Jacques. 1972. *The Politics of God and the Politics of Man.* Grand Rapids, MI: Eerdmans.

Emerson, Michael. 1997. "Explaining Racial Inequalities: Are the Views of Evangelical Protestants Unique?" Paper presented at the annual meeting of the Association for the Sociology of Religion, Toronto, Canada, 9 August 1997.

Erickson, Millard. 1993. *The Evangelical Mind and Heart.* Grand Rapids, MI: Baker Books.

Eshel, Yohana, and Roni Dicker. 1995. "Congruence and Incongruence in Perceived Ethnic Acceptance among Israeli Students." *The Journal of Social Psychology* 135 (2): 251–73.

Etzioni, Amitai. 1988. *The Moral Dimension: Toward a New Economics.* New York: Free Press.

Farmer, Yvette. 1992. "Reference Group Theory." In *Encyclopedia of Sociology,* edited by Edgar Bargatta and Marie Bargatta, pp. 1624–26. New York: Macmillan.

Fenster, Mark. 1993. "Queer Punk Fanzines." *Journal of Communication Inquiry* 17, no. 1 (Winter): 73–95.

Fine, G. A., and S. Kleinman. 1979. "Rethinking Subculture: An Interactionist Analysis." *American Journal of Sociology* 85: 1–20.

Finke, Roger. 1989. "Demographics of Religious Participation: An Ecological Approach, 1850–1980." *Journal for the Scientific Study of Religion* 28, no. 1 (March): 45–59.

Finke, Roger, Avery Guest, and Rodney Stark. 1996. "Mobilizing Local Religious Markets: Religious Pluralism in New York State, 1855 to 1865." *American Sociological Review* 61, no. 2 (April): 203–19.

Finke, Roger, and Laurence Iannaccone. 1993. "Supply-Side Explanations for Religious Change." *Annals of the American Academy of Political and Social Science* 527 (May): 27–40.

Finke, Roger, and Rodney Stark. 1988. "Religious Economies and Sacred Canopies: Religious Mobilization in American Cities, 1906." *American Sociological Review* 53, no. 1 (February): 41–50.

———. 1989a. "Demographics of Religious Participation: An Ecological Approach, 1850–1980." *Journal for the Scientific Study of Religion* 28: 45–58.

———. 1989b. "Evaluating the Evidence: Religious Economies and Sacred Canopies." *American Sociological Review* 54, no. 6 (December): 1054–57.

———. 1989c. "How the Upstart Sects Won America: 1776–1850." *Journal for the Scientific Study of Religion* 28, no. 1 (March): 27–45.

———. 1992. *The Churching of America 1776–1990: Winners and Losers in Our Religious Economy.* New Brunswick, NJ: Rutgers University Press.

Fischer, Claude. 1975. "Toward a Subcultural Theory of Urbanism." *American Journal of Sociology* 80, no. 6 (May): 1319–41.

———. 1982. *To Dwell Among Friends: Personal Networks in Town and City.* Chicago: University of Chicago Press.

———. 1984. *The Urban Experience.* New York: Harcourt Brace Jovanovich.

———. 1995. "The Subcultural Theory of Urbanism: A Twentieth-Year Assessment." *American Journal of Sociology* 101, no. 3 (November): 543–78.

Fisher, Ronald. 1990. *The Social Psychology of Intergroup and International Conflict Resolution.* New York: Springer-Verlag.

———. 1993. "Toward a Social-Psychological Model of Intergroup Conflict." In *Conflict and Social Psychology,* edited by Knud Larsen, 109–22. Newbury Park, CA: Sage.

Foster, Richard. 1978. *Celebration of Discipline.* New York, NY: Harper and Row.

———. 1981. *Freedom of Simplicity.* New York, NY: Harper and Row.

Fowler, Robert Booth. 1982. *A New Engagement: Evangelical Political Thought, 1966–76.* Grand Rapids, MI: Eerdmans.

Gallup, George. 1978. *The Unchurched American Study.* Princeton, NJ: Princeton Religious Research Center.

Gasper, Louis. 1963. *The Fundamentalist Movement.* The Hague: Mouton.

Geertz, Clifford. 1983. *Local Knowledge.* New York: Basic Books.

Gerard, Harold. 1985. "When and How Minorities Prevail." In *Perspectives on Minority Influence,* edited by Serge Muscovici, Gabriel Mugny and Eddy Van Avermaet, pp. 171–251. Cambridge: Cambridge University Press.

Gerson, Judith, and Kathy Peiss. 1985. "Boundaries, Negotiation, Consciousness: Reconceptualizing Gender Relations." *Social Problems* 32: 317–31.

Gier, Nicholas. 1987. *God, Reason, and the Evangelicals.* Lanham, MD: University Press of America.

Gish, Arthur. 1979. *Living in Christian Community.* Scottdale, PA: Herald Press.

Glock, Charles, and Rodney Stark. 1965. *Religion and Society in Tension.* Chicago: Rand McNally.

Granberg-Michaelson, Wesley. 1987. *Tending the Garden.* Grand Rapids, MI: Eerdmans.

Greeley, Andrew. 1972. *Unsecular Man: The Persistence of Religion.* New York: Schocken Books.

Green, John C., James Guth, Corwin Smidt, and Lyman Kellstedt. 1996. *Religion and the Culture Wars: Dispatches from the Front.* Maryland: Rowman and Littlefield.

Gusfield, Joseph. 1963. *Symbolic Crusade: Status Politics and the American Temperance Movement.* Urbana: University of Illinois.

Hadaway, C. Kirk, Penny Long Marler, and Mark Chaves. 1993. "What The Polls Don't Show: A Closer Look at U.S. Church Attendance." *American Sociological Review* 58: 741–53.

Hadden, S., and M. Lester. 1978. "Talking Identity: the Production of 'Self' in Interaction." *Human Studies* 1: 331–56.

Handy, Robert T. 1960. "The American Religious Depression, 1925–1935." *Church History* 29: 2–16.

———. 1984. *A Christian America: Protestant Hopes and Historical Realities.* New York: Oxford University Press.

———. 1991. *Undermined Establishment: Church-State Relations in America, 1880–1920.* Princeton, NJ: Princeton University Press.

Hansen, Marcus L. 1952. "The Third Generation in America." *Commentary* 14: 492–500.

Harper, Keith. 1996. *A Quality of Mercy: Southern Baptists and Social Christianity, 1890–1920.* Tuscaloosa, AL: University of Alabama Press.

Hart, D. G., and John Muether. 1995. *Fighting the Good Fight.* Philadelphia, PA: Orthodox Presbyterian Church.

Hart, Stephen. 1992. *What Does the Lord Require? How American Christians Think about Economic Justice.* New Brunswick, NJ: Rutgers University Press.

Hatch, Nathan O. 1989. *The Democratization of American Christianity.* New Haven, CT: Yale University Press.

Haubert, Katherine. 1993. *Women as Leaders: Accepting the Challenge of Scripture.* Monrovia, CA: MARC.

Hein, Jeremy. 1994. "From Migrant to Minority." *Sociological Inquiry* 64, no. 3 (Summer): 281–307.

Henderson-King, Donna, and Abigail Stewart. 1994. "Women or Feminists? Assessing Women's Group Consciousness." *Sex Roles: A Journal of Research* 31 (9–10): 505–17.

Henry, Carl F. H. 1946. *Remaking the Modern Mind.* Grand Rapids, MI: Eerdmans.

———. 1947. *The Uneasy Conscience of Modern Fundamentalism.* Grand Rapids, MI: Eerdmans.

———. 1986a. *Conversations with Carl Henry: Christianity for Today.* Lewiston: Edwin Mellen Press.

———. 1986b. *Christian Countermoves in a Decadent Culture.* Portland, OR: Multnomah Press.

Henry, Carl F. H., and Kenneth Kantzer. 1996. "Standing on the Promises." *Christianity Today* 40 (September): 28–36.

Henry, Paul. 1974. *Politics for Evangelicals.* Valley Forge: Judson Press.

Hochschild, Arlie. 1973. *The Unexpected Community.* Berkeley: University of California Press.

Hofstadter, Richard. 1955. "The Pseudo-Conservative Revolt." In *The New American Right,* edited by Daniel Bell, pp. 33–55. New York: Criterion.

Hoge, Dean R., Benton Johnson, and Donald Luidens. 1994. *Vanishing Boundaries:*

The Religion of Mainline Protestant Baby Boomers. Louisville: Westminster/John Knox Press.

Hogg, Michael. 1992. *The Social Psychology of Group Cohesiveness.* New York: New York University Press.

Hogg, Michael, and Dominic Abrams. 1988. *Social Identifications.* New York: Routledge.

Hollinger, Dennis. 1983. *Individualism and Social Ethics: An Evangelical Syncretism.* Lanham: University Press of America.

Hout, Michael, and Andrew Greeley. 1987. "The Center Doesn't Hold: Church Attendance in the United States, 1940–1984." *American Sociological Review* 52: 325–45.

Hunt, Scott, and Robert Benford. 1994. "Identity Talk in the Peace and Justice Movement." *Journal of Contemporary Ethnography* 22, no. 4 (January): 488–518.

Hunter, James. 1983. *American Evangelicalism: Conservative Religion and the Quandary of Modernity.* New Brunswick, NJ: Rutgers University Press.

———. 1987. *Evangelicalism: The Coming Generation.* Chicago: University of Chicago Press.

———. 1997. "The Changing Locus of Religions." *Partisan Review* 64, no. 2 (Spring): 187–96.

Hutchison, William. 1968. *American Protestant Thought.* New York: Harper and Row.

———. 1976. *The Modernist Impulse in American Protestantism.* Cambridge, MA: Harvard University Press.

———. 1986. *Liberal Protestantism.* Cleveland, OH: Pilgrim Press.

Hyman, Herbert, and Eleanor Singer, eds. 1968. *Readings in Reference Group Theory and Research.* New York: The Free Press.

Iannaccone, Laurence. 1988. "A Formal Model of Church and Sect." *American Journal of Sociology* 95: 241–68.

———. 1990. "Religious Practice: A Human Capital Approach." *Journal for the Scientific Study of Religion* 29, no. 3 (September): 297–315.

———. 1992. "Sacrifice and Stigma: Reducing Free-Riding in Cults, Communes, and Other Collectives." *Journal of Political Economy* 100: 271–92.

———. 1994. "Why Strict Churches Are Strong." *American Journal of Sociology* 99, no. 5 (March): 1180–1212.

Jackson, Dave, and Neta Jackson. 1974. *Living Together in a World Falling Apart.* Carol Stream, IL: Creation House.

Jenkins, Richard. 1994. "Rethinking Ethnicity." *Ethnic and Racial Studies* 17, no. 2 (April): 197–224.

John, Daphne, Beth Anne Shelton, and Kristen Luschen. 1995. "Race, Ethnicity, Gender and Perceptions of Fairness." *Journal of Family Issues* 16 (3): 357–80.

Kane, Paula. 1994. *Separatism and Subculture.* Chapel Hill: University of North Carolina Press.

Kanter, Rosabeth Moss. 1972. *Commitment and Community: Communes and Utopias in Sociological Perspective.* Cambridge: Harvard University Press.

Kelley, Dean. 1972. *Why Conservative Churches Are Growing.* New York: Harper and Row.

———. 1978. "Why Conservative Churches Are Still Growing." *Journal for the Scientific Study of Religion* 17: 165–72.

Kelley, Jonathan, and M. D. R. Evans. 1995. "Class and Class Conflict in Six Western Nations." *American Sociological Review* 60 (2): 157–79.

Kelly, Jeffrey A., Kathleen Sikkema, Laura Soloman, Timothy Heckman, L. Yvonne Stevenson, Ann Norman, Richard Winett, Roger Roffman, Melissa Perry, and Laurie Desiderato. 1995. "Factors Predicting Continued High-Risk Behavior among Gay Men in Small Cities: Psychological, Behavioral, and Demographic Characteristics Related to Unsafe Sex." *Journal of Consulting and Clinical Psychology* 63 (1): 101–8.

Kornhauser, William. 1959. *The Politics of Mass Society.* Glencoe, IL: Free Press.

Kraybill, Donald. 1978. *The Upside-Down Kingdom.* Scottdale, PA: Herald Press.

Kriesberg, L. 1982. *The Sociology of Social Conflicts.* Englewood Cliffs, NJ: Prentice-Hall.

Kruse, Holly. 1993. "Subcultural Identity in Alternative Music Culture." *Popular Music* 12, no. 1 (January): 33–42.

Land, Kenneth, Glenn Deane, and Judith Blau. 1991. "Religious Pluralism and Church Membership: A Spatial Diffusion Model." *American Sociological Review* 56: 237–50.

Lasch, Christopher. 1986. "What's Wrong with the Right." *Tikkun* 1, no. 1: 23–29.

Lenski, Gerald. 1954. "Status Crystallization: A Non-Vertical Dimension of Social Status." *American Sociological Review* 19: 405–13.

LeVine, Robert, and Donald Campbell. 1972. *Ethnocentrism: Theories of Conflict, Ethnic Attitudes, and Group Behavior.* New York: John Wiley and Sons.

Lightner, Robert. 1978. *Neoevangelicalism Today.* Schaumburg, IL: Regular Baptist Press.

Lipset, Seymour Martin. 1960. *Political Man.* New York: Doubleday.

———. 1963. "Three Decades of the Radical Right: Coughlinites, McCarthyites, and Birchers." In *The New American Right,* edited by Daniel Bell, pp. 166–233. New York: Criterion.

Longfield, Bradley. 1991. *The Presbyterian Controversy.* New York: Oxford University Press.

Lorentzen, Louise J. 1980. "Evangelical Life Style Concerns Expressed in Political Action." *Sociological Analysis* 41 (2): 144–54.

Lowney, Kathleen. 1995. "Teenage Satanism as Oppositional Youth Culture." *Journal of Contemporary Ethnography* 23, no. 4 (January): 453–85.

Lyon, Larry. 1987. *The Community in Urban Society.* Chicago: Dorsey Press.

Macaulay, Susan Schaeffer. 1984. *For the Children's Sake.* Wheaton, IL: Crossway Books.

Maine, Henry. 1905. *Ancient Law.* London: Murray.

Marsden, George. 1970. *The Evangelical Mind and the New School Presbyterian Experience.* New Haven, CT: Yale University Press.

———. 1973. "The Gospel of Wealth, the Social Gospel, and the Salvation of Souls in Nineteenth-Century America." *Fides et Historia* 5, no. 1 (Spring): 10–21.

———. 1980. *Fundamentalism and American Culture: The Shaping of Twentieth-Century Evangelicalism, 1870–1925.* New York: Oxford University Press.

———, ed. 1984. *Evangelicalism and Modern America.* Grand Rapids, MI: Eerdmans.

———. 1987. *Reforming Fundamentalism: Fuller Seminary and the New Evangelicalism.* Grand Rapids, MI: Eerdmans.

———. 1989. "Unity and Diversity in the Evangelical Resurgence." In *Altered Landscapes: Christianity in America, 1935–1985,* edited by David Lotz, Donald Shriver, and John Wilson, pp. 61–76. Grand Rapids, MI: Eerdmans.

———. 1994. *The Soul of the American University.* Oxford: Oxford University Press.

Marshall, Susan. 1986. "In Defense of Separate Spheres: Class and Status Politics in the Anti-Suffrage Movement." *Social Forces* 65: 327–51.

Marwell, Gerald. 1996. "We Still Don't Know if Strict Churches Are Strong, Much Less Why: Comment on Iannaccone." *American Journal of Sociology* 101, no. 4 (January): 1097–1104.

May, Roy. 1991. *The Poor of the Land.* Maryknoll, NY: Orbis Books.

McCarthy, Rockne, James Skillen, and William Harper. 1982. *Disestablishment a Second Time: Genuine Pluralism for American Schools.* Grand Rapids, MI: Eerdmans.

McCulloch, Ann, and David Wilkins. 1995. "'Constructing Nations Within States." *The American Indian Quarterly* 19, no. 3 (Summer): 361–89.

McEvoy, James. 1971. *Radicals or Conservatives? The Contemporary American Right.* Chicago: Rand McNally.

McGrath, Alister. 1995. *Evangelicalism and the Future of Christianity.* Downers Grove, IL: Inter-Varsity Press.

McMahon, Felicia. 1991. "Forging 'The Adirondacker.'" *Western Folklore* 50, no. 3 (July): 277–96.

Mead, Frank, and Samuel Hill. 1990. *Handbook of Denominations in the United States.* Nashville, TN: Abingdon Press.

Melton, J. Gordon. 1992. *Religious Bodies in the United States.* New York: Garland.

———. 1993. *Encyclopedia of American Religions.* Detroit: Gale Research.

Melucci, Alberto. 1985. "The Symbolic Challenge of Contemporary Movements." *Social Research* 52: 781–816.

———. 1989. *Nomads of the Present: Social Movements and Individual Needs in Contemporary Society.* Philadelphia: Temple University Press.

Milgram, Stanley. 1970. "The Experience of Living in Cities." *Science* 167: 1461–68.

Miller, Arthur, Christopher Wlezien, and Anne Hildreth. 1991. "A Reference Group Theory of Partisan Coalitions." *The Journal of Politics* 54, no. 4: 1134–50.

Miranda, Jose. 1974. *Marx and the Bible.* Maryknoll: Orbis Books.

———. 1987. *Communism in the Bible.* Maryknoll: Orbis Books.

Moberg, David. 1977. *The Great Reversal.* Philadelphia: Lippincott.

Monsma, Stephen, and Christopher Soper. 1997. *The Challenge of Pluralism: Church and State in Five Democracies.* Lanham, MD: Rowman and Littlefield.

Moore, Raymond, and Dorothy Moore. 1979. *School Can Wait.* Provo, UT: Brigham Young University Press.

Mott, Stephen. 1982. *Biblical Ethics and Social Change.* New York: Oxford University Press.

Murphy, Larry, J. Gordon Melton, and Gary Ward, eds. 1993. *Encyclopedia of African-American Religions.* New York: Garland.

Muscovici, Serge, Gabriel Mugny, and Eddy Van Avermaet. 1985. *Perspectives on Minority Influence.* Cambridge: Cambridge University Press.

Nagel, Joane. 1994. "Constructing Ethnicity: Creating and Recreating Ethnic Identity and Culture." *Social Problems* 41: 152–77.

Nash, Ronald. 1987a. *Evangelicals in America: Who They Are, What They Believe.* Nashville, TN: Abingdon Press.

———. 1987b. *Evangelical Renewal in the Mainline Churches.* Westchester, IL: Crossways.

Neitz, Mary Jo. 1987. *Charisma and Community: A Study of Religious Commitment within the Charismatic Renewal.* New Brunswick, NJ: Transaction.

Nelson, Rudolph. 1987. *The Making and Unmaking of an Evangelical Mind: The Case of Edward Carnell.* New York: Cambridge University Press.

Newman, William M. 1993. "The Meaning of a Merger: Denominational Identity in the United Church of Christ." In *Beyond Establishment: Protestant Identity in a Post-Protestant Age,* edited by Jackson Carroll and Wade Clark Roof, pp. 296–308. Louisville, KY: Westminster/John Knox Press.

Nieburh, H. Richard. 1937. *The Kingdom of God in America.* New York: Harper and Row.

Noll, Mark. 1994. *The Scandal of the Evangelical Mind.* Grand Rapids, MI: Eerdmans.

Noll, Mark, and David Wells. 1988. *Christian Faith and Practice in the Modern World.* Grand Rapids, MI: Eerdmans.

Olson, Daniel. 1993. "Fellowship Ties and the Transmission of Religious Identity." In *Beyond Establishment: Protestant Identity in a Post-Protestant Age,* edited by Jackson Carroll and Wade Clark Roof, pp. 32–53. Louisville: Westminster/John Knox Press.

———. 1995. "Religious Pluralism Versus Subgroup Identity: Explanations of Religious Commitment." Paper presented at the annual meeting of the Society for the Scientific Study of Religion, St. Louis, Missouri, October.

Olzak, Susan. 1983. "Contemporary Ethnic Mobilization." *Annual Review of Sociology* 9: 355–74.

Page, Ann, and Donald Clelland. 1978. "The Kanawha County Textbook Controversy: A Study of the Politics of Life Style Concern." *Social Forces* 57, no. 1 (September): 265–81.

Payne, Wandell, ed. 1991. *Directory of African-American Religious Bodies.* Washington, DC: Harvard University Press.

Perrin, Robin, and Armand Mauss. 1993. "Strictly Speaking . . .: Kelly's Quandary and the Vinyard Christian Fellowship." *Journal for the Scientific Study of Religion* 32, no. 2 (June): 125–36.

Peshkin, Alan. 1986. *God's Choice: The Total World of a Fundamentalist Christian School.* Chicago: University of Chicago Press.

Pizzorno, Alessandro. 1978. "Political Exchange and Collective Identity in Industrial Conflict." In *The Resurgence of Class Conflict in Western Europe Since 1968,* edited by C. Crouch and A. Pizzorno, pp. 277–98. New York: Holmes and Meier.

PRRC. 1996. "Just How Many Evangelicals Are There in the U.S. Today?" *PRRC Emerging Trends* 18 (April): 1–2.

Pulis, John W. 1993. "Up-full Sounds: Language, Identity, and the World-View of Rastafari." *Ethnic Groups* 10(4): 285–301.

Quebedeaux, Richard. 1974. *The Young Evangelicals.* New York: Harper and Row.

Radecki, Carmen, and James Jaccard. 1995. "Perceptions of Knowledge, Actual Knowledge, and Information Search Behavior." *Journal of Experimental Social Psychology* 31 (2): 107–39.

Rasmussen, Larry L. 1993. *Moral Fragments and Moral Community.* Minneapolis, MN: Fortress Press.

Redfield, Robert. 1930. *Tepoztlan, a Mexican Village: A Study of Folk Life.* Chicago: University of Chicago Press.

Reed, John. 1982. *One South: An Ethnic Approach to Regional Culture.* Baton Rouge: Louisiana State University Press.

———. 1986. *The Enduring South: Subcultural Persistence in Mass Society.* Chapel Hill: University of North Carolina Press.

Reeves, Thomas C. 1996. *The Empty Church: The Suicide of Liberal Christianity.* New York: Free Press.

Regnerus, Mark, and Christian Smith. 1998a. "Selective Deprivatization among American Religious Traditions: The Reversal of the Great Reversal." *Social Forces* (forthcoming).

———. 1998b. "Who Gives to the Poor?: The Role of Religious Tradition and Political Location on the Personal Generosity of Americans Toward the Poor." *Journal for the Scientific Study of Religion* (forthcoming).

Ridderbos, Herman. 1975. *Paul: An Outline of His Theology.* Grand Rapids, MI: Eerdmans.

Ritzer, George. 1993. *The McDonaldization of Society.* Thousand Oakes, CA: Pine Forge Press.

Rogers, Jack, ed. 1977. *Biblical Authority.* Waco: Word Books.

Rogers, Jack, and Donald McKim. 1979. *The Authority and Interpretation of the Bible: An Historical Approach.* San Francisco: Harper and Row.

Rohter, Ira. 1969. "Social Psychological Determinants of Radical Rightism." In *The American Right Wing*, edited by R. Schoenberger, pp. 193–237. New York: Holt, Rinehart, and Winston.

Roof, Wade Clark. 1993. *A Generation of Seekers: The Spiritual Journeys of the Baby Boom Generation.* San Francisco: HarperCollins.

Roof, Wade Clark, and William McKinney. 1987. *American Mainline Religion: It's Changing Shape and Future.* New Brunswick, NJ: Rutgers University Press.

Rudin, A. James, and Marvin Wilson. 1987. *A Time to Speak: The Evangelical-Jewish Encounter.* Grand Rapids, MI: William B. Eerdmans.

Sandeen, Ernest. 1970. *The Roots of Fundamentalism.* Chicago: University of Chicago Press.

Sandel, Michael. 1982. *Liberalism and the Limits of Justice.* New York: Cambridge.

———. 1984. "The Procedural Republic and the Unencumbered Self." *Political Theory* 12:93.

———. 1987. "The Political Theory of the Procedural Republic." In *Reinhold Niebuhr Today*, edited by Richard John Neuhaus, pp. 19–32. Grand Rapids, MI: Eerdmans.

Sapp, Stephen, and Wendy Harrod. 1989. "Social Acceptability and Intentions to Eat Beef: An Expansion of the Fishbein-Ajzen Model Using Reference Group Theory." *Rural Sociology* 54 (3): 429–39.

Savells, Jerry. 1993. "The 'Cajun' Subculture." *International Journal of Comparative Sociology* 34, no. 1–2 (January): 113–22.

Schaeffer, Francis. 1984. *The Great Evangelical Disaster.* Westchester, IL: Crossways.

Schaffner, Julie Anderson. 1995. "Attached Farm Labor, Limited Horizons and Servility." *The Journal of Development Economics* 47 (2): 241–71.

Schermerhorn, John, James Hunt, and Richard Osborn. 1994. *Managing Organizational Behavior.* New York: John Wiley and Sons.

Schmitt, Raymond. 1972. *The Reference Other Orientation.* Carbondale, IL: Southern Illinois University Press.

Schmalzbauer, John, and C. Gray Wheeler. 1996. "Between Fundamentalism and Secularization: Secularizing and Sacrilizing Currents in the Evangelical Debate on Campus Lifestyle Codes." *Sociology of Religion* 57: 241–57.

Schnachenburg, Rudolf. 1968. *Christian Existence in the New Testament.* Volume I. Notre Dame, IN: University of Notre Dame Press.

Schutz, Alfred. 1971. *Collected Papers: The Problem of Reality.* Vol. 1. The Hague: Martinus Nijhoff.

Schwalbe, Michael L., and Douglas Mason-Schrock. 1996. "Identity Work as Group Process." *Advances in Group Processes* 13: 113–47.

Shaull, Richard. 1988. *Naming the Idols.* Oak Park, IL: Meyer-Stone.

Sherif, Muzafer. 1966. *In Common Predicament: Social Psychology of Intergroup Conflict and Cooperation.* Boston: Houghton Mifflin.

Shibley, Mark A. 1996. *Resurgent Evangelicalism in the Untied States: Mapping Cultural Change Since 1970.* Columbia: University of South Carolina Press.

Short, James. 1995. "Subcultures." In *The Social Science Encyclopedia*, edited by Adam Kuper and Jessica Kuper, pp. 855–56. Leiden, The Netherlands: Routledge and Kegan Paul.

Sider, Ronald. 1979. *Christ and Violence.* Scottdale, PA: Herald Press.

————. 1980. *Cry Justice.* Downers Grove, IL: Inter-Varsity Press.

————. 1990. *Rich Christians in an Age of Hunger.* Waco: Word.

Sikkink, David. 1996. "Just Call Me a Christian: Symbolic Boundaries and Identity Formation among Churchgoing Protestants." In *Reforming the Center: American Protestantism, 1900 to the Present,* edited by Douglas Jacobsen and Vance Trollinger. Grand Rapids, MI: Eerdmans.

Sikkink, David, and Christian Smith. 1996. "The Meaning of Commonly Used Labels among Churchgoing Protestants: An Analysis of the Construction of Religious Identity." Paper presented at the Society for the Scientific Study of Religion annual meeting, Nashville, TN, November 1996.

Simmel, Georg. [1908] 1955. *Conflict* and *The Web of Group-Affiliations.* Glencoe, IL: The Free Press.

————. [1905] 1957. "The Metropolis and Mental Life." In *Cities and Society,* edited by P. K. Hatt and A. J. Reiss, pp. 635–46. New York: Free Press.

Skocpol, Theda. 1985. "Cultural Idioms and Political Ideologies in the Revolutionary Reconstruction of State Power: A Rejoinder to Sewell." *Journal of Modern History* 57, no. 1 (March): 86–96.

Smedes, Lewis. 1966. "The Evangelicals and the Social Question." *The Reformed Journal* 16 (February): 9–13.

Smidt, Corwin. 1988. "The Mobilization of Evangelical Voters in 1980: An Initial Test of Several Hypotheses." *Southeastern Political Review* 16: 3–33.

Smith, Christian. 1996a. *Resisting Reagan: The U.S. Central America Peace Movement.* Chicago: University of Chicago Press.

————, ed. 1996b. *Disruptive Religion: The Force of Faith in Social-Movement Activism.* New York: Routledge.

Snow, David, and Leon Anderson. 1987. "Identity Work Among the Homeless." *American Journal of Sociology* 92, no. 6 (May): 1336–71.

Snow, David, and Richard Machelek. 1982. "On the Presumed Fragility of Unconventional Beliefs." *Journal for the Scientific Study of Religion* 21: 15–26.

Soper, J. Christopher. 1994. *Evangelical Christianity in the United States and Great Britain.* New York: New York University Press.

Stark, Rodney. 1971. *Wayward Shepherds.* New York: Harper and Row.

Steedman, Carolyn. 1995. "Inside, Outside, Other." *History of Human Societies* 8, no. 4 (November): 59–77.

Stein, Arthur A. 1976. "Conflict and Cohesion." *Journal of Conflict Resolution* 20: 143–72.

Stein, Maurice R. 1960. *The Eclipse of Community.* New York: Harper and Row.

Stearns, Lewis French. 1890. *The Evidence of Christian Experience.* New York: Charles Scribners.

Stone, Jon. 1996. "Defining Protestant Orthodoxy." In *Religion and the Social Order,* edited by Lewis Carter, pp. 67–92. Greenwich: JAI Press.

Stringfellow, William. 1977. *Conscience and Obedience.* Waco, TX: Word.

Strong, Josiah. 1963 [1886]. *Our Country: Its Possible Future and Present Crisis.* Cambridge: Harvard University Press.

Su, Yang. 1996. "Plausibility Structure of Evangelicalism: The Subculture in a Modern Society." Paper presented at the 91st annual meeting of the American Sociological Association. New York City.

Sumner, William Graham. 1906. *Folkways.* New York: Ginn.

Swartz, David. 1996. "Bridging the Study of Culture and Religion: Pierre Bourdieu's Political Economy of Symbolic Power." *Sociology of Religion* 57, no. 1 (Spring): 71–86.

Sweeney, Douglas. 1992. "Fundamentalism and the Neo-Evangelicals." *Fides et Historia* 24 (1): 81–96.

Sweet, Leonard, ed. 1984. *The Evangelical Tradition in America.* Macon, GA: Mercer University Press.

Swidler, Leonard. 1987. "Jesus Was a Feminist." In *Border Regions of Faith,* edited by Kenneth Aman, pp. 30–38. Maryknoll, IL: Orbis Books.

Szasz, Ferenc. 1982. *The Divided Mind of Protestant America, 1880–1930.* University, AL: Alabama University Press.

Tajfel, Henri. 1982. *Social Identity and Intergroup Relations.* Cambridge: Cambridge University Press.

Tajfel, Henri, and John Turner. 1986. "The Social Identity Theory of Intergroup Behavior." In *Psychology of Intergroup Relations,* edited by Stephen Worchel and William Austin, pp. 7–24. Chicago: Nelson Hall.

Taylor, Charles. 1989. *Sources of the Self: The Making of Modern Identity.* Cambridge: Harvard University Press.

Taylor, Verta, and Nancy Whittier. 1992. "Collective Identity in Social Movement Communities." In *Frontiers in Social Movement Theory,* edited by Aldon Morris and Carol Mueller, pp. 104–29. New Haven: Yale University Press.

Terry, Deborah, and Michael Hogg. 1996. "Group Norms and the Attitude-Behavior Relationship: A Role for Group Identification." *Personality and Social Psychology Bulletin* 22 (8): 776–94.

Thurow, Lester C. 1996. *The Future of Capitalism.* New York: William Morrow.

Tidball, Derek. 1994. *Who Are the Evangelicals: Tracing the Roots of Today's Movement.* London: Marshall Pickering.

Tönnies, Ferdinand. 1963. *Community and Society.* New York: Harper.

Touraine, Alain. 1985. "An Introduction to the Study of Social Movements." *Social Research* 52, no. 4: 749–87.

Turner, John, with Michael Hogg, Penelope Oakes, Stephen Reicher, and Margaret Wetherell. 1987. *Rediscovering the Social Group: A Self-Categorization Theory.* New York: Basil Blackwell.

Turner, Jonathan. 1986. *The Structure of Sociological Theory.* Chicago: The Dorsey Press.

Urry, John. 1996. "Reference Groups." In *The Social Science Encyclopedia (Second Edition),* edited by Adam Kuper and Jessica Kuper, pp. 723–25. New York: Routledge.

USCC. 1986. *Economic Justice for All.* Washington, DC: National Conference of Catholic Bishops.

van Knippenberg, Ad. 1989. "Strategies of Identity Management." In *Ethnic Minorities: Social Psychological Perspectives,* edited by Jan Van Oudenhoven and Tineke Willemsen, pp. 59–76. Amsterdam: Swets and Zeitlinger.

Vogt, Virgil. 1982. *Treasure in Heaven.* Ann Arbor, MI: Servant Books.

Wacker, Grant. 1984. "Speaking of Norman Rockwell: Popular Evangelicalism in Contemporary America." In *The Evangelical Tradition in America,* edited by Leonard Sweet, pp. 289–315. Macon, GA: Mercer University Press.

———. 1996. "Travail of a Broken Family: Evangelical Responses to Pentecostalism in America, 1906–1916." *Journal of Ecclesiastical History* 47, no. 3 (July): 505–29.

Wald, Kenneth, Dennis Owen, and Samuel Hill. 1989. "Evangelical Politics and Status Issues." *Journal for the Scientific Study of Religion* 28, no. 1 (March): 1–17.

Wallis, Jim. 1976. *Agenda for Biblical People.* New York, NY: Harper and Row.

———. 1981. *The Call to Conversion.* New York, NY: Harper and Row.

Walter, J. A. 1979. *Sacred Cows.* Grand Rapids, MI: Zondervan.

Warner, R. Stephen. 1993. "Work in Progress Toward a New Paradigm for the Sociological Study of Religion in the United States." *American Journal of Sociology* 98: 1044–93.

Wasserman, Ira. 1990. "Status Politics and Economic Class Interests: The 1918 Prohibition Referendum in California." *Sociological Quarterly* 31, no. 3. (Fall): 475–85.

Webb, K. 1983. "Social Movements: Contingent or Inherent Phenomena?" Paper Presented at Feltrinelli Foundation Conference. Milan.

Webber, Melvin. 1963. "Order in Diversity: Community Without Propinquity." In *Cities and Space,* edited by Lowdon Wingo, pp. 23–54. Baltimore: Johns Hopkins.

Webber, Robert. 1978. *Common Roots: A Call to Evangelical Maturity.* Grand Rapids, MI: Zondervan.

Weber, Max. 1958. *The Protestant Ethic and the Spirit of Capitalism.* New York: Scribners.

———. 1964. *The Theory of Social and Economic Organization.* New York: Free Press.

Wellman, Barry, and Barry Leighton. 1979. "Networks, Neighborhoods, and Communities." *Urban Affairs Quarterly.* 14, no. 3 (March): 363–90.

Wells, David. 1993. *No Place for Truth: Or Whatever Happened to Evangelical Theology?* Grand Rapids, MI: Eerdmans.

Wells, David, and John Woodbridge. 1975. *The Evangelicals: What They Believe, Who They Are, Where They Are Changing.* Nashville, TN: Abingdon Press.

West, Candace, and Don Zimmerman. 1987. "Doing Gender." *Gender and Society* 1: 125–51.

Wilkinson, Loren. 1980. *Earth Keeping.* Grand Rapids, MI: Eerdmans.

Wilson, Kenneth, and Louis Zurcher. 1976. "Status Inconsistency and Participation in Social Movements." *Sociological Quarterly* 17, no. 4: 520–33.

Wirth, Louis. 1938. "Urbanism as a Way of Life." *American Journal of Sociology* 44: 3–24.

Wood, Michael, and Michael Hughes. 1984. "The Moral Basis of Moral Reform: Status Discontent vs. Culture and Socialization as Explanations of Anti-Pornography Social Movement Adherence." *American Sociological Review* 49, no. 1: 86–99.

Woodberry, Robert, and Christian Smith. 1998. "Fundamentalists, et al." In *Annual Review of Sociology,* edited by John Hagan. Palo Alto, CA: Annual Reviews.

Woodbridge, John, Mark Noll, and Nathan Hatch. 1979. *The Gospel in America: Themes in the Story of American Evangelicals.* Grand Rapids, MI: Zondervan.

Woodward, Kenneth L. 1993. "Dead End for Mainline?" *Newsweek,* August 9, 1993.

Worchel, Stephen, Dawna Coutant-Sassic, and Frankie Wong. 1993. "Toward a More Balanced View of Conflict: There Is a Positive Side." In *Conflict Between People and Groups,* edited by Stephen Worchel and Jeffrey Simpson, pp. 76–89. Chicago: Nelson-Hall.

Worchel, Stephen, E. Lind, and K. Kaufman. 1975. "Evaluations of Group Products as a Function of Expectations of Group Longevity, Outcome of Competition, and Publicity of Evaluations." *Journal of Personality and Social Psychology* (31): 1089–97.

Wuthnow, Robert. 1987. *Meaning and Moral Order: Explorations in Cultural Analysis.* Berkeley, CA: University of California Press.

———. 1988. "Sociology of Religion." In *Handbook of Sociology,* edited by Neil Smelser, pp. 473–509. Newbury Park, CA: Sage.

———. 1989a. *The Struggle for America's Soul: Evangelicals, Liberals, and Secularism.* Grand Rapids, MI: Eerdmans.

———. 1989b. *Communities of Discourse.* Cambridge, MA: Harvard University Press.

———. 1994a. *Sharing the Journey: Support Groups and America's New Quest for Community.* New York: Free Press.

———. 1994b. *God and Mammon in America.* New York: The Free Press.

Yamane, David. 1997. "Secularization on Trial: In Defense of a Neosecularization Paradigm." *Journal for the Scientific Study of Religion* 36, no. 1 (March): 109–13.

Yoder, Howard. 1971. *The Original Revolution.* Scottdale, PA: Herald Press.

————. 1972. *The Politics of Jesus*. Grand Rapids, MI: Eerdmans.

Yu, Jiang, and Allen Liska. 1993. "The Certainty of Punishment: A Reference Group Effect and Its Functional Form." *Criminology* 31 (3): 447–64.

Zurcher, Louis, and R. Kirkpatrick. 1976. *Citizens for Decency: Antipornography Crusades as Status Defense*. Austin, TX: University of Texas Press.

Zurcher, Louis, R. Kirkpatrick, R. Cushing, and C. Bowman. 1971. "The Anti-Pornography Campaign: A Symbolic Crusade." *Social Problems* 19 (Fall): 217–38.